London's War

London's War

A Traveler's Guide to World War II

*20 memorable walking tours
through the sites of
Central London*

**Sayre
Van Young**

Ulysses Press

Published by:
Ulysses Press
P.O. Box 3440
Berkeley, CA 94703
www.ulyssespress.com

ISBN 1-56975-382-2
ISSN 1544-1415

Printed in Canada by Transcontinental Printing

10 9 8 7 6 5 4 3 2

Editorial Director: Leslie Henriques
Managing Editor: Claire Chun
Copy Editor: Lily Chou
Editorial Associates: Kate Allen, Kaori Takee
Production: Steven Schwartz, James Meetze
Cartography: Pease Press
Design: Sarah Levin
Front cover photography: arttoday.com—Big Ben,
    Winston Churchill, flag; National Archives,
    Washington, DC—St. Paul's; London bobbie
    with girl
Back cover photography: Franklin D. Roosevelt Library

See page 342 for picture credits.

Distributed in the United States by Publishers Group West
and in Canada by Raincoast Books

This book is for those incredible women on my personal homefront:
Cathie L. Watts, Janet Fraser Jennings, Barbara Fraser Braun,
and especially Marin Van Young and Diane Davenport.

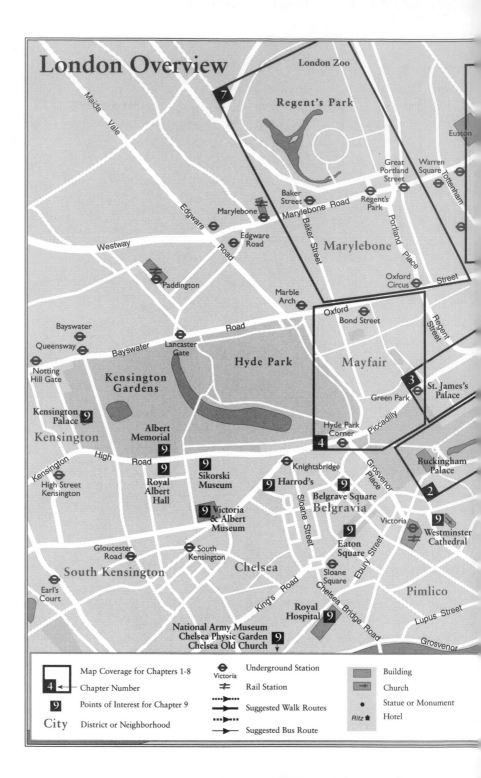

London Overview

London Zoo

Regent's Park

7

Maida Vale

Euston

Great Portland Street   Warren Square

Baker Street   Regent's Park

Marylebone   Marylebone Road

Edgware

Westway

Edgware Road

Baker Street

Marylebone

Portland Place

Paddington

Marble Arch

Oxford Circus   Street

Bayswater

Road

Oxford   Bond Street

Regent Street

Queensway

Bayswater   Lancaster Gate

Hyde Park

Mayfair

Notting Hill Gate

Kensington Gardens

3   St. James's Palace

Green Park

Kensington Palace **9**

Albert Memorial **9**

Hyde Park Corner

4

Kensington

High   Road **9**

Buckingham Palace

High Street Kensington

Royal Albert Hall **9**

Sikorski Museum **9**

Knightsbridge

Harrod's **9**   **9**

Belgrave Square

Grosvenor Place

2

Victoria & Albert Museum **9**

Sloane Street

Belgravia

Victoria   **9**

Westminster Cathedral

Gloucester Road   South Kensington

Chelsea

Eaton Square **9**

Ebury Street

South Kensington

Sloane Square

Pimlico

Earl's Court

King's Road

Chelsea Bridge Road

Lupus Street

Royal Hospital **9**

National Army Museum
Chelsea Physic Garden
Chelsea Old Church **9**

Grosvenor

Legend

Map Coverage for Chapters 1-8	Victoria ⊖ Underground Station	▦ Building
4 ← Chapter Number	⇌ Rail Station	✛ Church
9 Points of Interest for Chapter 9	▶ Suggested Walk Routes	• Statue or Monument
City District or Neighborhood	▶ Suggested Bus Route	Ritz ⛫ Hotel

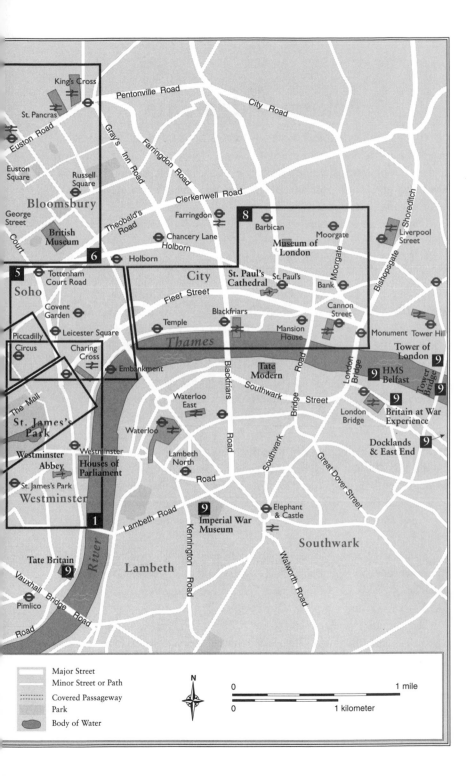

Map Legend

- Major Street
- Minor Street or Path
- Covered Passageway
- Park
- Body of Water

N

0   1 mile

0   1 kilometer

Map Labels:

King's Cross, St. Pancras, Pentonville Road, City Road, Euston Road, Euston Square, Russell Square, Gray's Inn Road, Farringdon Road, Clerkenwell Road, Bloomsbury, George Street, British Museum, Court, Theobald's Road, Farringdon, Chancery Lane, Holborn, Barbican, Moorgate, Shoreditch, Liverpool Street, Museum of London, Bishopsgate, 8, 6, 5, Soho, Tottenham Court Road, City, St. Paul's Cathedral, St. Paul's, Bank, Covent Garden, Fleet Street, Cannon Street, Moorgate, Piccadilly Circus, Leicester Square, Blackfriars, Temple, Mansion House, Monument, Tower Hill, Charing Cross, Embankment, Thames, Tower of London, 9, St. James's Park, The Mall, Waterloo East, Tate Modern, Blackfriars Road, Southwark Street, London Bridge, HMS Belfast, Tower Bridge, Waterloo, London Bridge, Britain at War Experience, Westminster Abbey, Westminster, Lambeth North, Houses of Parliament, Road, Docklands & East End, St. James's Park, Westminster, 1, Lambeth Road, Elephant & Castle, Great Dover Street, Tate Britain, 9, Imperial War Museum, Southwark, Vauxhall Bridge Road, Pimlico, River, Lambeth, Kennington Road, Walworth Road, Southwark Road, Road

Acknowledgments

It began simply enough, walking down a London street and wondering, "What was this like in the war?" It took awhile to find the answer, and then, of course, there was another street. And another. Along the way I've been given help and encouragement from friends, colleagues, Londoners, and librarians.

Ray Riegert and Leslie Henriques, friends and publishers, offered wise counsel and steady support throughout the long process from obsession to print. In fact, the entire staff of Ulysses Press—especially Claire Chun and Lily Chou—have effortlessly combined professionalism and fun, as did mapmaker Ben Pease, who smoothly performed cartographic miracles. Before them, Richard Davies brought his editorial talents to the manuscript.

Grateful thanks to all my colleagues at the Berkeley Public Library, especially Beth Benjamine, Diane Davenport, Tom Dufour, Jef Findley, Evelyn Gahtan, Francisca Goldsmith, Rosemary Hardy, Amy Kuo, Ann Lynn, Will Marston, Anne-Marie Miller, Lawrence Morris, Andrea Moss, Patricia Hoshi Nagamoto, Norine Nomura, Connie Reyes, Robert Saunderson, Jane Scantlebury, and Sura Wallace. The Library's Interlibrary Loan staff—Norma Bacchus, Leticia Dueñas Cendejas, and Linda Seward—went to the ends of the earth to find bibliographic resources. Cinema maven John Muller was extremely generous with his time and advice, as was children's book expert Elizabeth Overmyer. Co-workers Marcia Alpert, Alan Bern, Larry Fonteno, Melanie Lewis, Marti Morec, MaryLou Mull, Pat Mullan, and Yvette Pleasant were enthusiastic cheerleaders, particularly early on.

Speaking of cheerleaders, my thanks to the Chicago Bunch—Marlene Hellman, Lois Schwartz, and Paul Silver—and the Oregon/Washington Bunches: Barbara and Louis Braun, Carol and Ted Davenport, Donna and Bill Davenport, and Lynn and Chuck Koenig.

David Feld, Francie Kendall, Cathy McAuliffe, and Ken Stein made valuable suggestions—thank you all. Several people walked the walks, including Ellen and John Benson, Ann and Bob Lynn, and Diane Davenport, while Sarah Dentan stayed home and got all bleary-eyed staring at newspaper microfilm. Barbara Beatty, Jody Bush, Pam Grossman, Ethel Manheimer, Regina Minudri, and Carol Starr were stalwart supporters throughout—what great women and good friends.

Harve Niemela introduced me to Dorion Hull, a charming and loquacious Englishwomen transplanted to the States, just one of the many Londoners—most anonymously—who shared wartime memories in detail. A special thanks to Pamela Muffty and Richard Tames, two London guides who provided insight into the war years, and to postcard maven Brian Girling, whose advice was invaluable. That noted expert on the minutiae of London's war, Winston Ramsey, also weighed-in with helpful suggestions.

In London, my thanks to Ralph Smith at St. Martin-in-the-Fields, Malcolm Rooke at the Institute of Directors, Dorothy Cone at St. Anne's in Soho, Juanita Wise at St. Mary-le-Strand, Susan Gaskell and Joanna Gamble at Chelsea Old Church, and the helpful ladies of the Chelsea Physic Garden. Assistance was also kindly offered by Peter Bennett at Methodist Central Hall, Pamela Clark at the Royal Archives, Nadene Hansen at Harrods, Sam Giles at Fortnum & Mason, Claire Hart at the Royal Parks Central Services, Malcolm Smith at Gieves and Hawkes, and Christine Reynolds and Jackie Pope at Westminster Abbey. Michael Conway, Teresa Gomez, and Chris Mees all contributed helpful comments or resources, and in Teresa's case, a great place to stay.

The libraries of London are amazing. The collection of the Imperial War Museum is spectacular, of course, but Westminster City Archives, Westminster Reference Library, Guildhall Library, and the Museum of London held important pieces of the war-era puzzle. Emma Crocker and Janis Mullin at the Imperial War Museum's Photo Archives were particularly helpful, as were the photo experts at the U.S. National Archives and the FDR Library. Closer to home, the librarians of BALIS, the San Francisco Bay Area's systemwide reference center, helped me locate, verify, and corroborate. Nevertheless, any errors of fact or interpretation are mine alone.

Finally, this book never would have happened without my family. My daughter Marin Van Young never doubted; my partner Diane Davenport always believed. The two of them have provided more advice, fun, proofreading, support, emotional sustenance, enthusiasm, good meals, bad jokes, and love than I ever expected.

Sayre Van Young
January 2004

Time present and time past
Are both perhaps present in time future,
And time future contained in time past.
—T. S. ELIOT, *FOUR QUARTETS*

Contents

Footsteps of the Famous

Maps

Preface

*Do not be afraid of the past. If people tell you
it is irrevocable, do not believe them. The past, present,
and future are but one moment in the sight of God.
Time and space are merely accidental conditions of thought.
The imagination can transcend them.*

—OSCAR WILDE, *DE PROFUNDIS*

It may happen the first night you arrive in London. Intent upon avoiding jetlag, you've resolutely stayed awake ever since your plane landed. Getting to the hotel, cashing some travelers' checks, walking the neighborhood...it's four in the morning back home, but if you can just stay awake a little longer, you'll sleep well tonight. Unlike last night on the plane, when...what was that? What was that sound?

Was it just a police siren? Or was it some distant echo, some reprise of the sirens that wailed across London during the air raids of World War II? Could the buildings, the streets, even the oldest trees hold those sounds from long ago, and on certain nights, when the bombers' moon is up and the wind is down, could they let them softly fly across London, sounds of moaning air raid sirens and high-flying planes and hammering anti-aircraft guns?

I wish I could answer that question. I've imagined those same sounds— and not just when I was a little goofy from jetlag. But then I've "seen" barrage balloons in the sky too, and "heard" the static on the radio as King George delivered his New Year's message, trying manfully not to stutter. I've walked beside Winston Churchill up the steps to his Morpeth Mansions flat, and I've watched his funeral cortege pass slowly along the Strand towards St. Paul's Cathedral.

Supposedly travel is broadening, but sometimes the breadth is just too wide. Especially given the layers of history in London—literally a city of huts covered by cottages, then houses, then flats, then apartment towers—it's all too easy to become so overwhelmed by the past that one simply tunes out. (I once found myself mumbling, "That's a nice tomb.") After awhile, it can be just too much. I certainly found that to be true, and I set about refocusing and narrowing my interests in this sprawling and complex city.

I decided to investigate a small part of London's history in depth, to interpret the standard tourist venues through the historic lens of London's experience of World War II: finding what was bombed, what survived, where the shelters were, what was sandbagged, exactly how war on London's homefront sounded and smelled and felt. Did you know that two of London's largest and most popular museums still have very visible bomb damage? Or that one can still sit in a crowded bomb shelter and sing "Roll Out the Barrel" with fellow shelterers? Did you know that over 60,000 sandbags were once piled around the treasures of Westminster Abbey? Or that anti-aircraft guns once boomed away across the lawns of Hyde Park?

London's War takes the visitor to the best the metropolis has to offer, looking at the city as it is today and imagining it as it was six decades ago—Parliament Square strung with barbed wire, the Tower of London's moat planted in onions and carrots, Buckingham Palace's windows blasted out. This guide is aimed at today's traveler who wants to reach back into history to discover what London's war was really like.

Because the most involving way to see the metropolis is on foot and since the story of London's war is best seen up close, the book is arranged as walking visits to eight popular areas of central London, from Whitehall to Soho to Bloomsbury. Chapters begin with an overview of that neighborhood's experience of war, followed by information on the sights of today in the context of the war years. Shorter mini-walks take the traveler beyond the well-trod tourist attractions to less-frequented residential areas that offer insight into a war waged against ordinary citizens. An additional chapter guides the traveler who wants to investigate wartime sites in Greater London. Clear and readable maps lead off each chapter and mini-walk, and throughout, contemporary travel information is included: nearby Underground stops, hours, admission fees, and eating and restroom possibilities.

Travel and cultural preparations at the opening of each chapter suggest pre-trip activities, from checking the website of the British Museum to listening to Vera Lynn singing "A Nightingale Sang in Berkeley Square." Topical sidebars highlight the everyday icons of English travel (postboxes and telephone kiosks, tea time and buses), placing them firmly in the wartime setting while providing helpful information for today's traveler. Biographical sidebars visit the homes and haunts of well-known war-related figures, providing specific addresses and locations to guide the reader who can then "walk in the footsteps" of the players in the grand drama of World War II London. And watch for War Words, helpful definitions of perhaps unfamiliar terms.

The articulate voices of London's wartime experience— including Virginia Woolf, Andy Rooney, George Orwell, and Edward R. Murrow—dramatize the homefront years with comments on specific streets, sights, and sounds. A traveler's reprise concludes the book, revisiting many sites to see how  Londoners celebrated V-E Day, the day the war in Europe ended. Throughout, photographs suggest the physical changes London has experienced in the last sixty years.

This book talks not of war but of wartime, of a homefront that can still be seen and felt by the imaginative traveler. You'll find no dreary treks to depressing bomb sites here. Instead, *London's War* looks at the sights and events of a devastating conflict as experienced not by soldiers but by the ordinary citizens of London. No one can make war fun—who would want to?—but *London's War* brings the city's wartime struggle into the twenty-first century, providing a sort of demilitarized zone for readers where the past and present can mingle.

My choice of London in the war years wasn't totally random (I *did* hear that siren, after all), as the early 1940s are close enough to have personal meaning for many, myself included. Perhaps you and your family gathered around the radio to hear Edward R. Murrow broadcast the hurried footsteps of Londoners in the blackout, or perhaps years later, your dad—or your granddad—related stories of being stationed in England during the war. For me, the war and the experience of Londoners in it was an adventure told and retold by my mother and my great-uncle, one a gloriously patriotic Anglophile, the other an English businessman who'd go up to London weekly, then sit down to write his American family the war news.

I hope as you make your travel plans—weighing whether to go via Fodor's or the back door, whether to see wild Britain or walking Britain, whether to find cheap eats or cheap seats—you'll consider London's evocative windborne sounds. Others may hear Roman foot soldiers cursing the gluey swampland down by the river, or perhaps the clanking chains in the debtors' prisons, or even Elton John singing his sad song in the Abbey. *I* hear air raid sirens...be sure the lights are out, now, and let's get to the shelter.

Travel Basics

How to use this book: Each chapter travels one to three walking routes; several chapters also feature shorter mini-walks. Routes take two to three hours each, longer if there are sights to stop and visit. Mini-walks take from half an hour to two hours, and do not include as many stop-and-visit possibilities. Rest stops are suggested. Routes begin and end near Underground stations, although more as easily recognizable landmarks than as travel recommendations. Enjoy entire walks, partial walks, or chart your own itinerary and check the index as you go for specific attractions or areas.

Open hours can inexplicably change, and they're routinely shorter in winter. The last admission is often earlier than the actual closing time. Royal-connected establishments sometimes close without warning. Everything shuts down around Christmas and New Year's, and some attractions close on bank holidays. Call or web-check for details, or plan on being flexible and smiling through.

Admission fees vary; the fact that admission is charged is noted. Most attractions charge less for older visitors; several are free for disabled visitors and accompanying helpers. Even places offering free admission appreciate donations.

War Words: Bombers' Moon

During the early days of the blackout, Londoners welcomed the full moon bathing dark streets and pavements in helpful light. But once the Blitz began, a full moon was a **BOMBERS' MOON**—it meant a nighttime air attack was likely since the Luftwaffe pilots could more easily follow the silvery thread of the Thames toward the metropolis. As one Londoner put it, "There's no doubt about it—as soon as the moon is full, over they come." If your visit includes a clear sky and a full moon, consider taking a walk around the block to imagine the effect of that pearly light on a blacked-out London street, waiting for the evening's wailing sirens and the ominous thumps of exploding bombs.

> *I don't think that I have ever failed to appreciate a beautiful moonlight night before, but nowadays it has taken on a different meaning....Last night was a perfect night for the poet—unfortunately it was also a perfect night for the German planes.*
> —Anthony Weymouth, *Journal of the War Years*

Disabled access is noted where access is unusually quirky or problematic; otherwise consider access adequate. Don't hesitate to call for details, however, as in-depth information is beyond the scope of this book.

Telephone numbers changed with the millennium. The new style for London numbers is eleven numbers, including an "area code" of 020, followed by the number 7 indicating central London: 020 7123 4567. From the United States, drop the first zero and add the international calling code and city code. The number above, called from the States, would be 011 44 20 7123 4567. Called from London it would be 7123 4567. Called from Liverpool (for example), it would be 020 7123 4567.

Tourists (everyone else in line but you and me) are unavoidable. London is, after all, one of the world's most visited cities. Start out early, walk in the evening, or just be patient. If possible, avoid the entire month of August, when half of the Continent comes calling and many sights—especially churches—tend to close for a vacation themselves.

Churches, under-visited except for Westminster Abbey and St. Paul's Cathedral, provide a unique insight into London's history. Churches are generally open weekdays during the day for wandering about, and on Sunday for services only.

Money Basics:
How Much Is That in Real Money?

Britain moved to a decimal-based currency system in 1971, tossing aside the old scheme of pennies, shillings, and pounds along with the odd farthing, halfpenny, florin, half-crown, crown, and guinea. Overseas visitors today only have pounds and pence to figure out, at least until they try to compute how much something cost in 1940. Here's an overview of wartime money and a theory of equivalency.

In the war years, the most common English coins were the penny (written with a *d.*, from the Latin *denarius*), the sixpence (6d.), the shilling (equivalent to 12d.), and the pound (equivalent to 20 shillings or 240d.; written £ for *libra*, from the Latin for pound). There were also paper notes (at least early in the war) for £5, £10, £20, and so on.

Prices were quoted, for example, as two shillings and written as 2s or 2/-. An item costing two shillings and sixpence would be quoted as "2 and 6" and written 2/6. Most prices noted in this book are very straight-forward— £8, for example. However, when you see a figure like 3/6, re-member it's three shillings sixpence, not three-sixths.

Throughout this book, one wartime shilling is assumed to be equiva-lent to *about* twenty American cents based on the exchange rates circa 1940, so a £1 meal (i.e., 20 shillings) would be equivalent to about $4 in 1940. However, $4 in 1940 isn't equivalent to $4 today. And thus enters complexity.

Various economic sources suggest multiplying that 1940 figure by a factor of twenty to thirty, so a London wartime meal costing £1 would cost about £30 today or about $45. But remember, the average working-class Londoner made only about £3 a week right before the war started. So varying standards of living should also be factored in, plus changes in in-flation rates and cost of living over the course of the war and since. It *is* a miasma, and economic experts emphasize that the "factor of twenty or thirty" is only the most inexact of approximations. I agree wholeheartedly. Personally, I figure the American equivalent of a wartime shilling would have gotten me into an American movie in 1940, and that's all I need to know.

Maps help. The ones in this book, excellent as they are, will only guide you on the suggested walks herein. To strike off on your own, get a good readable map book and use it. No guilt or embarrassment in-volved—half of London carries maps.

Internet checking is useful, though not every London attraction has a website, relying instead on the travel, tourist, and accommodation mega-sites.

Construction happens. Scaffolding and pavement barriers can and do pop up unexpectedly, often directly between you and your destination. If building construction or heightened security measures block a route suggested in this book, be glad it isn't because of wartime bomb damage, then be creative in detouring to get back on course.

Spelling in *London's War*, as in London, tends toward the British, as does usage (petrol, for example, rather than gasoline), all in an effort to make war imaginings a bit more authentic.

Restroom locations are noted. Rail stations and larger Underground stations have public conveniences, though the cost is usually twenty pence—20p. Using the W.C. in a restaurant or pub is fine if you're eating there, but a little nervy if you just sweep in off the street. Several portable toilets have been set up in busy areas, including on Shaftesbury Avenue near Piccadilly, in Russell Square, and by the Guildhall. These loos are clean and convenient, once you get over the hurdle of thinking the door will open suddenly (it won't). They too charge 20p. And larger department stores have lavatories, though be prepared to leave a tip if there's an attendant. Careful readers of this paragraph will note that multiple synonyms for "the littlest room" have been used. Travelers can use any of these terms ("the littlest room" is a bit precious, though); just don't ask for the bathroom, unless, of course, you need to take a bath.

Writing about such a complex city and the experiences of the millions of Londoners who saw a lengthy war from so many perspectives inevitably means I may have missed something or perhaps misinterpreted scattered fragments of information. Please let me know *your* war experiences in and of central London—they'll make the next edition even more authentic and intriguing. I can be contacted by mail in care of the publishers, or at svanyoung@earthlink.net.

Introduction:
How War Came to London

For the second time in the lives of most of us, we are at
war...and war can no longer be confined to the battlefield.
—KING GEORGE VI, SEPTEMBER 3, 1939

World War II began, in a way, the day World War I ended. The Germans, humiliated by the Treaty of Versailles and embarrassed by their new world role (losers), were eager to throw off the draconian restrictions the treaty imposed. Austrian Adolf Hitler, that strangely charismatic veteran of World War I, rose quickly to postwar leadership, pledging to restore Germany's greatness. Hitler became Chancellor in 1933 and his National Socialists—the Nazis—soon injected themselves into every aspect of German life.

Throughout the 1930s, Hitler spearheaded German rearmament while European leaders looked the other way. Only Winston Churchill, no longer in the British Cabinet but still in Parliament, warned of the growing danger across the English Channel, and his views were belittled at best, ignored at worst. An exhausted nation, England was wrestling with depression, both economic and human, and wasn't much concerned with Herr Hitler and his once-defeated countrymen. An entire generation of young Englishmen had been lost in the trenches of France—dead, gassed, or haunted—and few of the survivors or their families could envision ever fighting again. They had won, it was over, and thank god, it had been the War to End All Wars.

Although Neville Chamberlain hadn't fought in World War I, he shared his countrymen's horror of conflict. The slow rise of this stolid bureaucrat up Britain's governmental ladder culminated in 1937 when he was named prime minister. The task of dealing with a rearmed and geographically acquisitive Hitler would fall to a man who would do anything to avoid war.

In the late 1930s, Hitler's machinations moved beyond Germany's borders. First the German Fuehrer wanted Austria. He got Austria. Then he wanted all of Czechoslovakia, but was willing to settle for the Sudetenland, the western part of Czechoslovakia bordering Germany. Hitler insisted the area was filled with Germans who rightfully should be part of Germany. Once the Sudetenland became Germany's, Herr Hitler assured European

Bomb Basics

High explosive bombs came in numerous sizes up to 4,000 pounds. The Germans most frequently used the general-purpose 500-lb. bomb and the 1,000-lb. variety. Bombs, usually dropped from about two miles above their targets, plummeted earthward at 600 miles an hour. Upon landing they would burst into thousands of fragments flying in all directions at 8,000 feet per second. One observer noted, "It makes a frightening noise while falling, a shattering thunder-clap on arrival, and sets up a blast so fierce that, landing 50 feet away from you, it is usually counted as a direct hit." The first effect was earth shock, like an earthquake, then the shock wave of blast above the earth, then bomb splinters whizzing through the air, and finally fire created by the intense heat of the blast. A 500-lb. bomb could easily demolish a house and make nearby homes uninhabitable. Of course, the 1,000-lb. version would do much worse.

    Incendiary or fire bombs were lightweight (two-and-a-half pounds) and small (thirteen to eighteen inches long), with a shell of magnesium alloy and a core of thermite priming composition. They ignited on impact and burned furiously for upwards of twenty minutes at 2,000°F. Larger German aircraft carried as many as 2,000 incendiary bombs, released in groups or in a "Molotov breadbasket," a cluster that fell as a unit until close to the ground. Given their momentum, incendiary bombs could easily penetrate roofs on impact. If they fell on roads or pavements, the bombs burned harmlessly; if extinguished quickly with sand or a stirrup pump, they were not dangerous. (Author John Dos Passos heard about a boy who put one out with a bag of Brussels sprouts.) If they fell unde-

leaders, his country's "legitimate" territorial needs would be assuaged. Chamberlain, determined to keep Britain out of war, did his best in a lengthy process of diplomatic appeasement that may have given Britain more time to rearm, but sold Czechoslovakia down the river.

So the Munich crisis of 1938 came and went—those tense weeks when Hitler threatened to send troops into the Sudetenland, and Chamberlain flew back and forth to Germany, promising, humoring, appeasing. Londoners feared war would break out at any moment. Dozens of defensive barrage balloons were put in place to rise above the city if needed, hundreds of men dug shelter trenches in London's parks and squares, and millions of gas masks were issued to worried citizens. The Munich crisis finally ended not with a bang but with a piece of paper, the agreement with Hitler that Chamberlain waved from the window of Number 10 Downing Street. The prime minister believed it meant peace; in fact, it only postponed war.

tected or in inaccessible areas, fire bombs could easily start a conflagration. On the night of May 10, 1941, over 86,000 incendiary bombs were
dropped on London.

Oil bombs were much larger than incendiaries, about a foot in
diameter. They carried an explosive charge, a detonator, and oil. When
they exploded, usually with a huge mushroom flame,
burning oil was splashed fifty to a hundred feet, a
messy and dangerous firestarter.

Parachute bombs were mines dropped
by parachute. They arrived silently and because of that were particularly terrifying.
They exploded on the surface—not deep
in the ground—producing a potent lat-
eral explosive force.

Unexploded bombs (UXBs) were
either high explosive bombs that failed
to detonate or bombs with timing
mechanisms set to explode after they
landed. Their presence necessitated the
immediate blocking off of streets and evacuation of anyone living nearby. Residents
were usually given a few minutes to gather ne-
cessities and then were restricted from returning
until there had been some resolution—either the removal of the bomb
elsewhere for detonation (often to one of London's more distant park
corners) or detonation where it had landed.

> *I marveled at
> the freaks of air
> raid damage and the
> unfathomable laws of
> blast....The entire frontage
> of the deserted business
> premises opposite was
> wrecked, and Milton's
> statue has been flung from
> its plinth. Yet the lamp-post
> was standing erect with no
> pane of its lantern broken.*
> —Cecil Beaton, *The Years
> Between, 1939–44*

Six months after the peaceful acquisition of the Sudetenland, German
troops invaded the rest of Czechoslovakia, and once again Chamberlain
and Britain failed to stand up to the Fuehrer. (One is reminded of
Churchill's definition, "An appeaser is one who feeds the crocodile, hoping it will eat him last.") Finally, realizing that Hitler's next step would
likely be toward the very large and very central country of Poland, France
and Britain signed an agreement offering unqualified support against any
action that might threaten Polish independence. Political tensions rose,
then rose some more. Clearly appeasement was no longer an option.

In the midst of the growing political strain, Germany and Russia unexpectedly signed a nonaggression pact, a blow to both England and France.
To the ordinary Londoner, the response was, "Wait—I thought they were
on *our* side." They (the Russians) were in a way, and would be again (rejoin-
ing the Allies in mid-1941), but the possibility of grabbing parts of Finland and Poland prompted the abrupt realignment of diplomatic alliances.

And then Hitler's troops marched into Poland on September 1, 1939, and the world turned upside down.

By the late 1930s, three out of four English homes had radios. Most were tuned to the BBC on Sunday, September 3, 1939, awaiting the important broadcast that had been hinted at for days. A thunderstorm had rattled windows in the night, but by 11:15am London's skies were quiet as Prime Minister Chamberlain began—"This morning the British Ambassador in Berlin handed the German Government a final note stating that unless we heard from them by eleven o'clock that they were prepared at once to withdraw their troops from Poland, a state of war would exist between us. I have to tell you now that no such undertaking has been received, and that consequently this country is at war with Germany."

For information on World War II books, check Stone and Stone's website (www.sonic. net/~bstone) with reviews, details on authors and booksellers, and links to other war-related resources.

Within minutes, a lone aircraft crossed the Channel toward England, setting off air raid warnings and hastily sending Londoners to shelters below ground. A false alarm (a French plane had not made its flight path known), the episode nonetheless suggested what was to come—a war fought not on distant battlefields but in England's skies.

After that adrenaline-producing false alert, London's war segued into months of boredom. Wartime measures were instituted—theatres and cinemas were ordered closed (they reopened twelve days later), petrol and food rationing was planned, identity cards were issued. Museums and art galleries evacuated irreplaceable treasures to safer locations beyond the range of Hitler's bombers. Although there was some fighting in Finland, for the British the period from September 1939 to April 1940 became known as the Phoney War.

The Phoney War ended abruptly in spring 1940 as Hitler began a *blitzkrieg,* or lightning attack, against Norway and Denmark, then Belgium, Luxembourg, and the Netherlands. One by one, some in a few days, some in a few weeks, each of these countries surrendered to the advancing German forces. A tired and worn Neville Chamberlain resigned, his hopes for peace irretrievably lost. Winston Churchill was named Britain's prime minister, offering his fellow citizens naught but "blood, toil, tears and sweat."

Meanwhile the British Expeditionary Forces, stationed in northwest France, were slowly driven back against the English Channel by German troops. Over 300,000 stranded soldiers were rescued from the beaches of Dunkirk by a flotilla of English craft, from ships to fishing boats, leaving

Some Common Misconceptions about London's War

- World War II did not start on December 7, 1941. For England, the war officially began on September 3, 1939, and for London, much of the worst bombing was over months before the Japanese attack on Pearl Harbor.

- Londoners did not "smile through." They did not believe "London can take it." They did not "carry on." And they did. The war lasted for almost six years, millions of Londoners of all social classes experienced it, and emotions and energies and focus ebbed and flowed for every one of them. The war was different and difficult for everyone, but for Londoners, the experience united them far more than it defeated or divided them.

- All Londoners did not shelter in the Tube. Sheltering options were many (see Chapter 3 for details). It's estimated that of those Londoners who elected to take shelter, only about 2 to 4 percent actually hunkered down alongside the Underground tracks during air raids.

- Not every London child was evacuated to safety, not every evacuee had a terrible (or wonderful) time of it, and not every child sent to a place of greater safety remained there the entire war. Early on, about one-and-a-half million children were evacuated from London to safer locations in the countryside. But when the first months of the war brought no bombs to the capital, London parents began to want their children back. The authorities were not happy (posters urged "Don't do it, Mother—Leave the children where they are"), but many of London's youngsters eventually came home to spend the war saving tin foil, picking up shrapnel souvenirs, and generally enjoying themselves.

- Greater London was not obliterated by bombs. One could drive for miles (petrol rationing permitting) and not see appreciable bomb damage. Conversely, one could turn a corner in the City or the East End and come upon acres of almost unimaginable devastation.

- Finally, a last notion worth disabusing oneself of—the understandable need to organize the horrors of war in some order of magnitude, sort of "my war was worse than your war." Was the Holocaust worse than the bombing of Nagasaki and Hiroshima? Was the carpet bombing of Dresden worse than the flattening of Coventry? Was the bombing of Berlin worse than that of London? Motives, methods, statistics, loss.... The miseries of war are unspeakably horrendous, and comparisons are by their very nature invalid. In the end, attempting to arrange destruction and death by degree of terribleness is fruitless because it all matters so much. As wartime poet Dylan Thomas wrote, "After the first death, there is no other."

behind an army's worth of equipment. As Churchill noted at the time, wars are not won by evacuations, but at least this dramatic exit saved the army to fight another day.

And then Italy joined in the military brouhaha, declaring war against both France and England. By mid-June 1940, France surrendered, and England stood alone as Germany's air force—the Luftwaffe—began to pound the Royal Air Force and its airfields.

Hitler's planned invasion of England in the early autumn—Operation Sea Lion—was predicated on mastery of Britain's air forces. White vapor trails floated thousands of feet above southeast England as RAF pilots dueled the Luftwaffe throughout the summer of 1940. Despite the sky-high carnage of the Battle of Britain, devastating to both sides, it's possible that if Hitler had continued the air battle, the Luftwaffe might well have prevailed. But inexplicably, just when the RAF pilots were most exhausted and British aircraft losses becoming most ruinous, Hitler changed his strategy. Allegedly outraged by bombing reprisals on Berlin, ordered by Churchill when German planes unexpectedly (and perhaps inadvertently) bombed London in late August 1940, Hitler ordered a halt to the attacks on RAF aircraft and airfields. Instead, the Luftwaffe retaliated with day-time attacks on the world's most populous city.

And so on September 7, 1940, the Battle of London began as German aircraft swept across the English Channel and headed up the Thames Estuary. By late afternoon the first formation of German bombers, accompanied by a fighter escort to ward off those pesky RAF Hurricanes and Spitfires, began to drop their bomb loads on London's eastern portion—West Ham power station, the Royal and Surrey docks, the ammunition dumps of Woolrich Arsenal, Rotherhithe, Canning Town, and Silvertown. As the keening moan of air raid sirens sounded across the capital, no one could know that this air strike heralded fifty-six more days of bombings.

For the first few Blitz raids, German planes concentrated on London's East End, packed with docks and shipyards and home to London's poor and lower classes. Here ramshackle tenements were squeezed together, flimsily constructed and overcrowded; the nearby warehouses and docks were filled with England's exports and imports—cooking oil, lumber, rum, sugar, and paint. Bombs falling here found an exceedingly flammable target.

But shortly, German strategy changed yet again as daytime raids were gradually curtailed in favor of nighttime attacks, with the primary target moving westward to central London. In retrospect, this was another inex-plicable strategic shift—by focusing on the slums of the East End, Hitler had a chance to drive a political wedge between London's unprotected and underserved lower classes and the well-protected well-off denizens of the West End. He failed to do so, and a great deal can be read into Queen Elizabeth's remark after the bombing of Buckingham Palace: "I'm *glad* we've been bombed. It makes me feel I can look the East End in the face." An opportunity to divide Londoners instead became a unifying force.

From September 7, 1940, to May 10, 1941, London's centers of government, commerce, culture, royalty, and religion were attacked—the Houses of Parliament, the City's Guildhall, the British Museum, the Tower of London, the shopping districts of Oxford Street, Buckingham Palace, St. Paul's Cathedral, and Westminster Abbey. During the first two months, an average of 165 bombers nightly

> Wartime censorship meant photos of bomb damage weren't published in daily newspapers immediately after air raids—they might provide information to the enemy. Instead, it was often months, sometimes years, before the photos appeared.

dropped 200 tons of high explosive bombs and hundreds of incendiary bombs. Several Blitz attacks were particularly memorable, for size, duration, targets, and effects:

September 7, 1940: "Black Saturday" marked the beginning of the Blitz; Hitler's bombers focused on the docks, warehouses, and homes of the East End. Over 430 Londoners died and 1,600 were badly injured.

October 14-15, 1940: Over 400 German bombers dropped 538 tons of bombs on the capital; more than 400 Londoners died and another 900 were seriously injured. Five of London's rail terminals were disabled.

December 8-9, 1940: Incendiary bombs from 400 bombers started 1,700 fires. More than 250 Londoners died and another 600 were injured.

December 29-30, 1940: The City—that square mile of history around St. Paul's Cathedral—took the brunt of the Luftwaffe's attack on "Red Sunday." High winds, low tide, broken water mains, and unattended warehouses and buildings meant small fires became large fires and large fires became conflagrations. In all, over 1,400 fires were started.

April 16-17, 1941: Known as "The Wednesday," this raid lasted more than eight hours and brought hundreds of German bombers over the capital, killing more than a thousand civilians and damaging thousands of homes, primarily in central and south London.

April 19-20, 1941: On "The Saturday," 700 Luftwaffe planes above London dropped 1,000 tons of high-explosive bombs and 4,500 canisters of incendiary bombs.

May 10-11, 1941: Generally considered the last and worst attack of London's Blitz, this five-hour raid saw Westminster Abbey aflame, St.

Text continued on page xxxii.

Neville Chamberlain

March 18, 1869: Arthur Neville Chamberlain is born in Birmingham.

1911: Chamberlain enters politics as a Birmingham council member and then as lord mayor. His next step is Parliament (1918). He marries Anne Vere Cole in St. Paul's, Knightsbridge. In 1920 the couple will move to 35 Egerton Crescent, South Kensington.

1923: As Chamberlain begins to rise in the government (Postmaster General, Paymaster General, Minister of Health), he and his wife purchase 37 Eaton Square, Belgravia. (A plaque notes their residence.) In the 1930s, German Ambassador Ribbentrop, a friend of the Chamberlains, will sublet the house.

1931: Chamberlain is named Chancellor of the Exchequer; the Chamberlains move into the Exchequer's official residence at 11 Downing Street.

May 1937: Neville Chamberlain, aged sixty-eight, succeeds Stanley Baldwin as prime minister, and soon moves into 10 Downing Street.

September 15, 1938: Mounting territorial demands of German Chancellor Adolf Hitler prompt Chamberlain to fly to Germany for a face-to-face meeting.

September 16–21, 1938: After returning to London, Chamberlain joins his cabinet in a flurry of meetings at 10 Downing Street amidst political and diplomatic maneuvers surrounding Hitler's plans to partition Czechoslovakia's Sudetenland.

September 22, 1938: Chamberlain and Herr Hitler meet again, this time in Godesberg, Germany. Hitler ups the ante with more extreme territorial demands. The two are unable to agree. A second inconclusive meeting follows the next day.

September 24, 1938: A worried Chamberlain returns to England, landing at Heston Airdrome and announcing to the somber crowd, "I trust all concerned will continue their efforts to solve the Czechoslovakia problem peacefully, because on that turns the peace of Europe in our time." Two days later, Hitler informs a British diplomatic representative that he plans to invade Czechoslovakia within forty-eight hours.

September 25–27, 1938: Britain moves closer to war. A state of emergency is declared. The country collectively holds its breath.

September 27, 1938: Chamberlain broadcasts on the wireless: "How horrible, fantastic, incredible it is that we should be digging trenches and trying on gas masks here because of a quarrel in a far-away country between people of whom we know nothing." Britain is not going to support Czechoslovakia's territorial integrity.

September 28, 1938: As the prime minister addresses the House of Commons regarding the miasma of the Czech situation, word is brought that Hitler has postponed troop mobilization and is prepared to meet with representatives of Britain (Chamberlain), Italy (Mussolini), and France (Daladier). No one from the Czech government will be included.

September 29, 1938: Chamberlain returns to Germany. A plan to effectively dismember Czechoslovakia is agreed upon, and the Munich Agreement is signed at 2am on September 30.

September 30, 1938: The prime minister greets cheering crowds at Heston Airdrome and declares that the agreement with Hitler is "symbolic of the desire of our two peoples never to go to war with one another again." Chamberlain confers with the king at Buckingham Palace, then returns to Downing Street, where he waves the piece of paper betraying Czechoslovakia and shouts to the crowd, "I believe it is peace for our time." Britain collectively breathes a sigh of relief.

March 15, 1939: Appeasement has not worked. Hitler ignores his agreement with Chamberlain and moves to occupy all of Czechoslovakia.

Early August 1939: Since Parliament is in recess, and despite the worsening diplomatic situation, Chamberlain leaves for a fortnight's salmon-fishing in Scotland.

August 23, 1939: The political situation deteriorates. Chamberlain returns to London and calls an urgent cabinet meeting. Political and diplomatic discussions continue almost nonstop for the next ten days. Britain again prepares for war.

September 1, 1939: German forces invade Poland. The next day the British government will send Hitler an ultimatum, demanding troop withdrawal from Poland.

September 3, 1939: At 11am, the ultimatum expires. Shortly after, Chamberlain sits before a microphone at 10 Downing Street and begins speaking: "[Hitler's] action shows convincingly that there is no chance of expecting that this man will ever give up his practice of using force to gain his will. He can only be stopped by force." Britain declares war on Germany.

September 4, 1939–early May 1940: The Phoney War follows. Chamberlain's political support gradually erodes.

May 10, 1940: After a too-narrow margin of victory in a Parliament vote of support, and facing his own inability to form a coalition government, Chamberlain resigns as prime minister. He will remain in the cabinet as Lord President of the Council.

November 9, 1940: Neville Chamberlain dies in Heckfield House, Odiham, Hampshire. A funeral is held in Westminster Abbey several days later, and the ashes of Arthur Neville Chamberlain are buried in the Abbey's nave.

Clement Danes gutted, Queen's Hall demolished. More than 1,400 Londoners were killed, another 1,700 were injured, and over 12,000 left homeless. Seven hundred acres of London were damaged by more than 2,200 fires, 20 of them major.

Even when the relentless Blitz raids ended, years of wartime lay ahead for London's civilians, a period filled with fewer bombing attacks but with the ongoing stress of threatened terror. That, combined with homefront challenges (rationing of food, clothing, and petrol, plus bureaucratic red tape and rules), ground the city and its inhabitants to a wartime gray. Everyone was war-involved: in the military or the Home Guard, serving as a firefighter or an air raid warden, driving an ambulance or running a lunch counter, volunteering to make tea for bomb-site workers or on-call for firewatching. Everything one did was war-influenced: when one got up, what one ate, what one bought and wore and read and listened to, how one moved about the metropolis, even when the curtains were closed—the nighttime blackout was strictly enforced. Plump sandbags were piled along London's streets and pavements, and tin hats and gas masks were as ever-present as the pillboxes and defense posts on city corners. War was everywhere, even when the bombs stopped.

The post–Blitz period brought more than stress to London—it also brought hordes of Allied soldiers. The largest group wore the khaki uniforms of the United States; the Yanks started arriving in quantity after Pearl Harbor and by 1944, well over a million GIs were in England. London pavements (and bars and hotels and shops) also overflowed with soldiers from France, Poland, Australia, Canada, New Zealand, and Holland.

Thirty thousand Londoners died in air attacks on the metropolis; another 30,000 civilians died elsewhere in Great Britain. But published photos showed just ruins and rubble with nary a body in sight.

European governments-in-exile found London safer compared to their embattled homelands, and several (including Norway, Poland, the Netherlands, Belgium, Czechoslovakia, Yugoslavia, and Greece) moved in for the duration. Perhaps the best-known expatriate was Charles de Gaulle (he once called London "the capital of the war"). Besides de Gaulle's Free French, other national movements worked out of London—the free Danish, free Rumanian, free Bulgarian, and free Austrian.

The respite from major bombing attacks—from mid-May 1941 through January 1944—ended with the aerial attacks of the Little Blitz in February 1944 and the rocket attacks of the war's last months. From mid-1944 to March 1945, thousands of deadly V-1 and V-2 rockets careened over London. At least the slower V-1s provided some warning—about twelve seconds from the moment the noisy spluttering stopped until the bomb exploded upon hitting the ground. Dubbed "doodlebugs," the V-1 pilotless bombs killed 5,000 and injured three times that number. The vastly more powerful and malevolent V-2 arrived swiftly (1,400 mph) and silently. The 500-plus V-2s that hit the metropolis killed almost 3,000 Londoners. Compared to the bombs of the Blitz, the V-1s and V-2s brought a new level of emotional stress. As Churchill put it, "Suspense and strain were more prolonged. Dawn brought no relief and cloud no comfort."

By war's end, Londoners had heard the warning sirens sound over a thousand times, an average of once every thirty-six hours from first to last bombing incident. Enemy planes had dropped 18,000 tons of high explosives on the metropolis and its citizens. Almost 30,000 Londoners now rested in the city's cemeteries, victims of German air attacks; another 50,000 had been seriously injured and twice that number slightly injured. Millions of homes were destroyed or damaged. In Bermondsey, east and south of London Bridge, 90 percent of the housing was affected; in Stepney (the Tower Hamlets area of East London) over 40 percent was affected.

Many political, economic, and military aspects of London's war haven't found their way into this travel book, including the treatment of refugees and aliens, the government's inadequate preparation for aerial bombings, even the role of radar. You'll find details on these issues in London at War *by Philip Ziegler, an excellent historical overview of the capital's wartime experience.*

On May 8, 1945, Londoners thronged the city's streets to celebrate Victory in Europe Day. Though the V-E revelers were certainly happy and relieved, they weren't nearly as exuberant as had been the celebrants at the conclusion of World War I. That, after all, had been the War to End All Wars. Londoners would never be so naïve again.

Postwar rebuilding began almost immediately, and the first to go was Winston Churchill; the prime minister lost the July 1945 election and was replaced by Labour's Clement Attlee. Then the capital's bureaucrats, businessmen, visionaries, preservationists, and architects settled in to wrestle over the spirit and look of postwar London. Many hoped that the cleared bomb sites might become green space, opening vistas in London's core, but it was not to be. Construction soon began and continues today. But amidst the office blocks and new streets of the ever-rebuilding metropolis lie evocative memories and more tangible reminders of a civilian battleground, where a war was fought and won by London's citizens. London's war can still be found.

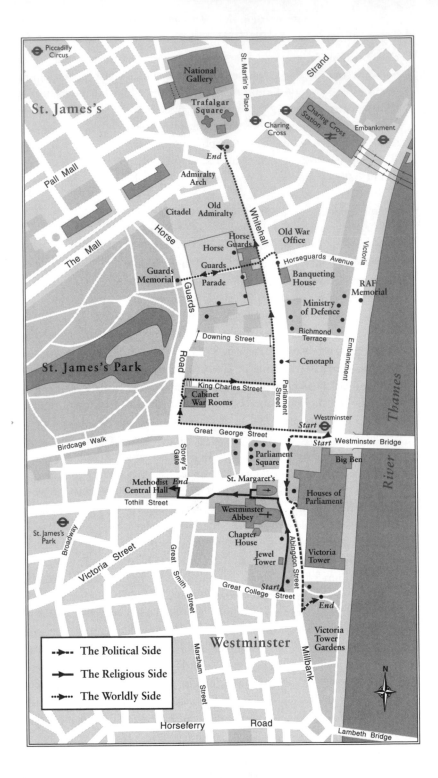

Piccadilly
Circus

National
Gallery

St. James's

Trafalgar
Square

St. Martin's Place

Strand

Charing
Cross

Charing Cross
Station

Embankment

End

Admiralty
Arch

Pall Mall

Citadel

Old
Admiralty

Whitehall

Old War
Office

The Mall

Horse

Horse
Guards

Horse
Guards

Horseguards Avenue

Victoria

Guards
Memorial

Guards
Parade

Banqueting
House

RAF
Memorial

Ministry
of Defence

Embankment

Richmond
Terrace

St. James's Park

Road

Downing Street

Cenotaph

Thames

King Charles Street

Parliament
Street

Cabinet
War Rooms

Westminster

Start

Birdcage Walk

Great George Street

Start   Westminster Bridge

River

Storey's Gate

Parliament
Square

Big Ben

Methodist *End*
Central Hall

St. Margaret's

Tothill Street

Houses of
Parliament

St. James's
Park

Broadway

Westminster
Abbey

Victoria Street

Great Smith Street

Chapter
House

Abingdon Street

Jewel
Tower

Victoria
Tower

Great College Street *Start*

End

Westminster

Victoria
Tower
Gardens

Marsham Street

Millbank

N

Horseferry   Road

Lambeth Bridge

At the Foot of Big Ben

Within a block of Big Ben, England's wartime prime ministers walked daily, war leaders were honored in somber funerals, and the endless drudgery of bureaucracy ground along behind blackout curtains and sandbagged windows.

Two nights brought the war home to the monuments and buildings in Big Ben's shadow. In late September 1940, an explosive bomb detonated in Old Palace Yard, leaving a gaping crater in the roadway, blowing out windows in Parliament, and damaging the statue of Richard the Lionhearted.

In mid-May 1941, German incendiary bombs rained down—and ignited. And as flames lit the skies, the next wave of heavy bombers had an even better view of the target. The Members' Lobby of Parliament was destroyed and the House of Commons meeting chamber totally gutted. Flames danced on the roof of Westminster Hall, and across the roadway, the towers of Westminster Abbey looked down on Abbey staff frantically fighting an inferno as the Little Cloisters, Deanery, and parts of Westminster School burned. Nazi bombs even found a slender Big Ben.

Six decades later, the environs of Big Ben seem untouched by World War II. But let's look more closely, starting from the Westminster Underground. The Bridge Street exit surfaces directly across from Big Ben in the middle of the three worlds of the Westminster/Whitehall district: the political landscape straight ahead toward Big Ben and Parliament; the religious realm to the right toward Westminster Abbey; and northward, at your back, the more worldly sphere of Downing Street, Banqueting House, and on towards Trafalgar Square.

While considering where to begin in this history-drenched area, some visual perspective may help. Turn away from the milling tourists at the Underground and head left across Westminster Bridge. Even though traffic pounds across this span, once at the bridge's mid-point you'll have the illusion of distance and quiet as you look back toward Parliament and the Abbey towers. This view has changed little in sixty years and, as pacifist and author Vera Brittain mused in August 1940 just before the Blitz began, has "the calm appearance of an old engraving delicately outlined against a tranquil sky," a calm that would miraculously survive the hell and chaos of London's war.

PART I

THE POLITICAL SIDE

This group of well-known, prominent buildings and towers between three major railway stations, with the river as a perfect guide by night and day, is the easiest of all targets....This building itself is not well constructed to withstand aerial bombardment. There is an immense amount of glass about the place.

—WINSTON CHURCHILL SPEAKING TO PARLIAMENT, 1939

Waiting for war.

Highlights: Big Ben, Parliament Square, Churchill statue, Palace of Westminster Complex (Parliament), Victoria Tower Gardens

Underground Station: Westminster

Photo Ops: Westminster's landmarks are close enough that you can easily—and dramatically—double up: Cromwell with Parliament behind, or Churchill with Big Ben. Alas, no photography inside Parliament.

BEFORE LEAVING ON YOUR TRIP

■ **Travel Scheduling:** During the summer recess, building tours of Parliament are offered. These are different from attending a Parliamentary session. Contact Firstcall Tickets (0870 906 3838, www.firstcalltickets. com). If you're willing to climb all 334 steps,

you can tour Big Ben. Write (at least three months in advance) to Clock Tower Tours, Parliamentary Works Services Directorate, 1 Canon Row, London SW1A 2JN. In late autumn, the State Opening of Parliament takes place. Londoners are a little ho-hum about this annual event, so a curbside view of the day's pomp is quite possible.

■ **Cultural Preparations:** Head down to the video store for *Hope and Glory* (1987). Although it has absolutely no scenes of this area, this entertaining movie is an accurate introduction to London's wartime experience. Plus you'll hear the rousing anthem "Land of Hope and Glory."

■ **Internet Best Bets:** Check Parliament's website at www.parliament.uk for updated details on tours and House sessions.

Standing on Westminster Bridge and looking back the way you came, you'll see the Palace of Westminster stretching almost 900 feet along the Thames. Starting at the far left, the plane trees of Victoria Tower Gardens hug the river, followed by a surprising number of Parliamentary towers. The largest and squarest, on the left, is Victoria Tower. Next is the Palace of Westminster itself, the center of Britain's parliamentary government, housing the House of Commons and the House of Lords. And almost straight ahead is Big Ben.

Big Ben's tolling at noon and midnight lasts just over a minute; the clock is accurate to within a second a year.

Big Ben is neither the clock tower nor the clock—it's the largest bell, the one that tolls the hours, named for the Commissioner of Works when the project was proposed in the mid-nineteenth century. Near the top of the clock tower, the Ayrton Light, named after yet another commissioner, is usually lit when either House is in nighttime session. The light was extinguished as a precautionary measure during the wartime blackout.

The only area of the tower seriously affected by German bombs is above the south-facing clock face, below the little rooflets. The ornamental ironwork and stonework were damaged in the mid-May raids of 1941, and the clock face on that side shattered. The following morning as John Colville, Churchill's private secretary, walked in the area, a fireman pointed out Big Ben's pocked and scarred face, then cheerfully described how a bomb had gone right through the tower. "The one thing that had given him great pleasure during the night was that Big Ben had struck two o'clock a few minutes after being hit. It was still giving the proper time."

In Whitehall-ese, a "private secretary" to a governmental minister is not the "type and file" sort but more of an assistant or aide.

Big Ben's four clock faces were not illuminated for most of the war. Glowing out across the river and a blacked-out metropolis, they would have provided an all-too-visible target for German bombers. It wasn't until spring 1945, when peace seemed assured, that the Speaker of the House threw the switch to relight Big Ben's clock faces; the war-weary crowd below cheered the return to normalcy. Today the clock faces continue to cast their warm light and give astonishingly accurate time. The bells have been silenced only for repairs, by extreme cold, and perhaps the most somber silence of all: the day of Winston Churchill's funeral, when Big Ben stood silent from 9:45am until midnight.

The sound of Big Ben can easily transport the listener to the days of Edward R. Murrow broadcasting to America. "This is London," he would begin his CBS radio report, Big Ben tolling in the background. From

Big Ben

Big Ben is assuredly one of the most recognizable of symbols. The clock tower's sturdiness during the Blitz and the tolling at the beginning of wartime radio broadcasts came to symbolize British steadfastness. Today Big Ben's image can be found in London souvenir shops on everything from tea towels to magnets to coffee mugs. More unusual Big Ben–related items (including models) are available at the Parliamentary Bookshop (12 Bridge Street, Westminster). Here's more information on this grand edifice:

Tower: The clock tower is 315 feet high, and each side is about 40 feet long. There are 334 spiral steps to the top. The tower was built without scaffolding in the mid-1850s.

Clocks: Each of the 4 clock faces is 23 feet in diameter with 312 pieces of opalescent glass. The numerals are 2 feet high, the minute hands (hollow copper) 14 feet long, the hour hands (solid gun-metal) 9 feet long. The clock mechanism is much like a grandfather clock, complete with pendulum (14 feet long and "ticking" every 2 seconds) and clock weights (2.5 tons each) that are raised by an electric motor.

Bells: There are 5 bells—4 quarter bells and Big Ben. The smaller bells range in weight from 1 to 4 tons. The big guy weighs just over 13 tons.

> *Big Ben still tolls the hours. Even as it strikes, another town joins the gallant list of those who have not bowed under the enemy's fiercest blows. After months of total war, London, England, Great Britain still stands firm.*
> —Bloody but Unbowed: Pictures of Britain Under Fire, 1941

Want to sing along? The hourly chime is based on a musical phrase in Handel's "I know that my Redeemer liveth" and is traditionally associated with the lines, "Lord, through this hour, Be thou our guide, That by Thy power, No foot shall slide."

If you'd like to hear Big Ben before your trip, Ralph Vaughan Williams' *A London Symphony* features the famous chimes in both the first and fourth movements, and in Eric Coates' *London Suite*, Big Ben solemnly strikes at the end of the second movement.

War Words: Blitz

BLITZ comes from the German *blitzkrieg*, "lightning war," used to describe the Nazi invasion of Poland, the Low Countries, and France. Capitalized, "the Blitz" is the worst period of German air raids on London—September 1940 through May 1941—although the word, usually lowercase, is sometimes also used for the catastrophic bombings of other areas: the Coventry blitz, for example.

George Orwell noted that by early 1941, "blitz" was used everywhere "to mean any kind of an attack on anything." Indeed, British civilians brought the most generic of nuances to the word. Phrases such as "a morning Blitz" or a "recent Blitz," meaning an individual bombing, were often heard. Diarist Vera Hodgson described how the queen took Eleanor Roosevelt "to see the blitz," that is, specific bomb damage. Hodgson even referred to a time of reduced attacks as being only "a bit blitzy this evening."

Armed forces personnel found additional uses. RAF pilots would "blitz," swiftly cleaning up selves and barracks for inspection. And a "blitz buggy" was an irreverent Air Force phrase for an ambulance, a phrase seldom used by London's beleaguered civilians.

autumn 1939 to spring 1941, as London sent her children to places of greater safety, as the blackout began, as the possibilities of gas attack were debated, and as the boredom of the Phoney War gave way to the reality of air raids, Murrow was the conscience of his American radio listeners. He vividly described the wartime look of London while subtly reminding his audience that London's streets were not so distant and that the city's experience would one day affect everyone listening.

To the west is **Parliament Square**, a grassy island in the midst of circling traffic. The political statues here, from Disraeli to Peel, are worth a look if you're willing to risk life and limb to cross the street. But remember, in New York City a car slammed into Winston Churchill when he looked the wrong way crossing Fifth Avenue. Be careful.

One statue is sufficiently large and dominating to be viewed without venturing across the roadway. On the square's northeast corner, facing Big Ben and his beloved Parliament, is a hulking bronze **statue of Winston Churchill**. Designed by Ivor Roberts-Jones, it was unveiled by Churchill's wife in a 1973 ceremony that included the

Royal Marines Band playing the prime minister's favorite Gilbert and Sullivan tunes.

In September 1939, before statues of Churchill were even conceived of, Harold Nicolson set out for Parliament after listening to Neville Chamberlain's broadcast announcing war. "Hardly had we left 28 Queen Anne's Gate when [an air raid] siren blows....The sirens scream all around us....We reach Parliament Square. As we enter it the crowd, which has massed itself against the railings, breaks up like a flock of pigeons....They cut across the grass plot where the statues are. We go on to Palace Yard."

> Most people find the statue of Churchill in Parliament Square just like the statesman, but Churchill's daughter Mary—who ought to know—once described it as "combining a somber likeness with considerable allegorical illusion."

Shortly after the announcement of war, Parliament Square was strung with barbed wire, rolls and rolls of it stretched over the lawn, intended to slow down the advance of the expected Nazi invaders. In 1941, a fake W. H. Smith bookstall—actually a concrete defense post—was installed here, and sandbags were piled on the same corner where Churchill stands today. When the invasion came, the local Home Guard, many of them Parliament members, would be expected to man the machine guns. In the meantime, the Parliament Home Guard often practiced marching in this area, shouldering their trusty (and antiquated) P17 Enfield rifles.

That's New Palace Yard at the near corner of the **Palace of Westminster complex**, the entrance for House of Commons members. Continue down St. Margaret's Street past New Palace Yard; ahead Oliver Cromwell stands, looking suitably humorless as he grips both sword and Bible, his back to Parliament. Cromwell was England's Lord Protector in the 1650s, when the English tested and found wanting a less regal style of government. Erected in 1899, the statue must have been a familiar sight to Neville Chamberlain, Winston Churchill, and members of the wartime Parliament.

Further along, in Old Palace Yard, rides King Richard, England's king in the late 1100s. This statue also survived the war's intense air attacks, although at least one blast elevated poor Richard from his pedestal. He settled back relatively unharmed. American journalist Ernie Pyle described the effects of that night's destructive bombings: "The entrance to the House of Commons is gone; there is some damage to the interior; and the same bomb damaged the rear end of Richard the Lionhearted's bronze horse and bent Richard's upheld sword, but he still rides on." Both the hole in the horse's tail and the rakish bend in Richard's sword have been repaired. The bomb, falling between the statue and the building behind, left a twenty-yard crater and blew out the window glass. The replacement window features the coats of arms or monograms of Parliament members and staff who died in the war.

The Palace of West-minster, a labyrinth of over a dozen buildings covering almost 9 acres, has 11 open squares and courtyards, 2 miles of corridors, 100 staircases, and 1,100 rooms.

The House of Lords entrance is at the back of Old Palace Yard, and Parliament members and staff can be seen briskly walking in and out. Just before that entrance is the gathering area for those waiting for admission to (free) sittings of either House. (See Visitor Details below for information on how and when the public is allowed in.)

The route to a session of **Parliament**, whether Lords or Commons, begins as you walk through St. Stephen's Entrance. Check out the painted panels inside, along the first of many staircases: to your right, a prewar map of London's public buildings and "amenities," to your left, a plan of the present building superimposed over the old palace. At the top of the stairway is a security checkpoint with Westminster Hall to the left—a look at it will have to wait until you leave. For now, visitors are ushered down St. Stephen's Hall to the octagonal Central Lobby, a room laden with decoration: mosaic floor, arches, stained glass, statues, a vaulted stone roof with more mosaics, all lit by a filigreed chandelier. In June 1940, while pacifist Vera Brittain lingered in this lobby waiting to hear Churchill address the Commons, she noted "how the coloured reflections from the windows

War Words: Incident

INCIDENT, the somewhat stilted and trivial term for the concept "what takes place when a bomb falls on a street," did not rise spontaneously as did many other wartime words and phrases. The Whitehall bureaucracy formally settled on "incident," which then filtered down to the Civil Defence forces and finally to the general public.

John Strachey, wartime Air Raid Precautions worker, rather mordantly described the linguistic process: "It cannot indeed be held to convey very graphically the consequences of a bomb. Just the contrary. The word is wonderfully colourless, dry and remote; it touches nothing which it does not minimise. And this, it may be supposed, is what recommended it conclusively to the authorities. It formed an important part of their policy of reassurance. For while anyone might be frightened of a bomb, who could be frightened of an incident?"

fall upon the sculptured shoulders of former statesmen, not one of whom was confronted with a situation remotely comparable to the present crisis."

Given a choice between attending a sitting of the House of Lords or the House of Commons, go for the Commons—debates are more interesting and lively. And in terms of the effects of the war, this is the place...or at least it *was* the place. Much of what's visible to the visitor has been rebuilt, for in that catastrophic bombing of mid-May 1941, the entire Commons chamber was destroyed, ravaged first by aerial attack and then consumed by fire.

The fire soon spread to the Members' Lobby, where the roof collapsed, and then the meeting chamber itself went up in flames. Harold Nicolson visited a few days later and found the Members' Lobby a mass of twisted girders. "So I went up by the staircase to the Ladies' Gallery and then suddenly, when I turned the corridor, there was the open air and a sort of Tintern Abbey [ruin] gaping at me." Only a shell of unroofed walls remained, filled with charred timbers, fallen steel beams, and broken chunks of masonry. On an emergency basis after this devastating raid, Parliament met in Church House near Westminster Abbey, then returned to meet in various other rooms in the Palace of Westminster until the rebuilt House of Commons chamber opened in 1950. The new chamber was designed by architect Giles Gilbert Scott in a clubby style

> *Winston Churchill, as always, put it memorably: "London will be ready, London will not flinch....You [Hitler] do your worst, and we will do our best."*

Text continued on page 13.

Walking the Queen Anne's Gate Neighborhood

Behind the urban façade of the well-traveled Parliament area is a little-known neighborhood of quiet Georgian streets, and a peaceful park where church bells once rang. The route begins across from Westminster Abbey and ends just a few blocks southwest of it.

Start at Storey's Gate and Tothill Street in front of the Methodist Central Hall, the ornate Edwardian structure that served during the war as both a place of worship and an air raid shelter. Across Storey's Gate is the modern Queen Elizabeth II Conference Centre (unredeemably ugly) and beyond it, Middlesex Guildhall. Despite the medieval look of the Guildhall, the building was completed in 1913. It saw wartime service as a court for military and maritime hearings of the Allied countries and continues today as a court building. Inside are panels signed by three monarchs grateful for the wartime use of the Guildhall—King Haakon of Norway, King George of Greece, and Queen Wilhelmina of the Netherlands. Visitor Alert: If you are carrying a camera, you will *not* be allowed inside, and no, you cannot leave the camera at the security desk. Trust me—charm will get you nowhere.

Walk north along Storey's Gate, then turn left down Old Queen Street, a near-alley at first that soon blossoms into a lovely Georgian-Victorian mix. Veer left then immediately right along Queen Anne's Gate, a near-perfect relic of Georgian London. Note the masks, fanlights, and hooded canopies over the doorways, the torch snuffers by some of the doors, and the boot scrapers. Stay on the northern (your right) side. Across the way at 1 Queen Anne Street, a plaque honors Sir Edward Grey, England's foreign secretary during World War I and the man who said, "The lamps are going out all over Europe; we shall not see them lit again in our lifetime." Well, they *were* lit again, only to be extinguished once more in World War II.

Mid-street, the marble statue of Queen Anne is a curious anomaly amidst all this charming domestic architecture. During the war, the queen was totally bricked in, a precautionary measure that ensured the statue's survival. Further along, on the northern side of the street, the faint trace of a shelter sign is visible midblock near Number 28. This was Ronald Tree's house (Conservative MP from 1933 to 1945), and it was here in 1939 that Harold Nicolson, together with Anthony Eden and others, heard the prime minister's wireless broadcast announcing the declaration of war.

Several blocks beyond our route is the Guards Chapel. A V-1 flying bomb falling there caused extensive damage in 1944 to the structures south of St. James's Park. Architectural historian James Lees-Milne lamented his blasted offices on Queen Anne's Gate: "All windows are out; parts of inner walls down, doors wrenched off, and ceilings down."

Queen Anne's Gate turns left and ends at St. James's Park Underground at 55

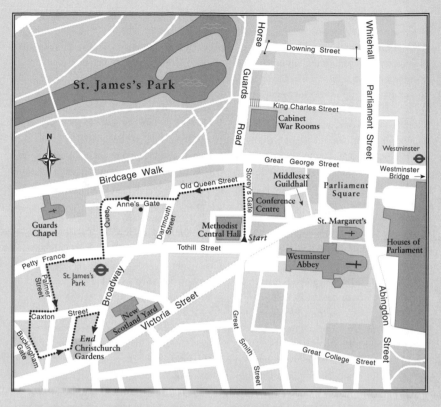

Map labels:

- Horse Guards Road
- Downing Street
- Whitehall
- St. James's Park
- King Charles Street
- Cabinet War Rooms
- Parliament Street
- N
- Westminster
- Great George Street
- Westminster Bridge →
- Birdcage Walk
- Old Queen Street
- Storey's Gate
- Middlesex Guildhall
- Parliament Square
- Anne's Gate
- Conference Centre
- Queen
- Dartmouth Street
- Guards Chapel
- St. Margaret's
- Methodist Central Hall
- Start
- Petty France
- Tothill Street
- Houses of Parliament
- St. James's Park
- Palmer Street
- Westminster Abbey
- Broadway
- Caxton Street
- New Scotland Yard
- Victoria Street
- Abingdon Street
- Buckingham Gate
- End Christchurch Gardens
- Great Smith Street
- Great College Street

Broadway. This gray behemoth, built in the late 1920s, is the headquarters for London Transport; note the relief sculptures high above ringing the façade. If they appeal, step inside to the tiny London Transport shop to purchase a set of postcards featuring the designs of Eric Gill, Jacob Epstein, Henry Moore, and others. Also inside is a display wall of information about the sculptures and building, next to the forbidding doors marked "Private," a reminder that this building houses offices as well as Tube travelers.

Exit St. James's Park station the same way you entered. Across the street to the right is the mansard-roofed 50-54 Broadway, once (1924 to 1966) headquarters of SIS, Britain's Secret Intelligence Service and known to espionage aficionados as MI6. To the left, on the corner of

Petty France and Queen Anne's Gate, is the bunker-like tower of the Home Office (1970s), replacing Queen Anne's Mansions, an intensely ugly residential building that graced the area from 1905 through the war.

Turn left from the Underground down Petty France, then left again on narrow Palmer Street to Caxton Street. A right turn here brings you to the small brick Blewcoat School building, sitting by Brewer's Green. This one-room treasure, almost 300 years old, once held a school for poor children of the area (note the statue over the door) and during the war years was an Army

The National Trust shop in Blewcoat School is open weekdays 10am to 5:30pm; Thursday 10am to 7pm.

warehouse. It now houses a well-stocked National Trust gift shop.

Exit the same door you entered and walk around the side of the building to Buckingham Gate, the wide avenue ahead. To the left is Rolls-Royce headquarters at Number 65, an unremarkable modern office building. Inside are bronze busts of Charles Rolls and Henry Royce, just visible through the smoked-glass window (or step inside and ask the receptionist for a closer look). Rolls-Royce designed and built Merlin airplane engines during the war, powering the RAF's Spitfires, Hurricanes, and Lancasters.

> *St. James's Park Underground served during the war as a place of safety for many who sheltered trackside when warning sirens warned of approaching German bombers.*

Continue along Buckingham Gate a short way, then turn left on Butler Place and cross Palmer Street (now just a narrow pedestrian passage) to the small park. Here in Christchurch Gardens once stood Christchurch, Westminster, built in 1843 on the site of a chapel founded by Charles I. It was gutted in April 1941 when showers of incendiaries set afire the roof of the small Gothic church. Despite the best efforts of the Civil Defence workers and the London Fire Brigade, only the tower could be saved. That final remnant was itself demolished in 1954, and the nearby post office/telephone exchange building erected on the site.

On a quick circuit of the park, note the distinctive marks on the low cement divider separating the gardens from the Victoria Street pavement, suggesting that iron railings were once embedded here.

Perhaps, even before the church's destruction, they were dismantled to be recycled into wartime armaments.

Across the street stands the eight-story Artillery Mansions (1895), operated before and during the war as "service flats," a sort of posh residential hotel. Artillery Mansions and the nearby Albert Pub (corner of Palmer and Victoria streets) are among the few wartime survivors in the neighborhood (and the Albert is well worth a visit if you're thirsty).

On the western side of the gardens, near where you entered, stands an upright scroll honoring the struggle of England's suffragettes. Read the lengthy inscription and perhaps say a silent thank you to those who fought to ensure the right of all to vote. Together with the women of World War II, who replaced men in jobs never before open to women, the suffragettes changed the gender landscape.

Facing the scroll, a right turn and a short walk toward Caxton Street bring you to Caxton Hall, formerly Westminster Town Hall and once a favored site for social gatherings and political meetings. Winston Churchill spoke here often during the war, as the wall plaque notes. His son Randolph was married in Caxton Hall in 1948 to second wife June.

Turn right and walk down Caxton Street, passing St. Ermin's Hotel on your left, a popular stopping place for American visitors in the early 1940s. Its upper floors were turned into offices, some with a whiff of wartime espionage.

Where Caxton Street meets Broadway is New Scotland Yard; up Broadway to the right is Victoria Street, a major thoroughfare that leads back to Westminster Abbey, just a few blocks away.

described as late Gothic or modified domestic Tudor; you'll see Scott's picture on the way to your seat.

After passing a final security checkpoint, strangers (that's us) sit in the rebuilt balcony gallery to watch the political process below. Members of Parliament (MPs) sit facing each other, about two swords' lengths apart, as indicated by the red lines on the carpeting. Members standing to debate must not cross the lines, a wise precaution as discussions can get heated. Pick up the free pamphlet that describes in detail how Parliament works and exactly what you'll see from the gallery high above.

The vault beneath Parliament's Central Lobby was used during the later war years as a construction area for the Ministry of Supply. MPs and staff volunteered here assembling wartime precision instruments.

The rebuilt archway into the Members' Lobby uses stonework from the original arch, as suggested by Winston Churchill, and is known appropriately as the Churchill Arch. It's been left rough and broken, also at his suggestion, as a reminder of the 1941 air raid. Here too is Churchill himself, a statue by Oscar Nemon unveiled in 1969, not visible to the visitors in the Strangers' Gallery but a common sight to MPs.

After a brief stay in the balcony (length depending on how many are waiting to get in), visitors are ushered down the winding staircase, back through the Central Lobby, back down St. Stephen's Hall, and past the entranceway security checkpoint again. Here **Westminster Hall** looms to one side, a gloomy and spectacularly cavernous area that's the oldest remaining part of the original Royal Palace. The enormous room (about 240 feet by 68 feet) is topped by its most stunning feature—the 600-year-old hammerbeam roof of Hampshire oak, its wooden arches still "blazon[ing] the ceiling like a Gothic dream." That Gothic dream took a direct hit from a Nazi bomb in mid-May 1941. The bomb and resulting fire destroyed some of the roof boarding and rafters, since restored, but the wooden trusses were not seriously affected. For centuries this hall has been used for courts of law, state trials, and state ceremonies, including Parliament's grand celebration of Winston Churchill's eightieth birthday in 1954. Just over ten years later, 300,000 mourners filed past Churchill's flag-draped coffin.

VISITOR DETAILS: Seating (free) in either House is usually available weekday afternoons and evenings, with seating in the House of Commons also available some Wednesday mornings and, for Lords, some Friday mornings. Myriad seating options exist, some based on what country you're a resident of—check Parliament's website. No eating facilities or restrooms. More information: 020 7219 4272 (Commons) and 020 7219 3107 (Lords), www.parliament.uk.

VISITOR DETAILS: Write in advance to Parliamentary Archives, House of Lords Record Office, London SW1A 0PW, or e-mail hlro@ parliament.uk. More information: 020 7219 3074, www. parliament.uk.

Victoria Tower anchors the southern end of the Palace of Westminster complex, the largest square tower in the world when it was built in 1858. The twelve floors house Parliament records and are closed to the public, although the Search Room is open by appointment if you need to peruse the Beaverbrook Papers or track down an obscure Churchill speech. Daytimes the Union Jack flies from the tower's flagpole if Parliament is in session.

Further south, as St. Margaret's Street becomes Abingdon Street, **Victoria Tower Gardens** offer a pleasant rest stop, but before settling down, check out *The Burghers of Calais* by Auguste Rodin, a bronze copy of the original in Calais. During the 1347 siege of Calais, the six burghers surrendered themselves to save the lives of their townspeople, hence their somewhat pained and conflicted expressions. The sculpture spent much of World War II safely crated and tucked away in distant Berkhampstead Castle.

PART II
THE RELIGIOUS SIDE

*Sunshine streaming in through a hole in the roof...lighted up
the damage, melancholy to look at, but not irreparable.
The marvel is that the Abbey survived.*

—LONDON *TIMES*, MAY 13, 1941

Westminster Abbey bomb damage.

Highlights: Abbey Gardens, Jewel Tower, George V statue, Westminster Abbey, St. Margaret's Church, Methodist Central Hall

Underground Station: Westminster

Photo Ops: Since photography isn't allowed inside Westminster Abbey, watch for photo possibilities outside, including the Abbey's towers silhouetted against London's dramatic clouds, or a different perspective from atop Methodist Central Hall.

BEFORE LEAVING ON YOUR TRIP

■ **Travel Scheduling:** If visiting in mid-September, consider attending the Battle of Britain Thanksgiving services at the Abbey. November visitors may want to schedule a visit near Remembrance Day.

■ **Cultural Preparations:** Music recorded in Westminster Abbey is especially appropriate. Watch for *A Millennium of Music from Westminster Abbey* or *Great Musical Occasions at Westminster Abbey*. If you don't find these before your trip, they're available at the Abbey Bookshop. Churchill enthusiasts may want to drink a wedding toast to Winston and Clementine Churchill, married in St. Margaret's, with a glass of Churchill's favorite Pol Roger champagne, of course.

■ **Internet Best Bets:** Westminster Abbey's website at www.westminster-abbey.org has details of religious services and tour options; it's updated frequently. Check Methodist Central Hall's website for upcoming events: www.c-h-w.com.

Westminster Abbey, St. Margaret's Church, and Methodist Central Hall survived the war essentially intact, looking today much as they did before the war. The observant may note the addition of the Abbey's RAF Chapel or a wartime remembrance book or two. London's war had a dramatic impact here, however, and the visitor willing to re-imagine London's battleground will find lingering echoes and effects not immediately apparent.

It was Westminster Abbey that suffered the most. Until the very end of the Blitz, the Abbey and its surrounding cloisters, chapels, and school buildings had survived the Nazis' pummeling. In early September 1940, the Abbey's west window was damaged, and two weeks later a bomb blew out the windows of Henry VII's Chapel and punched a hole in the wall below. In late September and again in October, the Little Cloister area was struck.

Westminster Abbey.

But the Abbey's team of volunteer firewatchers and professional firefighters held the line, swiftly extinguishing blazes and cleaning up rubble.

But on "that dreadful night" of May 10, 1941, as the dean of the Abbey later often referred to it, Westminster Abbey was hit, over and over, and even the determined efforts of her devoted protectors were not enough. Incendiary bombs, designed to burn rather than blast, fell on the southern West Tower, on the Library, on the Deanery, on the houses in the Little Cloister. The Abbey's resident fire team of clergy, gardeners, and other staff rushed about wielding their stirrup pumps (a portable pump that could spray water on small areas from a sloshingly full pail) and buckets of sand. For awhile the firefighters kept up with the falling incendiaries and hopes were high that the Abbey would survive yet another wartime night.

Several factors worked against the Abbey's guardians. Most obviously, there was a full moon, a bombers' moon. The winding curve of the Thames reflected the moonlight and aided German airmen in spotting targets. And far below, the wooden roofs of London's oldest buildings—such as the Abbey—were often totally inaccessible to firefighters; if a blaze started there, reaching it quickly was impossible. Worse, the Germans had chosen a night when the river's tide was out. Usually when water pressure dropped because so many hydrants were in use or when the street-level water storage tanks (including several on the Abbey's grounds) were emptied, firehoses would be run to the Thames for additional water. On the night of

May 10, the river's water level had dropped twenty feet. For much of its width, the River Thames was mud flats; it would provide no relief.

A single incendiary bomb, falling through the lantern roof in the central part of the Abbey and onto the inaccessible wooden subroof below, eluded the vigilant firewatchers. Soon the lantern was ringed in flames, flames that "made many who saw them fear that the church was doomed." The roof broke away from the stone walls and the great flaming beams crashed down, breaking up the paving some 130 feet below, where the fire finally burnt itself out.

The surrounding structures were not so lucky. To the south and west where smaller ecclesiastical buildings had crouched alongside the Abbey, incendiary bombs wreaked havoc, burning several houses, melting lead roofs, and destroying centuries of history. The medieval Deanery was consumed, and five houses in the Little Cloister area perished. The Westminster School suffered significant damage; luckily its young students had been evacuated to Worcestershire. The seventeenth-century Ashburnham House, site of the wartime Churchill Club, survived unscathed, but College Hall (originally the dormitory of the Abbey's Benedictine monks) and College Dormitory went up in smoke. That same smoke settled thickly about the Abbey's gardens in the early morning of May 11, 1941, as the All Clear siren finally, blessedly, sounded.

Soon after the fallen timbers and medieval stones had cooled, a pair of rare black redstarts made their nest in the ruins.

Today, most visitors approach Westminster Abbey from the Parliament Square side, a route making for a hectic beginning—better the more leisurely approach from the south, starting just beyond Jewel Tower where the inside walkway meets Great College Street. This route provides a hint of the vastness of this ecclesiastical complex and offers a chance to get oriented to the Abbey's layout.

The large walled-in greensward to the south of Westminster Abbey is the **Abbey Gardens**, formally known as College Garden, over 900 years old and reputedly the oldest garden in England. For centuries this area provided food and medicinal herbs for resident Benedictine monks. The towering plane trees here, the oldest living things in the area and visible over the garden wall, are more than 150 years old.

Between the walkway and street sits a massive bronze sculpture by Henry Moore. Best known for such heavy rounded bronzes,

VISITOR DETAILS: Enter Abbey Gardens for free from Dean's Yard, on the far side of the Abbey. It's generally open Tuesday–Thursday 10am to 6pm in summer, 10am to 4pm in winter. Free band concerts on summer Thursday afternoons.

Text continued on page 20.

The Abbey's Neighbors

Just minutes from Westminster Abbey, this short side trip visits a quiet residential neighborhood with numerous World War II connections. Head south along Abingdon Street across from Parliament, a roadway that in pre-war years was considered "a magnificent specimen of real English ugliness," its long terrace of Georgian homes worn and shabby. Most were so badly damaged in the Blitz that they were quickly torn down after war's end. The lawn area is now called Abingdon Street Gardens, a favored spot for television interviews using the dramatic Parliament buildings as backdrop.

Turn right onto Great College Street. The Abbey buildings and garden are to the right behind a small door marked "1 The Abbey Garden," the first in a series of mysterious doors along this otherwise blank brick-and-stone wall. Portions of the wall were leveled in wartime bombings and have since been seamlessly rebuilt.

At the second corner, turn left onto Barton Street. Here at Number 1, Marie Belloc-Lowndes, sister of Hilaire Belloc and an author herself, spent the early

1940s (she'd lived at Number 9 from 1909 to 1922).

Barton Street wanders left and morphs into Cowley Street. On the first house on the left a plaque honors John Reith, resident here from 1924 to 1930. Reith guided the newly established BBC from 1922 to 1938, his policies setting the tone for wartime radio broadcasting. He also served during the war as Minister of Information and Minister of Transport.

The building at 17 Cowley Street is the former home of poet Laurence Binyon, a resident in the early 1900s. His poem to wartime dead, "For the Fallen," continues to be a prominent part of Remembrance Day and other memorial activities.

Cross Great Peter Street onto Lord North Street, a pretty block of cozy Georgian homes. Numerous war-era personalities trod this narrow street: Anthony Eden, wartime Secretary of State, rented 2 Lord North Street in the early 1920s (£250 a year!); Home Secretary John Anderson, responsible for the Anderson family shelter, lived at Number 4 during the war; Minister of Information Brendan Bracken lived at Number 8 in the 1930s and 1940s; and wartime society hostess Lady Sybil Colfax entertained small gatherings at Number 19, where her prewar guests included the Prince of Wales and his good friend, Mrs. Simpson. Mid-block, on both sides of the street, are several shelter signs.

At the end of this residential block stands St. John's, Smith Square. Constructed in the early 1700s as a church, this baroque building is now a musical venue, complete with a restaurant-in-a-crypt. In October 1939, Pamela Digby and Churchill's son Randolph were married here, their nuptials described by the *Daily Mirror* as "a real war wedding...all the

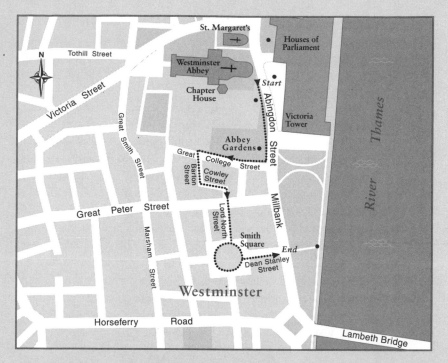

guests carried gas masks." Much of the structure was gutted in the 1941 air raids.

Number 4 Smith Square was briefly the postwar home of Kathleen "Kick" Kennedy, one of U.S. Ambassador Joseph Kennedy's children. At 3 Smith Square lived R. A. Butler (or Rab, as he was commonly known), the leading conservative in Parliament and Under-Secretary for Foreign Affairs and Minister of Education in the early 1940s. Like many government officials, he found this area convenient to Whitehall, though he did have to relocate when his home was blasted by a German bomb in 1940. On the square's southeast corner is Transport House, war-era headquarters of the Labour Party and now the headquarters of the Local Government Association. Finally, watch for 8-9 Smith Square, the inter-wars residence of Oswald Mosley, founder of the British Union of Fascists. Mosley was arrested in May 1940 and spent much of the war in jail.

Leave Smith Square down Dean Stanley Street. A block ahead is Millbank, with the lower part of Victoria Tower Gardens across the roadway. A dramatic High Victorian Gothic monument sits straight ahead in the gardens, commemorating the work of Thomas Fowell Buxton and others in the emancipation of the Empire's slaves in 1834. It stood in Great George Street by Parliament Square throughout the war (in fact since it was erected in 1865) and was moved here in the 1950s.

If you decide not to cross over to the gardens, a left turn on Millbank leads back toward the Abbey area; a right turn down the windy Millbank pavement leads past Lambeth Bridge to Tate Britain (formerly the Tate Gallery), the national collection of British painting. (See Chapter 9 for more on the Tate.) Along the way is Millbank Tower, the current headquarters of the Labour Party. Art and politics—just two of Westminster Abbey's many neighbors.

VISITOR DETAILS: Jewel
Tower is open daily in summer
10am to 6pm; closes earlier in
winter. Admission charged. No
disabled access. Light refreshments in the shop area; no
restrooms. More information:
020 7222 2219.

he also drew haunting sketches of human
forms sheltering along Underground tracks
during wartime air raids. (For more on
Henry Moore and the Tube shelterers, see
Chapter 3.)

Looking like a miniature moated castle,
Jewel Tower is a tiny reminder of the original Palace of Westminster. Once King Ed-
ward III's treasure house, Jewel Tower was first opened to the public after the
war and now houses an exhibition on Parliament past and present. The
war dealt Jewel Tower some shrapnel dinging but nothing catastrophic.

Beyond Jewel Tower and closer to Westminster Abbey stands a **statue
of King George V** in full field marshal regalia. His death set in motion
the abdication crisis of 1936 and eventually brought his second son, Albert
(King George VI), to the wartime throne. The other structure in the area,
7 Old Palace Yard, is a Parliamentary office building closed to the public.

Television viewers of the grand dramas bracketing the last half-century
(Queen Elizabeth's coronation and Princess Diana's funeral) have a lingering image of **Westminster Abbey**—spacious aisles and towering ceilings.
Only the latter is accurate. As Virginia Woolf invited, "Enter that strange
muddle and miscellany of objects both hallowed and ridiculous." Tombs,
statues, plaques, burial slabs, memorials, and monuments crowd the aisles,
fill the corners, and cover the floors, touching remembrances to people
you've probably never heard of, including over 3,500 British subjects, 8
prime ministers, and 24 British monarchs. And because of the crowds, visitors are briskly ushered along a set path.

Enter the Abbey's north door and head past the memorials honoring
English statesmen (Gladstone, Disraeli, and the like) toward the Chapel of
St. Edward the Confessor in the center of the ambulatory. To the left just
past St. Michael's Chapel is the unmarked door of the Nurses' Memorial
Chapel. To visit, talk to one of the helpful vergers. Particularly if a British
friend or relative served as a wartime nurse, the chapel is worth a look. Up
the staircase behind the locked door is a diminutive chapel, out of sight
from the main floor. Window badges honor various wartime nursing and
midwifery units, including the British Red Cross Society and the
Territorial Nursing Services. The window is by stained-glass artist Hugh
Easton, designer of numerous war memorial windows. Nearby, a remembrance book lists hundreds of nurses and midwives who died in the war.

Back down the chapel stairs (let the verger know you've left), a bevy
of royal tombs surrounds the Chapel of St. Edward the Confessor, including those of Edward I, Henry III, and Henry V, plus the Coronation Chair

itself, where all but two British monarchs have been crowned. During the war, the Coronation Chair was crated and sent to safety in distant Gloucester Cathedral. The Stone of Scone that had rested beneath the seat of the Coronation Chair for centuries was buried "somewhere" in the Abbey grounds. On the off chance that the Abbey itself would be destroyed and all staff knowing the stone's hiding place would be killed, the plan for locating the buried stone was secretly sent to the Canadian prime minister. The Stone of Scone, originally looted by the English from the Scots in 1296, was relocated to the Coronation Chair at the end of the war. In the 1990s, it was returned to Scotland.

Up several steps and filling the entire east end of the Abbey is the Henry VII Chapel (also called the Lady Chapel) with the colorful banners of the Order of the Bath hanging over the sixteenth-century wooden stalls. Short circular detours take visitors past the tombs of queens Elizabeth I and Mary I. Beyond the chapel's bannered section are several side chapels, the most dramatic, the **Royal Air Force Chapel,** at the far end. It was dedicated in 1947 to the memory of the 1,497 men of the RAF killed in the Battle of Britain.

Fire pump in action.

The original Tudor windows here were blown out in the same September 1940 attack that bent King Richard's sword across the road. Their colorful replacement is Hugh Easton's Battle of Britain memorial window, particularly stunning with morning sunlight streaming through it. The badges of the various RAF fighter squadrons that took part in the Battle of Britain surround the figures of four dashing airmen in blue flying suits and yellow scarves. Unless you're familiar with RAF squadron symbols, the window may appear dramatic but a trifle busy. Take a minute, though, to see if you can find the roaring tiger of Squadron Number 74, the elephant of Number 249, or the white hexagon of Squadron Number 85. At the window's base is the well-known Shakespearean phrase from *Henry V*: "We few...we happy few...we band of brothers." The multicolored rug features the emblem and motto of the RAF: *Per ardua ad astra* ("Through adversity to the stars").

The same night that the original windows were demolished, a fist-sized hole was smashed in the thick exterior wall just below the windows and to the left, about four feet from the floor. The hole has been preserved (though glassed over) as a further reminder of the war. Under the windows are the names of RAF wartime leaders—Douglas, Dowding, Harris, Newall, Portal, and Tedder. Floor stones mark the burial places of General

Trenchard, first air marshal of the RAF, and General Dowding, Chief of the RAF's Fighter Command during the Battle of Britain and leader of "the few."

The wooden case inside the chapel contains a roll of honor inscribed with the names of RAF airmen who died in the Battle of Britain. The long sad list includes the names of 47 Canadians, 47 New Zealanders, 35 Poles, 24 Australians, 20 Czechoslovaks, 17 South Africans, 6 Belgians, and 1 American.

Walk back along the south side of Henry VII's chapel and down the steps. Next is the south transept and Poets' Corner, a jumble of statues, busts, windows, and paving stones honoring British poets, writers, and musicians. For mobility's sake, visitors soon get over the habit of not walking on a grave, and anyway, many of the paving stones are memorials, not gravestones. Watch for floor stones honoring wartime poets T. S. Eliot and Dylan Thomas. If you're lucky, the day will be bright and sunlight will pour into this area. If it's gloomy, you may be reminded of the wartime boarding-up of the Abbey windows.

Westminster Abbey interior.

In the Abbey's central area, rest for a moment in one of the wooden chairs, perhaps looking toward the altar. Imagine sitting in this echoing stillness on a spring evening in 1941. One visitor wrote then, "In wartime, sightseeing in the Abbey is wonderfully simplified. The royal chapels are closed to the public, and peering through the gates they seem more mysterious....Many of the windows at the east end of the Abbey have been destroyed: and the asbestos that replaces them has created an artificial but romantic gloom. Where once were tombs of ormolu and alabaster we now see efficient sandbag pyramids."

Those sandbag pyramids, piled up both inside and out, were one reason relatively little damage was done to the Abbey and its contents. Over 60,000 were stacked outside around windows, doorways, and buttresses, and inside around nonremovable structures. Most smaller items—books, effigies, and artwork—were taken out of London or to locations of safety in the city, such as the Aldwych-Piccadilly Underground, a favored spot for wartime storage. Undamaged windows, including the resplendent west window, were taken down and the openings boarded over; windows already badly damaged were simply covered up. An efficient system of firewatchers was established among the staff, and a sturdy staff air raid shelter was built in the College Garden area.

In the racks behind each pew, worshippers found informational cards warning that the building was unsafe during air raids. American journalist Raymond Daniells reported, "The congregation was advised to seek shelter in a basement across the road [Methodist Central Hall]. In the event of an emergency, the card said, the choir would lead the way 'with all due reverent haste.'" Luckily, no crowds of worshippers had to seek safety during the late-night raid of May 10, 1941. If they had, they would have been sitting about where you are now. Directly above is the lantern roof area that burned and fell that night, depositing a mass of smoking debris and rubble around the altar and partially destroying the pulpit. On the morning of May 11, looking up you would have seen "a blue gap high above from which a few red cinders would occasionally drop."

At this point, visitors are directed outside of Westminster Abbey for a side trip to the **Cloisters**, moving from the Abbey's Gothic and neo-Gothic environs into its Norman and Benedictine monastic

The fourteen London bridges across the Thames suffered no serious war damage, which would have been catastrophic for civil defense, fire brigades, and ambulances. Just in case, three temporary bridges were built early in the war—at Westminster, Millbank, and Chelsea.

past. You can simply walk around the covered square of the Cloisters or pay the small admission fee to visit the attached Chapter House, Pyx Chamber, and the Undercroft Museum. Construction Alert: Repairs and refurbishment are ongoing in this area and one or more of these may be closed.

The first and largest is the **Chapter House**, an octagonal room just off the East Cloister walkway. Here monks met daily to hear the rules of St. Benedict read aloud. Built about 1250 for Henry III, the Chapter House was restored by George Gilbert Scott in the early 1870s. Walk slowly around the room, left to right, noting the captions at the bottom of each window. The last, back near the doorway, begins, "These windows were destroyed by blast from German bombs in 1941."

Further along the East Cloister are the Pyx Chamber and Undercroft Museum. The **Pyx Chamber** (a pyx is a storage chest), a low barrel-vaulted room, contains some of the Abbey plate. The larger **Undercroft Museum** collection is more varied, with exhibits of life-sized wax funeral effigies of various monarchs, armor, stained glass, coronation regalia, death masks, and similar Abbey-related miscellany. Note that all but the head of Henry VII was destroyed in the war. And check out the death mask of

Prewar Westminster view.

Edward III; after wartime bombing, the nose had to be replaced. But most of the effigies, particularly the larger ones, fared well, safely stored in the Aldwych-Piccadilly Underground. For part of the war, the Undercroft served as a medical dispensary and dressing room.

At one end of the Cloister walkway, it's possible to step outside into Dean's Yard. If the day is pleasant, take a quick turn around the tree-lined square (hang on to your ticket for readmission to the Abbey). **Church House** sits at the far end; here both houses of Parliament met at various times during the war when their own chambers were unavailable due to bomb threat or damage. To the left of the entrance porch a plaque commemorates the early United Nations' meetings held here soon after the war's end. **Ashburnham House**, a fourteenth-century building inside Little Dean's Yard and now part of the Westminster School, was the site of wartime (1943 on) meetings of the Churchill Club, a military networking spot for American, Canadian, and other Dominion forces.

Back in the Cloisters, watch for the tripartite statue and plaque honoring the submarine branch of the Royal Navy, the commandos, and members of the airborne forces and special air services who fell in the war. The monument was unveiled by Churchill in 1948. A nearby plaque honors Czechoslovak Army and Air Force personnel. This now-orderly Cloister area looked far different after the worst of the war's raids. The grassy square in the center, known as the Cloister Garth, was filled with building debris, and the surrounding walkways were flooded by firefighters' attempts to extinguish flames.

Returning to the Abbey, you'll enter about mid-nave on the south aisle. Guide ropes and walkways aren't a feature hereabouts; wander at will. Start by marveling at those towering ceilings (over a hundred feet high) featured on televised Abbey events. Then look around for the several war-related memorials in this open area.

On the south-central side of the nave, a floor stone marks the grave of Neville Chamberlain, Britain's prime minister from 1937 to May 1940 and architect of a vacillating political policy of appeasement with Adolf Hitler. Chamberlain's wartime funeral was held in Westminster Abbey, where a "huge congregation assembled, and froze as they sat beneath the shattered windows." Chamberlain's floor stone can be difficult to find as it's in the area for communion and is sometimes covered with chairs. If you can't immediately locate it, flag down one of the helpful staff for assistance.

Along the north aisle, floor stones mark the graves of Clement Attlee, Churchill's wartime deputy and successor as prime minister in 1945, and Ernest Bevin, Minister of Labour in the war cabinet. In the nave's north choir aisle, a memorial stone honors Edward Elgar, composer of *Pomp and Circumstance*. Known in the States as the "Graduation March," in Britain the tune is "Land of Hope and Glory," a rousing patriotic anthem heard during both world wars. Here too is a memorial stone for composer Benjamin Britten; his *War Requiem* received its London premiere in Westminster Abbey in 1962.

> *Poet Edith Sitwell was reading to a sizeable crowd at Ashburnham House when a V-1 rocket came spluttering overhead. She never paused ("Still falls the rain, still falls the blood...") as the rocket seemed to hover, then continued on to explode elsewhere.*

Watch for a display case containing the roll of honor of the Women's Voluntary Service. Unlike other remembrance books—depressingly long lists of names handwritten in beautiful calligraphy— these vibrantly colored drawings more closely resemble a modern illuminated manuscript. The artwork shows the WVS civil defense work, with captions explaining how arduously Britain's women labored during the war. The activities of the WVS, formed in 1938, ranged from staffing mobile canteens to setting up emergency clothing depots to running recycling drives.

In a corner near the west door is St. George's Chapel, also known as the Warriors' Chapel. In 1932 it was reconstructed and dedicated to the memory of the men and women killed in World War I, then after World War II, rededicated as a collective memorial to the dead of both wars. Abbey staff who served in either war are also honored here.

The most dramatic of the war memorials is the grave of the Unknown Warrior near the west door. Its black Belgian marble, flush with the floor, is always edged by brilliant red Flanders poppies (not real, incidentally). The tomb, erected in the 1920s, commemorates the dead from World War I. But like so many memorials for the War to End All Wars, the honor is shared by those who fought in the War After the War to End All Wars. Be sure to read the lengthy inscription, and watch for the ghostly young man some have seen here, his khaki uniform stained with mud.

Nearby, also embedded in the floor, a green-flecked marble stone reminds the viewer to "Remember Winston Churchill." The memorial was unveiled by Queen Elizabeth in 1965 on the twenty-fifth anniversary of the Battle of Britain. Every year afterwards, for the rest of her life, Clementine Churchill would lay flowers here on the anniversary of her husband's birth and of his death. Churchill isn't buried here, but for those unable to make the journey to his gravesite in Bladon Churchyard near Oxford, this is the place for silent tribute.

Another wartime leader, President Franklin Roosevelt, is commemorated with a marble wall tablet to the left side of the west door. Surmounted by an American eagle, the tablet was unveiled by Prime Minister Attlee in 1948 with Mrs. Roosevelt and Winston Churchill at his side. Beneath it are seven leather-bound volumes, books of remembrance to the homefront dead of World War II. One opened book is displayed at a time, and the pages are regularly turned. The brief entries—name, date, location, and circumstances of death—can make for sobering reading; the names of over 66,000 civilians appear here. If you seek a specific name, make an appointment with the Dean's Verger or contact the Commonwealth War Graves Commission, 2 Marlow Road, Maidenhead, Berkshire SL6 7DX (e-mail casualty.enq@cwgc.org).

Besides the services at Westminster Abbey attended by American soldiers in November 1942, there were also Thanksgiving services at Westminster Cathedral and the West End Synagogue.

Several other remembrance books or rolls of honor are maintained in public and private areas of the Abbey. If you're interested in any of these, ask a verger to see the memorials to the Metropolitan Police, the Royal Army Medical Corps, the Burma Campaign, the Commandos, the Queen's Westminsters, or the HMS *Barham*, a British battleship torpedoed and blown up in the Mediterranean in 1941.

Before leaving through the west door, turn and look back down the imposing nave. Imagine yourself a young and undoubtedly awed American soldier walking into Westminster Abbey for Thanksgiving services in 1942. It was the first time in 900 years that the building had ever been given over to another nation for a religious celebration. During the service U.S. Ambassador John Gilbert Winant read a Thanksgiving message from President Roosevelt, an American organist played, and a GI choir sang "America, the Beautiful." For a few moments, this was home for many a homesick Yank.

Outside, in a new memorial above the west door, each of ten niches has a small statue honoring a twentieth-century martyr, including Polish Franciscan saint Maximilian Kolbe and German theologian Dietrich Bonhoeffer, both killed by the Nazis, and American Martin Luther King, Jr. These are the only twentieth-century individuals represented by full-length statues in the Abbey.

VISITOR DETAILS: Westminster Abbey is open Monday–Friday 9:30am to 3:45pm (last admission), and until 7 on Wednesday; Saturday 9:30am to 1:45pm. Admission is charged; sound guides and guided tours available. No photography, except in the Cloisters and gardens. Coffee stand in the Cloisters; another outside on the Abbey's west side. No restrooms; head for the Westminster subway or the Broad Sanctuary public loo, opposite Methodist Central Hall. More information: 020 7222 5152, www.westminster-abbey.org.

If you've had enough of somber tombs and memories, visit the Westminster Abbey Bookshop outside. For those visiting early in the day, the shop may not yet be filled with London schoolchildren clambering over each other trying to find something they can afford. If, however, it's just too chaotic, head for the calm of nearby St. Margaret's.

St. Margaret's Church is somewhat overshadowed both historically and architecturally by the grand Abbey, but on the other hand, it's less hectic and quite charming on its own terms. This, the third church building to stand on this site, was consecrated in 1523 and serves as the parish church for the Westminster community and the House of Commons.

Cross the lawn paralleling the Abbey and head toward St. Margaret's unimposing doors. In the grassy areas here, fields of remembrance—areas dedicated to war dead—were traditionally covered with small crosses on

Remembrance Day at Westminster Abbey.

Armistice Day, a custom that continues today. In 1940, the "Fallen Soldiers of the Home Front" were memorialized here, members of the Civil Defence Services and civilians killed by the enemy. And while many such lawns in wartime London were turned over to garden allotments for the growing of vegetables, this churchyard was not. It served as a cemetery until about 1880, although the gravestones are long gone, and was considered not the best spot to grow a bumper crop of potatoes.

Unlike Westminster Abbey, with its side chapels and side-side chapels, St. Margaret's interior is straightforward: one central

St. Margaret's Church entrance.

aisle, two side aisles, wooden pews, and embroidered kneelers. Reputedly the church is the burial site of both early printer William Caxton (nearby Caxton Street is named after him) and Walter Raleigh; memorials to both men are here. Raleigh can also be seen spreading his cloak in the west window.

On the north wall a memorial honors Reverend James Palmer, vicar of St. Bride's Church in the early 1600s, with the addendum that the memorial was "irreparably damaged by an oil bomb 25 September 1940." A brass plaque on the southeast side of the altar surround honors St. Margaret's Church choristers who fell in the war.

The glorious east window was originally designed in Holland in the fifteenth century to celebrate the upcoming wedding of Arthur, son of Henry VII, to Catherine of Aragon. Alas, the window arrived too late (Arthur had died), and henceforth suffered "various vicissitudes" including being hidden during the Commonwealth. During World War II, it was hidden once more, the glass removed and taken to Putney for safekeeping.

In the September 1940 attack that so irreparably damaged Reverend Palmer's memorial, St. Margaret's roof was smashed, several pews were set on fire, and the pipe that carried the wind to the organ was severed. Author Phyllis Bottome, visiting soon after, found the "little silvery church was alive only in its outer fabric, within it smelt still of burned-out fires, and all its pews, its glass, and its hassocks and church ornaments were brushed up into little heaps."

The church's prewar stained glass was Victorian, apart from the east window, and almost all of it was blown out by German bombs. The incongruously modern windows now along the south aisle are by artist John Piper. He was also responsible for the stained glass in the new Coventry Cathedral, built after the catastrophic German bombing destroyed the original structure.

St. Margaret's has always been a favored site for weddings, and it was here that Winston Churchill married Clementine Hozier on September 12, 1908. Their daughter Mary Soames, writing in her biography of her mother, described the happy occasion: "Great crowds had assembled in Parliament Square, and both the bridegroom…and the bride were enthusiastically cheered as they arrived….St. Margaret's was a bower of palms and ferns, with white lilies everywhere….Mr. Lloyd George, the Chancellor of the Exchequer,

> **VISITOR DETAILS:** St. Margaret's is open Monday–Friday 9:30am to 3:45pm; Sunday 2pm to 5pm. More information: 020 7654 4840, www.westminster-abbey.org (yes, the Abbey website covers St. Margaret's).

signed the register, and Winston immediately set to talking politics with him." Check out the glass case to the right of the altar, as you face it, where items important to the history of St. Margaret's are displayed, including a copy of the marriage register signed by Winston Churchill ("a bachelor") and Clementine Ogilvie Hozier ("a spinster").

West of Westminster Abbey and St. Margaret's sits **Methodist Central Hall**, a chunky Edwardian block that, compared to its popular neighbors, seems at first glance both unvisited and unvisitable. Actually the hall is a remarkably impressive building with much war-related history and a welcoming reputation.

Soon after the 1891 centenary of the death of John Wesley, founder of the Methodist Church, church leaders embarked on a national project to raise one million guineas to finance various church developments, including the erection of a centenary memorial hall in London. The imposing building opened in 1912, a Viennese Baroque edifice of grace and elegance. Inside is a grand staircase and a surprisingly intimate meeting hall seating over 2,300. Outside, the steel-framed walls are faced with

Methodist Central Hall.

Portland stone and much decoration, all leading to the lead-covered dome. It was the strength and durability of the structure, plus the Methodist zeal for outreach and fellowship, that recommended Central Hall's use as a wartime air raid shelter.

Step inside the graceful foyer and explore a bit (ask at the desk about tours) or head downstairs to Wesley's Café, the location of the hall's air raid shelter. In the words of Margaret Sangster, daughter of the wartime Methodist minister here, "It became one of the biggest air raid shelters in the country, the permanent home of hundreds," housing homeless and bombed-out people from the Pimlico area plus passersby just ducking in for a few safe moments during raids. In contrast to the bomb and fire damage inflicted on its neighbors, Central Hall survived with only minor shrapnel damage.

VISITOR DETAILS: Methodist Central Hall is open daily 9am to 5pm. Free tours. Ramped disabled access at the Tothill Street side; elevators go to all floors (but not, alas, the roof). Wesley's Café offers cafeteria-style fare; open daily 10am to 4:30pm; restrooms. More information: 020 7222 6883, www.c-h-w.com.

In part because it was unscathed by the war, Methodist Central Hall easily shifted from shelter to meeting place and was selected as the site for the inaugural General Assembly of the new United Nations. On January 10, 1946, the fifty-one member countries of the UN began their work here, meeting in the Great Hall. Outside, on the south side near Tothill Street, two commemorative plaques mark the UN's opening and the fiftieth anniversary celebration in 1996.

One reason to tour the building (besides the historic aura of the Great Hall where both de Gaulle and Churchill have spoken) is an opportunity to rise above Westminster's streets for a different perspective. You can step out onto the deck area about three floors up (Vertigo Alert: This one is no problem) or go all the way to the top of the dome, over 200 feet from the pavement (Vertigo Alert: Skip this). Wartime firewatchers were stationed at both levels, extinguishing incendiary bombs before fire could take hold. Ask the tour guide to show you where firewatchers scratched their initials or brief messages into the soft lead of the roof.

Just 400 yards from the triad of religious sites in Big Ben's shadow sits 10 Downing Street, home to Britain's prime minister. Let's leave behind both the political and religious centers at the foot of Big Ben and head north, toward the more worldly district of the Cabinet War Rooms, Downing Street, Whitehall, and on toward Trafalgar Square.

PART III
THE WORLDLY SIDE

*Barbed-wire entanglements have been erected around
government buildings in Whitehall...troops in their
shirtsleeves were to be seen setting up sandbagged machine-
gun and observation posts near the Houses of Parliament,
watched by the usual expressionless group of loiterers....*

—MOLLIE PANTER-DOWNES, *LONDON WAR NOTES* 1939-1945

Wartime Tube shelterers.

Highlights: Cabinet War Rooms, Cenotaph, Downing Street, Banqueting House, Horse Guards Parade, Admiralty Citadel, Guards Memorial, Old War Office, Charles I statue

Underground Station: Westminster

Photo Ops: Bring along your camera for photos of military statues, ducks, and soldiers on horseback. Photography is discouraged in the Cabinet War Rooms, but excellent postcards are available in the shop.

BEFORE LEAVING ON YOUR TRIP

■ **Travel Scheduling:** If you're in London on the Sunday nearest November 11, Remembrance Day ceremonies at the Cenotaph are a must (arrive early). A high-

light of a June visit is the Trooping of the Colour in Horse Guards Parade; it's unlikely you'll get a seat, but the festivities are fun to watch even from a distance.

■ **Cultural Preparations:** The video *Churchill and the Cabinet War Rooms*, produced by the History Channel and the Imperial War Museum, is available from amazon.com or the Churchill Stores/Book Club at the Churchill Centre: 888-WSC-1874, www.winstonchurchill.org.

■ **Internet Best Bets:** Don't miss the Number 10 Downing Street website (www.number-10.gov.uk)—the wealth of interior photographs is as close as you'll get to the place.

If you've opted for Big Ben's more worldly neighborhood, turn right from the Westminster Underground and walk past the statue of Churchill along the northern side of Parliament Square. The incessant traffic here dramatizes the roundabout system, first introduced in 1926 and now a standard feature of English roadways. During the war, when petrol was rationed and fewer vehicles were on the road, it was far easier and safer to cross London streets...except during the blackout, of course.

Continue past Parliament Square (where a 400-person air raid shelter once stood) along Great George Street. At the park's edge, turn right onto Horse Guards Road. You can head directly for the Cabinet War Rooms or first take a stroll in St. James's Park. Prime Minister Chamberlain and his wife often set out from 10 Downing Street for a morning walk here, followed discreetly by a plainclothes detective. Churchill was also a regular park visitor, perhaps passing the sandbagged pillbox and uniformed sentries doing wartime duty at this corner. (See "A Walk in the Park" in Chapter 2.)

> The statue at the top of the steps near the Cabinet War Rooms is of Robert Clive, the man who brought India into the British Empire.

As the bombing raids of early autumn 1940 became more and more severe and with several near-misses in the area, it became clear that the prime minister's Downing Street residence was not safe. Further, although it was essential to find refuge from German bombs, it was imperative that no impression be given that the prime minister was abandoning London. "During the last fortnight of September," Churchill later wrote, "preparations were made to transfer my Ministerial Headquarters to the more modern and solid Government offices overlooking St. James's Park by Storey's Gate. These quarters we called 'the Annexe.'"

The "modern and solid" steel-framed building on the corner of Great George Street and Horse Guards Road provided the convenient and expandable site needed. A private apartment for the Churchills was constructed, complete with dining room and sitting room. A floor above were the offices of Churchill's science advisor and friend Professor Frederick Lindemann and the offices of various personal and military assistants. There was even a staff cafeteria. The stark Number 10 Annexe yielded somewhat to Clementine Churchill's decorating skills; visitor Harold Nicolson found it "very pretty with chintz and flowers and good furniture and excellent French pictures." But even the talented Mrs. Churchill couldn't make the small rooms seem spacious or camouflage the reinforcing iron girders.

As you stand on Horse Guards Road and look toward this corner building, the Churchills' wartime apartment would have been on the ground floor to the right of the building's entranceway. The windows

Welcome to the War Rooms.

were covered with steel shutters (long gone), and a reinforced concrete apron (still visible) was constructed along the west side, both meant to shield those inside from bomb blast and shell splinters.

Below the Churchills' apartment (and a three-foot concrete slab) was the labyrinthine underground area of the **Cabinet War Rooms**, including the War Room itself, the Map Room, dozens of offices, sleeping quarters, conference rooms, a radio broadcasting station, a canteen, a power plant—everything needed for a self-contained living space. After war's end, this underground site remained closed and untouched until some of the subterranean rooms were opened to the public in 1984. Today the place has the feel of Pompeii, as if assorted cabinet ministers and staff officers and civil servants—perhaps even the prime minister himself—have just stepped away from the wall maps, or the reports on the desks, or even the small room marked "Lavatory."

Enter through the faux-sandbagged doorway at the foot of Clive Steps and head downstairs, a different approach than that of a wartime visitor who would have been escorted down well-guarded steps from inside the building above.

After the introductory display rooms (watch for Churchill's own chromium-plated air raid helmet), the recorded tour leads visitors down a long passageway. First stop is the Cabinet War Room itself, where Beaverbrook, Morrison, Bevin, Reith, Attlee, and other war cabinet members sat, planning and arguing and undoubtedly chain-smoking for over a hundred meetings. The baize-covered table looks much as it did during those intense gatherings—note the sign Churchill placed mid-table. The prime minister's brown wooden chair sits at the center of the room's far side, in front of the world map. War cabinet members sat around the hollow square of the table, with Churchill's chiefs of staff sitting directly opposite him inside the square. Early on, when a German invasion seemed probable, Churchill grandly pointed to his chair and intoned, "This is the room from which I'll direct the war. And if the invasion takes place, that's where I'll sit—in that chair. And I'll sit there until either the Germans are driven back—or they carry me out dead." Such melodramatic pronouncements seem a bit over the top today, but in the midst of the nightmarish uncertainty of the early war days, Churchill's cocky bluster struck just the right note.

Here U.S. envoy Bill Donovan met Churchill, the latter probably wearing his favorite siren suit, a comfortable dark-blue one-piece overall zipped down the front. Donovan was quick to note the drama of the labyrinthine situation: "In these dungeons under Whitehall, you step into a Shakespearean play, with stage directions like 'Army Heard in Distance, Sound of Trumpets!'"

The Original London Walks Company infrequently offers both a Blitz walk and a Churchill walk. More information: 020 7624 3978, www.walks.com.

Down the hall is the "Lavatory," actually the Transatlantic Telephone Room, where Churchill spoke by telephone to President Roosevelt. Radio-telephony was then in its infancy, and the equipment needed to ensure safe communications by "scrambling" the message was so immense (weighing eighty tons) that it was housed across central London in the basement of Selfridges' Oxford Street store. The lavatory sign on the door was meant to confuse anyone who didn't really need to know when and how the two world leaders communicated. Part of the ruse included an actual toilet lock, still there, that could be switched from "Vacant" to "Engaged." Inside are the ubiquitous 1940s metal fan and a green shaded lamp. That may even be Mr. Churchill himself talking on the phone.

Next up are rooms used by the prime minister and Mrs. Churchill, plus the kitchen and the Chiefs of Staff room. One area not open to the public is the Dock, the sub-basement below the main level of underground rooms, although a glass window in the floor offers a peek into that subterranean world. Here emergency sleeping facilities were provided for staff reluctant to brave the falling shrapnel and explosive bombs outside. Because of its depth and the layers of concrete above, the Dock was considered a safe spot to spend the night during air raids, though the rats, all-night lighting, chemical toilets, and humming ventilation machinery made it unappealing to some. One Dock user noted that although it was certainly safe, the area "looked and smelt like a battleship and one emerged in the morning gasping for air."

Further along and around the corner, a dozen claustrophobic rooms house BBC transmitting equipment, a telephone/typing area, the stenographic typing pool, offices and sleeping quarters for various military personnel, and so on. Watch for essential wartime accoutrements: air raid helmets, gas masks, whistles, and candles (for power outages).

> *The underground rooms used by Churchill during the war were commonly known as "the bunker" or "the hole in the ground."*

Along a desk railing in the Central Map Room sits the "Beauty Chorus," a dozen or so black, red, green, and white telephones linked to the various Service war rooms. The white phone was a direct line to 10 Downing Street. Some phones had flashing lights rather than ringing bells, but even so, the noise level must have been high. Imagine these small offices crowded with dozens of workers and in the background the sound of ringing telephones, typewriters, office duplicators, shouting voices, and running footsteps.

Here, too, the room feels as if those who staffed the phones and plotted ship and troop movements on the wall maps have just stepped away, leaving behind the red painted box for cigarette ends, scribbled notes half-written on the desktops, and signs urging "Quiet Please." Although the Cabinet War Rooms were used primarily during the London Blitz, the Map Room remained in operation twenty-four hours a day until war's end.

> **VISITOR DETAILS:** The Cabinet War Rooms are open daily 9:30am to 6pm; open later in winter. Admission is charged. Free sound guides. Switchboard Cafeteria; restrooms near the exit. More information: 020 7930 6961, www.iwm.org.uk/cabinet/index.htm.

The prime minister's combined office and bedroom is furnished spartanly, with a narrow bed (nightshirt and cigar at the ready), bedside lamp, wall maps, and wire wastebaskets. Note the hand-wound wall clock, inkwell, and blotter. Churchill made several radio broadcasts from this room, perhaps glancing up from his notes to look at the maps—the curtains were to conceal them, as necessary, from prying eyes. Churchill spent only a handful of nights here. Even during the worst of the aerial attacks, he was much more likely to be watching than sheltering.

The tour concludes at an exhibit of Churchilliana, showcasing letters and telegrams and even the great man's hearing aids! Next—and last—is the shop, with many unusual items including Churchill-related postcards

Text continued on page 39.

Stand and Deliver:
A Walk among Westminster's Military Statues

This statue stroll begins along busy Whitehall, then moves to the relative quiet of the Victoria Embankment Gardens. There's little honor paid to homefront civilians here, but an important handful of military men are memorialized. Start at Raleigh Green, the lawn about a block south of Banqueting House, where three World War II heroes stand.

First—and closest to Downing Street—is Field Marshal Montgomery. The beret-clad Monty stands jauntily, arms behind his back, seemingly about to urge his men

> *Westminster's war began when a bomb fell on the south side of Horseguards Avenue on the afternoon of September 11, 1940.*

into the Battle of El Alamein. This charismatic (some would say arrogant) soldier led the 8th Army against Rommel in North Africa in 1942 and—in a dramatic reversal of Britain's military fortunes up to that point—routed the German forces. When I was last here, a small wreath lay at Monty's feet; the attached note read "Ex-8th Army Veteran Remembers Monty. A Great Leader."

Next comes Field Marshal Alan Brooke, Chief of the Imperial Staff from 1941 to 1946, and "Master of Strategy." The general was in charge of the homefront at the beginning of the war, helping the military—

and the country—prepare for the expected invasion, and rather effectively reining-in the inspired impetuosity of Churchill. (Some clarity: General, later Field Marshal, Alan Brooke chose the title of Lord Alanbrooke when raised to the peerage in 1945. Throughout this book, dealing with his pre-peer years, he'll be Alan Brooke.)

Last is a hero of the Burma Campaign, Field Marshal Slim, later Chief of the Imperial General Staff. The bronze statue shows a campaign-hatted Slim about to gaze across Whitehall through the soldier's ubiquitous binoculars. Incidentally, a fourth statue is planned for this area, honoring the women of World War II.

Head up Whitehall bast Banqueting House and turn right onto Horseguards Avenue past the statue of the Duke of Devonshire. Stroll one of my favorite London side streets—few tourists ever venture here, even though it's just yards away from the crowds of Horse Guards.

The Ministry of Defence is on the right beyond Banqueting House, its main entrance surmounted by two sculptures, *Earth* and *Water*. Across from the ministry stands the trusty Nepalese Gurkha soldier: "Bravest of the brave, most generous of the generous, never had country more faithful friends than you." Gurkha soldiers, perhaps the finest soldiers in the world, have fought in British military campaigns from 1816 to the late 1990s, including numerous World War II campaigns.

Take a quick down-and-back along Whitehall Court, past the Gurkha and the Royal

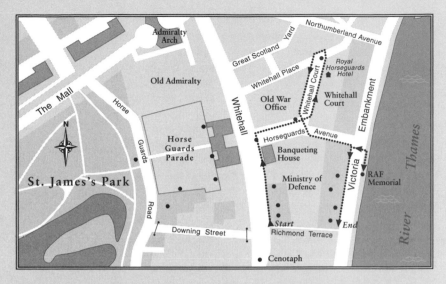

Horseguards Thistle Hotel, to see yet another military statue—five uniformed figures looking up the roadway. This affecting grouping honors the Royal Tank Regiment and the 5,000 men who died in action: "From mud through blood to the green fields beyond." On the corner nearby (away from where the soldiers are gazing) is the National Liberal Club, once called the "epitome of high-minded late-Victorian liberalism." Bombed in 1941, the Victorian-era building has since been rebuilt.

As you retrace your steps back to the Gurkha statue, that's the Old War Office to your right, a complex of offices that took several direct hits in the Blitz, although most damage, aside from shattered windows, was confined to the interior courtyard's stonework and upper levels.

At Horseguards Avenue, turn left toward the river. At the end of this short block is a stretch of green, with Queen Mary's Steps the first thing you'll encounter, up against the back of the ministry building. The steps, terrace, and river wall here were all part of the original Whitehall Palace, but over the centuries

the area was filled in and the river shore receded. The steps were uncovered in 1939 when evacuations for the Ministry of Defense building revealed the old river wall of the Tudor palace. Just beyond is a statue of General Gordon (different war), then a large flower bed commemorating those who fought in World War II.

Standing at the corner with the Thames directly ahead of you, turn and look back toward the long building that faces the river. This vantage point reveals the exuberant roofline of minarets, domes, turrets, and other architectural folderol of Whitehall Court, a residential building of spacious and expensive service flats. Before and during the war, playwright George Bernard Shaw lived here, his corner flat looking down on this garden and the river beyond. Shaw wrote a friend in 1940, "We also sleep through the raids. My wife does not give a damn for bombs, but dreads shelters and prefers death to getting up and dressing. After all bed is the proper place to die in." (She did, here, in 1943, though not during an air raid.)

Cross the Victoria Embankment and walk south along the river to the Royal Air

Force Memorial, a dramatic monument with gilded eagle, globe, and 54-foot stone column. The inscription honors members of the various British Air Forces "who gave their lives in winning victory for their King and Country 1914–1918." Lord Trenchard unveiled the all-too-familiar addition in 1946, in remembrance of the men and women of the air forces who fought—and died—in World War II.

Unless traffic is virtually nonexistent, walk back to the corner to cross the Embankment, then start along the opposite side of the street and its lineup of military men. Incidentally, up until the early 1950s, you would have had to watch out for trams speeding along the tracks here.

Statues of two Marshals of the Royal Air Force keep watch on the waterfront: Lord Portal and Lord Trenchard. First, Charles Portal, the Chief of Air Staff from 1940 to 1945, and one of the "architects of victory" in the war. Oscar Nemon's bronze statue of a determined Portal was unveiled in 1975; he might even be staring at the RAF memorial across the Embankment. Portal was friend and comrade to Lord Trenchard, who stands nearby (near the Fleet Air Arm monument, discussed below). "Boom" Trenchard is considered the father of the RAF. It was his philosophy of bombing raids developed earlier in the century that led in part to the

RAF Memorial.

British bombing concepts of World War II. The statue's plinth lists some of Trenchard's additional accomplishments.

Between Portal and Trenchard stands the Fleet Air Arm monument: a low white prow with a column rising above it, surmounted by a winged figure. It honors the men and women who died while serving in the Royal Naval Air Services and the Fleet Air Arm. The memorial column provides a long list of military campaigns, from 1914 to Kuwait 1991. And above? That spectacular angel is actually an air pilot.

Near the far corner of the grassy rectangle stands the Chindit Badge, honoring those who fought in North Burma with the Chindit Special Forces. The Chindits, commanded by Brigadier Orde Charles Wingate (check the back of this memorial), operated behind Japanese lines in Burma. Wingate called them Chindits after the Chinthe, the ferocious mythological beast at the top of the memorial, half lion and half griffin. A guardian of Burmese temples, the Chinthe here signifies the unusual cooperation between ground and air forces in the Burma campaign and is a reminder that "the boldest measures are the safest."

Wise words, though perhaps not the best for a pedestrian in London's streets. Straight ahead down the Embankment is Big Ben and the frantic traffic near Parliament. Be careful out there.

Whitehall's Cenotaph.

and posters, books, slides, medals, maps, Churchill Toby jugs, busts, and even bottles of his favorite champagne.

From the Cabinet War Rooms, turn right and head up the Clive Steps and along King Charles Street. If the evocative aura of the War Rooms still lingers, imagine getting off work some late wartime evening, perhaps after twelve hours spent underground taking dictation or typing or operating a switchboard. You're wearily trudging toward Whitehall to catch your bus home, the warning sirens are wailing, the sky is filled with cones of light from roving searchlights, and the discordant hum of approaching German aircraft can be heard. At any minute the anti-aircraft guns in the park will begin whumping, and you have to walk this long block between two very big and very bombable government buildings…in total darkness. Welcome to London's Blitz.

> The custom in the 1930s and 1940s was for gentlemen to doff their hats as they passed the Cenotaph.

Your wartime walk down King Charles Street ends at the Whitehall of today. The simple stone monument in the middle of the roadway to the left is the **Cenotaph**, unveiled on Armistice Day 1920 to honor the fallen of World War I. Every November since, the Cenotaph has been the focus for a salute to "the Glorious Dead" of all of Britain's wars.

Continue up Whitehall to **Downing Street**. Until terrorism reared its ugly head in the 1980s, visitors could stroll down Downing Street and view the unimposing brick exterior, black front door, and lion's-head door knocker of the prime minister's official London home. For security reasons the street is now closed ("Authorised persons only. All passes to be shown."), and tourists stand outside the gates and peer down the block, ever hopeful of seeing something or someone exciting. In the early 1940s, London visitors would have encountered a barbed-wire fence next to a sandbagged machine-gun nest, both located below the current "Downing Street" sign.

Cenotaph *comes from the Latin* cenotaphium, *meaning "an empty or hollow tomb."*

For decades, black limousines have lumbered around the corner here and beetled down the street, perhaps disgorging a private secretary or a cabinet minister at Number 10. On September 30, 1938, it was the limousine of Neville Chamberlain, coming from a showdown with Adolf Hitler, that turned onto Downing Street and sped the prime minister to his front door. Tired after his Munich efforts, Chamberlain entered his official residence, went to an upstairs window, leaned out, and waved the famous agreement with Herr Hitler at the cheering onlookers. He announced "peace with honor"—a haunting phrase—and added "I believe it is peace for our time."

In less than a year, Chamberlain would sit at a radio microphone in the Cabinet Room, grimly announcing the beginning of World War II. Eight months later, as the quiet of the Phoney War dramatically ended, Chamberlain resigned as prime minister.

When Chamberlain's successor, Winston Churchill, moved into his new home in mid-June 1940, he and wife Clementine found a charming though plain older London townhouse. Number 10, the residence of the prime minister, is interconnected with the residence of the Chancellor of the Exchequer at Number 11 and that of the Chief Whip at Number 12. The buildings look small from the street, but together they have upwards of two hundred rooms, including offices, private apartments, formal rooms, kitchens, and cellars.

The Cabinet Room and the prime minister's private office were on the ground floor of Number 10; one floor up was a large state dining room, and above that, various private rooms for the family. Photographer Cecil Beaton visited in September 1940 and later reported on the Churchill's family rooms: "Mrs. Churchill had typically arranged the rooms with her usual pale colours of pistachio green and palest salmon pink....The Prime Minister's bedroom

Number 10.

The Churchills' Chartwell home.

was simplicity itself. A small single bed: some drawings of his family and his mother by Sargent: a small bedside table mounted with telephones galore: boxes of cigars: a wash basin with shaving soap and brushes in evidence: a few books: some files of Parliamentary speeches, and that was all."

The Cabinet Room's french doors opened onto the walled garden between Horse Guards Parade and Number 10, a pleasant half-acre lawn edged with flower beds once fussed over by Neville Chamberlain. Very early in London's war the garden level, including the kitchen, was fortified and strengthened. Part was even outfitted as an air raid shelter, but it was small and deemed unsafe, so construction was begun on the Number 10 Annexe nearby. The Annexe was only partially finished in October 1940 when a bombing raid began and a huge explosion shook Horse Guards Parade. Although little damage occurred at Number 10, Churchill quickly instructed the kitchen staff to head to the garden-level shelter. Minutes later another bomb fell even closer. "The mess...was indescribable—windows smashed in all directions, everything covered with grime, doors off hinges and curtains and furniture tossed about in a confused mass."

Nevertheless, the small shelter at Number 10 had done its job: protected the prime minister and his staff. Churchill wasn't a great fan of shelters, and he grumbled endlessly when air raid wardens would insist on his seeking safety. But he did care about the safety of his staff and especially the king—George VI twice sought shelter in 10 Downing Street as a plaque in the Garden Room notes: "In this room during the Second World War His Majesty the King was graciously pleased to dine on four-

Text continued on page 46.

Winston Churchill

November 30, 1874: Winston Leonard Spencer Churchill is born in a small ground-floor room in Blenheim Palace, Woodstock, near Oxford. (The palace and grounds are open today to the public.)

February 1901: Churchill takes his seat in the House of Commons, elected as a Conservative MP from Oldham, Lancashire. For the next few years, Churchill lives in a bachelor flat at 105 Mount Street, Mayfair (still flats).

August 11, 1908: A nervous Winston proposes to Clementine Hozier in the Temple of Diana on the grounds of Blenheim Palace. (The temple still stands.)

September 12, 1908: Over 1,000 guests attend the wedding of Winston Churchill and Clementine Hozier at St. Margaret's Church, Westminster, "the most popular and interesting wedding of the year," according to the *Daily Mirror*. The couple honeymoon in Italy. They return to Winston's tiny bachelor house at 12 Bolton Street, later staying briefly between moves at 22 Carlton House Terrace, home of Churchill's cousin.

Spring 1909: The Churchills move to 33 Eccleston Square near Victoria Station, leasing it for £195 a year. They'll remain until 1913, and later briefly return in 1916. Daughter Diana (1909) and son Randolph (1911) are born here. (The building has a plaque, confusingly placed somewhat closer to Number 34.)

October 1911: Churchill is named First Lord of the Admiralty. The family moves into Admiralty House, Whitehall in 1913. Daughter Sarah (1914) is born here.

May 1915: Churchill leaves the Admiralty in disgrace over his failed Dardanelles plan. The family stays with Winston's brother Jack at 41 Cromwell Road, Kensington (still standing), until autumn 1916, then returns to Eccleston Square until spring 1917.

November 1915: Major Winston Churchill leaves for France to join his regiment.

Spring 1917–January 1924: The Churchills live in several London residences, including 16 Lower Berkeley Street (1918), 1 Dean Trench Street, Westminster (1919–1920), and 2 Sussex Square, north of Hyde Park (1920–1924; destroyed in the Blitz; there's a plaque at the site). Daughter Marigold

Winston Churchill.

(1918) is born at 3 Tenterden Street, Mayfair, but dies tragically of septicaemia three years later. The same day daughter Mary (1922) is born, Churchill spends £5000 to buy Chartwell in Westerham, Kent, south of London. The house and grounds (open to the public) begin to occupy much of the Churchills' time, energy, and money.

October 1924: After being out of Parliament for two years, Churchill is elected to Parliament for West Essex (Epping), about twenty miles northeast of London; he represents this area for the next forty years.

November 1924: Prime Minister Baldwin names Churchill Chancellor of the Exchequer. The family soon moves into 11 Downing Street, the Chancellor's official residence, where they live until April 1929, when the new prime minister, Ramsay Macdonald, fails to include Churchill in his government. For much of the 1930s—his years in the political wilderness—Churchill lives at Chartwell.

December 1931: Out of the cabinet (though still a member of Parliament), Churchill sails to the U.S. for a lecture tour. He looks the wrong way while crossing a New York City street and is struck and badly injured by a car.

1930: Churchill leases a top-floor flat at 11 Morpeth Mansions, Morpeth Terrace, close to Parliament. This is his city home until late 1939. (The building, now pricey flats, has a plaque noting Churchill's residence.)

September 3, 1939: At Morpeth Mansions, the Churchills listen to Chamberlain's wireless announcement of war. When an air raid siren sounds, Churchill arms himself with brandy and "other appropriate medical comforts" and heads to a nearby basement shelter. The Churchills may have sheltered in the vaults of The Priory at Willow Place and Francis Street at the east end of Morpeth Terrace, or perhaps in the shelter on Carlisle Place, a street away, where a shelter sign can still be seen.

September 4, 1939: Prime Minister Chamberlain names Churchill First Lord of the Admiralty. The Churchills return to Admiralty House.

October 4, 1939: The Churchills attend son Randolph's wedding to Pamela Digby at St. John's, Smith Square, Westminster.

May 10, 1940: Neville Chamberlain resigns as prime minister; King George asks Churchill to form a new government.

June 1940: The Churchills move into 10 Downing Street. They remain here and in the Number 10 Annexe at Horse Guards Road until July 1945.

Mid-to-late 1940: Churchill's war cabinet meets regularly at the Down Street Underground (not in use then or now) while construction continues on the underground War Rooms. Accommodations are quite comfortable and Churchill often entertains and occasionally sleeps here. (The now-sealed street entrance is next to the small market at 24 Down Street.) Once the underground War Rooms are completed,

Churchill will hold over a hundred meetings there, but spend only a handful of nights. (Open to the public, at King Charles Street and Horse Guards Road.)

1940–1945: Throughout the war the prime minister visits the smashed and blasted streets of London and the bombed cities beyond: Battersea, Coventry, Dover, and Bristol among them. He meets President Roosevelt several times in Washington and

at Casablanca, Teheran, and Yalta. Churchill often spends working weekends at Chequers near Aylesbury in Buckinghamshire, the country residence of England's prime ministers, where his grandson Winston (1940) is born.

June 30, 1943: The battle of North Africa over (and won), the City of London confers the Freedom of the City on Churchill. He rides to the Guildhall ceremony in an open carriage with his wife and two of his daughters.

June 6, 1944: D-Day. Churchill spends time in the underground Map Room following the progress of the Normandy landings. Twice he walks to the House of Commons to speak of the day's events.

June 12, 1944: Churchill lands in Normandy, where he lunches with Montgomery at the general's headquarters. He visits Normandy twice more this summer.

November 11, 1944: Armistice Day. With General de Gaulle, the head of the Provisional French Government, Churchill walks down the Champs-Élysées in Paris as emotional crowds shout "Chour-cheel!"

May 8, 1945: Standing in an open car, Churchill makes his slow way through the jubilant crowds to Whitehall. Later, in a break with royal protocol, he stands with the Royal Family on the Buckingham Palace balcony, waving to the crowds below.

July 26, 1945: Churchill resigns in defeat after the general election, and King George asks Clement Attlee to form a new government. Churchill leaves Number 10 immediately, moving into a suite at Claridge's Hotel, Mayfair.

October 1945: After a brief stay at Number 67 Westminster Gardens, Marsham Street (a flat loaned by son-in-law Duncan Sandys), the Churchills move into 28 Hyde Park Gate, Kensington. They later buy Number 27 and combine the two homes into one. (The building has a plaque noting Churchill's residence.)

June 8, 1946: Although now a mere MP, Churchill sits with Prime Minister Attlee and other dignitaries in the viewing stand of London's Victory Parade.

October 1951: Aged seventy-seven, Winston Churchill is again named prime minister and returns to 10 Downing Street.

Spring 1953: Churchill is made a Knight of the Garter; he is now Sir Winston Churchill.

October 1953: The Nobel Prize for Literature is awarded to Churchill for "his mastery of historical and biographical description and for the resplendent power of speech with which he presents himself as a defender of high human rights." Because he's attending the Bermuda Conference at the time of the ceremony, Clementine Churchill accepts the award on her husband's behalf in Stockholm.

November 30, 1954: On his eightieth birthday, Churchill is honored by Parliament in a formal ceremony at Westminster Hall. A large oil painting of Churchill painted by Graham Sutherland is presented to the statesman.

April 5, 1955: Winston Churchill goes to Buckingham Palace to resign as prime minister; Queen Elizabeth asks Anthony Eden to form a new government.

April 9, 1963: Churchill is made an honorary United States citizen; son Randolph accepts the honor on his father's behalf at the White House.

January 24, 1965: Shortly after 8am, Winston Churchill, age ninety, dies at 28 Hyde Park Gate, on the seventieth anniversary of the death of his beloved father. London prepares for a state funeral, only the fourth ever held in the metropolis.

January 27, 1965: Churchill's flag-draped coffin lies in state in Westminster Hall. More than 300,000 people file past, paying homage to the wartime leader.

January 30, 1965: Churchill's coffin is placed on a gun carriage, used before in the funerals of four British monarchs, then in military slow time the funeral procession moves from Westminster Hall. Big Ben is silenced and remains so until midnight. The cortege proceeds to St. Paul's Cathedral via Whitehall, Trafalgar Square, the Strand, Fleet Street, and Ludgate Hill; as many as a million silent mourners line the streets. Ignoring royal etiquette, the queen stands on the steps of St. Paul's, awaiting England's greatest statesman. The service concludes with the playing of the "Last Post" by a trumpeter standing high above in the Whispering Gallery. Leaving St. Paul's, the funeral procession passes Tower Hill, moving via Cannon Street toward the river as artillery gun salutes echo through the City. The coffin is placed on the ship *Havengore* at Tower Pier and taken to Festival Hall Pier, then travels by hearse to Waterloo Station. Here it's moved on board the funeral train heading to Bladon, Oxfordshire, less than a mile from Churchill's birthplace. The body of Sir Winston Leonard Spencer Churchill is buried in the churchyard of St. Martin's Church. Only two wreaths are placed on his grave: one from his wife and one from his queen.

A Churchill coin—the crown, equivalent to five shillings—was minted by the millions after the prime minister's death. No longer officially in circulation, they can often be purchased at London street markets and make a portable and unusual gift.

December 12, 1977: Clementine Hozier Churchill (now Baroness Spencer-Churchill of Chartwell), age ninety-three, dies in her London flat at 7 Prince's Gate. Her ashes are buried in her husband's grave in Bladon.

teen occasions with the Prime Minister, Mr. Churchill…on two of those occasions the company was forced to withdraw into the neighbouring shelter by air bombardment of the enemy."

Horse and Guard.

Downing Street environs were bombed several times and Number 10 survived some very near misses, the worst in February 1944 when bombs exploded on the corner of Downing Street, on Horse Guards Parade, and near the Guards Memorial. By war's end, Number 10 was scarred inside and out. Repairs began almost immediately, and by the early 1950s the prime minister's official residence once again looked presentable.

Continue up Whitehall another block or so. Across the street is a grassy area with several statues, but you can save these for later. (See "Stand and Deliver: A Walk among Westminster's Military Statues" on page 36.) On the left side of the street, where the crowds are, is Horse Guards. We'll come back in a moment, but first cross Whitehall to **Banqueting House**, a smaller wonder often overlooked in the drama of the nearby Abbey and Parliament. Even the brochure headlines this as "a hidden Royal treasure." It's beautiful, it's quiet, and it's open, unlike any other building along this stretch of history.

Designed by Inigo Jones in 1622, Banqueting House is all that's left of the original Whitehall Palace. The building's main feature is Banqueting Hall with its marvelous ceiling paintings by Peter Paul Rubens. In the early twentieth century, the Rubens' ceiling had been mounted on laminated board, making it relatively easy at the outbreak of war to remove the paintings for safekeeping in a distant quarry. At war's end, the panels were restored and retouched by the Ministry of Works before being returned to the Banqueting Hall ceiling. The building itself sustained little wartime damage.

The museum of the Royal United Services was located here from the 1890s to the mid-1960s, its collection illustrating the history of the British armed forces. Wartime visitors were welcome, admission one shilling, free to service personnel in uniform. Military standards of famous British regiments and

> **VISITOR DETAILS:** Banqueting House (barring some ceremonial function) is open Monday–Saturday 10am to 5pm. Admission is charged. Free sound guides. Wheelchair access to the Banqueting Hall is tricky but doable; call 020 7839 8918. Ramp to the Undercroft Museum. Restrooms in the Undercroft. More information: 020 7930 4179, www.hrp.org.uk.

ships were displayed, with engravings and weapons on the walls and small display cases dotted about. Some of these same items are now on display in the Undercroft Museum.

Even if you decide not to visit, step inside the entranceway and check out the "outline contingency plan for the proposed wedding/coronation of Edward VIII and Mrs. Simpson," dated November 7, 1936, on the wall to the right.

Cross Whitehall once again to investigate the small courtyard where two of the Queen's Horse Guards are mounted on horseback, surrounded by hordes of camera-toting folks, with passing tour buses slowing for a look. Though this seems a très touristy spot, it's a hardhearted visitor who won't sneak a photo of those stoic young men. Watch for the schedule posted on the fence-railing; it lists upcoming ceremonial Army events such as gun salutes and includes a monthly schedule of the Changing of the Guard at Buckingham Palace.

> **VISITOR DETAILS:** The Changing of the Guard at Horse Guards takes place daily at 11am; Sunday at 10am. Inspection is at 4pm daily.

Walk through the archway at the back of the Horse Guards area to **Horse Guards Parade**, a vast open space surrounded by government buildings (and in early June filled with viewing stands for the annual Trooping of the Colour). To the north, your right as you face the park, is the **Admiralty Citadel**, an ivy-covered and windowless monolith that's always aroused a sort of bemused distaste from Londoners. The incredibly strong structure, with foundations extending thirty feet below ground, was erected in 1940 to provide protection for the communications operations of the Admiralty; reputedly it could withstand a 1,000-lb. bomb. Politician Harold Macmillan, who served in Churchill's wartime

Horse Guards Parade.

government and was later prime minister, once described this hulking fortress as the building "which still graces, or defaces, Horse Guards Parade." It was quickly christened Lenin's tomb.

Other structures visible from the Parade Ground are all sturdy office buildings, most built in the eighteenth century and run together in an architectural tangle. Looking around from north to south, the building next to the Citadel is the Old Admiralty (1725) where Churchill twice served as First Lord of the Admiralty. It's generally open only to groups for tours, and then by appointment only; note the seafaring-themed lamp standards outside, though. Starting in May 1940, barbed-wire barricades surrounded the Admiralty and khaki-clad soldiers with bayoneted rifles guarded all entrances. German soldiers had parachuted into the Netherlands and Belgium as part of their invasion forces, and the authorities felt it best to be prepared for that possibility in London. And of course this huge open space had a barrage balloon moored in it.

Next is the brick Admiralty House (1788), then the Paymaster-General's Office (1732). The latter was bombed at least five times in the war, losing a massive chunk of its Whitehall frontage to an October 1940 bomb; the adjacent Horse Guards Building was also hit by wartime bombs. To the south is the Scottish Office in Dover House (badly damaged by Nazi bombs), the old Treasury, and then the brick backs and gardens of the buildings facing onto Downing Street. All these structures survived the war, though pockmarked and dingy on both the Whitehall side and this back side.

> Wartime humor: Two American GIs were walking down Whitehall. They stopped an English Tommy and asked, "Which side is the War Office on?" "Blimey," replied the English soldier. "I 'ope it's on ours."

Two of the four military statues on the Parade Ground's southern side are worth a quick visit—one of Lord Mountbatten, the other of Field Marshal Kitchener. Naval captain Mountbatten skippered the destroyer *Kelly* early in the war and was later named Chief of Combined Operations, then Supreme Allied Commander in South East Asia, and eventually First Sea Lord. The bronze statue was unveiled by Queen Elizabeth in 1983.

The statue of Kitchener—the man who bristled out of recruiting posters: Your Country Needs You!—backs onto the garden behind 10 and 11 Downing Street. The statue received shrapnel damage late in the war, primarily to the stone screen behind it. Watch for repaired chips and dings. Visitor Alert: Heightened security measures may disallow upclose scrutiny, as both statues are close to Downing Street's backyard.

The **Guards Memorial** stands across Horse Guards Parade on the edge of St. James's Park. Unveiled in 1926, it honors the soldiers in His

Majesty's Regiments of Foot Guards who died in World War I. The five bronze figures, cast from captured German guns, stand above a typical addendum seen on war memorials: "This memorial also commemorates all those members of the Household Divisions who died in the Second World War." The five guardsmen represent (left to right as you look at them) the Coldstream, Irish, Welsh, Scots, and Grenadier Guards. One Guardsman's leg was pierced by a fragment of a bomb that exploded in Horse Guards Parade; I've never been able to figure out which leg, but perhaps you can.

Guards Memorial.

Retrace your steps back through the Horse Guards archway and past the horses and the crowds, and turn left, up Whitehall toward Trafalgar Square. Across the street is the **Old War Office**, opened in 1900, a huge building that suffered several wartime bombing attacks. At least one explosive fell in the War Office's interior quadrangle, shattering windows and shaking loose masonry.

To your left ahead is the marquee of the Whitehall Theatre, a worldly element indeed in the Westminster/Whitehall mix. Opened in 1930, the theatre has offered a long string of comedic plays and reviews including the Whitehall Follies in 1942. The Follies featured Phyllis Dixey who can best be described as a stripper—but one with special talents. Total nudity was permitted on London's stages, but only if the performer didn't move. Miss Dixey joked and kidded with the audience as she slowly disrobed, and then…stillness in the Whitehall Theatre.

> For many Londoners, one of the worst aspects of the Blitz was the loss of sleep. It was much like jetlag…weeks and weeks of jetlag.

At the top of Whitehall on a traffic island across from Trafalgar Square stands an equestrian **statue of Charles I**, England's king from 1625 to 1649. Even before the war, this statue had a wandering history. Cast in 1633, it originally stood in Roehampton; in 1642, it was moved to the churchyard at St. Paul's, Covent Garden, and, with the coming of the Commonwealth, was sold as scrap to be melted down. The crafty buyer offered souvenirs supposedly made from the statue but, in fact, he hid it, producing the statue in 1660 at the restoration of the monarchy. It eventually was erected here in 1675. Charles I spent part of World War II at Lord Rosebery's estate in Mentmore, Buckinghamshire,

Great Churchill Reads

Any of these books, read in concert with a London visit, will enhance your understanding of the war's greatest statesman. For more on the Churchill bibliographic bonanza—there are dozens of books in print on Churchill—contact the Churchill Centre at 1150 17th Street NW, Suite 307, Washington, DC 20036, or www.winstonchurchill.org.

Churchill: A Biography (2001) by Roy Jenkins is an insightful political appraisal of Churchill, "with all his idiosyncrasies, his indulgences, his occasional childishness, but also his genius, his tenacity, and his persistent ability...to be larger than life," and declares him simply the greatest human being ever to occupy 10 Downing Street.

Sir Martin Gilbert is Churchill's official biographer, and he writes prolifically and well. *Churchill: A Life* (1991) parallels, but is not a condensation of, Gilbert's much larger "official" biography, which at eight biographic volumes and over a dozen companion volumes is more than most will want to take on. This shorter biography (1,000+ pages) provides a solid foundation in Churchill's background, family, and war experience.

In *Family Album: A Personal Selection from Four Generations of Churchills* (1979) by Mary Soames, more than 400 photographs (many never before published) plus lengthy commentary by Churchill's youngest daughter make for a charming album, filled with baby pictures, snapshots of family pets, photos of Churchill family homes, and glimpses of relatives and close friends.

Settle in for an in-depth read of Churchill's droll humor and intelligent wit gathered in *Irrepressible Churchill: Stories, Sayings, and Impressions of Sir Winston Churchill* (2000), an anthology of quips, quotes, and anecdotes selected and compiled by Kay Halle, a close Churchill family friend. The chronological arrangement makes it particularly easy to find comments related to World War II. A lighter collection is *The Wit and Wisdom of Winston Churchill* compiled by James Humes (1995).

The Last Lion: Visions of Glory, 1874–1932 (1983) and *The Last Lion: Alone, 1932–1940* (1988) by William Manchester provide the reader with much biographical background, but even better, a compellingly readable style (one reviewer calls it lyrical—you may find yourself, as I did, reading passages aloud to anyone who'll listen). The author recently suffered two strokes, so, sadly, the planned third volume covering the years 1940 to 1965 may never appear.

The letters and notes in *Winston and Clementine: The Personal Letters of the Churchills* (1999) offer a very personal and intimate look at a loving couple, enmeshed in a close relationship during chaotic political and economic times. I started this book, edited by Mary Soames, intending to limit my reading to the war era and ended up devouring every letter.

the bronze king being hauled there rather ignobly on a truck. The well-worn plinth, the base for the statue, remained boarded-up throughout the war. For a time it sported a humorous sign reading "Closed on Sundays—not open all the week." Charles was returned to his plinth in early 1946. Some statue trivia: The statue is signed on the left front foot of the horse, the armor the king is wearing is in the Tower of London collection, and all distances from London are traditionally measured from this point.

Having visited the three different worlds surrounding Big Ben—the political, the religious, and the worldly—consider a fourth: the hungry. During the late 1930s and the early 1940s, you might have had tea at the Lyons teashop next to the Westminster Underground, or perhaps enjoyed a pint at St. Stephen's Tavern and Restaurant nearby. Both the Lyons teashop and St. Stephen's Tavern are gone, alas, but several other pubs and eateries are nearby. Try the Red Lion (48 Parliament Street), good if you fancy a quick pint, and the closest pub to 10 Downing Street. Who knows who might walk in. Other possibilities: Café Churchill (49 Parliament Street) for morning coffee or lunchtime sandwiches, or the Clarence, Old Shades, or Silver Cross pubs. The Lord Moon of the Mall on the west side of Whitehall also serves lunch. Whether you enjoy a pint of bitter or a cup of coffee, a full ploughman's lunch or a quick sandwich, enjoy a restful moment waxing nostalgic about the wartime ambience at the foot of Big Ben.

> *The name of St. Stephen's Tavern can still be seen, incised overhead on the building between the Parliamentary Bookshop and Canon Row.*

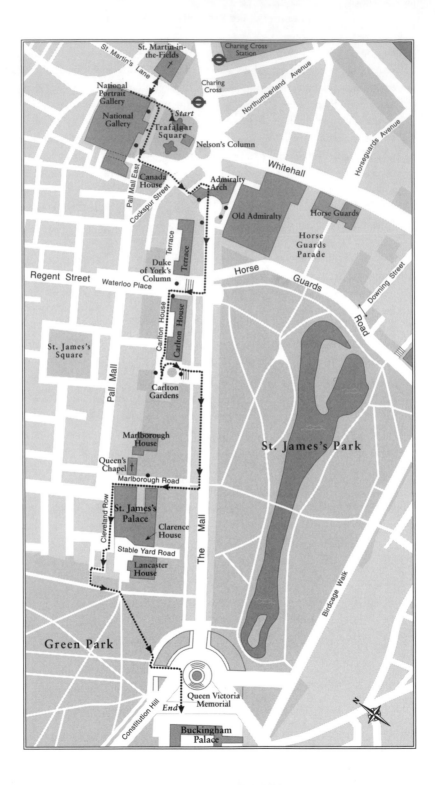

St. Martin's Lane

St. Martin-in-
the-Fields

Charing Cross
Station

Northumberland Avenue

National
Portrait
Gallery

Charing
Cross

National Gallery

Start

Trafalgar
Square

Nelson's Column

Whitehall

Horseguards Avenue

Pall Mall East

Canada
House

Cockspur Street

Admiralty
Arch

Old Admiralty

Horse Guards

Horse
Guards
Parade

Terrace

Terrace

Duke
of York's
Column

Horse

Guards

Downing Street

Regent Street

Waterloo Place

Road

Carlton House

Carlton House

St. James's
Square

Pall Mall

Carlton
Gardens

St. James's Park

Marlborough
House

Queen's
Chapel

Marlborough Road

Cleveland Row

St. James's
Palace

Clarence
House

The Mall

Stable Yard Road

Lancaster
House

Birdcage Walk

Green Park

Constitution Hill

Queen Victoria
Memorial

End

Buckingham
Palace

N

2
Trafalgar Square to Buckingham Palace

I never knew Trafalgar Square was such a vast open space until the first time I crossed it during a night-blitz. Gave me a feeling of nakedness.

—ENGLISH NEWSPAPERMAN IN A WARTIME LETTER

Post-Luftwaffe clean-up at Buckingham Palace.

Highlights: Trafalgar Square, Nelson's Column, St. Martin-in-the-Fields, National Portrait Gallery, National Gallery, Canada House, Admiralty Arch, The Mall, Carlton House Terrace, de Gaulle statue, George VI statue, Marlborough House, St. James's Palace, Clarence House, Lancaster House, Canadian Memorial Fountain, Queen Victoria Memorial, Buckingham Palace

Underground Station: Charing Cross

Photo Ops: At one end of this walk are the pigeons of Trafalgar Square, at the other the equally over-photographed Buckingham Palace. Consider buying postcards of these and focus instead on the simplicity of St. Martin-in-the-Fields or the out-of-the-way statues of George VI and Charles de Gaulle.

BEFORE LEAVING ON YOUR TRIP

■ **Travel Scheduling:** Buckingham Palace displays its State Rooms in late summer. You may want to schedule your trip accordingly. If you visit during the holiday season, check out the enormous Christmas tree in Trafalgar Square, a gift from Norway made annually since the end of World War II.

■ **Cultural Preparations:** Track down Myra Hess playing Beethoven. *Dame Myra Hess: A Cameo* Includes "Jesu, Joy of Man's Desiring," a piece Hess frequently played in the wartime National Gallery concerts. While CD shopping, watch for the French national anthem, "La Marseillaise." Playing of the anthem was forbidden in France and French territories throughout the German occupation. Remember that scene in *Casablanca* when the crowd in Bogie's bar defiantly stands to sing?

■ **Internet Best Bets:** Royal watchers will particularly enjoy www.royal.gov.uk, with its great photos of the Queen Mum and various palatial royal homes.

The Trafalgar Square area has changed little since the war. Particularly early on a Sunday morning, it's easy to picture a 1940s swirl of black cars, red buses, and innumerable bicycles here. One can imagine George Orwell sitting on a fountain ledge, ignoring the traffic and pigeons while engrossed in a Penguin paperback. On the far side, perhaps, literary critic Cyril Connolly and poet Stephen Spender stroll toward the National Gallery, deep in conversation about the upcoming issue of *Horizon* magazine. And might that be British General Alan Brooke, quartered nearby, briskly striding across the square? Even Virginia Woolf, early in the war, might be seen here on one of her long meandering walks.

Today **Trafalgar Square** is Tourist Central, one of the busiest spots in London. Most visitors know about the pigeons, Admiral Nelson high atop his column, and the lions at its base. You may want to peruse the lesser-known statues and busts including that of World War II Admiral Lord Cunningham—note his striking resemblance to American president Lyndon Johnson. The busts of Lord Jellicoe and Lord Beatty, although completed before the declaration of war, were stored for safety and erected later. The two central fountains, built in the 1840s and later remodeled by architect Sir Edwin Lutyens, were here during the war, although the bronze dolphins, mermaids, and mermen are postwar additions, as is the blue tile lining the fountain basins.

Nelson's Column, the square's high point, was erected in 1843 to honor England's greatest naval commander, the hero of the Battle of Trafalgar; the bronze lions at the base were added in the 1860s. Admiral Nelson, a patch over his missing eye and his empty sleeve pinned up,

Trafalgar Square and Nelson's Column.

War Words: Queue

Throughout the war, long lines of shoppers wound down the street from the fishmonger's shop or the greengrocer's doorway. Unrationed food items were sometimes scarce, and when word circulated that Mr. Potter down at the corner might have a few extra lemons available, Mum and Aunt Ethel and Mrs. Davis next door would all grab their shopping baskets or bags (there was seldom extra paper available to wrap purchases in) and head for the **QUEUE**. Often passersby would join a queue without even knowing what they were queuing for. But a line must mean something good and/or hard to get was at least momentarily available. Today the habit lives on, perhaps because rationing on some items continued well into the mid-1950s. You'll see patient queues at bus stops, ticket lines, and films. Next time you're waiting for a London bus, take your place in line, and remember Mum's patience.

watched London's wartime homefront from his 170-foot-high perch, surviving that conflict, at least, untouched. The base was boarded up, but the column and the statue itself couldn't easily be protected. Nelson fared well; steeplejacks, clambering up the column in 1946 to see if any bomb damage had been done, reported, "He looks quite nice." The lions at the base were less successful in dodging German bombs. See if you can tell which of the four Landseer lions had to have its paw replaced after the war. The same lion received a gaping wound in its stomach, also since repaired.

Political demonstrations occurred here frequently in 1942 in support of the opening of a second front—an Allied landing in France to take pressure off the Russians fighting Germany. Trafalgar Square also served as a focused location to encourage Londoners to donate money or time to wartime campaigns. Activities for War Weapons Week or Salute the Soldiers Week or Wings for Victory Week were centered here, and usually featured a tank or warplane display to encourage donations. At one point a thatched house stood in the square to attract volunteers to help with the fall harvest.

Author James Pope-Hennessy looked about Trafalgar Square in 1941 and optimistically noted, "Except for the long brick [bomb] shelters by the fountains and the war-savings slogans about the base of Nelson's column, there is no suggestion of war here." Well, except for the "craters and pitfalls" that many, including Churchill's private secretary John Colville, would encounter when crossing the square on a dark night. And the ever-present barbed wire, a sharp reminder of the wartime ambience. Despite Pope-Hennessy's bravado, by 1941 the Trafalgar Square area had become

Gas and Gas Masks

The enemy's use of poison gas in World War I haunted the British; mustard gas had melted the lungs and ravaged the breathing of the young soldiers who survived it. As war clouds gathered again across Europe, the expected use of gas on London's civilians prompted a variety of defenses, the most obvious being the civilian respirator, or gas mask.

Gas masks were first issued to Londoners in autumn 1938 during the Munich scare. American journalist Martha Gellhorn noted, "There are forty million gas masks already stored in government depots, and all over England people are being fitted with the ordinary civilian gas mask....a small rubber affair, with isinglass over the eyes, a boxlike snout that contains the filter to keep out gas...and a narrow face-covering to keep the mask on."

One's mask was to be carried at all times, either in the small brown cardboard box provided, with the addition of a string carrier, or in a more stylish container, perhaps from Harrods or Selfridges. Fashionable London  ladies sported velvet gas-mask cases, each with an envelope-shaped handbag attached to the top, where lipstick, vanity case, and cigarettes could be stashed.

Bearded men faced a problem: gas masks were not designed to accommodate longer beards. The feisty playwright George Bernard Shaw refused to even consider shaving: "I am certainly not going to cut my beard off and I am rather skeptical about gas-masks. I dislike the style of their appearance." Less truculent youngsters were issued child-size masks, baby-size gas-hoods, or baby bags.

In Richmond, local signboards asked passersby during Poison Gas Week, "Have you brought your Gas Mask?" and admonished "Don't be a Gasualty." In Kensington, Gas Mask Week posters noted times to get masks tested at the local first aid station or Town Hall. Cloakroom signs in

yet another homefront battleground, with civilians listening for the evening's warning siren while carefully stepping over rubble from last night's attack, ready to duck into that nearby shelter if necessary.

It had been different a year earlier, before the wholesale bombing of London had begun. In late summer 1940, the band of the Coldstream Guards stood on the shelter roof playing Gilbert and Sullivan tunes for the warm-weather crowds. The hoardings (billboards) around the base of dance halls cautioned: "You are advised to keep your gas-mask with you." And everywhere, wartime posters ominously reminded Londoners that "Hitler will send no warning—so always carry your gas mask."

Nevertheless, the lost gas mask was a frequent occurrence. Transit Lost Property Offices had stacks of gas masks turned in every day, despite the warning printed on the back of every ticket. Most Londoners soon found carrying cases uncomfortable and cumbersome, and their contents far more of a nuisance than a protection. By mid-war, most gas masks had been lost or were left at home, perhaps in the refuge room many Londoners had dutifully prepared early in the war, sealing all air openings in at least one room in the household as a place of safety in case of gas attack.

However, and particularly early in the war, the threat of poison gas was very real, and the authorities instituted measures to detect toxic fumes. The tops of red postboxes were painted with a yellow gas-sensitive paint, a covering that supposedly would change color when in contact with gas. In some areas of London small flat boards covered with gas-sensitive paint were mounted on waist-high posts. Even loco-motive cab windows had detector paint on them. The train engineer was expected to continue on, but to warn the next signalman by sounding his train whistle continuously. Air raid wardens carried special wooden gas rattles to warn if gas was detected—"Don't be caught without your gas mask when the Wardens sound their rattles." Happily, except for practice exercises, warning rattles were never needed.

> *Public ingenuity has occupied itself... with the problem of how to carry the by now familiar cardboard container. A neat canvas case worn slung from the shoulder makes the whole thing as innocuous as a Kodak....It has been observed that Queen Elizabeth, on her numerous smiling visits to the various women's organizations in London, carries her gas mask this way.*
> —Mollie Panter-Downes, *London War Notes 1939–1945*

Nelson's Column pictured a waving Union Jack and urged "Buy National War Bonds...Join the Crusade." Even with gas-masked soldiers on the rooftops armed with rifles and bayonets, even with South Africa House "swarming with Grenadier Guards who, indeed, frequented every pill box in and around Whitehall," Londoners felt some optimism. Hadn't the British Expeditionary Force survived Dunkirk? Wasn't the RAF standing up to the Luftwaffe? In fact, news vendors' chalked signs compared the

daily "score" of planes shot down to a cricket game: "Biggest raid ever, score 78 to 26. ENGLAND STILL BATTING."

The cataclysm was coming closer, but for most Londoners strolling across Trafalgar Square, late summer 1940 was still a time of confidence. It *is* easier to feel assured in the daylight, in a crowd, with your gas mask slung jauntily over your shoulder. Of course, a quick word with the Almighty never hurts. Walk up the stairs at the northeastern corner of Trafalgar Square and head for **St. Martin-in-the-Fields**.

The medieval fields are long gone but the name remains, a reminder of what this area once was. St. Martin's, with its spire and impressive portico, was designed by Scottish architect James Gibbs and completed in 1726, though there's been a church here since the twelfth century. If the building looks familiar, it's because a similar design graces many New England villages.

The iron railings are a postwar addition to keep pedestrians from drifting off the narrow walkways, but the well-worn steps (across the southern side especially) have long been here. And here, broadcaster Edward R. Murrow stood one Blitz night, sirens wailing mournfully in the background as he bent low with his heavy microphone to record the sound of Londoners' footsteps as they sought safety. Many of the passersby were heading into the church—its eighteenth-century crypt served as a public shelter.

"St. Martin's among the Tombstones" it was called by some, offering wartime sleeping facilities for upwards of 500 persons in the crypt's six large vaults. A canteen served tea, buns, and sandwiches, and billiard and ping pong tables offered recreational possibilities. Today the crypt's sturdy pillars and brick-vaulted ceiling provide a dramatic setting for a cafeteria-style Café-in-the-Crypt, still serving much the same menu (plus soup, lunch plates, English puddings, and wine). A rest stop here provides an opportunity to consider what it was like sharing a night below ground with 499 other souls, as sirens wailed outside and the muffled pom-pom-pom of anti-aircraft guns resounded and the whoomp of nearby bombs shook the walls.

Check out the rest of the catacombs: the shop, London Brass Rubbing Centre, and small art gallery. In the shop, note the dates at the top of the pillars; both the one dated "1937" and the one with "1941" have interesting plaques below, though the latter inscription is half-obscured by a bookcase.

In the Dick Sheppard Chapel near the Duncannon Street stairs, a wall plaque honors pacifist Vera Brittain. Unveiled by Brittain's daughter Shirley Williams in 1993 (Williams was then in Parliament, but as a youngster during the war she was evacuated to the States), the understated plaque reads "Vera Brittain / 1893–1970 / Writer & Reformer / Blessed are the Peacemakers."

Climb the steps to the church interior or up the stairs of the Duncannon Street exit, but don't wander off without spending some time in the church itself. On the front portico's main entrance doors, brass doorknobs show the church's patron saint, St. Martin, sharing his cloak with a beggar. And those huge keyholes in the doors? Yes, there are corresponding keys, some weighing almost a pound. Inside, the Admiralty Box is to the right of the altar (note the flag) and the Royal Box to the left, both at gallery level. This is the parish church of the sovereign, and Queen Mary was a regular prewar visitor (her box even had a fireplace). On the northern wall a memorial honors the Far East Prisoners of War and the civilian internees who died while in Japanese hands.

St. Martin-in-the-Fields survived the war in good shape, although a large explosion along the southern wall, about where the crypt exit is today, smashed the railing and masonry wall beyond and blasted out windows. Even before the war, St. Martin's was well-known for its remarkable compassionate connection with the community; this was—and is—a good works church. Homespun American journalist Ernie Pyle wrote in 1941, "When you see a church with a bomb hole in its side and 500 fairly safe and happy people in its basement, and girls smoking cigarettes inside the sacred walls without anybody yelling at them, then I say that church has found a real religion."

> **VISITOR DETAILS:** St. Martin-in-the-Fields is open daily 8am to 6pm, reopening at 7pm for evening concerts. The shop, Brass Rubbing Centre, and gallery are open similar hours. Midday concerts are free; admission is charged for evening concerts. The Café-in-the-Crypt is open Monday–Wednesday 10am to 8pm; Thursday–Saturday 10am to 11pm; Sunday noon to 8pm. Full food service may not be available all those hours. Restrooms. More information: 020 7766 1100, www.st.martin-in-the-fields.org.

From the church portico, walk up St. Martin's Place to the **National Portrait Gallery** on the northeastern side of the National Gallery. This collection of portraits, sculptures, caricatures, drawings, photographs, and other visual representations of Britons, established in 1856, includes over 9,000 works. To view it all chronologically, take the escalator to the second level and work your way down through the Tudor, Elizabethan, Romantic, and Victorian eras. Alternatively, skip the distant past and head directly to Room 31 on the first floor, featuring figures from the post–World War I years. Whatever your route, don't miss the Royal Family gallery on the first-floor landing, an intimate look at Britain's monarchy, particularly the twentieth-century members.

VISITOR DETAILS: The National Portrait Gallery is open Monday–Wednesday 10am to 6pm; Thursday–Friday 10am to 9pm; weekends 10am to 6pm. Charge for special exhibits. Sound guides available. Large shop (great postcards); bookshop in the basement. Portrait Café; rooftop restaurant. Both open much the same hours as the gallery, with the restaurant open later on Thursdays and Fridays. Restrooms on the top and lower ground floors. More information: 020 7312 2463, www.npg.org.uk.

In "The Armistice to the New Elizabethans" gallery (Room 31), watch for the large oil painting of Lord Beaverbrook, the Canadian who served in Churchill's wartime cabinet. Other war-related images feature Neville Chamberlain (yes, he has his umbrella); RAF pilot Richard Hillary; plastic surgeon Archibald McIndoe, who treated Hillary and hundreds of other severely burned airmen; the martial Monty; Noël Coward; and a small sketch of Churchill by Graham Sutherland. This early 1950s work was a preliminary sketch for the larger oil painting presented to Churchill by Parliament on his eightieth birthday, a painting so hated by the prime minister that his wife eventually had it destroyed. Watch too for busts of George VI, Churchill, T. S. Eliot, and George Bernard Shaw. And sooner or later you'll come upon an image captured by photographer Cecil Beaton, whose dramatic portraiture memorialized dozens of war-era personalities. Visitor Alert: Themes stay the same, but specific art works can and do come and go.

Like many of London's major museums and galleries, the National Portrait Gallery was emptied of art during the war. The collection was transported to distant Mentmore, the Buckinghamshire home of Lord Rosebery. The 1896 building itself survived the war with little damage aside from the ubiquitous shattered windows.

From the National Portrait Gallery, turn right and backtrack a bit to the **National Gallery** (yes, a little unexpectedly, that *is* a statue of American president George Washington in front). The National Gallery, here since

the 1830s, houses Western European paintings from the thirteenth century
to the end of the nineteenth, obviously not the period of World War II.
But this stop is particularly important for what occurred here during the
war years, though do take time to view the impres-
sive art. Visitor Alert: Grand plans are in the works
to transform the entranceway of the National
Gallery—expect construction and changes ahead.

> *Sooner or later, just
> about everyone in the
> wartime metropolis
> attended a National
> Gallery concert—
> Virginia Woolf went in
> January 1940.*

As the clouds of war grew darker, the Gallery
trustees and director Sir Kenneth Clark (later familiar as host of the TV documentary *Civilisation*)
decided the irreplaceable art works would not be
safe in Target London. On August 23, 1939, the
gallery closed its doors to the public and the big move began. Most of the
3,000-plus pictures were packed in sponge-rubber-padded railway
coaches for transport to a secret destination in North Wales, with 100
smaller works traveling to safety in distant Gloucestershire. It took eleven
days to pack and move; the last artwork left London on September 2,
1939, the day before war was declared. And the move was a wise one; the
National Gallery was bombed nine times during the war.

Immediately following the declaration of war, the BBC radio
announcer began reading the new emergency orders in effect, including
the closure of all cinemas, theatres, and concert halls (a "wanton" black-
ing-out of culture, according to the *Times*). Within days, London resident
and classical pianist Myra Hess, bored with her volunteer work helping in
the evacuation of schoolchildren, approached Clark and suggested a way
to alleviate the cultural blackout—public concerts in the now virtually
empty galleries.

For the opening concert on October 10, 1939, almost one thousand
Londoners climbed the steps of the National Gallery, paid a shilling apiece,
and settled in on folding chairs or on the floor to hear Hess play. Perhaps the
most moving music of that first concert was Beethoven's "Appassionata
Sonata."

"I am sure we all wept," the usually stoic Clark wrote later. "It was an
assurance that all our sufferings were not in vain." Hess concluded that
first concert with her arrangement of "Jesu, Joy of Man's Desiring." Clark,
again: "[The audience] had come with anxious, hungry faces, but as they
listened to the music and looked at Myra's rapt expression, they lost the
thought of their private worries. I had never seen faces so transformed."
The lunchtime concerts, with Hess at the piano, a string quartet, a violinist,
or other professional musicians, continued, five days a week, through the
Phoney War and into the Blitz.

The written concert programs soon carried an added message: "In case of air raid warning the audience will proceed downstairs where adequate protection is available." By September 1940, daylight bombings made it necessary to re-locate from the glass-roofed gallery area to the "adequate protection" of the downstairs shelter room, a claustrophobic area holding only about 350 people. Concerts continued there until June 1941, with one brief move to the distant east wing.

The basement shelter had none of the austere panache of the lofty galleries above—here buckets caught the drips from the leaky roof and, since all the windows were blown out and the heating system didn't work, the room could be extremely cold. In mid-October 1940, a time bomb fell in the courtyard area near what is now Room G in the lower floor, and the entire building had to be evacuated (the bomb exploded six days later). The long string of consecutive performances would've been broken had the High Commissioner not offered the use of the library in nearby South Africa House, the large building on the eastern side of Trafalgar Square.

> Not every painting in the National Gallery was spirited off to safer quarters. A few remained and were regularly rotated about the near-bare galleries. Every night the "Painting of the Month" would be returned to a basement storeroom for safety.

The close quarters hereabouts created some unexpected problems. Early on, concertgoers were frequently disturbed by the church bells of St. Martin-in-the-Fields, interrupting both the regular concert and the Tuesday and Thursday afternoon repeat performances. Constant negotiations and some strained compromises ended after the ringing of church bells was nationally forbidden, since they were to be the warning signal of invasion.

And remember the Coldstream Guards band performing atop the air raid shelter in Trafalgar Square? August 1940 featured War Savings Week and the Guards loudly entertained the gathered crowds. The gallery's open windows meant quite a clash between the "Colonel Bogey March" in Trafalgar Square and Mozart in the National Gallery. The compromise this time: the Guards stopped playing at 1:30, the gallery concerts started at 1:30, and shy pianist Myra Hess made a speech urging War Savings, standing on the wing of a B-36 bomber parked in the middle of Trafalgar Square.

For six years—1,698 performances—Hess organized chamber and orchestral concerts, performing over 140 times herself. Since there was little opportunity for artists to perform elsewhere during the war, the National Gallery concerts were an opportunity eagerly sought after by professional musicians. For wartime Londoners, the music was deeply moving: "The clear voice of reason in a crazy world...one's belief in the worth of man was thus restored—at the cost of a shilling." Even the queen attended, alone and with her daughters. In all, over 800,000 people climbed the National Gallery stairs for an hour or so of musical relief from the fears and drabness of London's war zone.

Today as you enter the National Gallery and head upstairs to the galleries, note the floor mosaics on the stair landings. Created by Boris Anrep, a peripheral Bloomsburyite, the figures are based on "the intellectual life

Firefighting with stirrup pumps.

of the modern age." Watch for Virginia Woolf, T. S. Eliot, Bertrand Russell, and (hint: rather centrally) Winston Churchill, complete with siren suit, tin helmet, and "V for Victory" sign. More of Anrep's mosaics can be found at the Tate Britain and in Westminster Cathedral.

At the top of the National Gallery stairs, turn right through the wooden doors into the east wing. Before enjoying the delights of Canaletto, Reynolds, and Turner, think for a moment of what this gallery must have looked like in 1940. Imagine a wartime stroll through a gallery of bare walls, "where only discolored squares...show the position of one's old favorites." And over there would be Myra Hess, sitting at the grand piano, waiting for the overflow crowd to quiet so she could begin the opening chords of the "Appassionata Sonata."

If perchance you didn't cross over to the National Gallery's Sainsbury Wing while inside the National Gallery, stop for a visit, particularly if paintings from 1260 to 1510 interest you. The lobby's scale model of the Trafalgar Square area offers some directional

> **VISITOR DETAILS:** The National Gallery is open daily 10am to 6pm; Wednesday 10am to 9pm. Charge for special exhibits. Sound guides available. Small shop near the main entrance staircase; larger shop in the Sainsbury Wing. Self-service café; Sainsbury Wing restaurant. Check the free map for restroom locations. More information: 020 7747 2885, www.national gallery.org.uk.

bearings, and even the local pigeons appear in miniature form. The Sainsbury wing opened in 1991, after the Sainsbury brothers commissioned the building as a gift to the nation. It sits on the long-vacant site of Hamptons, the builders, decorators, and furniture suppliers who assured their customers in the decade before the war that they stood ready to provide "interesting and original interpretations of the modern style." Their

Text continued on page 66.

FOOTSTEPS OF THE FAMOUS

Pianist Myra Hess
at the National Gallery

Summer 1936: Concert pianist Myra Hess moves into "a delightful little house" north of central London on Hampstead Heath at 48 Wildwood Road.

September 3, 1939: With the declaration of war, the Home Office orders all cinemas, theatres, and other places of entertainment closed and all performances cancelled.

September 5, 1939: Hess, foregoing a planned American concert tour, signs up for ARP (Air Raid Precautions) and begins assisting the WVS (Women's Voluntary Service) in the evacuation of London children to the countryside, a useful but boring task.

Mid-September 1939: At a gathering of Hess's friends, the casual suggestion is made to hold chamber music concerts in the emptied National Gallery.

Mid-September to early October 1939: Hess meets with Sir Kenneth Clark, director of the National Gallery, to suggest regular concerts. He embraces the idea and together with the gallery trustees begins organizing various committees to oversee the details.

The National Gallery and St. Martin-in-the-Fields.

September–October 1940: In the park opposite Hess's Wildwood Road home, six anti-aircraft guns nightly produce an inferno of artillery. This cacophony, plus bombs, flares, and roaring airplane engines, makes piano practicing impossible. Worse, a neighbor's house across the street is demolished by a direct hit from a German bomb.

October 4–9, 1939: Feverish activity in the National Gallery: One of the main galleries is prepared for a new purpose, with a raised wooden platform and a large Steinway piano.

October 10, 1939: Over a thousand Londoners attend the first lunchtime concert at the National Gallery, so many that a second concert is scheduled for the afternoon. Myra Hess, her dark hair in a bun and dressed as always in black, sits at the piano beneath the gallery's domed ceiling and plays Scarlatti, Bach, Chopin, Brahms, and Beethoven.

October 24, 1939: Queen Elizabeth first attends a concert at the National Gallery.

November 1940: Hess moves temporarily to a quieter and somewhat safer area, 54 Abbey Road, St. John's Wood, west of Regent's Park. She will return to her Wildwood Road home in spring 1941.

April 27, 1941: Hess performs at Queen's Hall near Broadcasting House. A few weeks later, the hall is destroyed by the fires from a single incendiary bomb.

June 1941: Myra Hess is made a Dame Commander of the Order of the British Empire.

January 17, 1942: Hess is presented the Royal Philharmonic Society's gold medal in ceremonies at Royal Albert Hall, Kensington.

July 23, 1943: At the 1,000th National Gallery concert, Hess plays Mozart. Queen Elizabeth attends and warmly congratulates the pianist.

April 10, 1946: The final wartime concert—number 1,698—is played at the National Gallery. Hess, fearing she will be overcome by emotion, attends as a concertgoer, not a performer. Sitting in the front row, she hears the Griller Quartet perform Beethoven's Quartet, Opus 59, Number 3. John Masefield in his poem "Remembering Dame Myra Hess" will later write, "She who played perceived / The world undying, that composers know / At moments, as reward for years of woe, / She touched the deathless world and we believed."

many Mayfair customers must have been particularly distressed when the structure was gutted in an early morning attack in November 1940. High explosive bombs partially demolished the store, which was then swept by fire. General Alan Brooke, Chief of the Imperial General Staff, was staying at the nearby Army and Navy Club down Pall Mall and was awakened by the conflagration: "Hamptons caught fire and burned nearly most of the night with noisy arrival of fire engines…it was a weird sight looking east to see the end of the street one blaze of flame." For decades, this remained one of the most visible reminders of the war: a scraggly empty lot, primarily used as a car park, in the center of London.

From the National Gallery, cross Pall Mall East and head down the western side of Trafalgar Square, pausing to take in the new look of the area—until 2002, Pall Mall East continued as a roadway directly in front of the National Gallery. Much traffic rerouting has produced a safer and more elegant pedestrian experience.

Along this side of the square looms **Canada House**, a somewhat ponderous building (or majestically imperial, depending on your viewpoint) erected in the 1820s. In mid–October 1940, a bomb exploding at the back of Canada House caused extensive damage, since well-repaired. Canada House was a home away from home for Canadian soldiers, with an officers' club, the popular Beaver Club for noncommissioned officers, and frequent parties held for departing or returning Canadian troops. Enter on the south side—the red-and-white Maple Leaf flag flies over the entrance. When King George and Queen Elizabeth visited here in October 1939, they were welcomed by a scarlet-uniformed Canadian Mountie, but you can expect a more low-key greeting; check in at the information desk to get a brochure and map and to find out what Canadian-related exhibits or films are available for the day. Architectural buffs, watch for the Ionic columns, marble floors, ornate mahogany doors, and tulip wood chandeliers.

VISITOR DETAILS: Canada House is open Monday–Friday 10am to 5pm. More information: 020 7258 6600.

Cross Cockspur Street at the light and walk down Spring Gardens, a short byway that jogs left; jog left with it, then turn right at the end— ahead is the triumphal **Admiralty Arch**, a structure that loses much of its triumph due to the press of buildings around it and the rush of traffic through it. Erected in 1910 as part of the national memorial to Queen Victoria, the massive structure provides a dramatic frame for a view down the Mall. One generally tends to look *through* it, however, rather than *at* it, so take a moment to savor office-building-as-arch—complete with chimneys, skylights, and curtains.

Admiralty Arch.

Traditionally, the center of the three larger iron gates is opened only for ceremonial occasions; during the war, this archway remained closed, with a makeshift guardhouse nearby and coils of barbed wire surrounding it. Traffic flowed through the two side archways, being stopped at times by the vigilant wartime guards to check identification, and pedestrians used the smaller outside arches. The volunteers staffing the guardhouse were World War 1 veterans, recruited from several of London's nearby gentlemen's clubs. In an early morning raid in mid-April 1941, a high explosive bomb badly damaged the top right of the arch (the corner nearest Canada House), blowing out windows and taking off a corner overhead, about where the medallion next to the Roman numeral date is. Luckily neither the veteran guards nor any passersby were killed.

Together with Admiralty Arch, the reddish roadway of the half-mile-long **Mall** provides a dramatic processional to Buckingham Palace. It's the buildings and monuments along the Mall's northern side that provide the war-era interest here. For more on St. James's Park to the south, see "A Walk in the Park" elsewhere in this chapter. And incidentally, that's "Mall" to rhyme with "Hal."

Once past Admiralty Arch and looking west along the Mall, you'll encounter two statues actually standing a bit behind you; *Navigation* and *Gunnery* are located on the ends of the semi-circular swath of Admiralty Arch. Across the Mall, beyond the freestanding bronze figure of Captain Cook, is the Old Admiralty (1725) and the wartime addition of the Admiralty Citadel (1940), with pigeons now roosting on the narrow gun-slit window ledges. I once spoke to a woman who worked as a telephone operator here during the war; she said the Citadel had been unbelievably crowded inside. Now this grim-looking structure is covered with tenacious ivy and in summer resembles a gigantic hedge. (For more on the Admiralty and the Admiralty Citadel, see Chapter 1.)

On the northern side of the Mall, straight ahead, a monument honors the Royal Marines who died in South Africa and China in 1899 and 1900. A century later the statue was rededicated by Prince Philip in honor of all Marines, with a new bronze caption set in the pavement around the base. Incidentally, you may wonder (as did I) how wreaths from royalty are signed. I checked out the wreath after the prince placed it here—the elegant white card attached bore only a typed name: "Philip."

As you continue down the Mall, **Carlton House Terrace** rises on the right, once considered the most fashionable address in town. It was designed in part by architect John Nash in the 1830s and was a favored residence for London's great and wealthy. Winston Churchill, then neither great nor wealthy, stayed at Carlton House Terrace briefly in spring 1909 at cousin Freddie Guest's home.

In the 1930s, the London social season (roughly May through July) featured parties on the lower rooftops, and at least one observer was smitten by "the spell of early summer twilight, a string quartet playing Mozart, listeners and fair women picked out in the lit terrace setting, and young green foliage illuminated overhead." But even before the war, these cream-colored stucco homes were slowly being transformed into government offices, both domestic and foreign—the German Embassy and the German Consular Department, for example, were located here when war broke out.

I've always hoped the stereo of a Carlton Gardens resident would be loudly playing "La Marseillaise" as I wandered the ghost-filled sidewalks, but so far I've been disappointed.

In April 1941, as a German bombing raid thundered around him, entertainer and playwright Noël Coward headed home to Belgravia, his taxi calmly motoring down the Mall. Looking back some years later, he rather unemotionally recalled the experience: "The sky above Carlton House Terrace was red with the reflected glow of fires, presumably in the Piccadilly district, and the rooftops were etched black against it. There was a lot of noise and gunfire, and every so often, a shattering explosion." By war's end, both blocks of Carlton House Terrace were well-battered, exposing their shoddy construction. Post-war renovation soon began, in part because this roadway serves as one of the grand boulevards of London. Unfortunately the Mall is so wide (over a hundred feet) and so pastoral (double rows of trees but no shops) that some find it a trifle soulless, except on Sundays when it's closed to traffic and London comes strolling.

Carlton House Terrace's long bank of row houses is divided in two by Waterloo Place, up whose broad steps you'll see the Duke of York's Column, over 120 feet high and even more imposing when one is at the bottom of the stairs. At the top of the granite column stands a bronze statue of Frederick Augustus, the somewhat disreputable second son of George III. As with Admiral Nelson in Trafalgar Square, the height of this column and statue precluded any wartime protective measures. Nevertheless, the Duke survived.

Climb the steps on the left side, past the Duke's column and left through the iron gate, to view what is considered by some to be London's only Nazi monument. In front of the plane tree is a diminutive glass-and-wood-encased tombstone honoring Giro, the dog of Hitler's ambassador to England; alas, Giro died in 1934. The stone reads *Ein treuer begleiter*, a faithful companion. That excitement out of the way, continue down Carlton Gardens, the street running parallel and behind the second bank of Carlton House Terrace buildings.

On one side of the circular drive at the end stands a **statue of General Charles de Gaulle**. The Frenchman poses proudly, "brilliant, dour, and difficult," as Churchill's daughter Mary Soames once described him. General de Gaulle worked at 4 Carlton Gardens for much of his time in wartime London, his offices the headquarters of the Free French government-in-exile.

In June 1940, as the German forces swept across France, General de Gaulle had escaped to England, accepting neither the French surrender to Germany nor the new Vichy government. He slowly gathered a band of French exiles, expatriates, and supporters around him and, also very slowly, built a fighting force. Partly because de Gaulle was incredibly stubborn, arrogant, and focused, he succeeded, but then again, no one else had the nerve to do what he did. One Englishwoman working in the Free French offices during the early war years characterized the atmosphere as "a hotbed of intrigue and cross purposes," and given the emotion-laden times, the stakes involved, and the larger-than-life persona of de Gaulle, one can

Text continued on page 72.

Exiled: Charles de Gaulle and the Free French

June 9, 1940: Charles de Gaulle, at forty-nine the youngest general in the French Army, flies to London, lunches at the French Embassy (2 Albert's Gate, on Hyde Park's south side), and meets with Prime Minister Churchill at 10 Downing Street. During this, their first meeting ever, de Gaulle urges the British leader to release RAF resources to aid France. Churchill refuses, and a glum de Gaulle returns to France.

June 14, 1940: German troops enter the outskirts of Paris. The Nazi flag replaces the French tricolor on Parisian monuments and buildings.

June 16, 1940: General de Gaulle returns to London. He takes a room at the Hyde Park Hotel near the French Embassy, then meets with Churchill at the Carlton Club (then at 94 Pall Mall). The Frenchman proposes an Anglo-Franco Union, creating joint wartime bodies including the unification of the two war cabinets. Later, de Gaulle waits at Downing Street while Churchill and the British war cabinet discuss his proposal. Given the nod from the prime minister, de Gaulle returns to Bordeaux hoping to check the French descent toward a humiliating armistice with Germany. He arrives too late and, worse, orders for his arrest are issued.

June 17, 1940: General de Gaulle flies back to London, lunches at RAC, the Royal Automobile Club on Pall Mall, then joins Churchill in the garden at 10 Downing Street for more discussions.

June 18, 1940: General de Gaulle takes a taxi to Broadcasting House (Portland Place) and just before 6pm enters the BBC radio studios to deliver a brief impassioned address in French. "Whatever happens, the flame of French resistance must not and shall not die." Between 1940 and 1944, de Gaulle will make over sixty-five radio broadcasts.

June 19, 1940: A stream of expatriate and escaped Frenchmen, eager to join the cause of the Free French, come to de Gaulle's flat at 8 Seamore Place, a handsome building in an "elegant sort of dead end just off Park Lane" (now Curzon Place). The social headquarters for this community of exiles is Le Petit Club Français in the basement of 13 St. James's Place. The French Pub in Soho (49 Dean Street) also serves as a popular gathering place.

June 20, 1940: A dingy office suite in St. Stephen's House (since demolished) on the Victoria Embankment north of Big Ben becomes the temporary home of the Free French. Over the next few weeks, nearly 400 men will sign on with de Gaulle.

June 22, 1940: In a railway carriage in the Forest of Compiègne, near Paris, representatives of the new French government sign an armistice with Germany.

July 14, 1940: Bastille Day. General de Gaulle and several hundred Free French troops march down Whitehall, lay a wreath at the Cenotaph, and sing the French national anthem. The military parade continues around Parliament Square, down Victoria Street to Lower Grosvenor Gardens, near Victoria Station. At the statue of Marshal Foch, hero of World War I, de Gaulle lays a laurel wreath. (The statue, often with fresh wreaths at its base, is still in the same location.)

July 22, 1940: The Free French headquarters relocates to 4 Carlton Gardens.

Summer 1940: The *Deuxième Bureau*, the intelligence arm of the Free French, moves to 10 Duke Street near Selfridges. The Commissariat of the Interior (another intelligence operation) moves to offices in Hill Street, and the Free French navy moves to Stafford Mansions on Stafford Place, near Buckingham Palace (a plaque there honors the Free French Naval Forces).

August 2, 1940: General de Gaulle is tried *in absentia* by a French military tribunal, found guilty of insubordination and incitement to disobedience, and sentenced to death. He is, officially, a traitor to France.

August 6, 1940: Churchill and de Gaulle meet again at 10 Downing Street to discuss the Frenchman's proposal that the Free French be involved in the military campaign against Dakar in French West Africa. Churchill approves the idea. Free French officers, oblivious to the need for discretion, loudly drink to their expected success while dining at Le Coq d'Or on Stratton Street near Berkeley Square. A confident de Gaulle purchases tropical uniforms at Simpson's on Jermyn Street (still there). Both de Gaulle and his celebrating troops were overconfident. The campaign at Dakar will go very badly.

Late Summer 1940: De Gaulle stays at the Connaught Hotel (Carlos Place, near Grosvenor Square; still open). When his family arrives from France, they stay very briefly in the Hotel Rubens (still open) near the Royal Mews. The de Gaulles then move to a series of homes far from the center of London, and General de Gaulle commutes from Victoria Station. During the week de Gaulle stays in a flat at 15 Grosvenor Square and dines at the nearby Connaught Hotel—when he isn't eating at the RAC, the Savoy, or the Ritz. The General is usually driven to his office at Carlton Gardens but often walks home via St. James's, Piccadilly, and Berkeley Square.

June 18, 1942: General de Gaulle speaks at Royal Albert Hall, Kensington, on the anniversary of his stirring radio broadcast.

May 1943: General de Gaulle flies to Algiers; the seat of government for the Free French moves from British to French soil.

August 25, 1944: Paris is liberated. The French tricolor flies again from Paris monuments. General de Gaulle lays a wreath on the tomb of the [French] Unknown Soldier, then walks down the Champs-Élysées to Notre Dame, as hundreds of thousands of grateful French citizens wave, cheer, shout, clap, and cry.

easily imagine those dramatic eddies of political intrigue swirling about Carlton Gardens. (For more on de Gaulle, see "Footsteps of the Famous" elsewhere in this chapter.)

The statue of de Gaulle faces 4 Carlton Gardens, where a wall plaque marks the site as the wartime Free French headquarters. Another plaque bears the French text of the general's dramatic radio broadcast of June 18, 1940, calling for continued resistance by his besieged countrymen.

Walk down the stairs the general is eyeing—halfway along stands a bronze **statue of King George VI**, the wartime monarch looking rather gaunt and peaked as he keeps a watchful eye on the Mall and St. James's Park. Photographer Cecil Beaton once referred to the "raw, bony, medieval aspects of that handsome face," and this image brings out those haunting elements.

At the bottom of the steps, we're back on the Mall. Turn right, then right again onto Marlborough Road. St. James's Palace is ahead on the left, but first our route passes an art nouveau memorial and fountain honoring Queen Alexandra, wife of King Edward VII. Queen Alexandra long outlived her husband and was the beloved Queen Mum of her day. This memorial by Alfred Gilbert, the same man who designed the statue of Eros in Piccadilly Circus, was unveiled in the 1930s and survived Hitler's bombs unscathed.

Cross to the arched walkway of St. James's Palace (don't worry, the Royal Family won't mind), and look back eastwards, beyond Queen Alexandra's memorial to the red brick and Portland stone **Marlborough House**, built in the early 1700s by Christopher Wren for Sarah, the Duchess of Marlborough (and ancestor of Winston Churchill). This royal property has been home to many, primarily the royal widow. Here lived Queen Alexandra after the death of Edward VII, and Queen Mary (the last royal occupant) after the death of George V. During the war, as a royal property, Marlborough House had a sentry standing guard out front (the entrance facing Pall Mall), provided with a mini–bomb shelter to duck into at times of flying bombs or splintering shrapnel. Now the headquarters for the Commonwealth Secretariat, it's not generally open to the public.

The arched walkway you're standing in is part of **St. James's Palace**, the monarch's official residence from the time of William III (1680s) until the ascension of Victoria (1837). When the Royal Court at Whitehall burned in the 1690s, the court was moved here; although no longer the monarch's residence, it's technically still the royal court: diplomatic ambassadors to Britain are presented "to the Court of St. James's." That's Friary Court directly across from Queen Alexandra's memorial, on the Mall side of the arched walkway. From the balcony overlooking Friary Court, every new sovereign is officially proclaimed, a delightfully retro custom. The

official proclaimers were kept busy in 1936 when a new king was twice announced: in January when George V died and his eldest son, the Prince of Wales, became a reluctant King Edward VIII, and again in December when Edward abdicated and his younger brother, Albert, became King George VI. You can walk around Friary Court if you'd like, but unless a new monarch is being proclaimed, there's not much to see.

St. James's Palace.

Continue down the passageway to Pall Mall (blending with Cleveland Row in the St. James's Palace forecourt), then turn left toward the gatehouse, one of the few remaining original parts of St. James's Palace; much of the palace was rebuilt after a fire in 1809. At the gatehouse and clock tower, a stony-faced guard stands at attention at the "front door." Actually, the palace has many doors, an architectural feature that the resourceful Prince of Wales exploited in the mid-1930s to slip out unseen to meet his American ladyfriend, Wallis Simpson. He lived in York House, the section of the palace west (to the right) of the gatehouse as you face it.

Londoners, who still consider St. James's Palace "not only the most approachable of our palaces, [but] one of the more satisfying of architectural sights," were particularly heartsick at the wartime destruction here. Incendiary bombs caused serious fire damage in March 1941, although the palace's faithful firewatchers prevented a disaster. Two months later a high explosive bomb fell near Friary Court and destroyed several rooms. And in the Little Blitz of early 1944, Londoners found St. James's "sadly knocked about, the clock awry [the hands wrenched off], the windows

Text continued on page 76.

A Walk in the Park: St. James's Park

London's parks provide an opportunity to trade views of asphalt, stone, and relentless traffic for vistas of grass, lakes, and trees. This mini-walk strolls through the eastern half of St. James's Park, the oldest of the Royal Parks. Its ninety-plus acres are bounded by the Mall to the north, Buckingham Palace to the west, Birdcage Walk to the south, and Horse Guards Road to the east.

Enter St. James's Park on the northern side at Marlborough Gate, across from Marlborough Road and St. James's Palace, and walk straight along to the footbridge over the lake. The view toward Whitehall looks much as the Wizard of Oz's Emerald City might have looked to Dorothy. Turning and facing the other way, the vista

> **VISITOR DETAILS:** St. James's Park is open daily 5am to midnight. The Cake House Café is open daily 9:30am to dusk, while the venerable Cake House is being overhauled. Snack trucks appear in tourist season. Public restrooms (wheelchair accessible) near Marlborough Gate; a second batch is northeast of the café.

toward Buckingham Palace is just as impressive, especially on moonlit nights. The bridge itself is a mid-1950s replacement of a Victorian-era span.

Wartime changes would have been obvious to a park visitor in the early 1940s. Temporary buildings were dotted about, and shelter trenches crisscrossed the lawns—early on a rash of them had been dug near the German Embassy across the Mall. Before the park's gates and railings were removed to be recycled into arma-

ments, they would be locked to prevent access if an unexploded bomb (UXB) had fallen nearby. After the park's ironworks were gone, visitors were warned of unexploded bombs by ropes and sawhorses. Charles Ritchie, serving with the Canadian government in London, grumbled in spring 1941, "The grass is green at last in St. James's Park, but the gates are locked and one is not allowed in because it is full of time-bombs. I look through the railings at the deserted paths and lawns. Even the ducks seem to have been moved away." (They hadn't been.) Later in the war, photographer Cecil Beaton, on the other hand, found the park without its Victorian iron railings positively sylvan.

After war's end, several unexploded bombs were discovered buried here. In one incident, a 1,000-lb. UXB was found in the lake at the northern end of the bridge. The lake was drained (it's only about four feet deep), pedestrians kept away, the windows at Buckingham Palace and Marlborough House opened to reduce breakage in case of an explosion, and the bomb (nicknamed Baby Blobs) defused.

A second UXB—this one called Annie—was later found under a park footpath, more than fifty feet below ground. It had quietly lain buried since April 1941. A shaft was dug down to it, but the bomb disposal squad was unable to defuse Annie and decided to detonate the bomb. On an April evening in 1946, after two days of ominous ticking, Annie exploded, leaving a crater forty feet wide and twenty feet deep.

Continue on this cross-park footpath (perhaps walking a bit more gingerly) almost to Birdcage Walk, the southern bor-

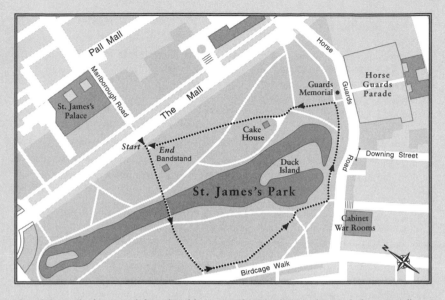

der of the park, then turn left and amble along beneath the London plane trees. Since St. James's Park is so close to Whitehall, civil servants and MPs often relax here, and both Chamberlain and Churchill frequented these walkways. And on London's warmer days, today as sixty years ago, everyone stretches out in the midday sunshine.

At the lake, continue right toward Duck Island and its cottage. The island is maintained as a breeding ground for waterfowl and includes water treatment facilities and pumps for the lake and fountains. When wartime sirens sounded, the caretaker of the cottage and his wife took

refuge in their Anderson shelter, partially dug into the lakeside ground. In one May 1941 raid, a high explosive bomb fell on this eastern edge of the lake and its explosion drenched Duck Island Cottage (with a gigantic splash), smashing the chimney down through the roof tiles. The explosion caused "much slaughter amongst the birds, and those which survived were so nervous that they would not even come for their food." Their descendents have overcome any hesitations in this area.

Just before you get to the Guards Memorial (covered in more detail in Chapter 1), turn left again back toward Marlborough Gate. Along the way, you may spot the more unusual avian inhabitants of St. James's Park: the barnacle goose, the chiloe wigeon, the ruddy shelduck, the green finch, and especially the swans, geese, and pelicans. Watch too for foxes and hedgehogs who've made the park their home, and especially watch out for unexploded bombs.

VISITOR DETAILS: The interior of St. James's Palace is not open to the public, but the perimeter along Marlborough Road and Pall Mall/Cleveland Row is walkable. If you're visiting in autumn or winter, check the church listings in the Saturday *Times*. The Chapel Royal holds public Sunday services, a unique opportunity to go to church in a palace. Check www.royal.gov.uk (link to Art & Residences).

gaping, and shrapnel marks on the wall." All the stained glass on the northern side and in the Chapel Royal (the chapel inside the palace) was blown to pieces. Through all these attacks, palace inhabitants suffered an ongoing problem: no air raid shelters, a need understandably unforeseen by Henry VIII when he built the Tudor palace in the 1530s.

Until quite recently, St. James's Palace has been the London residence and office of Prince Charles (see Clarence House, below). Princess Anne lives here, as does Princess Alexandra and members of the royal household. The guard in front of the Gatehouse is changed hourly during the day, such a low-key ceremony that you may find yourself the only visitor watching.

At the western end of St. James's Palace, Stable Yard Road leads back to the Mall, although this roadway is closed to the public. Look past the barricade to see two structures, one once the home of the Queen Mother and the other once the home of London's own museum.

Clarence House (1820s) on the left of Stable Yard Road was renovated after the war for use by Princess Elizabeth and her new husband, Prince Philip; their daughter Princess Anne was born here in 1950. The Queen Mother moved in after her daughter moved on to Buckingham Palace, and lived at Clarence House for the rest of her life. Prince Charles and his sons have since taken up residence here, after much building renovation, and a suite of rooms has been readied for royal friend Camilla Parker Bowles.

VISITOR DETAILS: Clarence House opened briefly to the public soon after the prince moved in; this may become an annual event. More information: www.royal.gov.uk.

Just visible along the right side of Stable Yard Road is **Lancaster House** (1825). Built for the Duke of York (the same duke atop the Waterloo Place column) and once regarded as the finest private residence in London, Lancaster House is now primarily used for government receptions and conferences. From 1914 to 1943, the London Museum was housed here, but became homeless when the government requisitioned the place for wartime offices, then refused to return the premises for the museum's use at war's end. The building suffered extensive wartime damage, since well-repaired. Lancaster House is not open to the public.

Westward, down the walkway between Number 8 and Selwyn House, is Number 13, Stornoway House, home of William Maxwell Aitken (bet-

Canadian Memorial Fountain.

ter known as Lord Beaverbrook) from 1929 until the building was bombed in 1941. The Canadian Beaverbrook made a fortune in the New World, came to England and entered politics, became a Lord in 1911, and went on to become a lord of the newspaper world, owning both the *Daily Express* and *Evening Standard*. When Churchill needed a go-getter to spur airplane production early in the war, he chose Beaverbrook to head the new Ministry of Aircraft Production. In fact, in those hectic early days when office space was at a premium, ministry offices were maintained here. At about the same time, the building's attractive iron railings and awnings were dismantled and sent off for salvage (and the awnings, at least, never replaced). One American magazine captioned a photo of Beaverbrook's denuded entranceway: "Instead of plowshares to swords, it's iron fences to guns and bombs in this war." The house was gutted by Nazi bombs, prompting the resourceful Beaverbrook to move into a flat on the first floor of the *Evening Standard* building.

To the right of the Stornoway House drive and car park is Bridgewater Passage, a narrow path leading to the pavement (Queen's Walk) along the eastern edge of Green Park. Wend your way along this almost hidden pathway, then turn left onto the Green Park walkway.

Buckingham Palace, our eventual destination, is ahead, but if it's time for a short park break, Green Park provides an opportunity for either a bucolic stroll or rest stop. If you're more interested in the latter and you're visiting on a sunny day, relax in one of the park's canvas deck chairs, but expect a chair-rental fellow to suggest you pay the nominal rent—60p or so—before sitting down (it was 2d. in the war years). If you'd rather amble about, head for the **Canadian Memorial Fountain** in this same corner of Green Park.

Text continued on page 80.

London's Parks in Wartime

Given the regenerative nature of London's parks, World War II reminders are difficult to spot sixty years later. Rather than seeking long-gone structures or filled-in bomb craters, consider the following wartime park trivia.

Early on, most park railings were removed as scrap metal to be made into various armaments, a war consequence that was almost universally applauded. Some ornamental gates, such as Green Park's Devonshire Gates, were dismantled and taken to safer locations; others were left to take their chances. In parks with strict hours, including Kensington Gardens, park groundsmen continued to call "All out" at closing time, even though there were no railings; they would then solemnly close the big iron gates.

Beginning September 1938, central London's larger parks and squares had shelter trenches dug across their lawns, "raw brown mole-heaps on the green grass." Trenching was generally done by legions of shovel-wielding men or less often by steam shovels. Amenities were later added—canvas curtains at the door, boards covering the dirt floor, and wooden benches along the sides. Another early war measure was the stretching of coils of barbed wire around many London squares and open areas, giving the impression of invasion readiness. As the coils became rusted and entwined with overgrown grass, the effect was somewhat more disheveled than defensive.

Anti-aircraft batteries were stationed on the lawns of several parks, most centrally in Hyde Park. Each gun sat in a ring of sandbags perhaps twenty-five to forty feet in diameter and piled as high as a man's head. London's open spaces also served as wartime bases for barrage balloons,

with balloon personnel quartered in nearby military huts. In Green Park the all-women crew holding down the balloons lived in temporary huts, later destroyed by a flying bomb. Luckily the balloon tenders had already moved on, leaving behind their vegetable garden carved out of a corner of the park. In fact, most London parks turned areas over to allotments: in Albert's shadow in Kensington Gardens, in the Inns of Court, or near the debris tips (dumping areas) in Hyde Park. Entire families would descend on Sundays, spades and forks in hand, "to dig and plan, and dream of beans and carrots and lettuces." A particularly un-usual "crop" was coal, stockpiled on the lawns of Regent's Park in the last war winter, as authorities feared extreme winter weather would delay fuel transport.

Military bands performed regularly: Fridays in St. James's Park and Sundays in Hyde Park, Green Park, and Regent's Park. In fact, most summer evenings, Hyde Park strollers would hear military tunes drifting over the lawns.

American soldiers stationed in England brought their sports with them: touch-football teams played in Regent's Park and Hyde Park, and soft-ball games were frequently held. GIs cir-cled the running track at Regent's Park, played tennis at Hyde Park (hourly court rental from 9d. to a shilling), or worked out in the Primrose Hill gymnasium near Regent's Park.

Sooner or later every London park got bombed.

> *The grass is long and shaggy—people have trodden paths across what used to be smooth preserved lawns. There are cigarettes boxes and papers everywhere, but the trees are in full magnificence and there are lovers on the grass and solitary ladies reading lending library books in their deckchairs...and everywhere soldiers.*
> —Charles Ritchie, *The Siren Years*

Larger bomb craters and areas that had been dug up to provide sand for sandbags were filled with debris from London's blitzed and blasted build-ings. Crumbling bricks, wood, and old doors were piled up in these debris tips. Mixed in was the detritus of London home life, and distant park cor-ners became cemeteries of bedsteads, bathtubs, electric stoves, and water tanks. Materials were sorted and recycled as possible, and some rubble was carted away to be used in the manufacture of airfields, gun sites, and ordnance factories, according to the *Times*. London alone supplied 1,250,000 *tons* of "hard core," materials used in the building of fighter and bomber station runways. After the war, much of the remaining debris was removed from the parks, although the rolling green lawns may still harbor buried reminders of London's war.

Turn right through the first break in the park railings as you walk toward the Mall and the palace and continue until you spot the fountain. Actually, "fountain" is a misnomer—don't expect splashing spraying jets of

VISITOR DETAILS: Green Park is open daily 5am to midnight. During tourist season a snack truck parks on the palace side. Restrooms on the northern side, near the Green Park Underground. Check the posted map for more information.

water. Instead, a low-lying sheet of water spreads across a divided inclined base, the bottom part imprinted with large maple leaves, leaf outlines that merge with real leaves in autumn. A bronze and stone caption circles the flat medallion in front: "In two world wars, one million Canadians came to Britain and joined the fight for freedom. From danger shared, our friendship prospers." Unveiled in 1994, this memorial remains one of the lesser known but more somber war-related monuments in London.

On to Buckingham Palace. Whether leaving your deck chair or the Canadian Memorial Fountain, walk toward the Mall and the area in front of Buckingham Palace. In the center of this heavily trafficked area (formerly an island in the middle of a chaotic traffic circle, but now much safer for pedestrians) is the **Queen Victoria Memorial**, a statue abrim with Victorian allegorical nuance. The elaborate eighty-two-foot-high memorial, unveiled by King George V in 1911, includes a marble basin

Queen Victoria Memorial.

and fountains. On the east side looking down the Mall and away from the Palace sits a thirteen-foot-high Queen Victoria, carved from a single block of marble. Virginia Woolf aptly described her: "Victoria, billowing on her mound." The good queen holds an orb with a tiny St. George and the Dragon atop it and, in the German fashion, wears her wedding ring on her right hand. On the opposite side facing the palace is a mother with three children. Truth and Justice can be found on the remaining two sides. There are also figures representing Courage and Constancy, with the winged gilt figure of Victory at the very top. Watch for the bronze mermaid and merman, the lions, and the figures representing Progress (think torch carrier) and Peace (think olive branch). Agriculture and Manufacture are also there, and Neptune, and…well, you get the idea. All 2,300 tons of marble, plus uncounted pounds of metal, were on their own during the war and survived in good shape, despite several very near misses.

Buckingham Palace under a bomber's moon.

Beyond the Queen Victoria Memorial is **Buckingham Palace**, the official London residence (and office) of the monarch, a building best described as more big than beautiful. And big it is, with almost 600 rooms, including 19 state rooms, 52 royal and guest bedrooms, 188 staff bedrooms, 92 offices, and 78 bathrooms and lavatories, plus an enormous basement. It was a long time in the making—construction began in 1703, the venerable John Nash did alterations in 1825, and the relatively modern Portland-stone look was completed in 1913 as part of the national memorial to Queen Victoria.

The view from the iron gates is actually the back of the palace; the true front is in the inner courtyard, a sheltered quadrangle seen by very few. For decades Buckingham Palace was off-limits to all but invited guests arriving to dance to a military band in the ballroom, kneel before the sovereign while being knighted, or stroll the forty-acre grounds at a lavish royal garden party. Today, when the State Rooms of the palace are opened to the general public in late summer, thousands of visitors view the queen's tapestries, works of art, and furniture. The regal and plush State Rooms *are* well worth a visit, but for a more war-related experience, spend a few solitary moments outside the gates, considering the look and memories of the palace six decades ago.

On a summer afternoon in mid-1944, the London visitor viewing the façade of Buckingham Palace would see a worn and tired building, one that had experienced at least fourteen wartime "incidents." High explosive bombs, incendiaries, and flying rockets had all taken their toll, and just about every window was blasted out. Starting in October 1941, over

Text continued on page 85.

A Walk in the Palace Neighborhood

Many London visitors watch the Changing of the Guard, then drift away down the Mall or Birdcage Walk, off to lunch or an afternoon of shopping or museums. As an alternative, consider a walk amongst the queen's neighbors.

Begin facing Buckingham Palace, then turn left and walk to the end of the iron gates. Continue down the roadway along the Palace's south side. Buckingham Gate merges into Buckingham Palace Road as the brick-and-stone wall to the right goes on seemingly forever, but eventually there's a rather plain entrance to the Royal Mews shop. Buy a ticket here for entrance to the mews themselves, a large quadrangle of buildings housing the monarch's horses and royal processional gear.

During the war, the Royal Mews stood silent—most horses and carriages had been evacuated to Windsor Castle. The Coronation Coach stayed safely at Lord Rosebery's distant country home in Buckinghamshire. Such provident measures meant little damage was done to animals or equipment when a German bomb exploded here in November 1940. If horses intrigue you, or if you're eager to know the difference between a landau and a barouche, then a visit to the queen's working stables is definitely in order.

> **VISITOR DETAILS:** The Royal Mews are open daily, March–October, 11am to 4pm, and until 5pm in August and September. Admission is charged. Large shop open daily 9:30am to 5pm. More information: 020 7766 7302, www.royal.gov.uk.

As you leave the Royal Mews, turn right and continue along Buckingham Palace Road, originally the dividing line between the fashionable Belgravia district to your right and the somewhat less fashionable South Belgravia/Northwest Pimlico to your left. A wartime RAF pilot, having knocked a German bomber from the skies over Victoria Station, was forced to bail out around here, coming down near the Victoria Station train tracks, His plane, however, crashed and reputedly still lies buried somewhere under Buckingham Palace Road.

At Bressenden Place, turn left across Buckingham Palace Road to the Rubens Hotel. This was home to the Polish General Staff during the war; there's a plaque near the entrance. Walk up Bressenden Place— between and beyond the soulless glass towers and the colorful street art on your left was once the site of Watney's Stag Brewery. Postwar, a windswept plaza replaced the brewery's bombed buildings, and recent additional construction has now replaced the plaza. In fact, it may not be possible to cross this area. If so, return to Bressenden Place, turn left and walk to Victoria Street, then turn left onto Palace Street, and a final left brings you back to the route.

Rooftop firewatchers at Watney's Stag Brewery found waiting for incendiary bombs "like sitting on the bull's eye of a darts board whilst play is in progress." If that thought's just too much for you, perhaps it's time to consider a rejuvenating pint at one of the neighborhood pubs.

And remember, during wartime if you weren't a regular customer, many London pubs would have expected you to bring your own glass. You'd also be urged to drink draught (draft) beer: "Help your country by saving: glass, rubber, timber, petrol, labour—draught beer is good." In mid-1940, author John Lehmann found "a

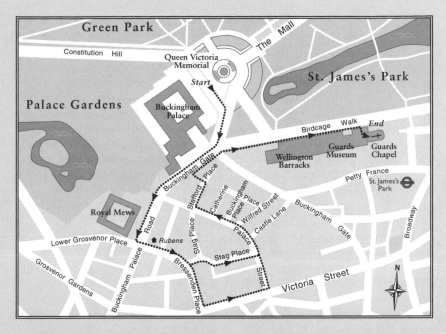

scene of vigour and high spirits in the pubs around Victoria way," perhaps a direct result of aiding the war effort by consuming draught beer. Later in the war, beer availability became limited and alcohol content dropped, undoubtedly contributing to a reduction in the "vigour and high spirits" of local pub-goers.

Palace Street, on the far side of Stag Plaza, is a quiet roadway with several even quieter residential lanes branching off to the right. Stroll past (or down and back) Castle Lane, Wilfred Street, and Buckingham Place. Streets like these always set me to imagining their wartime residents opening the front doors after a nightlong air raid, wondering what they'd find outside. The fourth side street is Catherine Place; Winston Churchill's son Randolph and his second wife June lived in Number 12 in the late 1940s.

Last is Stafford Place, a residential cul-de-sac. Turn right and watch for the plaque on the wall of Stafford Mansions, carved with one of General de Gaulle's incisive wartime exhortations to "mes camarades."

The Free French Naval Forces headquarters were housed here from 1940 to 1945.

Further down the street, Number 16 Stafford Place is the blue-plaqued wartime home of Leslie Hore-Belisha, Minister of Transport from 1934 to 1937 and the man who introduced Belisha (that's "be-LEE-sha") beacons, those flashing yellow lights at crosswalks. The plaque, however, honors his service as statesman; Hore-Belisha was Secretary of State for War from 1937 to 1940. As you nip up this short street to view his former residence, ruminate on the catty comments of fellow-politician "Chips" Channon, who found the house "a horror," with "astounding lack of taste or humour. Wedgwood plaques cover the walls...old ones, small ones, good ones, bad ones."

Near the end of Stafford Place almost directly across from Hore-Belisha's home, a narrow passage opens onto Buckingham Gate. Head down this, turn right, and continue along Buckingham Gate (the palace will be on your left). Cross onto Birdcage Walk, paralleling St. James's Park.

Wellington Barracks, the headquarters of the Household Brigade, are to your right. The palace sentries are stationed here—the Grenadier and Coldstream Guards, and the Scots, Irish, and Welsh Guards. The barracks themselves aren't open to the public, but the Guards Museum and the Guards Chapel are—the entrance is at the far end of this complex.

While walking this long stretch, consider the setting here on a quiet Sunday morning in mid-June 1944. Over 180 service personnel had walked, bicycled, or driven to the Guards Chapel for Sunday services, an opportunity to give thanks for the early success of the invasion of the Continent. From inside the chapel the liquid strains of organ music drifted out across St. James's Park. Heads were bowed in prayer as the Grenadier Guards' Lieutenant-Colonel read the lesson. The worshippers were inside a sturdy masonry building modeled on a Greek temple, its four Doric columns at attention across the front portico; most worshippers probably didn't hear the spluttering sound of an approaching V-1 rocket. The rocket's engine stopped suddenly, and the missile plunged earthward. The resulting explosion destroyed the chapel roof, upper walls, the massive columns, and the portico, leaving a tangle of timbers, girders, marble, and bricks, with a fine white dust floating silently upwards. Hundreds of windows in the neighborhood—many in the streets we just walked—were shattered by the blast. Far worse, 121 of the worshippers died and dozens were seriously injured in the first major tragedy resulting from the newest of German weapons.

Just over a year later, the Guards held Christmas services in a large hut set up outside the ruins of the once-proud Guards Chapel. Reconstruction moved very slowly,

but in December 1963 the new chapel, with the original and unscathed apse appended to one side, was finally opened. Today a visit provides one more reminder that war can be as vicious on the homefront as on the battleground. On the outside walls framing the entrance are incised the names of those honored by memorials in the old chapel, memorials vaporized by that V-1 explosion. Step inside to view dozens of newer memorials, books of remembrance, and some dramatic regimental standards.

The nearby Guards Museum—across the plaza and down the steps—is a must for anyone intrigued by military pomp and circumstance. Arranged by conflict (Peninsular Way, Sudan War, Great War, and so on), displays here feature uniforms, weapons, battlefield dioramas, and the miscellany of military life. If you're lucky, the retired Guardsman tending the front desk may ply you with stories of his World War II experiences in London.

> **VISITOR DETAILS:** The Guards Museum is open daily 10am to 4pm. Admission is charged. The Guards Chapel (free) is generally open the same hours. Steps down to the museum; call ahead to make lift arrangements. More information: 020 7414 3428.

For a lighter military moment, visit the nearby Guard Toy Soldier Centre and Shop. Hundreds of metal and plastic figures, both military and nonmilitary, are on display and for sale, plus CDs, postcards, and children's Guards uniforms.

Through the iron gates head right down Birdcage Walk—there's still time for a late lunch, or perhaps some shopping or museums.

twenty tons of iron railings had been removed as part of the national scrap-iron campaign for metal, taken away to be melted down and used in the building of armaments. (The gates in front were *not* removed.) Rifle pits had been dug around the palace and were manned as a protection against parachute attacks. The red-coated sentries had put away their brilliant uniforms and mounted guard in khaki battledress. The garden entry area, the swimming pool, and the chapel had been bombed, the North Lodge gutted, and several other areas inside the palace destroyed. The central balcony, so familiar as the gathering place for members of the Royal Family to greet the crowds gathered beyond the gates, would be empty in 1944 and not particularly safe—repeated bombings had undermined the structure. In any case, until the war ended, there would be little reason to cheer.

King George and Queen Elizabeth had moved into Buckingham Palace after Edward VIII abdicated the throne and a life of royal duties in favor of an American divorcee. The political reverberations of the 1936 abdication rocked both the British monarchy and government, and the relatively unknown Prince Albert—the new King George VI—was looked to to re-establish the monarchy's royal solidity. The new Royal Family *did* bring a regal realness to the monarchy, still royal but not quite so unapproachable as the Victorians and Edwardians had been. The early reign of King George featured the usual opening of schools and factories and libraries, but with the declaration of war, the monarch's public duties changed drastically. Now, instead of honoring a building project with the royal presence, the king and queen visited devastated neighborhoods and bombed cities, honoring the grit and stubbornness of the British people. And except for visits to such areas of destruction and time spent at Windsor Castle to be with their evacuated daughters, the king and queen stayed in London. The Royal Standard, indicating that the monarch was in residence, flew over Buckingham Palace.

The first palace bombing incident occurred early on September 9, 1940, when a delayed-action bomb fell near the swimming pool at the northwestern corner of the palace, about sixty feet from the queen's sitting room and seventy feet from the king's study. The area was roped off and the wait began. The royal couple headed off to the usual day's work of visiting London's bombed citizens. Here the London *Times* struck a rather melodramatic note: "Even as the King was touring East London,...as he went round saying a cheerful word to some of the poorest of his people, the King knew that lodged in his own home was this heavy bomb which sooner or later would explode." *New York Times* correspondent Raymond Daniell described the outcome: "A heap of rubble now lies beneath the

Text continued on page 89.

The Royal Family

December 14, 1895: Albert Frederick Arthur George, the second son of the then-Duke of York and grandson of Queen Victoria, is born in York Cottage on the Royal Family's Sandringham Estate, Norfolk.

August 4, 1900: Elizabeth Angela Marguerite Bowes-Lyon is born, probably at St. Paul's, Walden Bury in Hertfordshire (although sources differ about the location).

Early Summer 1920: At a small party at 7 Grosvenor Square, Mayfair, the Duke of York meets Lady Elizabeth Bowes-Lyon. A romantic courtship will follow…eventually.

April 26, 1923: The happy couple marry at Westminster Abbey. The Yorks honey-moon first at Polesden Lacey, the mansion of Mrs. Ronald Greville in the Surrey countryside, then at her family's Scotland home, Glamis Castle, and finally at Frogmore, just a mile from Windsor Castle.

June 1923: The Duke and Duchess of York live at White Lodge in Richmond Park but soon decide to move closer to the city. (White Lodge is now home to the Royal Ballet School.) They settle on a handsome row house at 145 Piccadilly, near Apsley House. While the Piccadilly house is being renovated, the royal couple stays with her family at Glamis Castle and St. Paul's, Walden Bury, and with his family at Sandringham and Chesterfield House in London. When 145 Piccadilly is finally ready (1926), the Yorks will happily reside there for a decade. (Gutted in the war and not totally demolished until the 1950s, it's now the site of the Four Seasons Hotel.)

January 26, 1926: The young couple move temporarily into her parents' home at 17 Bruton Street, Mayfair, to await the birth of their first child. The site is now part of the northern wing of Berkeley Square House.

April 21, 1926: Elizabeth Alexandra Mary is born at 17 Bruton Street (a plaque marks the event). Four years later (August 21, 1930) Margaret Rose is born at Glamis Castle.

January 20, 1936: King George V dies at Sandringham; his eldest son becomes King Edward VIII. The new king continues his romance with the American divorcee, Wallis Warfield

Simpson. Insurmountable ethical, religious, and political conflicts surround his inten-tion to marry Mrs. Simpson, and by year's end King Edward decides to abdicate.

December 11, 1936: Prince Albert, Duke of York, officially becomes King George VI. That night the former king broadcasts to his subjects: "I have found it impossible to carry the heavy burden of responsibility and to discharge my duties as King as I would wish to do without the help and support of the woman I love."

May 12, 1937: The Royal Coach, carrying King George VI and Queen Elizabeth, passes through the gates of Buckingham Palace and down the Mall, through Admiralty Arch, onto Whitehall and Parliament Street, and pulls up in front of Westminster Abbey as Big Ben strikes 11am. The Royal Coronation begins.

June 3, 1937: The Duke of Windsor, the former King Edward VIII, marries Wallis Warfield Simpson in the Château de Candé in Touraine, near Tours, France.

June 22, 1939: The king and queen return from a seven-week trip to Canada and the U.S. Arriving at Waterloo Station, they motor to the palace via Parliament Square, where the bells of St. Margaret's peal a welcome and members of Parliament stand and cheer.

Late June 1939: In preparation for a possible German invasion, the king begins rifle practice in the palace grounds. The queen sharpens her skills with a revolver.

September 3, 1939: At 6pm King George broadcasts to his people from Bucking-ham Palace, asking them to stand "calm and firm and united." From now until war's end, the king and queen embark on a full calendar of military inspections, munitions factory tours, hospital visits, walks in devastated London neighborhoods, and trips to England's bombed cities: Plymouth, Liverpool, Southampton, Bath, Sheffield, Hull, Portsmouth....

September 4, 1939: Queen Mary, the King's mother, is "evacuated" from her London home at Marlborough House to Badminton, Gloucestershire.

May 10, 1940: Prime Minister Neville Chamberlain resigns; King George summons Winston Churchill to Buckingham Palace and asks him to form a new government.

May 1940: Princesses Elizabeth and Margaret leave for the safety of Windsor Castle, about twenty miles west of London. Their parents spend many weeknights and, later in the war, some weekends with their daughters. The castle is gloomy, its win-dows covered with blackout curtains and wire net. The war efforts of the princesses during the next five years include vegetable growing in the royal gardens, knitting woolen scarves and socks for England's sailors, and collecting tinfoil and scrap iron.

September 9, 1940: A delayed action bomb falls on Buckingham Palace, the first of over a dozen attacks on the royal residence. The king and queen spend the day visit-ing bombed-out victims in London's East End.

September 10, 1940: Regular Tuesday luncheon meetings between King George and Prime Minister Churchill begin and will continue throughout the war. During air raids and later during the rocket attacks, the luncheons are held in the royal air raid shelter in the palace basement.

September 13, 1940: A Luftwaffe pilot zooms up the Mall and bombs Buckingham Palace, destroying the Royal Chapel and blasting huge craters in the roadway.

November 16, 1940: Two days after the devastating raid on Coventry, King George visits the city and its gutted cathedral, stepping carefully over the still-smoking rubble.

August 25, 1942: The Duke of Kent, the king's younger brother, dies when his RAF plane, headed for Iceland, crashes into a Scottish hill near Sutherland.

September 19, 1942: King George institutes a drastic fuel savings plan at Buckingham Palace and Windsor Castle: no more than five inches of water in the bathtubs, only one light in each bedroom and the removal of all unessential corridor lights, and no bedroom heat at all (unless by doctor's orders).

October 1942: Eleanor Roosevelt, wife of the American president, visits Buckingham Palace, staying in a drafty and gloomy suite with most of the window panes broken out and covered with isinglass. Later she learns she has been given the queen's suite.

Autumn 1944: The king walks through the palace gardens toward Hyde Park Corner to inspect the damage from a V-1 rocket that fell during the night.

Spring 1945: Princess Elizabeth receives an honorary commission as a second subaltern in the ATS (Auxiliary Territorial Service). She trains in Camberley, west of London, learning how to change spark plugs and do vehicle maintenance.

May 8, 1945 (V-E Day): It is Tuesday and the king and the prime minister lunch together, as usual. In the early evening, the Royal Family will repeatedly come out on the palace balcony to wave to the jubilant throngs below. About 5:30pm, Churchill joins them. The princesses (Elizabeth in her ATS uniform) slip out a side door to join the cheering crowds.

February 6, 1952: King George VI dies in his sleep at Sandringham. His body lies in state in the family church there, then is brought by train to London. The coffin, draped with the royal standard, lies in state in Westminster Hall and then is taken to St. George's Chapel, Windsor, for the funeral. Elizabeth II becomes queen.

October 21, 1955: A bronze statue of King George VI is unveiled by his daughter, Queen Elizabeth II, near St. James's Park.

August 4, 2000: The Queen Mother celebrates her 100th birthday, ending a summer-long celebration of parties, parades, and World War II aircraft fly-overs.

February 9, 2002: Princess Margaret dies in London, aged seventy-one.

March 30, 2002: The Queen Mother dies peacefully in her sleep at Royal Lodge, Windsor, aged 101. Her body lies in state at Westminster Hall before her funeral at Westminster Abbey. She is buried next to her husband in St. George's Chapel, Windsor.

windows of the Queen's sitting room and the swimming pool built for the Princesses in the old conservatory wing is in ruins. Under four plane trees…where royalty receives its guests at its annual garden party there is a crater fifteen feet deep and twenty feet in diameter."

The bomb blew out every window on the northern side of the palace, damaging doors, and splattering ceiling plaster, glass splinters, and debris everywhere. Various stone pillars were smashed, with some of the pieces being thrown onto the palace roof. A chunk of Portland stone weighing almost two tons was tossed twenty feet, yet incredibly, no one was hurt. The king and queen moved to other rooms, facing the inner quadrangle.

Later in the same week, a Luftwaffe pilot (reputedly a former pilot of the London-Berlin air service) dove down through the balloon barrage to about 1,000 feet, then sped up the Mall to bomb Buckingham Palace. This attack wrecked the small Royal Chapel in the southern wing of the building ("blown to flinders," as a wartime diarist put it), originally built during Queen Victoria's reign. Two bombs also damaged the inner quadrangle, blasting large craters, breaking a water main, and causing a ten-foot fountain of water. The royal couple had been in the king's sitting room just before lunchtime when "all of a sudden we heard an aircraft making a zooming noise above." They looked out the window and saw the bombs falling into the central courtyard. "We looked at each other & then we were out into the passage as fast as we could get there.…We all wondered why we weren't dead." With admirable royal quickness, they then moved to the palace's air raid shelter, the housemaids' former sitting room in the basement. Here, in what the *Illustrated London News* called "their refuge from Hitler's spiteful and murderous attacks," the king and queen of Great Britain waited for the bombs to stop. This was the attack that prompted the queen's famous remark: "I'm *glad* we've been bombed. It makes me feel I can look the East End in the face."

Two bombs also fell in the roadway in front of Buckingham Palace, one of them a time bomb. Workers piled a wall of sandbags around it, but even so, when the bomb finally exploded the next day, a deep crater was blown in the street. The areas damaged were in front (the public side) of the main gates, between the gates and the Queen Victoria Memorial. Amazingly enough, the memorial itself, though showered with debris, was undamaged.

In March 1941, Buckingham Palace was bombed again; this time North Lodge—and sadly, a patrolling policeman—fell victim to Nazi bombs. North Lodge is the columned one-story wing extending to the right as you look at the palace from the Mall. When it received a shattering direct

When asked why the two princesses hadn't been evacuated abroad to safety, the queen replied, "The Princesses could never leave without me—and I could never leave without the King—and, of course, the King will never leave."

hit on that cold March night, most of the columns and the balustrade above were destroyed; what you see now has been completely rebuilt. During that same raid, three bombs fell into the forecourt between the palace and the front gates, leaving three large craters each about thirty-five feet from the next.

There were other wartime raids in the immediate area, including a November 1940 attack on the Royal Mews and an August 1944 flying bomb that fell on the palace grounds, destroying a number of trees and smashing what windows were left in the palace. The royal policy of dealing with windows as every other Londoner did (no new glass, cover it as best you could) meant that by war's end, palace windows were covered with internal wood shutters, thick black tarpaper, isinglass, boards, roofing felt, or whatever else came to hand. It looked shabby, like "an unkempt tenement house." It looked like there was a war on.

The royal response to shattered glass was just another effort by the king to show his countrymen that their war was his war, that his home was no more immune to attack than theirs. The Royal Family used food and clothing ration cards, they filled the bathtub with only a few inches of water, they recycled palace railings and cooking pans to make weapons, they turned off all unneeded lights. "It was pressed home vividly upon the consciousness of every Englishman that all were in the same boat, king and commoner, soldier and civilian." Undeniably, the royal boat was more comfortable and elaborate, but to the extent they could, the Royal Family willingly shared wartime hardships and privations with their countrymen.

VISITOR DETAILS: The exterior of Buckingham Palace can be viewed anytime. The Changing of the Guard takes place in the palace forecourt daily, April through July, at 11:30am, and on alternate days the rest of the year. The State Rooms are open early August–September (dates vary from year to year); admission is charged. For ticket information, call 020 7766 7300, stop by (summertime only) the Green Park ticket booth, or check www.royal.gov.uk. A snack cart parks in Green Park during tourist season. The queen would rather you didn't use her bathrooms; plan ahead.

The mid-1944 visitor, standing idly outside the gates and looking at those multi-patched wartime windows would not have known that within a year thousands of jubilant Londoners would stand here chanting "We want the king! We want the king!" The war would end, the common peril would be survived, the windows, would be replaced, and life would go on.

Royal Succession

Royal succession...royal confusion. Perhaps this will help. Don't memorize it—just refer back here when the monarchs begin to blur together.

Queen Victoria reigned from 1837 to 1901; her husband (officially the prince consort) was Prince Albert. Victoria's eldest son Edward was Prince of Wales.

When Queen Victoria died in 1901, her eldest son Edward became **King Edward VII**; Edward's wife was Queen Alexandra. Edward's eldest (living) son George was Prince of Wales. Edward VII reigned from 1901 to 1910.

When King Edward VII died in 1910, his eldest son George became **King George V**; George's wife was Queen Mary. George's eldest son Edward (David to all the family) was Prince of Wales; George's second son Albert was Duke of York. George V reigned from 1910 to 1936.

When King George V died in January 1936, his eldest son Edward (David) became king and took the name **King Edward VIII**. Edward VIII reigned in 1936.

When King Edward VIII abdicated in December 1936, his brother Albert became king and took the name **King George VI**; George's wife was Queen Elizabeth. George's daughters were Princess Elizabeth and Princess Margaret. David (the former King Edward VIII) was named Duke of Windsor. George VI reigned from 1936 to 1952.

When King George VI died in 1952, his daughter Elizabeth became **Queen Elizabeth II** (Elizabeth I reigned from 1558 to 1603); her husband is Prince Philip. Elizabeth's son Charles is Prince of Wales. Elizabeth's mother, the former Queen Elizabeth, was known as the Queen Mother. Elizabeth II has reigned from 1952 to the present.

Queen Victoria.

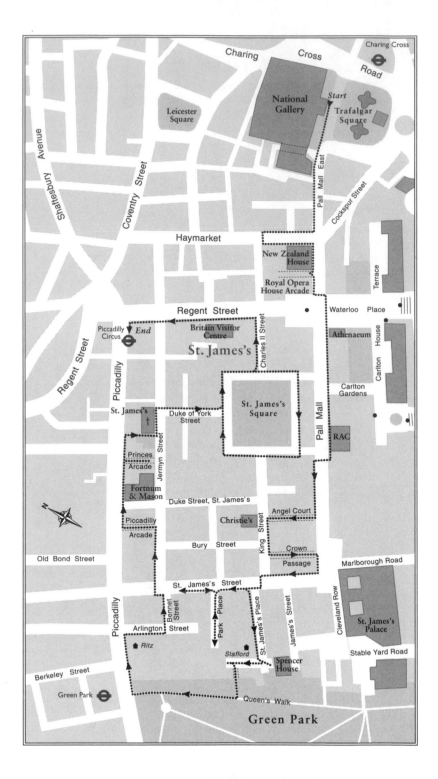

Charing Cross Road

Charing Cross

Leicester Square

National Gallery

Start Trafalgar Square

Pall Mall East

Cockspur Street

Shaftesbury Avenue

Coventry Street

Haymarket

New Zealand House

Royal Opera House Arcade

Terrace

Regent Street

Piccadilly Circus *End*

Britain Visitor Centre

Charles II Street

St. James's

Waterloo Place

Athenaeum

Carlton House

Regent Street

Piccadilly

St. James's †

Duke of York Street

St. James's Square

Carlton Gardens

Jermyn Street

Princes Arcade

Fortnum & Mason

Pall Mall

RAC

Duke Street, St. James's

N

Piccadilly Arcade

Christie's

Bury Street

King Street

Angel Court

Old Bond Street

Crown Passage

Marlborough Road

St. James's Street

Bennet Street

Park Place

St. James's Place

James's Street

Cleveland Row

St. James's Palace

Piccadilly

Arlington Street

Ritz

Stafford

Spencer House

Stable Yard Road

Berkeley Street

Green Park

Queen's Walk

Green Park

3

St. James's

*There is a large bomb crater in the road just outside what is
left of St. James's, Piccadilly; it's deep, all London clay and
with fountains of water cascading down into it from broken
mains; smells of gas and burning everywhere.*

—POET STEVIE SMITH

A less-than-elegant Jermyn Street, 1941.

Highlights: Carlton Hotel site, shopping arcades, Pall Mall, Clubland, Christie's, Crown Passage, Spencer House, Green Park, Ritz Hotel, Jermyn Street, Fortnum & Mason, St. James's Church, St. James's Square and Gardens, Astor home, Norfolk House, London Library, Canadian service clubs, Piccadilly Circus, Stage Door Canteen

Underground Station: Charing Cross

Photo Ops: The nooks and crannies of St. James's garden offer some unusual statuary and endearing handmade signs.

BEFORE LEAVING ON YOUR TRIP

■ **Travel Scheduling:** Spencer House is closed January and August; Green Park's

spring bulbs explode in late March and early April; London's best sales are in January. If you're hoping to fit in tea at the Ritz, make reservations early. Finally, if you're in London on a Sunday, stroll Piccadilly's street market.

■ **Cultural Preparations:** For a look inside a London gentlemen's club in the between-war years, read *The Unpleasantness at the Bellona Club* by Dorothy L. Sayers. The mystery begins on Remembrance Day in the Bellona Club, modeled somewhat on Piccadilly's In and Out Club, where an aged clubmember has nodded off...or has he?

■ **Internet:** Provisions from Fortnum & Mason are just a mouse click away: www.fortnumandmason.com.

In a morning's brisk outing, the determined walker could easily stride every street in the compact district of St. James's, but we shall travel more selectively and slowly, looking for wartime reminders amidst sedate gentlemen's clubs, elegant shops, hidden passages, and aristocratic town houses.

The St. James's area is bounded by Piccadilly and Pall Mall, Green Park and Regent Street. Our walking route starts in the southeastern corner of this tidy rectangle in the depths of Clubland, then heads west and north with stops at Spencer House, the Ritz Hotel, the south side of Piccadilly, and several shopping arcades. We'll spend time at St. James's Church (badly damaged in the Blitz) and take a turn around St. James's Square (where wartime cabbages grew and Ike had his headquarters), ending back on Regent Street for a visit to the Piccadilly Circus Underground (a wartime air raid shelter).

If you roam Waterloo Place on statue patrol, watch for Sir Colin Campbell. The angel and lion at the base were overthrown by a German bomb and tumbled face down onto the pavement. Though they've since been returned to their spot on the statue's plinth, bomb pitting on both the marble and stone plinths is a reminder of their travails.

Shopping interludes are encouraged, but don't expect many opportunities to step behind the stolid anonymous façades of London's social, professional, and political clubs. These are members-only clubs, and the casual visitor is not encouraged (or allowed) to wander in. Happily there are a handful of exceptions to this rule. We'll also enjoy the exteriors of many other London clubs and consider their success in surviving the war, from bombs in the sleeping chambers to whale meat on the dining table.

From Trafalgar Square head west past the Sainsbury Wing of the National Gallery along congested Pall Mall East (pronunciation hint: more "pell mell" than "pawl mawl") toward Waterloo Place. Across Haymarket on the corner is the site of the long-gone **Carlton Hotel**, a sumptuous hostelry built in the 1890s. After a direct hit by a Nazi bomb, the Carlton Hotel was a scene of ghastly desolation with twisted and charred beams strewn about, acrid smoke rising from the over 160 gutted rooms, and firemen's hoses snaking through the ruins. The gaunt shell remained, empty and abandoned, until it was demolished in the late 1950s and eventually replaced by the toweringly ugly New Zealand House.

If matters theatrical delight you, take a quick detour up Haymarket to admire the columned façades of the Theatre Royal Haymarket on your right and Her Majesty's Theatre across the street, both here in the war years (although the latter was *His* Majesty's Theatre then).

Returning to Pall Mall East, don't miss the **Royal Opera House Arcade**, London's oldest shopping arcade (circa 1818) and perhaps the prettiest. Step up, step in, and enjoy a browse in the bow-fronted shops arrayed along just one side of the arcade under hanging plants and lamps. New Zealand House and some modern shop windows are all that's along the other side.

Past Haymarket, Pall Mall East imperceptibly becomes plain **Pall Mall**, the preserve of London's gentlemen's clubs. In the late 1930s, a London guidebook listed over ninety "exclusive and luxurious institutions" in and around Pall Mall and Piccadilly, bastions of tradition whose membership was almost entirely a function of social status, even if the clubs' focus might be more varied. There was the Alpine Club (for climbers) and White's ("social, non-political"); there were clubs for journalists and for tennis players, for military officers and for "public school men," for bridge players and for those interested in matters dramatic, literary, and artistic. Another twenty or so similar groups served London's club ladies, although these were centered in the more residential areas of Mayfair and Belgravia. But this stretch of Pall Mall and St. James's Street beyond was **Clubland**, an unofficial but apt name. Here gentlemen could gather behind closed doors to dine with their peers, read the *Times*, enjoy a relaxing after-dinner smoke, discuss matters of importance, perhaps take a brief nap or even spend the night, and most importantly, simply *belong*.

A particularly grand Clubland stretch is ahead, starting with the building at Waterloo Place and Pall Mall on the southeastern corner. This was once the **United Service Club**, known among London's cognoscenti as "the Senior" to distinguish it from the *Junior* United Service Club. The club was established in the early 1800s for officers from the Napoleonic wars and served its members throughout World War II (and until it was disbanded in the mid-1970s), despite incendiary bombs that set the roof afire and sent concrete ceiling slabs crashing to the floor below.

The since-repaired and now impressive building houses the Institute of Directors (IoD), a membership association of business men and women. Since it's no longer a private club (now more of a quasi-

Norwegian Corner.

private club), this building is one of the few in Clubland you can enter. Ask at the front desk to see the ground-floor public areas (only on weekdays and only when lunch isn't being served), particularly the simple plaque in the restaurant/lounge noting the Norwegian Corner where Norway's exiled King Haakon and his officers met during the war.

Across Waterloo Place stands the elegant **Athenaeum**, founded in 1824, with a blue-and-cream frieze above the main windows and a golden statue of the goddess Pallas Athena standing watch. One postwar writer found great satisfaction in the Athenaeum's exterior, so different from the somber gloom of other Clubland fixtures: "Its stucco front is never allowed to grow dingy....In the drab years after the war, the appearance of the building kept up one's faith in London's eventual recovery from its wounds, dirt, and general slatterliness." Despite its spiffy front even during the war years, it also had an inelegant surface shelter plunked down directly in front of it on Waterloo Place.

> Older volunteers from several gentlemen's clubs, including the Travellers and Brooks, helped staff the Admiralty Arch guard post during the war years.

The Athenaeum has always been considered the most intellectually elite of London's clubs, as a bit of dialogue from Noël Coward's play *Present Laughter* suggests: "You ought never to have joined the Athenaeum Club. It's made you pompous." The reply: "It can't have. I've always been too frightened to go into it." Perhaps more evidence of the club's elite attitude: the basement air raid shelter was lined in part with leather-bound copies of the London *Times*.

Mid-block past the Athenaeum is the **Travellers** (106 Pall Mall), primarily a social club (that is, nonpolitical) founded in the early eighteenth century for world travelers—or at least those who had traveled 500 miles (now 1,000) from London. The Italian palazzo–style building was constructed in 1832, several of the rooms were destroyed by German bombs in 1940, and all was restored and refurbished in the early 1950s. If you're interested in what lies behind the anonymous façade of a London club, call to check on tours. The Travellers' morning room, smoking rooms, library, and dining room can flesh out one's imaginings of what club life is like behind the massive entrance doors.

> **VISITOR DETAILS:** The Travellers offers guided tours on autumn Saturdays. More information: 020 7930 8688.

Next at 104 Pall Mall was (and is) the **Reform Club**, "the premiere club of Liberalism," and a lucky building indeed. Although half its roof was burned by incendiaries, the club never had to close during the war years. Its escape from significant damage was not matched by its Tory neighbor across the street, the **Carlton Club**, which was destroyed by German bombs. The stark new building on the southwestern corner of Pall Mall and Carlton Gardens marks the former site of the Carlton, one of London's more famous, and conservative, political clubs. Past members included prime ministers Winston Churchill, Anthony Eden, and Harold Macmillan—in fact, Macmillan was in the smoking room one October

Wartime Shelter Signspotting

The metal shelter signs are long gone, but black stenciled notices marking wartime shelter locations still remain, and shelter signspotting is an intriguing travel activity for the homefront enthusiast. Some tips: Watch in residential, not business, districts. Focus less on buildings of stucco or Portland stone, or those with painted walls; watch more carefully along streets with brick or terra cotta residences. Generally, unless buildings have street-level stairs down to coal vaults or basements below, it's unlikely there'll be shelter signs—after all, there had to be somewhere to shelter. Here are a few to look for—and when you find more, let me know.

Mayfair
42 Brook Street
74 Brook Street
Near 43 Upper Brook Street

Westminster
41-50 Carlisle Place
Lord North Street (this short block
   has almost a dozen shelter signs)
28 Queen Anne's Gate

Pimlico
25 and 36 Longmoore Street

evening in 1940 when with a blinding flash the ceiling fell in, dirt and debris went everywhere, and shattered glass scattered over all. A direct hit and the club building essentially collapsed, sending chunks of masonry into the street, killing a pedestrian, and rendering Macmillan's car, parked just outside, "a battered heap of tin." Amazingly Macmillan and the forty or so others inside the club that night escaped serious injury. The 1850s building was so badly damaged that the club relocated to new quarters on St. James's Street.

Continuing along the southern side of Pall Mall, it's hard to miss the beflagged and belamped building at Number 89. The **RAC** (Royal Automobile Club) was founded in 1897 "for the Protection, Encouragement, and Development of Automobilism." The club moved into this French Renaissance structure in 1911, designed by the Ritz Hotel's architect. Honorary membership was offered during the war years to officers working in the War Office and others from the Dominions and the Allied Forces serving in London. General de Gaulle, Prince Olaf of Norway, and

Poland's General Sikorski all frequented the RAC. A number of wartime incendiary bombs fell here, primarily in the early raids of the Blitz and then again in the Little Blitz of 1944. All were quickly and efficiently dealt with by staff firewatchers, and no major damage was done, rather remarkable considering the building's size.

> After the battering of the Carlton Club in 1940, German communiques announced (as was their usual custom after bombing central London) that the bombers in daring low-flying attacks had once more hit a number of "important military objectives."

Time to cross Pall Mall to the **Army and Navy Club** at 36 Pall Mall. The club, usually known as the Rag, is situated in a 1960s building replacing the venerable Italian Renaissance–style structure that had long been the Rag's home. On this same less-imposing side of Pall Mall is a "club" of a different sort, the headquarters of the Royal British Legion at Number 48. This national organization safeguards "the welfare, interests, and memory of those who have served in the Armed Forces." They're also the folks who make and distribute poppies for Remembrance Day and for memorial wreaths.

Wander to the right, down Angel Court, a somewhat hidden and relatively bland passage, ending almost directly across from **Christie's** front door. One of London's two great auction houses (the other, Sotheby's, is on New Bond Street), Christie's has been on King Street since 1823. The entire block was badly bombed (or well bombed, if you were the Luftwaffe pilot involved) in 1941, and Christie's had to abandon their gutted premises ("burning like a baker's oven—too fiercely for there to be any smoke") for about a decade, spending part of that time in Spencer House (see below). Feel free to wander in and take a look at the auction galleries.

> **VISITOR DETAILS:** Christie's is open Monday–Friday 9am to 5pm; Tuesday 9:30am to 8pm; Sunday 2pm to 5pm. More information: 020 7839 9060, www.christies.com.

Return to Pall Mall along **Crown Passage**, a narrow passageway a block down King Street and known in the war years as Crown Court. Be prepared to step back in time, especially if you pause for liquid refreshment at the Red Lion Pub, reputedly London's last village inn and second-oldest continuously licensed house, making it about 350 years old; many a wartime pint was pulled here. The shops along this passage were much the same in the war years as today: then a hairdresser, hatter, and greengrocer, today a tobacconist, ironmonger, and millinery shop.

Head up St. James's Street along the east side. Berry Brothers & Rudd, wine and spirit merchants, at Number 3 served customers throughout the war years—in fact, for about the last 300-plus years. Duck down narrow and dark Pickering Place, another easy-to-miss passageway. The cul-de-sac at the end, with its plants, hanging lamps, brick walls, and unlabeled doors, offers a touch of mystery…though perhaps it wasn't the best spot to be during an air raid! Luckily, for both the architecture and the inhabitants, this quaint London corner, built in the 1730s, survived the German bombs.

Back on the street, Lock & Company Hatters is next, founded in 1676 and the oldest building along this stretch; it was *the* place to buy a top hat, bowler, or homburg during the 1930s and 1940s, when gentlemen still wore hats—King George VI himself was a customer. Next is John Lobb, Bootmakers, makers of fine footwear for royal and other feet for over 150 years.

Cross St. James's Street at the Belisha beacon; in a moment we'll head down St. James's Place, but first a slight detour past another clutch of men's clubs, including some of the oldest and most famous in London. At

War Words: Shelters

Two types of family shelters protected Londoners during World War II, both named after the war cabinet officials who spearheaded their development and use.

The **ANDERSON SHELTER**, somewhat similar to a small metal Quonset hut, was to be bolted together by the householder and sunk well into the ground in the garden—if there were a garden. Even Londoners with space, tools, and energy to erect one found it cramped, damp, even downright wet at times, and not particularly inviting. The Anderson shelter, named after Home Secretary John Anderson, could survive all but a direct hit, though, and many a homeowner was willing to endure the shelter's deficiencies in favor of its protection. Over 2,225,000 were distributed free to homeowners early in the war and were used by about 27% of those who chose to take shelter.

The **MORRISON SHELTER**, introduced later in the war for indoor use, looked like a cross between a very short cage and a very short table. In fact, many homeowners used it as a table when not sheltering under it. Imagine a double bed-sized structure, with stout legs a little over two and a half feet high, then add sturdy wire mesh wrapped from leg to leg. This contraption, named after Minister of Home Security Herbert Morrison, *did* provide protection from bombs and—especially—falling debris.

Both types of shelters were distinctly uncomfortable and claustrophobic. Late at night, hearing the sirens' rising moan, many Londoners would sleepily debate the pros and cons of leaving their warm beds and heading downstairs for the Morrison, or worse, trooping across the garden to the Anderson.

Then...

69 St. James's Street, near the southwestern corner of St. James's Place, stands the new quarters of the Carlton Club—refugees after being bombed out of their Pall Mall home, they settled here. Continue a short block to Park Place, a street that mystery writer Agatha Christie lived on early in the war. The basement dining room of the undistinguished-looking **Pratt's Club** (Number 14), provided an illusion of security during the Blitz and was a favorite stop of young Guards officers returning from leave. Further down Park Place is the St James Club (at Number 7, and no, there's no period in St). It's now a posh residential club/hotel, open to nonmembers. A quick peek inside suggests all the sturdy elegance of London's private clubs. The Royal Overseas League at the end of the street served as a wartime hostel for British Air Force officers.

Back on St. James's Street, on the northern corner of Park Place stands **Brooks**, an elegant blue-doored brick building with no indication of street number or occupants—if you're a member, you'll know where you're going. Across the street is **Boodle's** (Number 28), serenely here for over 200 years behind white columns, black iron fence, and wooden shuttered bow windows. It's a social, not political, club—the aforementioned London guidebook classified Boodle's prewar membership as "country gentlemen." English actor David Niven was a wartime member, and stopped by soon after a 1944 bomb demolished the back of the building. Niven found most of Boodle's windows boarded over and the interior very dark. One of the dining room staff, at least, was far more concerned about wartime food restrictions and substitutions, lamenting to Niven, "My members don't take to whale steaks at all." Another war-era member

...and now.

of Boodle's was Ian Fleming, who often lunched here, whale steaks and all. Careful readers of Fleming's James Bond stories may discern that M's club, Blades, is modeled on Boodle's.

A block ahead on the east side and almost at Piccadilly is **White's** (Number 37), the oldest (1693) London gentlemen's club of all. Wartime members included the irascible Randolph Churchill and the equally difficult Evelyn Waugh, both habitués of the club's bar and gaming room. We'll be back at this corner in a bit if you want to wait to look more closely at the building's exterior.

Enough clubs. Retrace your steps down St. James's Street to quieter St. James's Place, away from Clubland and traffic. This single lane seems to dead-end at a stark modern building, constructed after the war on a site obliterated by German bombs. But keep walking; near the end and slightly to the left is **Spencer House,** on a set-back block of fancy iron-

> The St. James's' Lyre and Piccadilly Gazette, *a mimeographed news-letter for shelterers,* noted some depressing food developments: *"St. James's, April 1941: Bananas, onions, oranges, and cheese unobtainable."*

work, torch snuffers, and intricate streetside lamps. Spencer House is London's finest surviving eighteenth-century private residence, built in the 1760s for the first Earl Spencer, an ancestor of Diana, Princess of Wales.

As with other London mansions, the between-war years meant a desperate struggle to keep Spencer House in the family as costs escalated. Lord Spencer finally sublet the building to the Ladies' Army and Navy Club in the mid-1920s. Just before the Ladies moved in, Spencer removed all the building's furniture and artwork to Althorp, the family home, then returned at the onset of the Blitz to take everything else: mahogany doors and door cases, marble chimney pieces, baseboards, woodwork, and more. On one hand, the image of stripping a building is disturbing; on the other, the possibility of losing all that splendor to a German bomb is equally unsettling. And the bombs did come, gutting buildings to either side. The windows of Spencer House were blasted out, plasterwork shaken from the walls as ceilings sagged and threatened to collapse, the façade blackened from smoke, and the top floor badly burned by incendiaries. The Ladies having left mid-war, slapdash repairs made it possible to temporarily turn the building over to the National Nursing Agency for the remainder of the war.

> During the inter-war years, it could cost as much as £20,000 a year to maintain a London mansion.

Once hostilities ended, Lord Spencer set about seeking long-term tenants, eventually discovered just blocks away. Christie's Auction House, burned out of their premises on King Street, found Spencer House a convenient location once it was spruced up a bit. Christie's stayed for several years, using the Great Room and Lady Spencer's Dressing Room for displays and the Dining Room for auction sales. For a look inside, plus details on the painstaking restoration, stop by for the guided tour.

> **VISITOR DETAILS:** Spencer House is open Sunday 10:30am to 5:30pm; closed August and January. Admission (by timed ticket) is charged; guided tour. No children under 10. Restrooms in the basement. More information: 020 7499 8620, www.spencer house.co.uk.

From Spencer House, walk straight ahead down the jog of St. James's Place toward the Stafford Hotel, on your right and exactly where it was in the war years. Past it on the opposite side is 21 St. James's Place, the site of Henry "Chips" Channon's home before he moved to Belgravia, where we'll meet him again. American Channon came to London, married money, won a Parliament seat, kept a detailed diary of the capital's political and social scenes, and gossiped and partied his way through prewar and wartime London. He strolled along St. James's Place mid-war, lamenting that Number 21 had been leveled: "All that remains is rubble, some remnants of the basement, and a few daffodils which I myself planted in the once so charming garden." John Colville, Churchill private secretary, walked here too, finding "the whole street of charming houses is laid waste." Well, not everything—but Number 21 was certainly gone. To get an idea of what was destroyed, check out Number 20.

Exit via the narrow covered passage across from the Stafford Hotel, about where Channon's daffodils must have been. Head down it to the Queen's Walk, Green Park's eastern boundary.

A Wartime Cuppa

During the war, the English were simply awash with tea. It was the standard palliative for anxious moments as the warning sirens went off and the usual restorative as the All Clear sounded. Some householders were even known to desert their damp garden shelters mid-raid to slip back into the house to brew a quick cuppa. And on the post-raid scene, the canteen wagons of the volunteer services offered tea to excavation workers, ambulance drivers, air raid wardens, dusty survivors, and curious passersby.

...the tea ration hits the English hardest of all the restrictions. Tea, even stewed so that it tastes like nothing at all, is their panacea for all griefs and trials, spiritual and physical.
—I. A. R. Wylie,
Flight to England,
1943

Rationing put a crimp in the national consumption of tea, limiting individuals to two ounces of loose tea a week, a third of the prewar consumption and equivalent to about sixteen of today's teabags (though the teabag itself wasn't introduced to Britain until after the war). The brew was very hot and "strong enough to walk on," and the teapot of choice was usually the squat ceramic Brown Betty.

Visit Twinings on the Strand, a well-stocked tea shop selling over 150 varieties of tea; a tiny tea museum is tucked at the back of the shop. Near the Tower Hill Underground, the Bramah Tea and Coffee Museum offers a social and commercial history of tea (admission charged).

Green Park—unimaginatively but appropriately named—has no flower beds, unlike its well-manicured neighbor, St. James's Park. Unless you visit during spring bulb season, you might think it was nothing but rolling lawns, trees, and office workers eating their lunches. But springtime's daffodils are magical and the park's 900-plus trees are always a delight. We wandered the Buckingham Palace corner in Chapter 2, and the route here visits just the northeast corner, so if you'd like to spend more time in Green Park, come back for an exploratory walk of its fifty-three acres.

VISITOR DETAILS: Green Park is open daily 5am to midnight. During summer, a snack truck parks along the Buckingham Palace side. Restrooms are located near the Green Park Underground.

Linger at the frenetic juncture of Queen's Walk and Piccadilly but briefly, only long enough to locate and read the inscription on the corner wall, noting that the **Ritz Hotel** was inspired by Swiss hotelier César Ritz, designed by

The Ritz.

Charles Mewès and Arthur Davis (at a cost of more than a million pounds), and opened May 25, 1906.

Here's one of the world's most prestigious hotels sitting amidst the tumult of Piccadilly. The chaos was likely a causative factor in the move of the hotel entrance from the elegant walkway to the quiet around the corner. Walk through the Ritz colonnade along Piccadilly, then turn down Arlington Street. The hotel's top-hatted doorman reminds one of the Ritz's century of elegance, even during the war years. It was, of course, a war elegance, with a doorman *and* sandbags at the entrance, utility tablecloths on the dining room tables, and a stylish basement air raid shelter stocked with camp beds. The steel-framed Ritz, like Mayfair's Dorchester Hotel, was considered a safe refuge from wartime blasts. The management closed the hotel's top two floors, assuming bomb damage to the roof would extend no further than two levels. It was a wise move: in October 1940 the hotel's top story *was* struck by a German bomb; though messy, the damage wasn't horrendous. A basement shelter was also established—guests not wanting to use it could still move up the safety scale somewhat by sleeping in the hallways on *chaises longues* set up by management.

And who found the sturdiness of the elegant Ritz so appealing? Society matron Emerald Cunard lived here (before moving on to the Dorchester), as did the exiled Albanian Royal Family headed by King Zog. King George of Greece and King Peter of Yugoslavia stayed briefly, and seemingly everyone in town dined or drank here: Chips Channon, the Churchills (father and son), Evelyn Waugh, Dr. Edward Benes (Czech president and leader of the Czech government-in-exile), Nancy Mitford, American author William Saroyan, Louis Mountbatten, Brendan Bracken, Countess This and Lord That, and countless others, London's society having found an extremely pleasant venue in which to be both safe and seen.

Continue down Arlington past the Jaguars, Mercedes, and taxis pulling up at the Ritz, then turn left onto Bennet Street. Within a block and

> **VISITOR DETAILS:** For a très elegant afternoon tea, the Ritz Hotel's Palm Court is the place. Reservations recommended (you can make them online); spiff up a bit. More information: Call 020 7493 8181 when in London or 877-748-9536 toll-free from the States, www.theritzhotel.co.uk.

across St. James's Street, Bennet becomes **Jermyn Street**. (Pronunciation hint: That's "Jermyn" as in "German.") We were on this corner a while back, surveying the exterior of White's.

This narrow shopping precinct is the home of the bespoke tailor, providing the discriminating gentleman with custom-made suits, shirts, shoes and boots, ties, silk scarves, and gloves. Umbrellas, perfumes, jewelry, fine art, and antiques round out the offerings along this most stylish of shopping boulevards. Jermyn Street was somewhat less so, however, after wartime air raids—essentially, it was a shambles, particularly the western end between Duke and Bury streets, where almost every building was gutted, burned, and blasted. It was here that jazz singer Al Bowlly was killed late one night in April 1941 when his flat was hit by a land mine. That same attack completely destroyed the famous Hamman Turkish Baths and badly damaged the Cavendish Hotel at the next corner (81 Jermyn). The old hotel was the fiefdom of the legendary and eccentric Rosa Lewis, who ran the exclusive hotel with an iron hand and a great deal of idiosyncratic warmth. The new Cavendish Hotel (officially the DeVere Cavendish), a bland tower built in the 1960s, serves afternoon tea in the lounge or, for something stronger—perhaps even legendary—try the Sub Rosa pub downstairs.

> *The Jules Club for American officers was located at 20 Jermyn Street.*

> *For more on Rosa Lewis, eccentric proprietor of the Cavendish Hotel, read Evelyn Waugh's Vile Bodies. The character of Lottie Crump, who runs Shepheards' Hotel in the book, is based on Lewis.*

On the northern side of the street in an area heavily affected by German bombs is the splendidly restored **Piccadilly Arcade**, built in 1910 and today offering arcade shoppers yet more consumer opportunities. Check out the Armoury of St. James's, with hand-painted model soldiers and other figures, including policemen, RAF pilots, Life Guards, and even Mr. Churchill himself.

Walk through the arcade from Jermyn Street to Piccadilly, and turn right toward **Fortnum & Mason** on the corner of Piccadilly and Duke Street, St. James's. This elegant "provision merchant" was established in 1707 by Mr. Fortnum (a grocer) and Mr. Mason (a footman to Queen Anne) and soon became the royal grocers. Clothing and furnishings have been added to the wares offered, but for today's traveler (and picnicker), the ground-floor food hall is still the main draw.

Even during the war, Fortnum & Mason's skills as provisioners proved useful; they sold "active service gift boxes," costing from 10/6 to £3. Each was filled with canned and dried foods, wine, medical supplies, insect powder, cigarettes, and Cox's Orange Pippins—perfect to purchase before you went overseas, or to send to a relative at the front. Here's where members of the Forces could find military uniforms and footwear, plus camp equipment, binoculars, waterproof map cases, shoe cleaning kits, even sleeping bags and Fortnum & Mason's own Service Chocolate.

The building escaped major damage although an April 1941 Luftwaffe visit caused some problems, blocking nearby Jermyn Street with rubble and shattered glass—it was the same evening that Al Bowlly was killed, the nearby Turkish Baths destroyed, and the Cavendish Hotel leveled.

Past Fortnum & Mason on Piccadilly are the bow-fronted windows of Hatchards Booksellers (187 Piccadilly), one of London's best bookshops, and with such clubby ambience you'll think you've entered a Clubland outpost. Check out the excellent travel and map sections plus the wall of biographies with a special section for Churchilliana.

Fortnum & Mason patented an interesting wartime invention, the "Fortknee." It was a short stocking designed to cover the knees and lower thighs of lady drivers in the services. Tight ribbing at either end kept the stocking tube in place.

Princes Arcade is next, beyond Hatchards along Piccadilly, and it's filled with waistcoat makers, jewelers, elegant candy shops, art galleries, and more. A good arcade stop is S. Conway Shirtmakers. They can whip up classic made-to-measure shirts plus braces (suspenders) featuring U.S. and British flags, if you're feeling particularly patriotic.

Retrace your steps, leaving Princes Arcade on Piccadilly and turning right. Less than a half-block ahead is **St. James's, Piccadilly**. A plaque on the brick wall along the pavement notes the church's garden was donated by Viscount Southwood, proprietor of the *Daily Herald*, to commemorate the wartime courage and fortitude of the people of London, suggesting a war-link lies ahead through the iron gates and down the steps.

This parish church was built by Christopher Wren, one of his few efforts outside the City, with a spire added by a local carpenter—it leaned several feet to one side: a leaning tower of London, as it were. An open pulpit, with a stone canopy overhead, stood in one corner of the churchyard together with the tall brick rectory. Outside, St. James's was "neat and severe," Wren having economized; inside, the church was a single gorgeous room adorned with a vaulted ceiling, a carved marble font, and intricate wood carvings over the altar and around the organ, all by Grinling Gibbons. From the eighteenth century on, St. James's Church was one of the most fashionable places for weddings and baptisms in the West End. As one Londoner rather archly put it, St. James's received "the patronage of the people of quality."

Peace in St. James's Garden.

The plaque on the church's exterior wall notes only that St. James's was damaged by enemy action on October 14, 1940. The *Evening News* more graphically described the attack: "One of Hitler's furious bombs landed in the forecourt, grievously shattering the fabric of the church and demolishing...the rectory." Those furious bombs also killed the verger in his kitchen, wounded his wife, and reduced the open-air pulpit to a pile of debris. The leaning spire disappeared, and the roof was almost completely destroyed. The bell overhead, calling Londoners to worship since 1686, smashed to the floor, its supporting timbers splintered and pulverized. St. James's Church was a charred, blitzed skeleton. The October 1940 attack was just one of several raids that slammed about St. James's. Another in April 1941 left a large crater in the middle of Piccadilly in front of the church and splashed heavy debris onto both St. James's and the churchyard.

> *St. James's flagstoned churchyard, a burial ground until 1852, nowadays hosts a small market (Tuesday through Saturday).*

Postwar restoration work soon began, helped along by the donation and opening of the garden of remembrance in 1946. The garden, originally part of the churchyard and once covered with tombstones, is now a flower-filled sanctuary. Wander past the social services trailer parked by the stone fountain to discover the hidden statue of Peace.

By 1954, major restoration was completed although the rebuilt spire, straight this time and made of fiberglass, wasn't added until the 1960s. Step inside St. James's to see the result: simple wooden pews, white and gold columns, and the stunning carved altarpiece by master woodcarver Gibbons, back in place after wartime evacuation to Derbyshire. Watch too for the marble plaque honoring

> **VISITOR DETAILS:** St. James's is open daily. Free lunchtime recitals. No eating facilities or restrooms in the church itself. The adjoining café is open Monday–Saturday 8am to 7pm; Sunday 10am to 6pm. Restrooms toward the back of the café (customer use only). More information: 020 7734 4511, www.st-james-piccadilly.org.

choristers who died in the war. Lunchtime concerts here offer an opportunity for a rest, some good music, and a chance to consider this building's wartime experience...and survival.

Exit via the church's (or café's) back door and cross Jermyn Street. Straight ahead is **St. James's Square**, built in the 1670s. King William III rides in the center of the garden, a bronze statue by John Bacon erected almost 200 years ago and moved to wartime safety at Berkhampstead Castle. Garden allotments, planted around the empty plinth, soon filled with cabbages and other vegetables.

This square was once given over completely to town houses of the well-to-do, then gentlemen's clubs moved in, and then business offices. After that, it was the U.S. military—most visitors to St. James's Square are vaguely aware that General Eisenhower had his headquarters here, but few realize that there are several other important war-era connections.

As you enter the square, turning left from Duke of York Street, Number 4, the **Astor home** is straight ahead, once home to millionaire William Waldorf Astor II and his American wife Nancy from 1912 to 1942. Lady Astor had been a society hostess in the century's early years, but when her husband moved from the Commons to the House of Lords after the death of his father, she decided to enter politics. She was elected in 1919 representing Plymouth and became the first woman to sit in Parliament; she remained an MP until 1945, through six general elections. Lady Astor's reputation was as a strong-willed, impatient, outspoken, somewhat naïve, conservative-leaning politician and a strong supporter of the Temperance Movement. She seemed to particularly annoy Winston Churchill, and several apocryphal anecdotes have long circulated, generally featuring acerbity on her part and wit on his. One of the best-known exchanges has Lady Astor saying, "Winston, if I were married to you, I'd put poison in your coffee," and Churchill replying, "Nancy, if I were married to you, I'd drink it."

The United States of America recognizes the selfless service and manifold contributions of General Dwight David Eisenhower, Supreme Allied Commander, 1944-1945. At this site, General Eisenhower, on behalf of freedom loving peoples throughout the World, directed the Allied Expeditionary Forces against Fortress Europe, 6 June 1944.

This plaque was dedicated by a United States Department of Defense delegation and the Eisenhower family on 4 June 1990 during the Centennial year of his birth and the 46th Anniversary of Operation OVERLORD.

The Astors entertained often, and guests as disparate as Gandhi, Sean O'Casey, and Charles Lindbergh walked up the steps of 4 St. James's Square. Joachim von Ribbentrop was a luncheon guest here in 1936, right before he was named German ambassador to Britain. The occasion did not go particularly well, however, especially when the forthright Nancy Astor asked to hear more about Hitler, "although I must warn you that anyone with a Charlie Chaplin moustache is never going to be taken seriously by the British public." Stunned into silence, von Ribbentrop excused himself soon after.

The Astor's country home, Cliveden (pronunciation hint: "CLIVED-in," to rhyme with "LIVED-in"), was the prewar scene for frequent gatherings of a gaggle of well-heeled appeasement-minded guests, giving rise to the damning phrase, "the Cliveden set." In truth, many of the appeasers in the bunch reversed their opinions once war broke out.

The Naval and Military Club recently moved into the Astor's former home. At their previous headquarters on Piccadilly, the club had erected pillars at either end of the entrance drive clearly marked "In" and "Out" to insure that vehicles entered and exited safely, and in fact the club came to be commonly known as the "In and Out Club." Rather cleverly, the pillars on either side of the club's entranceway in St. James's Square are similarly painted.

Turn right and continue around the square. Number 31 rates two plaques, both providing background on the wartime importance of **Norfolk House**. The first notes that American General Dwight Eisenhower formed the Allied Force Headquarters (1942) here, then planned and launched Operation Torch, the campaign for the liberation of North Africa. Early in 1944, Eisenhower also planned and launched Operation Overlord from this location, the D-Day invasion that led to the liberation of northwest Europe. The present Norfolk House is a brick-and-stone neo-Georgian edifice built in the late 1930s and replacing the original Norfolk House, the first building constructed in St. James's Square.

Popular wartime reading included novels by Anthony Trollope, Jane Austen, Charlotte M. Yonge, and James Hadley Chase's thriller No Orchids for Miss Blandish.

Continue toward Number 20 where Queen Elizabeth, the Queen Mother, lived from 1906 to 1920. The building was damaged by wartime oil bombs but has been well-restored. Numbers 17 and 16 were the wartime home of the East India and Sports Club, though the officers of the Canadian Army also used it as a service club. After the war, the club amalgamated with two others, becoming the East India, Devonshire, Sports, and Public Schools Club, a name that doesn't quite trip off the tongue like "Boodle's" or "Brooks."

Number 14 houses the **London Library**, a private subscription library founded by author Thomas Carlyle in 1841 after an unpleasantly lengthy bibliographic wait for requested books at the British Museum. Over 400,000 volumes were on the shelves when war broke out, in what

Text continued on page 112.

Public Shelters

By war's end, most Londoners had sheltered from German bombs in dozens of locations: at home under a table wedged beneath the stairs with sofa cushions piled about, or down a damp cellar, or under a Morrison "table" shelter, or in the garden's Anderson shelter.

Out in the world, public sheltering possibilities included the informal and not particularly safe: under one's desk at work, in doorways and down covered passageways, or beneath railway arches.

More organized though still not particularly safe possibilities included slit trenches in the parks or communal surface shelters. Hundreds of these long rectangular brick buildings, topped with concrete slabs, were erected in the middle of London streets, each holding about fifty people. Unfortunately the building specifications were incorrect (not enough cement mixed in with the lime and sand mortar), and the shelters were notoriously shaky and apt to collapse. Add in their dankness, darkness, and general smelliness, and  few Londoners rushed to use surface shelters when the sirens sounded. For an idea of what they were like (minus the damp and smell), your Blitz Experience at the Imperial War Museum begins with a few moments in a communal shelter.

Another possibility was semi-private shelters: perhaps Mrs. Birch down the street had cleared out that storage space next to the coal bin, in the vault half under the street, and she and her neighbors and anyone else passing by would hurry down the steps when sirens warned of approaching bombers. Signs for this type of shelter can still be seen today—see "Wartime Shelter Signspotting" elsewhere in this chapter.

Larger stores provided public shelters in their basements, and shoppers (and others) would line up for hours waiting to get in. But the public shelter of choice for many was along the train platforms of the Tube, as deep underground as possible.

Government authorities early on made several misjudgments about the anticipated aerial attacks—they expected brief but very intense day raids and not nightlong raids, they feared encouraging a "deep shelter mentality," and they assumed no one would need to or want to crowd together for warmth and comfort. Worse, organization and efficiency got mixed up with policy and politics, and the goal of saving civilian lives became mired in arguments about morale, psychological effects, practicality, shortages of labor and materials, and so on.

The people just lined up for Tube tickets, sometimes long before the sirens sounded. They brought their rolls of bedding, tea and snacks, perhaps a deck of cards or a magazine, and settled in alongside the train platforms. Seventy-nine of the Underground stations in daily use served as evening shelters. Later in the war, several unused Underground stations and track extensions were also put into use. Pictures of jolly Londoners (or sleeping ones) under station signs reading "Elephant & Castle" or "Piccadilly" are one of the most enduring of homefront images.

Artist Henry Moore ensured that the image of the Tube-sheltering Londoner would persist. His haunting sketches of sleeping cocoon-like shelterers are considered to be some of the most profoundly symbolic images to have emerged from the war.

Despite the urban myth that the Underground stations were safe, many were not. Six hundred shelterers died at the Balham station when blast, crowding, and flooding combined, and closer to central London, a tremendous explosion in the intersection in front of the Royal Exchange killed over a hundred Londoners sheltering below in the Bank station. And despite the perception that practically all London was huddled below ground, only about 2 to 4 percent of sheltering Londoners consistently used the Underground stations.

> *The sleepers lie packed together making a continuous layer of bodies from one end of the platform to the other. They sleep in a blaze of lights and their coloured blankets and patchwork quilts, their sandwiches and mouth-organs, give almost a Bank Holiday atmosphere.*
> —Louis MacNeice, "London Letter," 1941

Some Tube shelters started out—and stayed—totally formless, with no leadership and hence no recreational, medical, or social services or amenities (the overflowing bucket serving as a loo for hundreds appears in many shelter accounts). Other shelters soon had volunteer marshals organizing songfests, lectures, and contests; ensuring sanitation; allocating spaces in newly built bunks; and promoting a communal togetherness that—much more than that overflowing bucket—is the image that has persisted for many Londoners.

one London guidebook lauded as that "invaluable institution to literary workers and lovers of books."

The war years for the library meant evacuating irreplaceable materials to the countryside, instituting a staff schedule of firewatchers outfitted with stirrup pumps and buckets of water, covering windows with sticky criss-crossed tape to reduce flying glass in the event of blast, and then waiting. In February 1944, a 500-lb. high explosive bomb fell directly on the library's west wing, ripping off the back of the building and part of the roof and twisting the steel girders of the book stacks. The façade facing St. James's Square was hardly marked but behind the front door lay a quagmire of torn volumes, broken glass, crumpled shelves, and rubble. Over 16,000 books were destroyed despite the desperate efforts of author Rose Macaulay, architectural historian James Lees-Milne, and others who scrambled amidst the distorted steel, attempting to rescue volumes on shelves hanging out in the air above the bomb crater. The bust of founder Thomas Carlyle lay on the floor, decapitated. The library closed for five months, a notice on the front door reading "Members are Requested not to ask for Books or Return them until Further Notice."

> **VISITOR DETAILS:** The London Library is open only to members. Various temporary membership possibilities are available, however, worthwhile options for dedicated bibliophiles. More information: 020 7766 4720, www.london library.co.uk.

Nearby, Number 11 St. James's Square saw wartime duty as the United Nations Forces Fellowship Club, offering sleeping accommodations to noncommissioned officers and merchant seamen of the Allied Forces for just 2/6 a night (about 50 cents).

Having been once around the square, take a break in the garden amidst the trees and carefully tended flower beds while considering how this garden must have looked decked out with reinforced concrete air raid shelters.

Next, amble eastward out of St. James's Square along Charles II Street. If your heart doesn't beat faster at the heady prospect of re-discovering **Canadian service clubs**, just turn left from Charles II Street onto Regent Street and catch up with us in a few paragraphs at Piccadilly Circus.

> **VISITOR DETAILS:** The gardens of St. James's Square are open Monday–Friday 10am to 4:30pm.

Number 1 Regent Street housed offices of the Canadian Army Medical Corps and the British Columbia Services Club, a welcome stop for Canadians on leave in London. Today the building is British Columbia House, home to the British Columbia government in London and to the

Piccadilly Circus in wartime.

Britain Visitor Centre. The Knights of Columbus managed another wartime service club at 11A Regent Street.

Across Regent Street at 13 Charles II Street was Ontario House, the London offices of the Canadian province of Ontario. The Canadians leased the building in 1944, knowing that it lacked windows, electricity, plumbing, and telephones, but also fully aware that it possessed a hundred-bed emergency air raid shelter. This proved an appealing bonus, given the harassing bombs of the Little Blitz of 1944 and the rocket attacks of the war's final months.

Back on Regent Street toward Piccadilly Circus, at the southeastern corner of the Jermyn Street intersection, the Ontario Services Club offered all ranks and services the use of snack bars and lounges, cafeterias, and a check room (a perk today's traveler would enjoy), plus the Canadian Girls' Hostel.

Ahead is the transit hub of **Piccadilly Circus**, filled with taxis and buses, cars and brave bicyclists whirling about, though no longer whirling *around*. Major postwar street modifications moved the Eros fountain to the southern pavement, making this a no-ring circus. During the war the boarded-up monument stood in the middle of circling buses, bicycles, and pedestrians, including many "Piccadilly Warriors" or "Piccadilly Commandos." These were ladies of the night who were often just as evident during the day, a parade of prostitutes enthusiastically plying their trade among the hordes of new customers the war brought to London. (Their open-air counterparts were known as the Hyde Park Rangers.)

The wartime blackout meant that nighttime walking in Piccadilly Circus was difficult indeed, the pavements so dark that the prostitutes car-

Text continued on page 116.

Sculptor and Artist Henry Moore

July 30, 1898: Henry Spencer Moore, son of a coal miner, is born at 30 Roundhill Road in Castleford, Yorkshire. (His early home is demolished in 1974.)

February 1917: Moore arrives in London, spending the night in Chelsea at 38 Oakley Crescent (now Oakley Gardens) before heading off to enlist in the Civil Service Rifles of the 15th London Regiment.

1917–1919: Moore trains in a camp on Wimbledon Common, then is sent to the Western Front. Toward the end of the war he returns to Wimbledon, serving as a specialist in bayonet training.

1919–1924: Moore studies sculpture at Leeds College of Art and later at London's Royal College of Art. He continues his education amidst London's museums: "Not far away I had the National Gallery and British Museum and the Victoria and Albert...."

1929: His first public commission is a relief sculpture symbolizing the West Wind for London Transport headquarters at 55 Broadway, Westminster. One of a series of reliefs on the building, Moore's female wind is located on the northern face of the building's east wing.

July 1929: Moore marries Irina Radetzky at St. John's Church, West Hendon. Moore leaves his bachelor home at 3 Grove Studios, Hammersmith, to move with Irina into a studio at 11A Parkhill Road, Belsize Park, in north London. They will live there until mid-1940.

Early 1930: Moore is named head of the department of sculpture at Chelsea School of Art, remaining until the start of the war when the school is evacuated to Northampton.

September 3, 1939: Moore goes swimming with his wife and a friend by Shakespeare Cliffs at Dover. The day's feelings of apprehension will later be replicated in Moore's "September 3 1939," a disturbing sketch of eight gas-masked bathers standing in blood-red water near ominous cliffs.

Late summer 1940: The Moores move from Parkhill Road to the nearby 7 Mall Studios, recently vacated by artists Ben Nicolson and Barbara Hepworth.

September 1940: Returning home after a night out in the West End, Henry and Irina are stuck on the platform at the Belsize Park Underground during an air raid alert, Moore's first close-up experience with Tube shelterers. "I spent the time looking at the rows of people sleeping on the platforms. I had never seen so many reclining figures, and even the train tunnels seemed to be like the holes in my sculpture." The figures of this subterranean world are the subjects of the Shelter Drawings, two sketchbooks filled with stark images of the blanket-shrouded figures, and several larger drawings. Soon after, Moore is named an Official War Artist, working for the War Artists' Advisory Committee headed by the National Gallery's Sir Kenneth Clark.

Knife Edge: Two Piece near Parliament.

October 1940: The Moores visit friends in Perry Green, Hertfordshire, about twenty miles northeast of London. Driving home they're stopped at a roadblock, and a policeman warns of unexploded bombs, confiding that Moore's studio has been bombed "flat to the ground."

Actually, it was Moore's former studio that had been hit, but the explosion was near enough to make his current studio unusable. The Moores return to Perry Green and within weeks find a home nearby, Hoglands, where Moore will live for the rest of his life. He soon joins the local Home Guard, going out on night duty "patrolling the country lanes twice a week."

1941–1942: Moore travels to the mines of Castleford, Yorkshire, to sketch coal miners, a second commission from the War Artists' Advisory Committee.

September 1943: Moore revisits the London Underground (Holborn Station) for the filming of *Out of Chaos*, a documentary about war artists.

August 1963: Moore is awarded the Order of Merit by the queen at Buckingham Palace.

March 1984: Moore's last commission, *Mother and Child*, is installed in St. Paul's Cathedral.

August 31, 1986: Artist and sculptor Henry Moore dies at Hoglands, aged eighty-eight; he is buried in the nearby churchyard. Several months later, a service of thanksgiving for the life and work of Henry Moore is held in Westminster Abbey.

Piccadilly Circus.

ried flashlights. Lamp standards and street bollards were painted with black-and-white stripes for better visibility, and there were no globes or lights atop the lamp standards—lights couldn't be turned on in the blackout, and it was feared the globes might shatter and fall during air raids. And of course all the illuminated advertisements were not—no "Guinness is good for you," no "Bovril," no "Schweppes Tonic Water" lighting up the night. Piccadilly Circus lights were turned off for the duration and stayed off even after war's end as a fuel economy measure.

American actor Douglas Fairbanks, Jr., called Piccadilly's wartime prostitutes the "ladies of the blackout." And broadcaster Edward R. Murrow thought them the bravest people in London—"They stayed out on the streets in the heaviest raids."

The boarded-up fountain at the center of all this was covered with signs that encouraged "Take up the challenge! Buy National War Bonds" or asked "What can I buy? War Savings, of course!" And atop the monument in the early 1940s? Nothing more than a little boxed-in knob. The beloved aluminum statue had been taken to the safety of the English countryside.

The statue, unveiled here in 1893, was officially meant to represent "The Angel of Christian Charity," but it was almost immediately dubbed Eros. The threat of German bombs meant Eros was evacuated, "taken to a refuge in the country like the other children of London," as the *Times* put it, with an almost audible catch in the editorial voice. Eros returned to his vantage over this busiest of intersections in mid-1947. Remarkably enough, the winged archer could have spent the war safely atop his fountain; no bombs fell on Piccadilly Circus.

Below the frenetic vehicular traffic here lies another busy transit level, the Piccadilly Circus Underground. An entrance is just ahead, at the top of Regent Street. Even if you're not ready for an Underground trip, make a brief detour down the Tube steps to imagine a little of the wartime atmosphere. This station, in the early 1940s the city's largest and busiest with upwards of thirty-two million passengers a year, also sheltered more than 3,000 Londoners on Blitz nights. Imagine lining up outside for hours before being allowed in to claim a cramped spot along a station platform; settling in, perhaps with a thermos of tea and a few sandwiches; unrolling a blanket brought from home; and then trying to sleep, crammed in with hundreds of others, being stepped over by passengers (the Tube didn't stop running until late), and wondering what you would find when you went home in the morning. Those were very long nights.

Early in the war, author Malcolm Muggeridge celebrated the absence of traffic by driving the wrong way around Piccadilly Circus in his camouflaged Austin.

Come up the Tube steps—the same ones you went down a moment ago. Our last stop requires circling back a ways, down the south side to 201 Piccadilly, site of the **Stage Door Canteen**. It opened September 1944 in a former Lyons Café and closed just over two years later, but not before three million Allied troops and dozens of celebrities, government representatives, and various royalty had visited. For some reason, even though a late arrival on the wartime entertainment scene, the Stage Door caught the imagination of many. Anthony Eden formally opened the canteen; Fred Astaire, Bing Crosby, Noël Coward, Hermione Gingold, and Bea Lillie performed here; filmmaker Arthur Rank guaranteed two years of rent payments; the Queen Mother brought young Princess Margaret for a visit; and the Crown Prince of Norway, the Belgian ambassador, and the Polish Foreign Minister all came by. It's now a Boot's drugstore, a far cry from those wartime nights when young soldiers partied and dreamed of home.

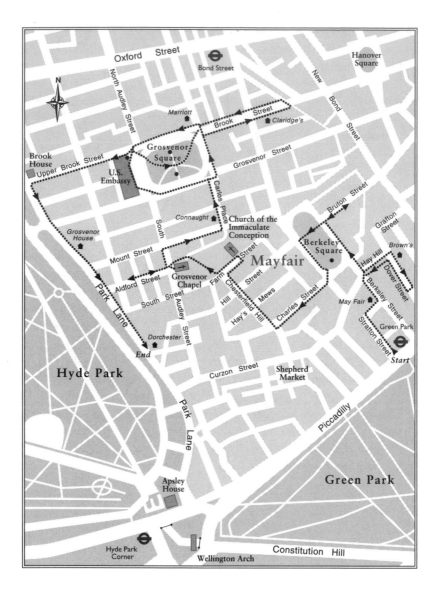

Elegant Mayfair

We walked around [Mayfair] the other night before the raid
began, about 6:30, and it needed a painter to do it justice—the
big houses with windows blown out and torn white curtains still
streaming out, and trees and railings down here and there....

—ACTOR JOHN GIELGUD

Berkeley Square railings go to war.

Highlights: May Fair Hotel, Brown's Hotel, Arts Club, Berkeley Square, Bruton Street, Lansdowne House, Charles Street, Church of the Immaculate Conception, Grosvenor Chapel, Grosvenor Square, Eisenhower statue, FDR statue, American Eagle Squadrons' Memorial, Claridge's Hotel, Brook House, Hyde Park, Park Lane, Grosvenor House Hotel, Dorchester Hotel

Underground Station: Green Park

Photo Ops: Some statue favorites: FDR in Grosvenor Square, and FDR and Churchill on New Bond Street. For less statuesque subjects, watch for the geese of Hyde Park, perhaps descendants of wartime park residents.

BEFORE LEAVING ON YOUR TRIP

■ **Travel scheduling:** If you're in London on the Sunday nearest July 4th or at Thanksgiving, consider attending evening services at the Grosvenor Chapel. The

American priest on the staff celebrates with a service on each of these most American of holidays. The Royal Academy of Art's summer exhibition runs from June to mid-August. And Mayfair's shopping streets are aglow with Christmas lights and displays during the holiday season.

■ **Cultural Preparations:** The romantic ballad from London's homefront, "A Nightingale Sang in Berkeley Square," offers a dreamy touch of enchantment. My favorite rendition is Vera Lynn's, available on her CD *Something to Remember—Wartime Memories*. And for more on the Mitfords, read *The Sisters: The Saga of the Mitford Family*.

■ **Internet Best Bets:** Mayfair's premiere shopping opportunities: Hamleys (www.hamleys.co.uk), John Lewis (www.johnlewis.com), Liberty (www.liberty.co.uk), Selfridges (www.selfridges.co.uk), and Sotheby's (www.sothebys.com).

Mayfair was London's most fashionable district well into the 1920s, home to the town houses of the very rich. Residences here were mansions, each well-staffed with servants and aglow with stylish grace. The très chic Mayfair shops provided Madame an opportunity to select the latest in haute couture, crystal, and fine art. But during the late 1920s and into the 1930s, inevitable changes in taxes, death duties, and the servant supply made the aristocratic lifestyle difficult to maintain. One by one the mansions were sold off, and throughout the inter-war decades, town house elegance was steadily eroded by office block mediocrity.

> By June 1944, 1,650,000 Yanks were stationed in Britain.

The long years of World War II brought two additional changes. Thousands of American servicemen were billeted in Mayfair, parking their Jeeps on the lawns, chewing gum as they leaned against corner lampposts, and engaging the area's prostitutes—the Piccadilly Commandos—in earnest conversation. The influx and influence of American military personnel centered on a Mayfair chapel, a square, an embassy, and a fancy hotel turned mess hall, but every part of this district was affected by the tides of boys in khaki.

And although relatively little bomb damage occurred in Mayfair (certainly when compared to the City or the East End), every street and square and hotel here holds wartime memories: Park Lane with the fashionable Dorchester Hotel on one side, its guests sleeping in the basement shelter, and Hyde Park on the other, its artillery guns blazing away above slit trenches and grazing sheep. Or the narrow lanes of Shepherd Market, where a single wartime bomb obliterated Mayfair's oldest house. And especially Grosvenor Square, bastion of the American presence in England and blasted by German bombs.

Begin at Stratton Street and Piccadilly, near the Green Park Underground exit. Piccadilly is the southern boundary of Mayfair, with Park Lane, Oxford Street, and Regent Street forming the other three sides. Across Stratton Street stands Stratton House, official headquarters during much of the war of both the Polish and Dutch governments-in-exile. Along the right side of the street, a direct hit in a May 1941 bombing demolished many of the buildings, and the blast plus falling chunks of masonry flattened vehicles parked here.

Stratton jogs right at the charming red brick building; at block's end is the **May Fair Hotel**, opened in 1927 by King George V and Queen Mary—note the plaque by the entrance. The hotel's original name (it's now the May Fair Inter-Continental) is a reminder that this fashionable area was named after a rowdy street fair, described in one prewar guidebook as "an annual scene of debauchery suppressed at the end of the eighteenth century." (Think jugglers and puppet shows, tightrope walkers and pickpockets, fire-eaters and eel-divers, with gambling and drunkenness thrown in.) The site for this spectacle was nearby Shepherd Market, where the notorious fair was held annually the first two weeks of May, starting in the late 1680s. It became enough of an event that its name was given to the then-rolling countryside to the west of the City and Westminster. (See "Shepherd Market and Wellington Walk" elsewhere in this chapter.)

Turn left onto Berkeley Street (that's "BARK-lee") heading toward Berkeley Square, although aficionados of the life and times of President Franklin Roosevelt might want to take a short side trip. If so, turn right off Berkeley Street at the light, onto and up Hay Hill to Dover Street. Turn right— that Union Jacked building across the street is the elegant **Brown's Hotel** where FDR and his bride honeymooned in 1905. The Roosevelts also walked and shopped tirelessly in the area, which even then was filled with swanky stores; young Franklin gleefully wrote to his mother in New York that he had purchased thousands of dollars worth of new clothes. The young couple stayed in the Royal Suite at Brown's; the 1905 tariff is lost in the proverbial sands of time, but today the suite would set back newlyweds (or anyone, for that matter) around £840 ($1400) a night.

> *A wartime double room with private bath at the May Fair Hotel would have cost you 32 shillings (about $7). Special terms were available for members of His Majesty's Forces and their families, who also enjoyed nightly dancing (Sundays excepted, of course) to Jack Jackson and His Orchestra in the official air raid shelter–cabaret.*

Brown's was also the London waystation for American aviator Charles Lindbergh and his wife, author Anne Morrow Lindbergh. Lindbergh noted during the 1938 Munich crisis that "people on [the] streets are talking war....There is an A.R.P. gas mask station on Piccadilly, around the corner from our hotel. Makes one think, to see gas masks being fitted in the center of London." Unfortunately for Lindbergh, it did not make him think enough. He is remembered by many as a German-favoring appeaser, although he had excellent taste in hotels. Undoubtedly the Lindberghs (and probably the Roosevelts too) enjoyed afternoon tea at Brown's Hotel, and you may want to do the same.

Down Dover Street at Number 40 is the **Arts Club**. This gentlemen's club, here since 1896, was founded in 1863 to "facilitate the social intercourse of those connected either professionally or as amateurs with art,

Text continued on page 126.

Shepherd Market and Wellington Walk

Shepherd Market is a picturesque jumble of streets in the southwestern corner of Mayfair, just off Piccadilly, although our approach along Curzon Street will add additional wartime nuance. This walk begins just two blocks from the Green Street Underground and ends, several twists and turns later, at the western end of Piccadilly.

From Curzon and Bolton streets, head west along the northern (right) side of Curzon Street. Down Clarges Street, *Stars and Stripes* correspondent Andy Rooney temporarily found a flat, although the risqué activities of a Piccadilly Commando upstairs kept him awake; Rooney soon moved to Bayswater Road. Rentals hereabouts often included wartime perks: two rooms at 13 Clarges Street, for example, came with private bathroom and access to an air raid shelter. Most of the bomb-damaged eighteenth-century houses along the eastern side of the street were subsequently demolished and rebuilt.

> Recreation opportunities at American Red Cross clubs ranged from dancing, movies, and lectures to country rambles, London sightseeing tours, variety shows, "krazy karnivals," bingo, and boxing lessons.

Number 6 Curzon Street is the Washington Hotel, opened in July 1942 by U.S. Ambassador Winant as the Washington Club for American Officers. The hotel had been damaged in the early Blitz and after repairs were completed, it was turned over to the American Red Cross to provide officers with a place for a quick snack (doughnuts, hamburgers, and American coffee), dinner, and a night's rest (2/6 a night or about 50¢).

G. Heywood Hill's bookshop at 10 Curzon Street is a bibliographic oasis. One imagines that the narrow aisles were just as book-filled in the war years when Nancy Mitford worked here. Mitford was one of six Mitford daughters (and one son), children of Lord and Lady Redesdale; each offspring chose a vastly different path in life. Americans may be most familiar with the very left-wing Jessica Mitford, author of *The American Way of Death*. Far to her right was sister Unity, all too enamored with Herr Hitler. Unity's trips to Germany to sit at Hitler's side gained her a certain notoriety in Britain, especially when she attempted suicide soon after war was declared. Somewhat similarly placed along the political spectrum was Diana Mitford, married to British fascist leader Oswald Mosley; the Mosleys spent much of the war in British prisons. Nancy was oldest of the six, and as author and biographer, chose a less politically extreme path than her siblings.

Needing to support herself during the war, Nancy worked at G. Heywood Hill's, a Mayfair magnet for writers, booklovers, and intellectuals. Author Evelyn Waugh thought the bookshop "the one centre of old world gossip," and wartime book buyers (and gossips) Noël Coward, Lady Cunard, Cyril Connolly, Cecil Beaton, Chips Channon, and Edith Sitwell would have been seen here frequently. Then as now the stock in this very precious bibliographic haven focused on gardening, decorating, architecture, and the like. A plaque outside commemorates Mitford's bookshop service. (The shop was located at 17 Curzon Street until 1943, then at Number 10; Nancy Mitford worked at both locations.)

Next along the same side of Curzon Street, across Queen Street, is the cream-

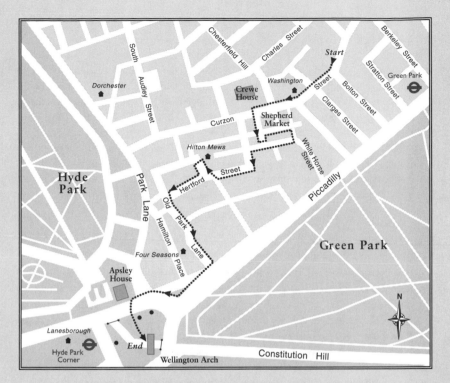

colored Crewe House, where Winston Churchill first met Clementine Hozier. The meeting did not go well. The normally voluble Churchill spoke not a word, but luckily the two would meet, more successfully, three years later. You'll know the Crewe House by its front lawn, an unusual feature in a neighborhood whose seventeenth-

The war years saw the usual upmarket businesses along Curzon Street: court dressmakers, estate agents, architects, and ladies' hatters.

and eighteenth-century homes and their lawns have been much redeveloped. Nancy Mitford served on firewatching detail on the roof of Crewe House, spending a night here every ten days on the look-out for incendiary bombs. The building now houses the Saudi Royal Embassy.

Crewe House was built by Edward Shepherd, who laid out the alleys and byways in this Mayfair corner in the 1730s, including Curzon Street. As it winds and turns across Mayfair, the street has a charming Georgian feel, a trifle more formal than the raffish atmosphere of nearby Shepherd Market. Several Curzon Street businesses have been part of this neighborhood for over a century, including George F. Trumper, gentlemen's hairdresser and perfumer.

Cross Curzon Street and enter Shepherd Market at Trebeck Street. Before turning down Shepherd Market (the street), check out the plaque—high up on the wall, mid-block on Trebeck past Shepherd Market—marking the original site of the historic May Fair. Then head down narrow Shepherd Market Street; it ends in a plaza-like area where it joins White Horse Street. Ye Grapes looms up to the left, a public house here since well before the war.

The brick market building across from Ye Grapes, with "Shepherd Market" carved overhead, reminds all that this is not *Shepherd's* Market. Turn west along Shepherd Street, passing the left side of the market building. Ahead, be prepared to yield to the inevitable desire to window-shop and wander; this maze of narrow streets and intriguing stores (and bistros and pubs) is perfect for dallying.

Shepherds Tavern comes up next, a "rather superior public house" in the words of one wartime resident, and another local pub slaking wartime thirsts. It was a favorite London rendezvous for Battle of Britain pilots, and after the Americans arrived, they too frequented it. If a wartime thirst overcomes you (or wartime hunger—food is served), step inside this mahogany and brass refuge and take a break.

Turn left down Hertford Street, which soon takes a jog to the right. Up Stanhope Row, the Hilton Mews Hotel sports a plaque marking an ending, not a beginning—the wartime loss of a simple archway and cottage. In fact, "The Cottage" was Mayfair's oldest house, circa 1618, "from where a shepherd tended his flock whilst Tyburn idled nearby." (Tyburn was not a lazy co-shepherd but rather the Tyburn River.) Destroyed in that same 1940 attack were a dozen small shops at the heart of this neighborhood: a greengrocer, butcher, fishmonger, two pubs and an oil and candle store.

Continue westward along Hertford Street as it drifts beyond the unofficial boundaries of Shepherd Market and back into the posh avenues of Mayfair. At the small tree-filled roundabout near Park Lane, take either Old Park Lane or Hamilton Place to Piccadilly.

Once there, watch for subway access to Apsley House and the Wellington Arch. Nearby, the two royal princesses once lived at 145 Piccadilly in a Victorian mansion standing east of Apsley House. The nine reception rooms and twenty bedrooms of Number 145 are gone now, bombed in 1940 by German aircraft. (The royal princesses and their parents had moved from Number 145 to the nearby palace late in the 1930s.) The site is now partially under the Four Seasons/Hotel Inter-Continental nexus.

Apsley House, home to the Duke of Wellington, is on the far side of Park Lane on a traffic-bound island. This is "Number 1, London," built in the 1770s, and filled with paintings of the Goya, Rubens, and Velásques ilk, and an eleven-foot-high statue of Napoleon (learn more than you want to know about Mr. Napoleon), plus some impressive table services. In a direct hit, wartime bombs next door damaged the façade of Apsley House, but the priceless contents went untouched. After this close call, many treasures were taken out of the big city to safety, although a mid-1943 photo on display shows furniture carefully covered but much of the art still on the walls and the oversize mirrors untaped or otherwise protected. Perhaps it was just the stunning table service that was evacuated.

Apsley House.

Descend to the convoluted but convenient subway, this time to cross to the neoclassical Wellington Arch (1828). The viewing platforms (Vertigo Alert: very secure, with high walls) offer impressive views of Piccadilly, Green Park, and Hyde Park, plus a close-up look at the bronze *Quadriga of Peace* sculpture overhead, added to the arch in 1912. An air raid siren was located between the chariot wheels during the war. The arch itself served as a police station from the 1830s into the 1950s.

Wellington Arch.

After visiting Wellington Arch, check out the other memorials marooned on this same green island, especially the massive Royal Artillery Memorial on the western side. Erected in 1925 (when memorials could be poignant and heartrending, as the figures on this one are), it commemorates the artillery gunners who died in World War I. The huge flat bronze plaques were added in 1949 to honor artillery soldiers of World War II.

Beyond the memorial, across the street, is the wartime site of St. George's Hospital, now the fashionable Lanesborough Hotel. In mid-1944, American author Ernest Hemingway ended up in St. George's after the car he was in lost a battle with a Fire Service static water tank in Lowndes Square in Knightsbridge. He was discharged shortly before two of Hitler's flying bombs hit the hospital, causing extensive damage. The hospital became a hotel in the 1980s.

Having walked from the 1700s through the early 1940s, now its down into the subway once more to choose your next destination; the Hyde Park Underground and bus stops are nearby for routes down Piccadilly, up Park Lane, over to Knightsbridge, or off to Victoria.

The howitzer barrel of the Royal Artillery Memorial points in the direction of the Somme in France, where many of the World War I soldiers memorialized here died in combat.

literature, and science." In September 1940 the rear of the building received a direct hit from a Nazi bomb, shredding much of the structure and leaving only the front rooms and the beautiful staircase standing. Staff sheltering in the wine cellar survived; unfortunately several staff members did not make it to the shelter in time. Note the stone plaque near the entrance.

Retrace your steps back along Dover and down Hay Hill toward Berkeley Street. American General Raymond Lee, walking near here one October 1940 evening, was reminded of how quickly a quiet Mayfair street could be transformed into a war zone. As he strolled along Hay Hill, he heard "the paralyzing swish of a bomb down the street." The bomb, exploding, splashed fragments onto the street and bounced steel pieces off the roof slates. General Lee was quite happy to escape the perilous Mayfair streets and retreat to his suite at Claridge's Hotel.

If you need a rest stop, head for the block-long shopping area at the bottom of Hay Hill and across Berkeley Street. Lansdowne Row provides a pleasant break, particularly on a sunny day, and features a Starbucks at either end if you can't go more than a block without a latte.

The nightingale of Berkeley Square originally appeared in Michael Arlen's short (and sad) story, "When the Nightingale Sang in Berkeley Square," published in 1923.

Even before the war, Berkeley Street saw great changes, an urban transformation viewed differently depending on one's feelings about architectural preservation. For this stretch, at least, the London *Times* came down firmly in favor of the renewal that modernization heralded: Berkeley Street in 1930 "has been converted in recent years from a rather plain and inadequately utilized frontage to a street of spacious and elegant showrooms." Unfortunately the price was the demolition of much irreplaceable Georgian-era architecture. And the *Times* would eventually regret this "orgy of destruction" among the historic buildings of London. Perhaps the lesson is that bombs alone do not remake the face of a metropolis.

Assuming one latte was enough, enter **Berkeley Square** at the corner near Hay Hill. The safest route is to cross at the light and start up the eastern, outside sidewalk. This area was once the center of Mayfair's world of aristocracy, fashion, and frivolity. A 1930 guidebook considered the square, "from the society point of view, the *crème de la crème*

Wartime Sounds

London's big city sounds are so expected as to be almost unheard: jets overhead bound for Gatwick or Heathrow, the constant hum of vehicles, a blaring horn or two. Wartime brought dozens of new sounds, very different from today's streetscape.

First, of course, were the sirens, two different wailings: the warbling, rising signal of warning and the more steady All Clear signal indicating "danger passed."

German airplane engines had a very recognizable desynchronized throb. Poet Louis MacNeice thought the uneven droning sounded like being "inside a mad beehive," Barbara Pym called it a "sinister purring sound," Graham Greene heard a repeated "Where are you? Where are you?"

Loudest and most frightening were the bombs, whining howling swishing sounds. Some Londoners even learned to differentiate the sounds of a 1,000-lb. bomb from a 500-lb. one. Incendiary bombs came with a rushing hiss, then a clattering on rooftops and pavements. And the anti-aircraft guns added a frightful baritone pom-pom-pom; journalist Ernie Pyle thought they sounded like thunder in a violent electrical storm. Falling shrapnel from the anti-aircraft guns contributed its own tinny sound, a pinging shower of steel fragments pattering down like rain. And was that the rat-a-tat of a German machine gun as a Luftwaffe pilot zoomed down the Mall?

There were whistles bleating, blown by vigilant police and air raid wardens. Clanging fire trucks. The howling of dogs, their ears aching from the sirens. Shouted voices, hurried footsteps. Worse, after the whistling screeching bombs came the bump and crump of the explosions, the ripping of roofs and beams and walls, the tinkling glass, the dripping water, the silence.

of residential London," but even then changes were beginning. At least twenty of the Georgian town houses built along the eastern side in the 1730s were demolished two hundred years later for the new Berkeley Square House, an immense block of shops and offices still despised by some ("a monstrosity in brown brick"). The wartime Special Operations Executive, the British government's sabotage and subversive section, was briefly housed here, and the Air Ministry took over the top floors. Enemy action (i.e., bombs) caused minor damage—the building is so huge it would have been hard to miss it—but all is now repaired. Today the lumbering structure contains offices above street-level banks and shops.

Continue along the east side of the square, then turn down **Bruton Street**, passing a wing of Berkeley Square House. Its construction neces-

Eleanor Roosevelt

1899–1902: Young Eleanor attends Allenswood School on London's outskirts near Wimbledon Common.

1905: Eleanor and Franklin Roosevelt honeymoon at Brown's Hotel, Mayfair. The newlyweds dine at the Carlton Hotel (at Haymarket and Pall Mall; destroyed in the war) and walk a great deal in the area.

October 23, 1942: Mrs. Roosevelt begins a tour of England, arriving at Paddington Station where she is met by King George and Queen Elizabeth. At Buckingham Palace the queen shows where a bomb had dropped "right through the king's rooms, destroying both his rooms and hers." Mrs. Roosevelt also notices "a plainly marked black line in my bathtub above which I was not supposed to run the water."

October 24, 1942: Mrs. Roosevelt and the queen view the destruction in the City, including the Guildhall and St. Paul's ("so that I could stand on the steps and see what modern warfare could do to a great city"). After Mrs. Roosevelt's press conference at the American Embassy in Grosvenor Square, she visits the Washington Club in Mayfair. The rest of her stay is spent visiting American soldiers and British war factories, though she finds time to attend a dinner party in her honor at 10 Downing Street.

April 12, 1948: Mrs. Roosevelt returns to London to unveil the statue of President Roosevelt in Grosvenor Square, Mayfair.

November 12, 1948: Mrs. Roosevelt unveils a marble plaque just inside the west door of Westminster Abbey honoring her husband, "A faithful friend of freedom and of Britain."

The king and queen greet their wartime guest.

sitated the demolition of 17 Bruton Street, the London residence of the Earl of Strathmore. His daughter had given birth here in 1926, and that event is so noted with a tablet high up on the wall in the approximate area where Number 17 once stood: "This plaque was dedicated in the Silver Jubilee Year of Her Reign to Her Majesty The Queen who was born here on April 21st 1926."

At 24 Bruton Street society hostess Sybil Cole-fax started an interior decorating business in the mid-1930s, then joined with John Fowler in the carriage-trade firm of Colefax and Fowler. They remained here for much of the war (undoubtedly a slow time for interior decorating), re-locating to Brook Street in 1944. The indefatigable Mrs. Colefax hosted small gatherings at her diminutive home in Westminster and entertained larger groups at the Dorchester Hotel, plus found time to serve with the Women's Voluntary Services in Belgravia.

> *Wartime shopping along Bruton Street offered much the same possibilities as today— sporting tailors, court dressmakers, couturiers, antique shops, furriers, and art galleries.*

The northern side of Berkeley Square offers little of note other than the plaque outside Number 27 commemorating the building's use during World War I as a hospital for British sick and wounded. You may want to just view it from afar and cut through the gardens to the west side.

Several older residences have been preserved near the southwestern corner. Check out the stylish Georgian details—fanlights, ironwork and stone balconies, and torch snuffers. Number 44 houses the private Clermont Club, perhaps the most exclusive gambling club in the country. That odd greenish affair to the left leads downstairs to Annabel's, a members-only club frequented by royals and film stars.

Number 45 was once the home of Robert Clive, the soldier/administrator who brought India into the Empire. You may remember seeing a statue of Clive near the Cabinet War Rooms; legend has it that you might also see him wandering near Number 45—he reputedly committed suicide here and his ghost has since been sighted. A plaque notes the illustrious former resident (Clive, not his ghost).

Nineteenth-century Tory politician and prime minister George Canning lived at Number 50, but more interesting is the current tenant, Maggs Antiquarian Booksellers. They settled here mid-war after being bombed out of their previous quarters, and narrowly missed being bombed out again; the house next to Number 50 was gutted by a German explosive. Maggs has a fine collection of maps, militaria, and travel books—but think first editions, rare and antiquarian, not Fodor's or Frommer's.

Last to be developed was the square's southern side. The original mansion here, designed by eighteenth-century architect Robert Adam, stretched across the area that's now Fitzmaurice Place. Over time the building was truncated and abridged in various ways—the drawing room ended up in Philadelphia's Museum of Art and the dining room in New York's Metropolitan Museum. In the years just before the war, the original building was set back forty feet, Fitzmaurice Place opened, and **Lansdowne House**, a large block of modern flats, was constructed—flats that were, in turn, replaced in the mid-1980s by the present building.

Wartime residents of Lansdowne House included American journalists Mary Welsh and Quentin Reynolds. Welsh had been living in distant Chelsea but found the daily trek to and from her Soho offices too arduous. In mid-September 1940 she rented a luxurious furnished flat on the seventh floor of Lansdowne House. On her first night here, a bomb exploded on the far side of Berkeley Square while she and Reynolds dined in the basement restaurant, shattering windows across the front of the building. Just a week later, as Lansdowne House shuddered from nearby explosive bombs, residents were warned of an additional threat—falling incendiary bombs. Welsh joined Reynolds and other colleagues "tossing sandbags on firebombs, the half-meter-long tubes hissing white-hot fire from one end. A whole clutch of the bombs had fallen on Berkeley Square as well as into our building and on surrounding roofs, and while we worked to save our grass and trees, the local fire brigade went after the more inaccessible sparklers."

Berkeley Square's gazebo is actually a pump house. The marble nymph with her pitcher-fountain is the work of Victorian sculptor Alexander Munro.

As wartime bombing continued, flats toward the top floors—as with many other higher-up flats in the West End—became far less desirable and therefore rented for much less. The frugal Welsh (and gutsy—she later married Ernest Hemingway) moved from the seventh floor to the top floor, paying one-third of her original rent. She and a friend lived there in early 1941, "in the chill English spring without windows or any prospect of getting them and the concomitant necessity of keeping our house lights very low in case a breeze ruffled the heavy window draperies and so allowed light to shine out." She was not at all upset when the Lansdowne House management notified tenants that the government needed the building for offices and it was time to move.

Spend a few moments in Berkeley Square's central garden, either for a leisurely end-to-end walk or a contemplative rest on one of the park benches. For those finding the "new" buildings here too modern, the garden's towering plane trees (the oldest planted over 200 years ago) provide some arboreal camouflage. However, they offer very little refuge for nightingales, who generally prefer lowland woods, tangled hedges, and moist thickets. Nevertheless, the song "A Nightingale Sang in Berkeley Square" will always be connected with this area, and many an American GI and his new English girlfriend captured some of Mayfair's romantic magic here.

As with other London squares, the railings of this once-private garden were dismantled and recycled early in the war, opening the lawns to overuse from tromping feet. "Who would ever have expected to see the cared-for emerald green of Berkeley Square emulate the Sahara in its sandy aridity, with trenches running through it and soldiers drilling there," wrote one wartime resident. An air raid shelter was constructed under the garden area and a steel water tank at the southeastern corner provided quick access to water for firefighting, completing the war-ification of this lovely garden.

As the war ground to an end, the buildings of Berkeley Square were shabby and dilapidated, exterior walls unpainted and shrapnel-dinged, their windows dirt-grimed or blasted out, the window boxes empty. There was little aristocratic, fashionable, or frivolous anywhere in Berkeley Square in 1945. (Or for several years after—in 1948 the *Times* lamented that the garden lacked color, the two tubs of geraniums having ended their season.) Today Berkeley Square has made the bumpy transition from mainly residential to mainly business, and the years since the war have brought a busier, better-kept aspect to the area.

> **VISITOR DETAILS:** Berkeley Square's garden is open daily 10am to dusk

Cross carefully at the square's southwestern corner and head west on well-preserved **Charles Street**. The brown-brick Georgian façades of Charles Street now hide not elegant residences but offices of architects, publishers, and businesses. The American Red Cross Service Club for Women was at 47/48 Charles Street during the later war years and the

War Words: Barrage

A **BARRAGE** was continuous firing from anti-aircraft artillery guns, blazing away from London's parks and open spaces. George Orwell started one wartime essay, "I began [writing] in the added racket of the barrage. The yellow gun-flashes are lighting the sky, the splinters are rattling on the house-tops." To more fully immerse yourself in the homefront experience, pronounce "barrage" with the accent on the first syllable (BAH-rahj), similar to the more familiar English pronunciation of "garage."

American Red Cross Officers' Club for Women was at Number 10. (For those unclear on the protocol of the armed forces, facilities for men and women were kept separate, as were those for officers and enlisted personnel of either sex, and often there were further divisions between junior and senior officers.)

At 37 Charles Street was (and still is) the English-Speaking Union at Dartmouth House, its flags suggesting this is a place offering "hospitality and contacts of every kind for visitors from the U.S.A.," particularly during the war to officers and men of the various Allied Air Forces. In Number 34, an extension of Dartmouth House, a wartime club and canteen for American and Dominion forces opened in 1943, with Mrs. Churchill performing the ceremonial formalities. Also in attendance was playwright George Bernard Shaw, who in his usual curmudgeonly fashion skipped the ceremony but grudgingly toured the facility with Lady Astor, Parliament member and good friend of Shaw's.

Society hostess Mrs. Ronnie Greville had her London town house at Number 16, a five-story obelisk-flanked building. Along with Emerald Cunard and Sybil Colefax, Mrs. Greville set the entertaining standard for a certain segment of London's prewar and, to some extent, wartime society (although Sir Kenneth Clark, at least, found her dinner parties "the dullest I can remember"). Here before the war Mrs. Greville entertained the Mountbattens, Brendan Bracken, and the Duke of Windsor, plus more politically suspect guests such as German ambassador Ribbentrop and Italian ambassador Count Grandi. The elderly and very rich Mrs. Greville retreated to Mayfair's Dorchester Hotel when the bombing got serious, finding the war "a vulgar inconvenience." After her death in September 1942, her Charles Street home stood empty for several years until the Guards Club, a gentlemen's club, moved in, only to move on in the 1970s to merge with the Calvary Club on Piccadilly. The building today contains offices.

Turn up Chesterfield Hill to Hill Street where British General Gort lived, the roadway bombed and cratered several times during the war, almost as if the Germans knew the location of his house. After the May 1941 bombing attacks, General Lee—whom we met earlier dodging bombs near Hay Hill—lamented that "a number of the mansions in Hill Street are simply brick shells still smoldering." He wasn't the only walker in the neighborhood noting the effects of enemy action. Author Somerset Maugham found it particularly grim "to saunter through the eighteenth-century streets of Mayfair and see a great gap where a fine old house had been and sometimes, precariously perched on a fragment of a bedroom floor, a chest of drawers or a coat hanging forlorn on a peg."

A short block further on from Hill Street, turn onto quiet Farm Street. A German bomb detonated in the middle of the road in October 1940, leaving a crater thirty feet across and blasting out windows on all sides, including those of the **Church of the Immaculate Conception**. Step inside (use the door to the left if the main door isn't open) for a look at the busy Victorian style of Decorated Gothic, all marble, mosaics, and polished granite pillars. Don't miss the altar by Victorian architect Pugin. The rose-window glass of Mayfair's only Roman Catholic church was destroyed in wartime blasts and has been replaced, its modern design by the Irish stained-glass artist Evie Hone.

> The Church of the Immaculate Conception was the Kennedys' parish church when they were in London.

As you leave the church, turn right, going west on Farm Street. Within a block, a narrow pedestrian walkway leads to the hidden Mount Street Gardens, where seemingly every bench faces south to catch the London sun. Watch for magpies, blue tits, and chubby wood pigeons, or check out some of the unusual trees including the Canary Island palm. Yes, a palm tree in London, and its success can be attributed to its sheltered location. If it's break time, this is a fine place to rest. Then follow the walkway around to the west (leftish from where you entered) to South Audley Street and Grosvenor Chapel.

Built in the early 1730s on a piece of rural land then known as the Gravel Pit Field, **Grosvenor Chapel** (pronunciation hint: "GROVE-nor") is one of several

Grosvenor Chapel.

smallish churches constructed hereabouts when society began to migrate
west from the City and Westminster. The war's bombing raids broke all the

VISITOR DETAILS: Grosvenor
Chapel is open Monday–Friday
8am to 6pm. Free lunchtime
concerts. More information:
020 7499 1684, www.
grosvenorchapel.org.uk.

chapel's windows and blasted holes in the
roof and front portico, but services continued. In fact, from 1943 on, the Protestant
chaplains of the American Armed Forces
used Grosvenor Chapel on Sundays, their
uniformed flock no doubt cherishing the
classic lines of such a New England–style
church. General Eisenhower himself worshipped here during his London
stays. A plaque on the exterior wall near the entrance commemorates the
wartime presence of the American forces.

In the final war years, American Ambassador John Gilbert Winant
rented a flat down Aldford Street, staying there until he returned to the
U.S. in 1946. A plaque on the diminutive two-story red
brick building notes his residence if you'd like to
stroll down this very quiet side street.

South Audley Street—running in front of the
chapel—was essentially a miniature Fifth Avenue
in the war, with GIs billeted throughout the area
and service clubs dotted about the neighborhood.
Today shoppers, not soldiers, provide the bustle here as
they peruse wares at South Audley's more unusual businesses—like the spy
shops on the street's western side, perfect if you're in the market for bul-
letproof vests, night scopes, recording briefcases, or telephone scramblers.

Turn right onto Mount Street at the next corner and walk to Carlos
Place, stopping for a break at the Audley pub if need be. On the south side

*So overwhelming was
the wartime American
presence in Grosvenor
Square that a song
parody soon grew
popular: "An English-
man Spoke in
Grosvenor Square."*

is 105 Mount Street, the home of bachelor Winston
Churchill in the early 1900s. Across the street is the
Connaught Hotel, its rooms and restaurant a popu-
lar destination for wartime travelers.

Head up Carlos Place two short blocks to
Grosvenor Square (and watch for Number 49,
just off the square and where Pamela Churchill
established a mini-salon in 1942 soon after her sep-
aration from Churchill's only son Randolph).

Grosvenor Square was laid out in the 1720s and the area has had close
connections with the U.S. government and various well-known
Americans ever since the 1780s.

Only two original Georgian buildings are left—Number 9 on the northeastern corner, the home of John Adams from 1785 to 1788 and badly damaged by wartime bombings, and Number 38 on the southern side, now the Indonesian Embassy. The remaining structures surrounding the six acres of this spacious square are neo-Georgian hotels (two large ones), residences (a few), and offices (mostly), with no shops.

Grosvenor Square, as with much of Mayfair, began a slow slide after World War I as the large homes emptied and were redeveloped into flats or offices. With the outbreak of World War II, redevelopment stopped and the Americans began to trickle in, becoming a deluge in mid-war when the U.S. Expeditionary Force requisitioned the entire square. This part of Mayfair became known as Little America, and the square itself, Eisenhowerplatz (and less frequently, Madison Square). The American Embassy, formerly at 14 Prince's Gate, relocated in 1938 to Number 1 on the southeastern side.

Number 7 Grosvenor Square was home to society hostess Emerald Cunard, who hosted many a lavish prewar party here. Like Mrs. Greville of Charles Street, social dowager Cunard moved into the Dorchester Hotel when war broke out (*her remarkably similar comment was "War's so vulgar"*). Part of her Grosvenor Square house was damaged in the early bombing, but she was able to offer two large rooms for the use of the Hyde Park Balloon Barrage. Lady Cunard filled her unfurnished hotel suite with much of her own furniture, and she continued entertaining, although on a reduced scale given the much smaller quarters. She remained at the Dorchester even after war's end, dying there in 1948 at age seventy-one. She did return to Grosvenor Square, however; friend and romance writer Barbara Cartland notes that the ashes of Lady Cunard were quietly scattered in the square's garden.

> *Wartime constraints brought many a local resident to more practical, less elegant measures than one would expect of this fashionable area. A 1942 letter to the* Times *proudly reported on the egg production of the six Light Sussex hens that lived "for the past nine months upon the leaden roof of my Mayfair home," where they provided an average of three eggs a day even during periods of snow and extreme cold. Given the restrictions of wartime food rationing, that was one happy hen owner.*

The American Red Cross London headquarters was at Number 12 (now subsumed by the London Marriott Hotel), a building so narrow that group meetings for new workers had to be held in rotation, with one small group brought inside at a time. Young Kathleen "Kick" Kennedy, daughter of former Ambassador Joseph Kennedy, could often be seen

Barrage Balloons

A merican sports events often feature an advertisement-festooned blimp drifting silently overhead, televising the competition below. Wartime London had its blimps too, just as silent but with neither advertising nor broadcasting facilities. To ward off low-flying enemy aircraft, pilotless barrage balloons floated a mile above England's wartime streets, parks, docks, and coast. Their silvery puffiness belied the danger of the steel cables hanging almost invisibly below. London's first barrage balloons floated skyward in October 1938, and by the Blitz over 450 hovered above the metropolis.

The hydrogen-filled balloons—the "nightmare of Nazi airmen"—were about sixty feet long and twenty-five feet in diameter, much smaller and squishier than today's advertising behemoths. The RAF's Balloon Command crews—as many as twelve men to a balloon—operated from fixed sites such as parks, from mobile trucks equipped with winches, and in coastal areas from ships. Newspaper ads soon pleaded for women "to take over the balloon barrage," enabling a soldier to fight at the front, and by midwar most of the balloon sites were staffed by the Women's Auxiliary Air Force (WAAF). In central London, barrage balloon sites were located anywhere there was open space, including Hyde Park, Green Park, Horse Guards Parade, Victoria Embankment Gardens, and Grosvenor Square.

The balloon's portly shape, pearly color, random windblown movements, and laudable purpose prompted an outpouring of endearing description ("like silver elephants with bloodhound's ears") and caring nicknames ("Bimbo" and "Bubbles"). Children's books starred the chubby blimps: *Blossom, The Brave Balloon* and *Boo Boo, The Barrage Balloon* were read to many a wartime tot. Today as you walk the capital's streets, look up and remember the time when the sky was patrolled by blimps glittering in the sunlight "like swollen fairy elephants lolling against the blue."

going in and out here, looking especially natty in her Red Cross uniform. American outposts included Eisenhower's army headquarters at Number 20 (watch for the plaque) and naval headquarters at Number 19, with additional military offices and installations, including overflow offices housing Embassy staff, filling the rest of the square.

John Gilbert Winant, former Republican governor of New Hampshire and good friend of President Roosevelt, replaced Ambassador Joseph Kennedy in early 1941. Winant and his wife lived in a comfortable third-floor apartment at 3 Grosvenor Square. A dedicated workaholic, Winant was essentially on duty twenty-four hours a day, especially given the time difference between London and Washington, and so was at his embassy desk late one April evening in 1941 when the nightly wail of sirens began. He continued working, only leaving when a bomb blast shattered his office windows. Winant and his wife then climbed to the roof to see the spectacle of London during a raid, with "guns roaring, bombers droning overhead, and high explosives bursting with terrific flashes," as described by the *Times*. They found, from high above Grosvenor Square, two of the houses on the square destroyed and many others on fire from incendiaries. On the far side a house had been sliced in half by a German bomb. Winant's sharing of difficult times with the British people endeared him to them, and in 1947, King George announced the award of an honorary Order of Merit to this loyal friend of Britain.

The current American Embassy is that modernistic white and gold building stretching along the entire western side of Grosvenor Square, designed by architect Eero Saarinen and opened in 1960. Note the bald eagle high over the Embassy's front, its golden wings spreading thirty-five feet. Near the northern corner of the embassy stands a figure in a familiar pose: **General Dwight Eisenhower's bronze statue** was unveiled in 1989 by Prime Minister Margaret Thatcher. On the back of the marble plinth is the Order of the Day, June 6, 1944, the words Ike sent to the boys of D-Day as they headed for the shores of France: "...the hopes and prayers of liberty-loving people everywhere march with you."

Cross into the hedged **Grosvenor Square garden**, in the prewar years a private gated area with tennis courts, dozens of plane trees, and manicured lawns and flower beds. But then the Americans arrived. In Ambassador Winant's wartime words, "The lovely garden in the centre of the square [was] turned to more practical use."

Military huts were erected, including several to house the WAAF operators of "Romeo," a barrage balloon. When a nervous young Andy Rooney, then working for the Army newspaper *Stars and Stripes*, visited Grosvenor Square, he noted four barrage balloons floating overhead. Rooney was convinced that "they made an obvious target of the headquarters building [at Number 20]. HERE! HERE! HERE! the balloons shouted to the bombardiers." Military vehicles, including the ubiquitous Army-drab American jeeps, used the lawns of Grosvenor Square as a parking lot and slowly turned the luxuriant green into dusty ruts. And at war's end, sixty-six trees were cut down as

Text continued on page 140.

1935: Young John Fitzgerald Kennedy (Jack to his family and friends) spends the summer in England; in London he and his father, Joseph Kennedy, stay at Claridge's Hotel, Mayfair. Jack hopes to attend the London School of Economics.

1937: Young Kennedy travels about Europe, ending up in London where he shops, inspects rooms a friend had recommended near Paddington Station, gets sick, and goes home.

January 1938: The appointment of Joseph Kennedy, patriarch of a large Boston Catholic family, financier and isolationist, as American ambassador to the Court of St. James's is approved by London authorities.

March 1938: Ambassador Kennedy arrives in England and settles in to the American Embassy at 14 Prince's Gate near Hyde Park.

Mid-March 1938: Kennedy's "attractive wife and long retinue of children" join their father in London. The two older boys, Joe Jr. and Jack, remain in the United States.

Mid-summer, older daughters Rosemary and Kathleen ("Kick") will be formally presented to the king and queen, part of the annual season for aristocratic London society.

February 1939: Jack Kennedy, now in London, writes home: "Am living up at the Embassy." (A plaque at 14 Prince's Gate notes his residence.)

Late August 1939: With war on the horizon, Ambassador Kennedy considers a refuge for the embassy outside of the city if the expected bombings of London prove too unpleasant. The London embassy itself has been moved, to 1 Grosvenor Square, Mayfair. Until shelter construction there is completed, Ambassador Kennedy and his staff will use the shelter at Claridge's Hotel, several hundred yards away down Brook Street.

September 3, 1939: At 10 Downing Street, Chamberlain shows Kennedy the text of his planned radio broadcast. That afternoon the ambassador, his wife Rose, Joe Jr., Jack, and Kick sit in the Strangers' Gallery in the House of Commons to hear Chamberlain formally make the declaration of war. That evening the ambassador phones President Roosevelt and laments, "It's the end of the world, the end of everything."

September 1939: Rose Kennedy and the younger children return to the United States early in the month. Daughter Kick remains in London and will eventually volunteer with the Red Cross and be assigned as a program assistant at an officers' club in Hans Crescent, Knightsbridge. Jack volunteers as an air raid spotter at the American Embassy, where he goes to the roof well-equipped with binoculars, steel helmet, and gas mask. At month's end he'll fly home, eventually joining the Navy and embarking upon a new career.

September 7, 1940: Heavy nighttime raids on London begin. Ambassador Kennedy walks down Piccadilly with author Harvey Klemmer and asserts, "I'll bet you five to one...that Hitler will be in Buckingham Palace in two weeks."

October 1940: Ambassador Kennedy returns to the States and meets with President Roosevelt, who is not particularly happy with his outspoken isolationist ambassador.

November 1940: Young Jack Kennedy's Harvard thesis is published; *Why England Slept* becomes an immediate bestseller. The same month, his father resigns as ambassador.

May 6, 1944: Kick Kennedy marries Billy Cavendish, the Marquess of Hartington and heir to the Duke of Devonshire, at the Chelsea Register Office. Cavendish will be killed five weeks later on the front lines in Europe.

August 12, 1944: The oldest Kennedy son, Navy pilot Joe Jr., having volunteered to fly a hazardous mission against German rocket bases, dies over the English Channel when his B-17 explodes in flight.

1947: The only remaining Kennedy in England, daughter Kick, moves into 4 Smith Square, Westminster. She will die a year later when the small plane she is in crashes into a French mountainside.

1965: A bust of John Fitzgerald Kennedy is unveiled at the International Students' Hostel at Park Crescent near Marylebone Road.

the square was opened up to become a backdrop for a **statue of President Roosevelt**.

The sudden death of America's president in April 1945, just as the European war was grinding to a conclusion, shocked and surprised the

British. The government quickly moved to honor FDR: the Roosevelt Memorial Bill provided for the erection of a statue of the president in Grosvenor Square and the laying-out of the square as a public garden. The statue was funded by public donations, limited to no more than five shillings per person, and the required sum (£40,000) was easily raised in a few days.

The ten-foot-high bronze statue by sculptor William Reid Dick stands on the square's northern side atop a plinth of Portland stone. The stone walls surrounding the two fountains are inscribed with Roosevelt's Four Freedoms: Freedom from Want, Freedom from Fear, Freedom of Speech, and Freedom of Worship. A cloaked FDR leans on a cane, and even in the 1940s, contentious discussion arose as to how the disabled president should be pictured, foreshadowing the arguments around the statue of Roosevelt recently erected in Washington, DC. Eleanor Roosevelt made the final decision—FDR would be shown standing. The statue was unveiled in April 1948 in an emotional ceremony attended by his widow, King George, Queen Elizabeth, and Mr. Churchill.

FDR faces the **American Eagle Squadrons' Memorial**, a stone obelisk honoring the 244 American and 16 British fighter pilots and other personnel who served in the RAF Eagle Squadrons formed—and fighting—before America entered the war. Atop it is the square's second American bald eagle. On three sides of the obelisk, names of Eagle Squadron members are inscribed as are the mottoes and emblems of each squadron: "First from the Eyries" for the 71st Squadron, "For Liberty" for the 121st, and "Let Us to the Battle" for the 133rd.

From the northeastern corner of Grosvenor Square, take a short side trip along Brook Street to **Claridge's Hotel** at Number 53. Founded in 1855, the hotel has long been one of London's most prestigious. Even during the war the Claridge's doormen stood resplendent in livery and top hats beside the sandbagged entrance. The hotel's unrationed smorgasbord, served in the grill room, proved a draw to many, as did Claridge's air raid shelter. Queen Wilhelmina of the Netherlands and her son-in-law Prince Bernard were wartime guests, as were composer Irving Berlin; the kings of Norway, Yugoslavia, and Greece; FDR's personal envoy Harry Hopkins; author Daphne de Maurier; actor Douglas Fairbanks, Jr.; William J. Donovan, head of the American Office of Strategic Services, its London headquarters nearby at 68 Brook Street; and generals Montgomery, Clark, and Marshall. General Raymond Lee also occupied a corner suite here for much of the early war period. General Eisenhower's stay at Claridge's was far briefer; he left abruptly, annoyed by what he considered unsettlingly gaudy rooms.

> *Every government-in-exile in London had its own intelligence service, and the various operatives (i.e., spies) shadowed each other until, in the words of journalist A. J. Liebling, "Lunch at Claridge's or the Ritz Grill resembled a traffic jam of characters out of an Alfred Hitchcock film."*

A little further along Brook Street—a once-residential enclave now filled with property company offices, advertising agencies, lawyers, and posh shops—is Number 39, where Sybil Colefax and John Fowler moved their interior decorating firm in 1944. The firm, innovators of the elegant "English country house look," is still there. Prince Charles's good friend, Camilla Parker Bowles, reputedly worked here briefly.

Cross to the northern side of Brook Street and return to Grosvenor Square. Along the way, watch for barely visible shelter signs a bit past Number 42 and at 74 Brook Street. At the Belisha beacon cross over to Ike and continue along Upper Brook Street, another stretch with several shelter signs stenciled on brick walls (plus several very posh restaurants). At the northern corner of Upper Brook Street and Park Lane rises the site of **Brook House**, its penthouse (two floors, thirty rooms) the prewar home of Louis and Edwina Mountbatten; we saw his statue on Horse Guards Parade in Whitehall. The move out of Brook House was a wise decision for the Mountbattens. In November 1940 a bomb slammed through the roof, wrecking much of the top floors of the building.

Turn left onto Park Lane and head south, noting the rolling greens of **Hyde Park** just beyond the eight lanes of traffic. The park's 350 acres provided a sylvan backdrop to wartime

Holocaust Memorial.

proceedings. Trench shelters were dug near the Serpentine just over the rise (and the lake partially drained so that a German bomb in the area wouldn't flood Knightsbridge), anti-aircraft artillery guns in sandbagged bunkers nightly loosed off salvos against the high-flying Luftwaffe, and great gashing excavations scarred the lawns, the contents used to fill sandbags and the resulting craters filled with rubble from bombed buildings. All this amidst peacefully blooming lilacs, crocuses, chrysanthemums, and lupins, grazing sheep (a herd of 500 was maintained in the park), and geese…well, doing all the things geese do, even in wartime.

Hyde Park is considered by some "the lungs of London," by others "the heart of London." It's definitely a visceral relationship. Londoners love Hyde Park and use it well—from political demonstrations to family picnics (sometimes interrupted by dramatic gun salutes honoring a royal occasion). Find time during your London visit for a park wander, watching especially for two simple World War II memorials.

The first, just before the café at the eastern end of the Serpentine, is the understated Holocaust Memorial Garden—several boulders set in gravel ringed by silver birch trees. The inscription from Lamentations reads, "For these I weep, streams of tears flow from my eyes because of the destruction of my people." As terrible as some aspects of London's home-front experience were, a few silent moments here considering the six million noncombatant victims of the Holocaust offers some important perspective and a reminder of man's inhumanity to man.

VISITOR DETAILS: Hyde Park is open daily dawn to dusk. Access from the Park Lane side is via subways under the traffic lanes. Café generally open weekdays 10:30am to 6pm; weekends 10am to 6pm. Check the posted maps for restroom locations and additional park features.

A second war memorial is located northwest of the Serpentine boathouse. Here stand the Norwegian Stones of Commemoration, large boulders (one almost seven feet high) erected by the Royal Norwegian Navy to thank the British people for friendship and hospitality during the war. This was far more than "come in, have a cuppa" hospitality. Their country occupied by Germany, the Norwegian fleet of merchant ships headed for—and was welcomed at—British naval bases.

As you walk along **Park Lane**, don't let the throb of passing vehicles conceal that this roadway was once much narrower, less busy, and more fashionable. Like much of Mayfair, Park Lane's history is one of mansions demolished and hotels and flats superseding them, a process that began before—and was accelerated by—the war. A prime example is the

Grosvenor House Hotel, on Park Lane between Upper Grosvenor and Mount streets.

In 1927, the incredibly palatial Grosvenor House, home of the Duke of Westminster, was demolished and the Grosvenor House Hotel built in its place. Palatial in its own right, the nine-story hotel opened to enthusiastic fanfare and civic pride: here was "the latest and greatest contribution to the art of comfortable living that a modern world has conceived." The west façade, designed by architect Sir Edwin Lutyens, has a modernistic 1930s look featuring rose-colored brick and stone colonnades and pavilions. Not every Londoner found the building pleasing—one critic, dubbing it "Park Lane Cliffs," considered it nothing more than a huge unappealing pile built in a typical American style. Worse, the hotel's upper floors were "utterly devoid of all external decoration, and more suggestive of some huge warehouse or penitentiary than a block of luxury flats in Park Lane." Whew.

> Number 75 Grosvenor Street was the birthplace of Clementine Hozier, later better known as Mrs. Winston Churchill.

The modern interior touches, at least, garnered more enthusiasm. All 500 rooms had a telephone (unusual at the time), every floor had a mail box and room service, and the bathrooms were the very latest in luxury. For one thing, every suite had one—no wandering down the hall to the shared facilities while staying in a Grosvenor House Hotel suite.

In those last elegant years just before the war, the hotel's Banqueting Hall could serve as many as 2,000 guests at a time, quickly becoming *the* place for the most important entries in society's calendar. For especially large crowds, when motor shows, antique dealers' fairs, or mammoth society receptions were held, the indoor ice skating rink could be quickly covered, adding 16,000 square feet of space. By 1939, the hotel employed over 1,150 men and women, but war meant hundreds traded in their hotel uniforms for those of artillery gunners, ambulance drivers, or company

Park Lane just after the war.

Text continued on page 147.

Along Piccadilly's Northern Side

A walk down Piccadilly's northern side—the southern border of Mayfair—toward Piccadilly Circus passes gentlemen's clubs, soldiers' hangouts, and art and shopping possibilities. Start at Piccadilly's west end near where Park Lane meets the Hyde Park Corner roundabout.

First up is London's Hard Rock Cafe, on the corner of Old Park Lane, a place wartime GIs would have loved. Instead, soldiers could eat at several American mess halls and service clubs in the area or explore the more upmarket offerings of central London's restaurants. Nearby wartime possibilities included the Berkeley (with dancing), the Liaison Club (great name *and* dancing), L'Auberge de France, and closer to Piccadilly Circus, Oddenino's or Scott's, the world-famous fish restaurant.

Several ponderous buildings hereabouts are or were gentlemen's clubs. Watch for the Royal Air Force Club at 128 Piccadilly (founded in 1917 and still in operation) and the Calvary and Guards Club at Number 127. The Royal Aero Club was at Number 119 in the war years (since moved), and the St James's Club was at Number 106 before moving to Park Place. (For more on London's men's clubs, see Chapter 3.)

The Athenaeum Court, a block of service flats at 116 Piccadilly (now the Athenaeum Hotel) offered wartime occupants a protective steel and concrete residence. Author John Lehmann found refuge here after his Bloomsbury flat had been done-in by enemy action, and Vera Brittain moved in after her Chelsea home had its roof opened by a Nazi bomb. Cyril Connelly lived in a top-floor flat at Athenaeum Court for a time; from here he and George Orwell watched the fires in London's East End on the first night of the Blitz.

The bar at the Park Lane Hotel at 111 Piccadilly was a popular stop for members of the Allied Forces during the war, as was King George's Club for Officers nearby at Number 105 in the Hotel Splendide.

Piccadilly looking east.

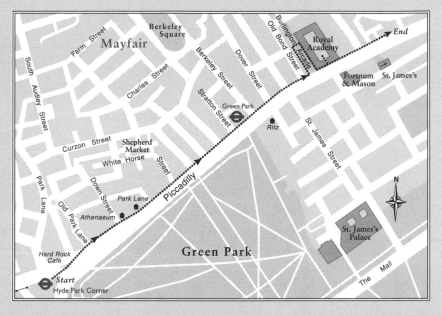

Past White Horse Street, that large building set back from the sidewalk was once the In and Out Club. Officially the Naval and Military Club (founded in 1862), its street gate pillars marked "In" and "Out" long ago gave the club its nickname. In an early Blitz bombing, a handful of high explosive bombs smashed the club façade and gutted the interior. Another fell toward the back, killing two residents, and a third explosive, falling on Half Moon Street, obliterated much of the eastern corner. The club wasn't completely restored until 1958, when its large premises included forty-five bedrooms, a library, a card room, and a ladies annex plus drawing rooms, cocktail bar, and private dining room. Incidentally, the In and Out Club recently moved to St. James's Square; its building on Piccadilly sold as a private home for £50,000,000.

Across Piccadilly are two London landmarks. The Devonshire Gates almost directly opposite the In and Out Club once graced the forecourt of the long-gone eighteenth-century Devonshire House.

They were dismantled and stored "in a safe place" from March 1941 until the end of the war. And coming up on Piccadilly's south side is the mansard-roofed Ritz Hotel. This perspective allows a look at the hotel's western wall, with dings and pittings that look remarkably like shrapnel damage.

Harold Macmillan, conservative politician and later prime minister, stayed in Green Park Chambers at 90 Piccadilly when in London, finding the only problem with his flat was that "it was in the mansard roof at the top of the house, and the noise of the German bombers prowling around was rather distracting." This was resolved one night early in the Blitz when his rooms were blown-in by those prowling bombers. Macmillan moved to a first-floor flat, loaned to him by author Hugh Walpole.

Past Dover and Old Bond streets is the Burlington Arcade (1819), a Regency-era diversion with some great shopping of its own. Built for "the gratification of the public and to give employment to

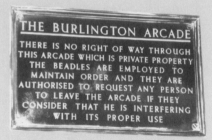

those red telephone kiosks in the entrance archways? They're quite possibly the oldest in London, prototypes of Sir Giles Gilbert Scott's earliest model.

industrious females," this covered passageway holds dozens of classy shops. Watch for oldtimers such as Penhaligon's Perfumers (established in 1870) and newer shops that carry older items (like the war-era fountain pens at Penfriend). In 1940, the entire northern end of the arcade was destroyed when a high explosive bomb fell twenty-five yards away. In fact, most of the walkway and shops at that end were "reduced to a shambles," in Somerset Maugham's words, but repairs started in 1952 and Burlington Arcade is now as good as new.

Nearby is the Royal Academy of Arts in Burlington House. Stop in if the current show is of interest (check the banners festooning the building's street side), but at least wander into the courtyard and enjoy the pleasing Palladian architecture. Across the courtyard on the wall near the entrance is a memorial to the glorious memory of the fallen members of the Artists' Rifles in World War I, with the usual sad addition for the war losses of the 1940s. And

Closer to Piccadilly Circus and a bit hidden stands the courtyard of the Albany, a block of brown-brick Georgian "bachelor apartments" constructed in the early 1800s. The Albany has been home to hundreds of well-known gentlemen (primarily) over the decades, including Byron, Macaulay, and Gladstone. Prewar and war-era residents included authors J. B. Priestley and Aldous Huxley, and actress Edith Evans.

At 35 Piccadilly, across from St. James's Church, once stood the Fifty Shilling Tailors, a casualty in the raids that so decimated Wren's church. Here was a building whose loss was little lamented. In fact, a local shelter newsletter hoped "never again will such eyesores like the building of the 'Fifty Shilling Tailors' be permitted. There has been some destruction which has seemed almost worthwhile."

Piccadilly Circus is just ahead, but for details of that central point from which so much of London radiates, check Chapter 3 (for Eros, the Underground, and the Stage Door Canteen) and Chapter 5 (for the eastern side). For now, you're in Transit Central, with a dozen bus routes and the Underground nearby.

cooks. The remaining staff struggled with wartime demands: covering the hotel's thousands of windows with five miles of blackout material, and piling 30,000 sandbags around the exterior walls to provide blast protection. The Turkish Baths were transformed into a gas decontamination center, and two large air raid shelters were constructed—one above ground to protect upwards of 700 people and the second, built in an underground corridor, to shelter another 200.

When the air raids began, the mammoth Grosvenor House Hotel, so near to the bright gunfire flashes of Hyde Park's artillery batteries, became a prime target. One perilously close German bomb blasted out 1,000 panes of glass; a second a few weeks later blew out twice that number. A delayed-action bomb near the hotel's northern side meant evacuation for many guests until the bomb disposal squad could defuse it several days later. Meanwhile the Hyde Park anti-aircraft guns thundered away, shaking the hotel's crockery and rattling what windows were left.

The ice skating rink, covered permanently before the war and renamed the Great Room, took on wartime duties. It served early on as an emergency annex for the U.S. Embassy's immigration section as hundreds of English parents tried to obtain visas to send their children to safety in America. Throughout the war, the Great Room also served once a week as the Officers' Sunday Club, where thousands of Allied Forces' officers and guests were kept entertained. And it was the setting for distinguished speakers and important functions, including General Sikorski speaking on the peace to come, General de Gaulle addressing several gatherings of his countrymen, and the Netherlands' Queen Wilhelmina receiving members of London's Dutch Colony.

But to many American soldiers stationed in London, this very fashionable Park Lane building was a mess hall. In 1943, the Great Room was renovated and became Willow Run, one of the largest officers' messes in existence. At the time, Ford Motor Company operated a mile-long bomber-assembly plant near Detroit, and the vast space of the Great Room plus the assembly-line features of the cafeteria-style meals inspired the nickname. Meals cost two shillings or about forty cents, and as many as 6,000 were served in a day. By war's end, over 5,500,000 meals had been downed by hungry soldiers.

> **VISITOR DETAILS:** Now formally Le Meridien Grosvenor House, its Park Room Brasserie is open tea times. More information: 020 7499 6363, www.lemeridien.com (then click along until you get to their London hotels).

Officers and their guests ate sturdy American food: pork chops or chicken with mashed potatoes, canned corn, plus ice cream for dessert and real American coffee.

The Grosvenor House Hotel survived the war, securely sandbagged, with shuttered and shattered windows. It never closed its doors during six long years, and continues today as one of Park Lane's more upmarket hotels.

The next Park Lane hostelry is the **Dorchester Hotel**. It too was built on the site of a palatial home, Dorchester House, demolished in 1929. This opulent ultra-modern hotel opened two years later with 400 rooms, a fancy ballroom, bars, and plush banquet halls. So modern was the Dorchester that the bedroom walls were lined with cork in an effort to provide the best in soundproofed accommodations. But the building's reinforced concrete structure (2,000 miles of steel rods!) was the appeal for Londoners surveying the drastic effects of Hitler's early bombing raids. The Dorchester was soon touted as the safest hotel in London, and some of the city's wealthiest and most influential citizens flocked here, including Mrs. Ronnie Greville and Emerald Cunard. Lady Cunard, eschewing the Dorchester's air raid shelter, reputedly sat under a table during air raids and read Shakespeare.

Sybil Colefax was another society hostess who made wartime use of the Dorchester. Her tiny home in Westminster made entertaining large groups difficult so she held her monthly galas here. Colefax called them "Ordinaries," many called them boring, but the guests did pack the place even knowing she would send each of them a bill for 10/6 the next morning. Young Pamela Churchill, society-hostess-in-training, also stayed

Dorchester Hotel.

Wartime Beauty Tricks

Makeup was difficult to find in wartime shops. Author Theodora FitzGibbon became as creative as most London women: "We used Meltonian shoe cream for mascara…Trex or Spry cooking fat for cleansing cream…calamine lotion as a powder base, and sometimes even baby powder for face powder…we put Vaseline on our eye-lids and lips to achieve that 'dewy' look." FitzGibbon had tried moustache-wax for mascara but "it made my eyelashes look like furry spiders' legs."

here for a time. Her rooms on the top floor cost £6 a week, including breakfast. And it was at "the Dorch" that Ernest Hemingway stayed in 1944.

American correspondent Vincent Sheean was far less sanguine about the hotel's safety than were most of the guests. "What seemed a phalanx of…public characters lived at the Dorchester Hotel, seduced, I think, by the idea that it was the most modern of hotel structures and the one least likely to collapse under the bombs….I thought it merely lucky….It used to sway in the air like a tree in a storm." Author Somerset Maugham thought the Dorchester during bombing attacks "shook like a dog that's just come out of the sea." A cranky Nancy Mitford, who worked nearby on Curzon Street, had little patience with the "Dorchesterites" snug in their shelter: "A friend of mine paced out the shelter & found it is under that little pond & there are only a few inches of tarmac between them & certain death."

Despite the swaying and shaking (and some luck—the hotel was never seriously damaged), guests found the concept of steel-reinforced concrete extremely comforting. The Dorchester's basement Turkish Baths became an especially favored air raid shelter, with rows and rows of beds along the walls sporting name tags reserving the bed for a regular guest. Even the hotel's lounge drew the in-crowd, including many who stayed "in," remaining in the Dorchester until the All Clear sounded at dawn. There were, of course, standards to be maintained. At least one habitué, older and quite distinguished, scolded Somerset Maugham for appearing in the lounge in ordinary street clothes: "I can see no reason why, just because there's a raid, a gentleman shouldn't dress like a gentleman."

General Dwight Eisenhower, more used to bombing but impatient with ostentation, moved to the Dorchester after finding Claridge's

VISITOR DETAILS: For reservations for tea in the Dorchester's Promenade: 020 7629 8888, www.dorchester.com.

"whorehouse pink" rooms too unsettling. His smaller and more sedate suite here, available today as the Eisenhower Suite, nevertheless had some privacy and security problems—the balcony was all too close to the one next door. Prime Minister Churchill saw to it that a wall was built between the two balconies, a wall that remains today.

On the first anniversary of V-E Day, Princess Elizabeth attended a gala postwar dance at the Dorchester Hotel, her first public dance. But in the years following the war, the hotel gradually became outdated and worn. It closed in the early 1990s for a major overhaul, and today's flashy new Dorchester Hotel is more stylish than ever. It's a perfect spot for afternoon tea, a luxurious waystation in an aristocratic neighborhood.

Browsing for Memories: Mayfair's Shopping Streets

Shopping along one of Mayfair's major consumer corridors today is an experience far different from sixty years ago. For one thing, today's bargain hunters don't have to consider whether or not a store has an air raid shelter, and shop hours aren't curtailed by the evening's blackout. Rationing, coupons, utility clothing, and shortages are no longer factors, and signs declaring "More Open Than Ever" aren't seen on blasted-out, boarded-over shop windows.

Bond Street (New Bond and Old Bond)

Touted as London's premier shopping venue, Bond Street offers the serious consumer an adventure in specialized commercialism. Even if you can't afford anything here—like author Logan Pearsall Smith, who remarked shortly before the war, "I like to go down Bond Street, thinking of all the things I don't want"— the people-watching and window-shopping are outstanding. Enjoy this street of one-word stores: Armani, Baccarat, Chanel, Gucci, Hermès, Mulberry, Prada,

FDR and WSC.

Tiffany, and Varsace, of goldsmiths and silversmiths, art galleries and antique furnishings, glassware and fashion. Only a few shops remain from sixty years ago—old-timers like Sotheby's, Aspreys, Cartiers, and Fenwicks (that's "FEN-icks")—but even so, wartime memories can be found here.

The most obvious is at the intersection of Grafton Street, where Roosevelt and Churchill share a sidewalk bench. This bronze statue by American sculptor Lawrence Holofcener commemorates the fiftieth anniversary of V-E Day; it's located only a hundred yards from the hotel where the Roosevelts spent their honeymoon. Together, FDR and WSC have become one of the most popular photo opportunities in town.

Coty Parfums de Luxe (then selling cosmetics at 2 New Bond Street) had limited stock and short hours in common with many other wartime shops. For the 1941 Christmas season, Coty's opened only a few hours a day and long lines formed outside. Shoppers considered themselves lucky if they could buy a bit of face powder or a new lipstick. Gieves Men's Shop, then at 21 Old Bond Street, offered officers an upmarket location to purchase uniforms—at least until German bombs destroyed the building. Elizabeth Arden's Salon (25 Old Bond Street in the war years, now home to Tiffany's) was advertised as a place for members of the various wartime services to meet. Miss Arden also suggested that "Burnt Sugar" was the best lipstick to wear with anything khaki.

In October 1940, high explosive bombs blasted out most of the plate glass along this narrow boulevard. A few days later the bombers returned, and the Piccadilly end of the street suffered severe damage. One building, essentially vaporized, had only its basement remaining. This was made into a firefighting reservoir of water, so deep that a life-jacket was kept nearby. A pair of ducks soon arrived, settled in on the war-made pond, and calmly observed the Bond Street shoppers.

Oxford Street

Virginia Woolf observed, "Oxford Street, it goes without saying, is not London's most distinguished thoroughfare," a candid assessment that still holds true. The sidewalks are clogged with pedestrians negotiating a shopping venue that caters to rich and poor, window-shoppers and dedicated consumers. Oxford Street doesn't have the panache or charm of nearby Bond or Regent streets, but it has an energy and vigor the fancier streets lack. It also has 300 stores.

The bustle of a shopping day along Oxford is a far cry from the scene author Elizabeth Bowen viewed after the bombing raids of September 1940; she walked down Oxford Street one early morning with the charred dust still in the air from the previous night's explosions and fires. The whole street, empty from one end to the other, "looks polished like a ball-

Oxford Street.

room, glitters with smashed glass....The silence is now the enormous thing—it appears to amaze the street."

Selfridges, the block-long flag-bedecked department store near the Marble Arch end of Oxford Street, began the war as did most shopkeepers and householders—laying in supplies for the duration. In this case, 5,000 sandbags and tons of loose sand and timber to shore up walls, plus civil defense equipment: rubber boots, respirators, steel helmets, and waterproof overalls. Bomb shelters were prepared—the basement of the main building could hold several thousand people. The Phoney War came to a crashing end in autumn 1940 when a high explosive bomb slammed into the store's roof, destroying much of the fifth floor, blowing out most of the window glass, and knocking half of the store's elevators out of commission (they would remain so until war's end). In April 1941, an incendiary bomb set the third floor afire and badly damaged the Palm Court. One month later, in the last great German raid on London, the store was again badly assaulted by fire.

> *After Selfridges' elegant Roof Garden was blitzed, it was turned into a vegetable plot in response to the "Dig for Victory" campaign. The first growing season produced forty pounds of radishes, innumerable cabbages, and enough lettuce to supply the store's restaurant for weeks.*

Above the store's main doors on Oxford Street reigns an allegorical Queen of Time standing on a ship's prow. Hidden overhead, a three-ton bell tolls the hours. The Queen of Time remained here throughout the war, only slightly rattled by nearby bomb blasts, watching over the street below where sandbags and blast "baffle-walls" had been built around police boxes, store entrances, and shop windows.

The John Lewis building at 278 Oxford Street was totally gutted by high explosive, incendiary, and oil bombs in September 1940. One adjective-happy diarist viewed the devastation shortly after: "Gaunt girders already rusting enclosed here and there by unwilling masonry, ruined and blackened walls rearing crumbled tops out of shapeless debris, the whole street heaped with masonry from which…a thin plume of blue smoke was still spiralling." In other words, a shambles. Journalist Kingsley Martin more simply noted that the John Lewis building "stands today like the ruins of a Greek temple." The ruins were demolished and the store rebuilt in the late 1950s.

Several other large Oxford Street stores suffered damage, including Bourne and Hollingsworth, gutted by bombs, and Peter Robinson, near the top of Regent Street. A high explosive bomb smashed showrooms, windows, and offices in the area and put a nasty gash in the store's Oxford Circus frontage.

Regent Street

Regent Street was laid out in the early 1800s by architect John Nash, and its essence remains (though much rebuilt), a sweep of London architecture particularly dramatic the closer one gets to Piccadilly Circus. A ride along Regent Street atop a double-decker bus is an inex-

Regent Street.

pensive indulgence. Architecture buffs can eye the buildings, and shoppers anticipate their contents, while the wartime visualizer can call up
scenes of desolation, imagining the dilapidated look of smashed and
boarded-up windows and blackened
shopfronts, broken glass ankle-deep in the
street, and tired Civil Defence workers
gathered on the street corners.

*In 1939, wartime
shoppers seeking the
perfect gift for a
youngster could have
purchased a "Build Your
Own Maginot Line" set
at Hamleys.*

But since we're *walking* Regent Street,
the better to capture those wartime memories firsthand, start at Oxford Circus, preferably on the eastern side where the major
stores have tended to congregate. One of
the first large stores is Dickens & Jones, offering clothing for m'lady, though
m'lady in wartime might have been more interested in the deep shelter
here, so popular that queues would form outside for hours, hoping to secure a place far underground by the time the nightly sirens began wailing.

Next is Liberty. Duck down Great Marlborough Street to enter the
Tudor-style extension, a timbered interior filled with unique printed fab-
rics. Arthur Liberty founded the store in the 1870s, originally selling soft
colored silks from the Far East. Today it's a full-scale department store in a
warren of buildings and rooms off Regent Street. There's definitely a
Liberty look, better seen than described; start in the ground-floor rooms
and watch especially for fabric gifts. Shopper's Tip: Pick up a free store
map or expect to get lost.

Even if you have no children or grandchildren, or even godchildren—
even if you've never seen a child before in your life—Hamleys is worth a
visit, a multilevel toy warehouse for all ages and reputedly the world's
largest toy store. Although the latest,
trendiest playthings are stocked, the
wartime enthusiast will likely be most interested in the small metal cars, trucks, fire engines, and ambulances modeled after vehicles of the 1930s and 1940s. Watch too for
model kits including the *Queen Mary* luxury
liner (a troop carrier in the war) and *King
George V* (flagship of the Home Fleet when

*Burberry's on Regent
Street sold wartime
"service waterproofs,"
raincoats that "admit of
no retreat to rain, storm,
or chilling winds."*

she sailed to intercept the *Bismarck* in 1941), plus dozens of Spitfires,
Junkers, B-17s, and other war-era aircraft models.

Closer to Piccadilly Circus, the Café Royal has been a favorite hangout
for London's literati for over a century. Rebuilt and updated in the mid-
1920s, it remained a draw well into the 1930s and 1940s, and may draw
you in today. Regulars at the Grill Room in the between-war years in-

cluded the Prince of Wales and his brother the Duke of York; later T. S. Eliot, J. B. Priestley, H. G. Wells, Anthony Powell, Stephen Spender, and George Orwell dined and drank here.

Swan and Edgar, now Tower Records at the corner of Regent Street and Piccadilly Circus, was well-known as a meeting place throughout the war. The store also maintained a popular and very large air raid shelter where concerts, whist drives, and cinema shows were regularly held.

Savile Row

Home to London's best gentlemen's tailors, exclusive Savile Row fairly drips with cachet. Even if you're not in the market for expensive hand-made shirts and suits, this is a fine walking street where checking out the shoppers is as entertaining as shopping.

Number 1 Savile Row (pronunciation hint: "SAH-ville" not "suh-VILLE") is the venerable Gieves & Hawkes shop. Here an elegant dark blue tie featuring the rose of England and a woven-in gold outline of the British Isles is available, but only if you can prove you were an airman in the Battle of Britain; Gieves & Hawkes is the only retail outlet for the Battle of Britain tie. Watch too for Anderson & Sheppard at Number 30. Radio broadcaster Edward R. Murrow was a wartime regular here, shopping for his natty pinstripes.

After the autumn raids of 1940, Savile Row was simply battered to pieces. A particularly nasty attack demolished a four-story Savile Row building, the structure brought down in a heap of rubble, much of it falling into the basement area where a family of caretakers lived. The *Times* takes up the story: "Covered with dust and blinded by smoke, they climbed through the wreckage and forced a hole through which they got into the street, while other walls came crashing down as bombs exploded near them. A few minutes later fire broke out in the building they just left." On such a dramatic scene, let us close the book on Mayfair shopping.

SHOP SIGNS YOU WON'T SEE IN TODAY'S LONDON:
- "Straffed but not stumped."
- "Cremated but not defeated. We have taken our ashes to 101 Hatton Garden, where it's business as usual."
- "More open than usual."
- (At a barber's) "We've had a close shave. Come and get one yourself."
- (At a furniture shop) "They can smash our windows, but they can't beat our furnishing values."
- "Business as usual, Mr. Hitler."

Ike in London

May 1942: Military man Dwight David Eisenhower ("Ike") arrives in London; General Marshall has asked for recommendations on future operations of American forces in Europe. Ike leaves ten days later, disturbed by the laid-back American military presence.

June 1942: General Marshall appoints Ike commander of the American forces in the European Theater of Operations (ETO). General Eisenhower settles in at Claridge's Hotel, Mayfair, near his offices at 20 Grosvenor Square. Claridge's formality is not to the general's liking, and Ike moves to a simpler suite in the Dorchester Hotel on Park Lane.

July 1942: On a visit to Chequers, the prime minister's country home, Ike discusses matters military with Churchill. Later in the month Ike meets with King George at Buckingham Palace; they will confer several times during the war.

August 1942: Eisenhower is put in charge of Operation Torch, the invasion of North Africa. He begins to gather a staff at AFHQ (Allied Force Headquarters) at Norfolk House, 31 St. James's Square. Eisenhower moves into Telegraph Cottage in Kingston-upon-Thames, Surrey, about forty minutes by car from central London.

1943: Eisenhower spends much of the year in the Mediterranean (Algiers, Casablanca, Malta), returning to the U.S. at year's end, where President Roosevelt informs Ike he will command Operation Overlord, the Allied invasion of the Continent.

January 1944: General Eisenhower returns to England and 20 Grosvenor Square, now the London offices for SHAEF (Shared Headquarters, Allied Expedition Force). Once again life in London proves hectic and again Ike moves to the countryside, this time to a mansion in Kingston Hill near Bushy Park. Ike—not the mansion type— soon returns to nearby Telegraph Cottage.

May 15, 1944: The various invasion commanders—plus the king and the prime minister—meet with Eisenhower at St. Paul's School, West Kensington (then at Hammersmith near Brook Green), for a final review of invasion plans. The school is the 21st Army Group headquarters of General Montgomery.

June 2, 1944: Eisenhower and his staff move temporarily to the country estate of Southwick House, near Portsmouth, the advance command post for the Normandy landings. The next few days are filled with indecision regarding the timing of the D-Day invasion as the weather has turned extremely nasty.

June 5, 1944: In the mess room of Southwick House in the early morning, Eisenhower makes the final decision for the invasion: "Okay, let's go."

June 7, 1944: The day after the D-Day landings, Eisenhower views the beachhead from aboard the British minelayer *Apollo*. On June 12, he goes ashore at Omaha Beach, lunching on C rations at General Bradley's headquarters.

Mid-June 1944: V-1 flying bombs, aimed toward London by the Germans, have been landing in the rolling hills of Kent and Surrey. Churchill insists an air raid shelter be built near Telegraph Cottage, a resource Ike ignores until the rockets start landing several hundred yards away.

May 7, 1945: From his headquarters in France, General Eisenhower releases a simple message: "The mission of this Allied force was fulfilled at 0241 local time, May 7, 1945." The war is essentially over.

May 15, 1945: Eisenhower arrives in London, dines at the Dorchester Hotel, and attends the theatre (his first public appearance in three years).

June 12, 1945: Ike's stroll in Hyde Park is interrupted when grateful Londoners recognize him and crowd around. Later he rides in an open carriage to the scarred Guildhall, where he delivers a heartfelt and eloquent speech and is given the honorary Freedom of the City, only the fifth American to be so honored. Later in the day, King George confers the Order of Merit on Ike, the first American to receive the honor. General Eisenhower dines that evening at 10 Downing Street.

January 1953: Eisenhower is inaugurated as president of the United States. He will serve two terms, until 1961, when he retires to his farm in Gettysburg, Pennsylvania.

March 28, 1969: Dwight David Eisenhower dies in Washington, DC.

January 1989: Prime Minister Margaret Thatcher unveils a statue of General Eisenhower in Grosvenor Square, Mayfair.

Ike greeting the troops.

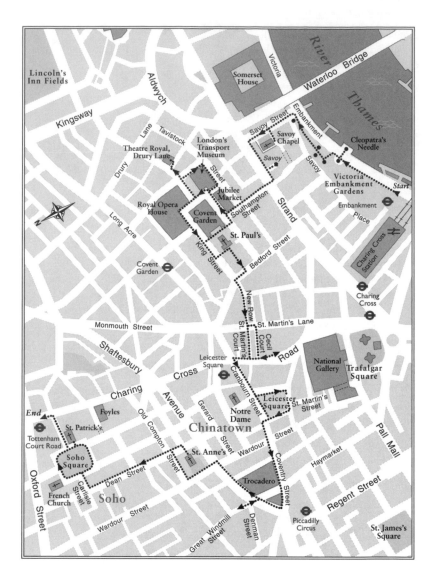

Lincoln's
Inn Fields

Kingsway

Aldwych

River Thames

Waterloo Bridge

Victoria

Somerset
House

Lane Tavistock

Drury Lane

Theatre Royal,
Drury Lane

London's
Transport
Museum

Savoy Street

Embankment

Savoy
Chapel

Savoy

Cleopatra's
Needle

Royal Opera
House

Street

Jubilee
Market

Covent
Garden

Southampton Street

Savoy

Victoria
Embankment
Gardens

Start

Long Acre

St. Paul's

Strand

Embankment

Place

Covent
Garden

King Street

Bedford Street

Charing
Cross
Station

Charing
Cross

Monmouth Street

New Row

St. Martin's Lane

St. Martin's Court

Cecil Court

Shaftesbury

Charing

Avenue

Cross

Leicester
Square

Road

National
Gallery

Trafalgar
Square

Foyles

Old Compton Street

Gerard Street

Cranbourn Street

Notre
Dame

Leicester
Square

St. Martin's
Street

End

St. Patrick's

Chinatown

Street

Pall Mall

Tottenham
Court Road

Soho
Square

St. Anne's

Wardour Street

Coventry Street

Haymarket

Oxford Street

Carlisle Street

Dean Street

French
Church

Soho

Wardour Street

Trocadero

Great Windmill Street

Denman Street

Piccadilly
Circus

Regent Street

St. James's
Square

5

Covent Garden to Soho

"Oh what a shabby city!" is one's first impression—
so many broken windows, so many windows boarded up,
the same old grime and mist but less colour, less traffic, fewer
people; gutted theatres still placarded with announcements
of forgotten shows; [and] huge and vulgar patriotic posters....
—LOUIS MACNEICE, "LONDON LETTER," JANUARY 1, 1941

The morning after...

Highlights: Cleopatra's Needle, Victoria Embankment Gardens, Waterloo Bridge, the Savoy Complex, Covent Garden area, St. Paul's Covent Garden, St. Martin's and Cecil courts, New Zealand Forces Club, American Eagle Club, Leicester Square, Café de Paris, Rainbow Corner, Windmill Theatre, Shaftesbury Avenue theatres, Chinatown, Soho, St. Anne's Church, French Pub, Soho Square

Underground Station: Embankment

Photo Ops: If you or a relative ever visited the Eagle Club or Rainbow Corner, you'll want to recapture some memories on the nearby streets.

BEFORE LEAVING ON YOUR TRIP

■ **Travel Scheduling:** Soho's Chinatown celebrates Chinese New Year in late January or February with a dragon parade and fire-

works. Covent Garden's Antiques Market is held year-round but only on Mondays.

■ **Cultural Preparations:** Music lovers, hasten to your local music store or public library for Eric Coates' *London Suite*. The first movement is a musical description of the animated market that once operated in Covent Garden. While you're shopping, pick up any Noël Coward CD that interests you, preferably one with "Don't Let's Be Beastly to the Germans" or "London Pride."

■ **Internet Best Bets:** Keep an eye on Soho and other London spots at www.camvista.com, a 24/7 webcam view. For London theatre information, try www.goodshow.com or www.officiallondontheatre.co.uk. Another possibility, www.theatremonkey.com, provides box office details, short irreverent reviews, and suggestions of best and worst seats.

This district, stretching from the Thames through some of the most relentlessly urban bits of central London, offers a variety of scenes and experiences: the tree-lined walkways of Victoria Embankment Gardens, the class of the Savoy Hotel, the bustle of Covent Garden, the quiet bookishness of Charing Cross Road bookshops, the sheer exuberance of Leicester Square, the swirl of Piccadilly Circus, the magic of Shaftesbury Avenue's theatre district, and the exoticness of London's Chinatown. Did I mention the bohemian *je ne sais quoi* of Soho? We'll visit all these and more, so put on your walking shoes. And with every step, we'll seek reminders of World War II, memories overlooked by most visitors. This is not an area of fancy houses or commemorative plaques or military monuments. Here people *worked*—in theatres and markets, in restaurants and bookshops, and we'll find some of those same locations sixty years on and see how the war came home to Covent Garden and Soho.

From the Embankment Underground, head along the Victoria Embankment, passing the "Public Convenience" in a small building that almost looks like a wartime surface shelter, albeit with a peaked roof.

Cross the Embankment roadway at the worn monument honoring Britain for taking in over 250,000 Belgian refugees in World War I. The large obelisk on the riverside—almost seventy feet high and weighing 186 tons—is **Cleopatra's Needle**. It was presented to Britain in 1819 and brought here from Alexandria as a gift from the viceroy of Egypt, though what a long strange trip it was. The granite monument, originally standing sentinel in Heliopolis in 1500 B.C., was eventually erected on the Embankment in 1878. Together with the bronze sphinxes on either side, which more traditionally as guardians of the column should be facing outward, Cleopatra's Needle has been on the Thames waterfront through two world wars.

> Cleopatra's Needle was cleaned in the 1970s, returning it to its original pinkish color; wartime observers would have seen a much grubbier Needle.

Watch for the plaque advising that the scars disfiguring the pedestal are of World War I vintage. A German bomb landed nearby in September 1917—the first air raid on London—and explosive fragments battered the obelisk, wrecked a passing tramcar, and killed three people. Even though they aren't World War II dings, the chips and pittings indicate just how damaging explosive bombs can be, even to sturdy stone monuments that have lain "prostrate for centuries on the sands of Alexandria" and been transported over the seas (and lost, then recovered). More of the saga of Cleopatra's Needle is presented on the several plaques on the base, so walk all the way around.

Back across the busy Embankment lanes, turn right at the Belgian monument, then enter the **Victoria Embankment Gardens** about seventy-five yards along. That imposing edifice behind and to the left of the statue of Robert Raikes is Shell-Mex House, built in the early 1930s. Most of the windows were blown out during the war, shattered by explosive bombs, but the building sustained no major damage. Incidentally, the clock face on the Shell-Mex tower is slightly larger than any of Big Ben's, although without the Victorian panache.

To the east of the Shell-Mex building is the Savoy Hotel complex, which we'll encounter again from the other side along the Strand. In the small garden memorial here, ringed with wooden benches, a sundial honors several theatrical folks including impresario Richard D'Oyly Carte, founder and proprietor of the Savoy Hotel and Theatre.

Opposite on the right side of the Embankment Garden walkway, a weeping muse mourns at the plinth of a bust of Arthur Sullivan, the music part of

The Embankment.

Gilbert and Sullivan, with a musical score, masque, and mandolin abandoned at one side. Gilbert and Sullivan staged the likes of *The Mikado*, *The Pirates of Penzance*, and other comic operettas at the Savoy Theatre. To add a touch of war-related interest to these essentially Victorian and Edwardian references, Winston Churchill was a great fan of Gilbert and Sullivan operettas.

Continue down the inner garden walk, then return to the Embankment pavement at the end. Straight ahead is **Waterloo Bridge**, a second-generation city crossing and the first all-concrete bridge to be built over the Thames. The original Waterloo Bridge—perhaps the loveliest bridge in Europe—was erected in the early 1800s, its name honoring Wellington's great victory. When in the early 1920s the bridge began to show "signs of weakening" (*such* an ominous phrase), a temporary bridge was hurriedly put up and lengthy bureaucratic discussions ensued about what to do next. Demolition of the lovely original finally began in the mid-1930s. Though construction was slowed somewhat by Mr. Hitler, the new Waterloo Bridge was officially dedicated in 1945, its completion seen by many as a symbol of London's determination to carry on despite the perils of war. The dismantled temporary bridge went to war, shipped to the front in Germany and eventually erected across the Rhine.

Turn left and walk up the incline of Savoy Street toward the Strand; on your left in front of the Institution of Electrical Engineers stands physicist Michael Faraday, inventor of the electric cell. You might want to nip down to the far west end of the IEE building, near the corner of Savoy Hill, to see the plaque noting the BBC's early history here.

Back on Savoy Street, head up the hill past the iron gates of the Savoy Cemetery and behind it the **Queen's Chapel of the Savoy**. This intimate chapel was built in the early 1500s as part of the Palace of the Savoy. Inside, a stained-glass window is dedicated to the memory of the Duke of Kent, youngest brother of King George VI, killed when his warplane slammed into the side of a Scottish mountain. The window features the RAF flag and the flag of St. George against a sky-blue background above the arms of the Duchy of Kent.

> **VISITOR DETAILS:** The Queen's Chapel of the Savoy is open Tuesday–Friday 11:30am to 3:30pm. Closed August and September. Guided tours available. More information: 020 7836 7221.

Once at the Strand, our route turns left— but first, a suggestion to return another time to visit Somerset House, to the right, housing the Courtauld collection of Impressionist paintings. In the courtyard a multitude of geysers set flat into the pavement lures visitors to tease and test the dancing waters. The cascading water provides a lively introduction to a classical eighteenth-century building, but one with relatively little war-related excitement except for those unfortunate bomb explosions along the waterfront that left a glaring gap in the riverside façade. So save the art and fountain of Somerset House for another day, and continue to the left along the Strand from the top of Savoy Street.

Next up is the **Savoy Hotel**. Even if you're not in the mood to step inside, do walk around the hotel's courtyard both to scan the half-dozen informative plaques and for a sense of the hostelry's personality. The Savoy was opened in 1889 by impresario Richard D'Oyly Carte, who soon lured César Ritz here as manager and Auguste Escoffier as chef, a one-two punch that meant it almost instantly became known as the capital's most elegant, luxurious, and expensive hotel. One of the earliest London hotels to be fitted with electric lights and elevators, the Savoy was also a pioneer in other areas: first hotel to install air conditioning and telephones in every room, first to have enough bathrooms (there were sixty-seven when the hotel opened, compared to the half-dozen in most large London hotels of the time), and allegedly first to mix a martini, naturally in the American Bar.

> *It wasn't just wartime journalists staying at the Savoy. Hollywood's best stayed here on their way to entertain the troops. Dinah Shore, Bob Hope, Marlene Dietrich, or Al Jolson might have been seen in the hotel's hallways or dining rooms.*

These comforts plus its central location made the Savoy a reporters' paradise during the war, serving as headquarters for dozens of American correspondents, from the *New Yorker's* Mollie Panter-Downes to *Collier's* Quentin Reynolds. Both the *New York Times* and the *Herald Tribune* moved

War Words: British Restaurants

BRITISH RESTAURANTS were a government-run nationwide chain of cafeterias providing nutritious and reasonably priced meals (a shilling or less) using unrationed foods. The original concept, at first called Communal Feeding Centres, was wisely renamed by Winston Churchill. Over 2,100 British Restaurants, serving over half a million meals a day, were in operation by September 1943. The quality of the two-course meals was...filling.

I suggest you call them "British Restaurants." Everybody associates the word "restaurant" with a good meal, and they may as well have the name if they cannot get anything else.
—Winston S. Churchill, writing to the Minister of Food, 1941

their offices here, and great clumps of journalists hung out at the American Bar, a "bazaar" for gossip.

Many of the resident journalists and those just stopping by for a drink while trolling for news would race back to their typewriters after watching German planes thread their way along the Thames, a view provided by the Savoy's rooftop. Unfortunately that same rooftop also offered an excellent target, and the Savoy easily won dubious honors as the most-bombed of the capital's major hotels.

Before the bombing began, Savoy management had made all the appropriate preparations—shutting the glass-domed restaurant at night, constructing blast walls, closing the hotel's top floors, establishing staff schedules for serving as air raid wardens and firewatchers, and building rooftop observation posts. In the guest rooms, heavy curtains provided protection from glass splinters, reduced the noise of the gun barrages, and were, of course, blackout-compliant. Several large banqueting rooms below ground level were reinforced with steel girders and transformed into shelters, each supplied with medical and nursing equipment...and curtained bunks. Here, in the words of one observer,

The Savoy's private forecourt is supposedly the only thoroughfare in England where traffic legally keeps to the right (in fact, by Act of Parliament).

was an "air-conditioned, gas-proof and sound-proof dormitory...equipped with its own maids and valets and waiters, with a room for coffee and a small bar one flight up." The Savoy, in its luxurious way, was ready.

The first weeks of the Blitz were relatively benign for the hotel—a high explosive bomb landed on neighboring Shell-Mex House and an oil bomb blazed merrily away nearby on the Embankment. These and other near-misses broke windows, cracked plaster, and smoke-streaked the Savoy's exterior walls. Meanwhile, guests steadily migrated from upstairs rooms to the basement shelters—the pom-pom-pom of anti-aircraft guns combined with the noise of German bombs made sleeping aboveground difficult. Then in November 1940 a late-night raid sent two high explosive bombs hurtling down on the Savoy. One damaged the hotel's northeast corner on the Embankment side, the other hit the hotel's front, then bounced down on the glass marquee in the forecourt, exploding and raining shards of glass down into the courtyard (about where you're standing if you circled the courtyard to read the historical plaques). Two people were killed, including a Belgian governmental minister. The war suddenly became very real for the hotel, its guests, and all the alcohol-enhanced journalists in the hotel's bar.

Theatregoers attending the Savoy Theatre in 1941 would have enjoyed Robert Morley in The Man Who Came to Dinner; *later war-era productions included* My Sister Eileen *and* The Last of Mrs. Cheyney.

In mid-April 1941, on the catastrophic night that came to be called The Wednesday, a land mine detonated along the river side, close enough that the whole building "staggered" when the mine exploded, as one eyewitness described it. Casualties from inside and outside the hotel were quickly attended to by the Savoy's medical staff; luckily there were no fatalities. More than fifty rooms had to be evacuated and closed temporarily, the hotel kitchen was a blackened shell, and the restaurant had been pulped, with over 5,000 glasses and pieces of china smashed. A major hole was punched in the exterior wall, about where the Embankment entrance now is, and every window on the Savoy's river side was shattered.

Bandleader Carroll Gibbons had most likely played "The Lady Is a Tramp" that night on his famous white piano. It was his signature tune and he performed it in many Savoy locations as changing air raid precautions and bomb damage moved the band from one hotel area to another. During Noël Coward's stay at the Savoy (he'd been bombed out of his home on Gerald Road), he volunteered to help entertain Savoy guests—probably with a rendition of his satirical "Don't Let's Be Beastly to the Germans." Alas, guest Margot Asquith (Lady Oxford) was least likely to join in the chorus. Bombed out of her Bedford Square home, the elderly Lady Oxford steadfastly remained in her Savoy room during air attacks, writing endless letters.

VISITOR DETAILS: Savoy Theatre box office: 020 7836 8888. Savoy Hotel: 020 7836 4343, www.savoy-group.co.uk/savoy.

The **Savoy Theatre**, on the west side of the Savoy complex, was opened by D'Oyly Carte in 1881, even before the hotel, and it too was a pioneer—it was the first public building in the world to be lit throughout by electricity, an innovation the audience cheered on opening night. The theatre was much rebuilt in 1929, with the main entrance moving from the Embankment side to the Savoy Hotel courtyard; the Victorian interior was totally redone in a slick and stylish Art Deco fashion.

In 1990, the theatre was consumed by fire, a modern disaster that must have reminded many onlookers of the Blitz: the theatre's roof collapsed, leaving "only blackened skeletal timbers…against the morning sky." An extensive restoration project recreated the 1929 splendor, and in 1993, with the Princess of Wales in attendance, a resplendent new Savoy Theatre opened.

Continue along the Strand to Southampton Street, then cross and head up the slight incline to **Covent Garden**. London's vibrant marketplace and entertainment center lies straight ahead, an area that has experienced several reincarnations in the last 400

> **VISITOR DETAILS:** Covent Garden piazza is open all the time; stores maintain varying hours, most in the Monday–Saturday, 10am to 5pm range. The cobbled road surface makes wheelchair use rough-going. Restaurants, cafés, and pubs abound; my personal favorite: Wagamama's, just south of the market. Restrooms are located between London's Transport Museum and Jubilee Hall; another set is across the piazza near the back of St. Paul's Covent Garden. More information: www.covent-garden.co.uk (with photos and sounds of the piazza) or www.coventgarden.uk.com.

years. At first it was a fashionable residential area, the site of mansions and town houses. In the 1670s a small fruit and vegetable market was established to provide the locals with fresh produce. This rapidly grew into a huge fruit and vegetable market (flowers too), and the surrounding environs slowly filled with more plebian brothels and taverns, coffeehouses and streetwalkers. Between the cabbages and the coffeehouses, the locals were squeezed out, and Covent Garden reigned as London's premiere produce market.

Covent Garden before wartime bombs and postwar changes.

They're Playing Our Song: Music of the War

As grim as wartime London could be—and imagine standing in a lengthy queue some rainy November morning, waiting to buy whale meat for tonight's dinner—music offered a relatively inexpensive gloom brightener. Some war-era music and oddball comic ditties are difficult to locate, never having been transferred from gramophone records to LPs or CDs. Finding "When Can I Have a Banana Again?" or "Thanks Mr. Censor" *can* be a challenge. But plenty of London's homefront favorites *are* available, especially the ballads and love songs a waiting sweetheart would have treasured.

Vera Lynn (The Forces' Sweetheart)—The clear sweet voice of the plumber's daughter from East Ham can still bring tears. Her CD *Something to Remember—Wartime Memories* includes such wistful standards as "The London I Love," "A Nightingale Sang in Berkeley Square," and "The White Cliffs of Dover." Another collection, *We'll Meet Again: The Early Years,* has songs recorded from 1936 to 1943.

Gracie Fields—"Our Gracie" was a much-loved Lancashire singer and comedienne whose endearingly cocky attitude could bring tears of laughter. Watch for *That Old Feeling* and *Our Gracie—23 Favorites 1928-1947* (with the rousing "Wish Me Luck as You Wave Me Goodbye"). Gracie is an acquired taste—not everyone finds "The Biggest Aspidistra in the World" knee-slapping hilarious, but her wacky insouciance was definitely a wartime morale booster.

Noël Coward—Urbane, suave, witty. Composer, lyricist, performer. These descriptions gather around one of England's great treasures. *The Songs of Noël Coward,* including "London Pride" and "Mad Dogs and Englishmen," highlights the wit of Coward's compositions.

George Formby—With his quirky smile and ukulele in hand, Formby was the epitome of British silliness. Two CD imports—*Formby Favourites* and *Ultimate Collection*—suggest his widespread appeal.

Anne Shelton—Shelton, only seventeen during her first BBC radio broadcast in May 1940, continued singing into the 1980s. Her rendition of "Lili Marlene," an anthem for both sides in the war, was popular throughout the 1940s. Watch for *Lili Marlene: The Early Years* and *At Last—*

And so it continued, a tough working-class market district for decades, including throughout World War II. But postwar sensibilities (and property values) changed, and developers began to look longingly at Covent Garden. In 1974, the market was moved to southwest London, leaving behind the piazza and market buildings—all ripe for redevelopment. It was a situation that could have gone horribly wrong (think tacky confer-

The Very Best of Anne Shelton, with "Kiss the Boys Goodbye" and "Coming in on a Wing and a Prayer."

Al Bowlly—For war-era dance music, you can't beat Bowlly's smooth swing singing in *Dance Band Years* and *Al Bowlly and the Great British Bands.*

Collections of wartime music offer a sampling of musical genres and performers. Watch for these CDs (the Imperial War Museum has a particularly good selection):

Favorite Wartime Songs: The Songs and Music That Lifted a Nation's Heart. Performers include Noël Coward, Arthur Askey, Anne Shelton, George Formby, Vera Lynn, and the Squadronnaires.

The Forces' Sweethearts: 23 Songs from the Heartthrobs of World War II. British and American heartthrobs sing out, including Vera Lynn, Anne Shelton, Deanna Durbin, Lena Horne, Ella Fitzgerald, and Judy Garland. Reminisce with such wartime standbys as "Say a Prayer for the Boys Over There" and "Stormy Weather."

Hits of the Blitz. Enjoy wartime hits performed by lesser-known musicians, including Geraldo and His Orchestra, Joe Loss, and Leslie Hutchinson.

Music from the 1995 Royal Tournament: Victory. Military bands play war standards, thematically arranged, starting with the outbreak of war ("There'll Always Be an England") through the Victory Parade ("Land of Hope and Glory"), with stops along the way to illuminate the unbroken spirit of Britain ("Who Do You Think You're Kidding, Mr. Hitler?" and "The Battle of Britain March").

Royal Music Collection: The Spirit of Britain. These well-loved tunes inspired a nation at war. Standards ("We'll Meet Again" and "Chattanooga Choo Choo") mix well with the less-familiar ("The Victory Polka" and "We Must All Stick Together").

Songs That Won the War. A slightly more diverse collection (Charles de Gaulle, after all, was probably not listening much to Vera Lynn or Gracie Fields), this features Edith Piaf ("La Vie en Rose"), Georges Thill ("La Marseillaise"), Anne Shelton, and several Americans—Dinah Shore, the Andrews Sisters, and Glenn Miller and His Orchestra. Many of the thirteen songs are musical tearjerkers, providing a hint of how very affecting homefront music could be, as it lifted the spirits and bolstered the will. It was almost enough to make whale meat palatable.

ence center or an Americanized mall), but luckily the move was toward an upscale specialty shopping center and entertainment district, bringing Covent Garden to yet another incarnation.

Today the piazza's central building is abuzz with trendy shopping areas—North Hall and Apple Market, Central Avenue, and South Hall. A newer and separate Jubilee Hall to the south (on the site of an older Jubilee Hall) houses several street markets during the week. The best is the Monday Antiques Market—watch for booths selling prewar London postcards or military medals.

Additional upmarket gift and clothing shops are located near the **Royal Opera House** in the covered arcade at the northeastern corner. The Opera House, home to both the Royal Opera and the Royal Ballet, suffered minor damage during the war but managed to carry on as the Mecca Dance Hall, with its seats covered with temporary flooring, two dance bands playing, and a soda fountain installed in one corner. The Opera House (with a great shop) has a serviceable entrance on the Covent Garden side, but for monumental drama, check out the columned portico on the Bow Street side.

VISITOR DETAILS: London's Transport Museum is open daily 10am to 6pm; Friday 11am to 6pm. Admission is charged; free for accompanied children under 16. Shopper Alert: Enjoy one of London's more varied shops, with an especially fine postcard collection. Café next door, restrooms nearby. More information: 020 7565 7299, www.ltmuseum.co.uk.

On the southeastern corner of Covent Garden the doors of **London's Transport Museum** swing open on an incredible collection of historic buses, trams, and trains, all housed in the old Flower Market building. The transportation war story in the metropolis involved far more than the Underground shelters—over one-and-a-quarter-million children were evacuated from the city via London Transport, and wartime buses and trains moved millions of Londoners on 400 different routes over a thousand miles of roadway…and all despite blackouts, detours and diversions, and bomb craters. The museum features plenty of hands-on opportunities plus archival photographs, videos, signaling apparatus, and antique transit vehicles to investigate or climb aboard.

Head a block east of Covent Garden on Russell Street to the **Theatre Royal, Drury Lane**, London's oldest theatre—in fact, England's oldest theatre still in use, and generally just called Drury Lane. This is the home of blockbuster musicals of the *My Fair Lady* and *Miss Saigon* genre. If you attend a performance, watch for the half-dozen or so statues honoring great English actors dotted about the corridors and staircases. But for now, step into the lobby and greet Noël Coward, cigarette in hand, languidly eyeing every arrival.

VISITOR DETAILS: Drury Lane's box office and lobby is open Monday–Saturday 10am to 8pm; the lobby itself is also open before, during, and after performances. For a theatre tour: 020 7494 5091. Drury Lane box office: 020 7494 5064.

Mr. Coward's wartime surroundings would not have been nearly as plush as they are today. One 1940 visitor found the war-scarred theatre looking dreary beyond words, with few lights in the entrance hall

War Words: Woolton Pie

Imagine a chicken pot pie, heavy on potatoes, cauliflower, turnips, and carrots; then remove the chicken. You'll have **WOOLTON PIE**, one of many dishes popular—or at least eaten—during wartime food rationing. Named after Lord Woolton, head of the Ministry of Food, Woolton Pie was a relatively filling and low-cost dish to prepare, and it yielded to the cook's imagination and rationing realities—if sausage were available it could be added, or more carrots or potatoes could be substituted when turnips or cauliflower were scarce.

> *And I can remember—which of my generation can't—the particular culinary horrors of war: Woolton Pie, composed of vegetables and sausage meat more crumb than sausage, and brown Windsor soup which tasted of gravy browning. And we got very tired of carrots.*
> —Mystery writer P. D. James

Woolton Pie was just one of many food treats touted in magazines or on the cookery hints program on the wireless every morning. (Other featured recipes included "swedes and turnips en casserole," oatmeal cheese rarebit, and grated carrot sandwiches.) Woolton himself was a favorite of Londoners, who were ready for reasonable food limitations if it would help the war effort. They cheered him on at a 1942 Christmas Potato Fair held in the Oxford Street bomb site of John Lewis's store, where faithguers were urged to sign the Potato Pledge: "I promise as my Christmas gift to the sailors who have to bring our bread that I will do all I can to eat home-grown potatoes."

and foyer and the grand staircase in semi-darkness. A German bomb had fallen through the roof, down through the gallery, the upper circle, and the grand circle, finally exploding at the back of the pit. But the show must go on, so the bomb crater was simply roped off and the roof shored up.

Drury Lane served as wartime headquarters for ENSA (Entertainments National Service Association), the government-sponsored organization established to provide entertainment to the troops. ENSA's army of actors, singers, dancers, and musicians entertained primarily the Armed Forces but they also strutted their stuff for workers at munitions plants, the new farm girls of the Land Army, and even wartime residents in prisoner-of-war camps, for a total audience by war's end of 500 million.

Head back to Covent Garden where the courtyard near St. Paul's provides a stage for an ever-changing assortment of fire-eaters, stiltwalkers, acrobats, magicians, jugglers, and other entertainers. The backdrop for the street performers is **St. Paul's Covent Garden**, looking much as it did when Professor Higgins first met flower seller Eliza Doolittle under the portico in Shaw's *Pygmalion*. The church is the oldest surviving structure

in Covent Garden, constructed in the 1630s by Inigo Jones and then much reconstructed after a fire in the 1790s. The false and nondescript door facing Covent Garden plus the building's "Tuscany Plain" architecture leave many visitors unaware that this is a church, and of those who do figure it out, many never find the front door.

Check the door immediately to the right of the church—if it's not open, walk out of Covent Garden on the north side past Dr. Martens. Halfway down King Street turn left into the covered passageway leading to St. Paul's secluded garden. It's several small steps down to

St. Paul's Covent Garden.

the flagstoned yard, a hidden spot that regularly fills with lunching office workers but is otherwise underpopulated...as is the church—I once wound my way through a hundred brownbaggers outside to enter the empty church, where I spent an hour totally alone.

Inside St. Paul's, the parish church of Covent Garden and long considered the Actors' Church, dozens of memorial plaques honor thespians, direc-

tors, stage designers, playwrights, and music hall performers—the likes of Noël Coward, Charlie Chaplin, Vivien Leigh, Ivor Novello, and Gracie Fields. Clemence Dane, a war-time playwright, author, and good friend of Noël Coward's, is memorialized here; she

VISITOR DETAILS: St. Paul's Covent Garden and church-yard are open Monday–Friday 8:30am to 4:30pm. More information: 020 7836 5221.

lived nearby on Tavistock Street. Several noted stage figures are buried in St. Paul's including Dame Edith Evans, yet another war-era thespian.

The church itself is a single rectangular room—no galleries, no side chapels—whose major attraction is all the plaques and memorials; plan on a circuit of the interior or perhaps a few quiet moments resting on one of the wood pews, looking eastward, where beyond the altar wall the Covent Garden performers entertain hundreds.

Walk out into the churchyard, then straight ahead down Inigo Place to Bedford Street. Turn right, and at the Belisha beacon, turn left and continue past the aptly named Round House pub, enjoying the intriguing shops along narrow New Row. Cross St. Martin's Lane and pause to explore either St. Martin's Court straight ahead or Cecil Court, parallel to it and a short block south.

The Victorian buildings nestled along **St. Martin's and Cecil courts** are filled with specialty bookshops, just as they were sixty years ago. You'll encounter no Books Etc. or Waterstone's here; instead, wander the cozy bookshops on these intimate streets, uncovering antiquarian, rare, and used dance folios, first editions, detective fiction, travel guides, P. G. Wodehouse novels, and children's books—perhaps a used copy of *Bulgy the Barrage Balloon* or *The Defence ABC Painting Book*. Both bibliographic lanes are vehicle-free and on a damp London afternoon, it's easy to imagine you're back in the early 1940s, perhaps seeking a Dorothy L. Sayers mystery to read tonight in the shelter. Remember, if the air raid siren sounds while you're shopping, there's a shelter in the basement of 4 Cecil Court, but meanwhile that half-crown is burning a hole in your pocket....

War-time maunderings over and purchases in hand, you'll find that both St. Martin's Court and Cecil Court end on Charing Cross Road.

Getting Your Pence's Worth

The wartime penny was a substantial copper affair about the size of an American fifty-cent piece. Though few items could be bought for just a penny, two pennies (tuppence), or even better, sixpence, could buy a great deal.

1 1/2d.	An Underground ticket
2d.	An issue of the London *Times* (the price would go up in 1941)
2d.	Rental of a park deck chair for a sunny Sunday afternoon
2d.	The latest BBC journal *Radio Times*
2d.	A postage stamp (the price would rise later in the war)
2d.	One packet of Smith's Potato Crisps
3d.	One Tobler National Service candy bar
3d.	A cup of tea at Lyons Tea Shop (4d. per pot, plus scones at 1 1/2d. apiece)
6d.	Sheet music for "They Can't Black Out the Moon"
6d.	Vim powder, for safe smooth cleaning, in a wartime economy pack
6d.	*Good Housekeeping*'s helpful booklet of "Thrifty War-Time Recipes"
6d.	Hot off the presses—the monthly *Boy's Own Paper*
6d.	Admission to Kensington Palace (1939)

The Ivy, at 1 West Street off Charing Cross Road, was a well-known lunchtime rendezvous for theatrical folk and Bloomsburyites. Perhaps it was the "whacking good" meals served early in the war, when Frances Partridge and Clive Bell, among others, ate smoked salmon, cold grouse, and chocolate mousse here. Such extravagance did not last.

Turn left and just before the Garrick Theatre enter the Charing Cross Library, to the left and up several steps—like so many older London buildings, this structure cannot easily be made wheelchair accessible. Inside, a brass plaque by the front desk notes that this building served as the **New Zealand Forces Club** during World War II; the adjacent Number 6 housed the New Zealand War Services Association. Prior to the war's outbreak, both Numbers 4 and 6 had been home to the Italian Club and several other Italian organizations; in fact, this area was well-populated by Italians. Once the war began, however, Italians were not looked on with great favor, and the government stepped in and seized the building.

Mrs. Churchill opened the New Zealand Forces Club in August 1940, and between then and 1945, busy volunteers provided over one-and-a-half-million meals and over five million snacks for visiting soldiers. The club welcomed service personal from any Allied country but an upstairs room was maintained exclusively for New Zealanders. Three years after war's end, the building opened as a public library. I'm always eager to wander any library, but I found this a very cramped facility—one wonders how all those hungry New Zealanders squeezed in here.

VISITOR DETAILS: Charing Cross Library is open on a varying schedule; check the sign. More information: 020 7641 4628, www.westminster.gov.uk/libraries/charing.

From the library's doorway, turn right to 28 Charing Cross Road, directly across from Bear Street. Today it's just offices jammed between a deli and a restaurant, but in the war years this was the **American Eagle Club**, a refuge for Americans ever since Thanksgiving Day 1940. It was taken over by the Red Cross in April 1942, renamed the Red Cross Eagle Club, and its services increased and focused on visiting GIs. Here they would find recreation rooms, inexpensive meals, hot showers, and an information bureau. This was one of several London ARC clubs; by January 1943 the clubs provided 3,000 beds nightly for American soldiers on leave, plus a variety of support services that made London manageable for the tourists in khaki.

Continue up Charing Cross Road a half-block to the corner streetlight, and cross to the **Leicester Square** area (pronunciation hint: "LESter"), London's semi-tawdry version of New York's Times Square, particularly along Cranbourn Street on the square's northern side. You'll

Leicester Square long ago.

encounter purveyors of cheap theatre tickets, outdoor cafés, espresso bars, a sex shop or two, street vendors, souvenir shops, movie theatres, restaurants, street entertainers, and every London visitor under the age of twenty-five. Oh yes, and a grassy square with the requisite quota of squirrels and statues. Officially laid out in the mid–1870s, though houses had been hereabouts since the 1600s, Leicester Square gradually developed into a "medley of variety theatres and cinemas, of charitable societies and billiard rooms; of propriety and impropriety." By the 1930s the cinemas began to dominate—the Odeon replaced the Alhambra Music Hall and the Empire Cinema replaced the Empire Music-hall. Together with its milk bars, foreign newspaper stalls, and restaurants, Leicester Square had become London's Cinema Square. Oh, and that billiard room—it was Thurston's, the billiard table manufacturers, to billiards what Wimbledon was (and is) to tennis.

Does the statue of Shakespeare in Leicester Square look familiar? It's a reproduction of one in Westminster Abbey. And if you're wondering why Newton, Reynolds, Hogarth, and Hunter rate busts at the square's corners, they all once lived in the neighborhood.

In October 1940, a land mine silently floated down onto Leicester Square and destroyed the entire southwestern corner, including Thurston's (Number 45). Adjacent buildings were flattened, the popular restaurant Perroquet badly damaged, the Leicester Square Theatre pockmarked by bomb fragments, and a deep crater plowed in the roadway. But saddest was Thurston's, where "in a pile of broken woodwork outside...could be seen torn fragments from the tables on which for 40 years the famous billiard and snooker players of the world had fought their battles."

Text continued on page 176.

Film Festival: Great Wartime Films

Homefront war movies span the cinematic range from classic tearjerk-ers (*Mrs. Miniver*) to documentaries (*Cities at War*) to contemporary features set in 1940s London (*The End of the Affair*). For a weekend film festival of your own, head to the video store or public library for these homefront stories. Note: All are available on video unless noted otherwise; check on DVD availability.

Battle of Britain (feature; 1969). Laurence Olivier as Hugh Dowding plus a bevy of British film stars don't quite pull this one off, but the flight scenes are impressive.

Cities at War: London, The First City (documentary; 1968). This documentary chronicles civilian life in London during the Blitz with dramatic seldom-seen footage of actual raids.

The Complete Churchill (TV documentary; 1991). A film festival in itself, this BBC production, written and presented by Churchill biographer Sir Martin Gilbert, depicts WSC's life with rare footage and personal interviews. Volume 2 features London's crisis years. [4-video set]

Dad's Army (TV feature; 1970s). Eighteen classic episodes of the very silly, very British, very funny BBC series focused on England's Home Guard. A movie spin-off was made (1971), but isn't available on video; the TV series was better anyway. [6-video set]

Danger UXB (TV feature; 1981). Experience tension and drama galore as the bomb disposal squad deals with unexploded bombs during London's Blitz. [Masterpiece Theater production; 5-video set]

The Dresser (feature; 1983). Had you forgotten this was set in the Blitz? Albert Finney, in a role best described as a "senile boozer," and Tom Courtenay star in this powerful wartime story of a traveling theatre company and its deteriorating star.

The End of the Affair (feature; 1999). A grim Blitz-era story based on the Graham Greene novel, this has all the biggies: love, religion, war, guilt, jealousy, and London. Ralph Fiennes, Julianne Moore, and Stephen Rea star in the 1999 film; an earlier version (1955) starred Deborah Kerr and Van Johnson.

Enigma (feature; 2001). Primarily set in Bletchley Park (though filmed elsewhere) but with a handful of London scenes, *Enigma* focuses on a codebreaking genius and his frantic efforts to crack the German code. This is my favorite Kate Winslet film; Tom Stoppard wrote the screenplay.

Foreign Correspondent (feature; 1940). Get out the popcorn and enjoy this dated but rousing Hitchcock spy drama. It follows an American journalist (Joel McCrea) sent to cover Europe's volatile war scene. Both Holland and London provide some nail-biting Hitchcock moments.

Forever and a Day (feature; 1943). These comic bits and dramatic moments, linked together by the story of a regal London house, star eighty Hollywood actors, many with British roots. Produced as a tribute to (and morale booster for) the people of England, it features Charles Laughton, Ray Milland, Claude Rains, Elsa Lancaster, and many more.

Hanover Street (feature; 1979). American pilot meets British nurse in an air raid, love blooms, complications arise. An early Harrison Ford flick, with sets "a bit too calculated an evocation of wartime London," put this toward the bottom of the must-see list.

Hope and Glory (feature; 1987). On the other hand, this engrossing story of a London family during the Blitz, as seen through the eyes of a young boy, should be at the very top of the must-see list.

In Which We Serve (feature; 1942). Noël Coward's Oscar-winning tale was inspired by the sinking of the English destroyer *Kelly*; the movie includes scenes in England of families left behind, including a very credible air raid.

It Happened Here: The Story of Hitler's England (feature; 1964). Here's London in 1944...if the Nazis won. A small movie, a haunting concept.

The Land Girls (feature; 1998). This bittersweet love story features several city girls going off to war—on a farm.

The Life and Death of Colonel Blimp (feature; 1943). Simply a great movie, following the life of soldier Clive Wynne-Candy from the Boer War to the Blitz. You'll know a lot more about the British after watching this.

The Lion Has Wings ("docudrama" feature; 1940). An interesting though dated combination of newsreel footage and feature film, this follows Britain's air defense against the Luftwaffe and stars Merle Oberon and Ralph Richardson. One reviewer called it "now quaint, but stirring wartime period piece." Sounds great

Listen to Britain and Other Films by Humphrey Jennings (documentaries; 1940–1951). A compilation of six short films by England's wartime documentary genius. Especially good: *London Can Take It* and *Fires Were Started*. Available on DVD only.

Ministry of Fear (feature; 1944). An atmospheric thriller set in wartime London from director Fritz Lang, this is based on a Graham Greene novel and stars Ray Milland.

Mrs. Miniver (feature; 1942). This Oscar-winning (six, including Best Film) Hollywood version of England's homefront features the stoic Mrs. Miniver and her family. It's flawed, sentimental, but moving nonetheless.

The 1940s House: Rediscovering Family Life in the 1940s (TV documentary; 2002). A 1990s family gets plunked down into wartime life, and we get to watch what happens. Contrived it is, but riveting and as emotionally powerful as any feature film. [2-video set]

Their Finest Hour (documentaries). Two multi-video sets with this title have been produced. The first and older, subtitled "The RAF and the Battle of Britain," includes an Oscar-winning turn by director Frank Capra focusing on London during the Blitz. Although not currently in print, it turns up in library collections and for sale on eBay. The more recent documentary, produced by WGBH and the BBC, uses archival footage, photographs, and personal stories to relate the story of Britain's wartime pilots.

Tonight and Every Night (feature; 1945). Rita Hayworth stars in yet another pilot-falls-in-love flick, but the interesting and almost-saving grace of this truly tepid story is that it's set at the "Music Box" (actually London's Windmill Theatre).

Waterloo Bridge (feature; 1940). Ballerina Vivien Leigh and aristocratic British officer Robert Taylor meet on Waterloo Bridge during a German air raid, then must part. Keep the Kleenex handy.

We'll Meet Again (TV feature; 1982). The U.S. Eighth Army Air Force moves into a quiet English town, and naturally the Yank major falls in love with the (married) English doctor. [Masterpiece Theater production; 5-video set]

Yanks (feature; 1979). GIs in Northern England prepare for D-Day, finding time to fall in love before bravely heading off to battle. Richard Gere, Vanessa Redgrave, and Lisa Eichhorn star.

Leicester Square again fell victim to German bombs a few months later, in spring 1941. This time it was the northeastern corner, and the local pub, the cake and bun shop, and the Café Anglais were obliterated. Shakespeare, standing in the square's center, lost his left hand, and three of the four corner busts (Newton, Reynolds, and Hunter) fell to the ground. The areas near the Odeon and the Empire were a sea of sparkling shattered glass. And in a chilling description of the time, "fragments of taxicabs hung from the trees."

Today the marble (and re-handed) William Shakespeare still stares at the Empire Cinema, just as he watched wartime Londoners flock to see *Gone With the Wind*, a movie so popular it was shown continuously here from 10am to 11:30pm, with long queues circling the theatre. Around him is a much renewed garden area with a very different look from the early 1940s—back then the walkway railings, dismantled and sent off to be made into armaments, were replaced with wicker stakes, and air raid shelters were dug beneath the weed-patch of a garden. After the war, the square became even more grungy and uninviting. Major refurbishment in the late 1980s rejuvenated the area and Queen Elizabeth was on hand in

1992 for the formal re-opening. Today the shady benches offer a still point in Leicester Square's turning world for people-watching or daydreaming, as you chose.

VISITOR DETAILS: Leicester Square is open pretty much all the time, though it's more pleasant earlier in the day before the empty soda cups and pizza crusts pile up. Several restaurants, cafés, and coffee shops ring the square; public restrooms are down the steps at the northern corners.

Leave Leicester Square at the northwestern corner, heading straight ahead onto Coventry Street; Piccadilly Circus is just a few blocks away. Instead of tourists, imagine this crowded street filled with waves of wartime soldiers, American and French, Polish and English, Dutch and Australian, all wandering from the service clubs (and friendly ladies) of Piccadilly Circus to the excitement of Leicester Square. Along this popular "Half Mile," those young soldiers would regularly pass by 3 Coventry Street along the north side of the street, a sign on the front warning "Danger—Unsafe Premises." It was once a popular destination for Londoners, with the Rialto Cinema aboveground and downstairs the **Café de Paris**, one of London's classiest nightspots. This subterranean nightspot attracted guests both royal and social with headliners such as Marlene Dietrich, Bea Lillie, and Maurice Chevalier.

By 1942, when hordes of American servicemen began to flood London, the elegance was gone, as were, tragically, both the Rialto Cinema and the Café de Paris. This "glittering night cavern" once advertised as the safest place to dance in town had been shredded by a German bomb on a busy Saturday night, March 8, 1941. Just before 10pm, Ken "Snakehips" Johnson and his band were playing "Oh Johnny" in the Café de Paris, with its two sweeping staircases modeled on the ballroom of the *Titanic* (some said the *Lusitania*—whichever, it was a ship that ended tragically). German land mines silently fell earthward, smashing through the roof of the Rialto and continuing down and down, into the club itself. One landed directly in front of the band, its explosion instantly killing dancers and diners, musicians and busboys. In all, more than

Although the air raid shelters below Leicester Square are long gone (destroyed when the electricity substation was built), Andrew Duncan in Secret London is convinced that the doorway down the men's restroom stairs in the northeast corner is an entrance to the former shelter.

eighty people died that night. After the bodies were taken away, and the rubble was cleared, the entranceway was shored up and that understated sign tacked up: "Danger—Unsafe Premises."

Three years after the horrific bombing of the Café de Paris, it reopened as a service club, an extension of the nearby Nuffield Center for British

Across from the Café de Paris stood the 400 Club, yet another wartime nightspot humming with "the bright intensity of American and British pilots on leave [and] socialites ready for an evening's entertainment."

service personnel. One wonders if any of those soldiers ever heard the ghosts of Snakehips Johnson and his band playing "Oh Johnny" soft and low, like a dirge. Incidentally and more recently a new nightspot, also called the Café de Paris, has opened here.

Straight ahead is Piccadilly Circus, long the hub of London's theatre and nightlife. Chapter 3 visited the Eros statue and the Underground, but several other war-related sites are in the vicinity. This was wartime London's amusement center, with cinemas and a dozen theatres within a block or two, and multitudes of dining and dancing opportunities. Even when the bright lights were off (as they were on wartime nights), Piccadilly Circus was London's most central, most exciting spot.

Just before the swirl of the Circus, the Trocadero looms on the right, now a "leisure centre" stretching from Coventry Street north to Shaftesbury Avenue. It was built in the 1890s and before the postwar tarting up, housed three popular eateries: the famous Trocadero (the "Troc"), a Lyons Corner House Restaurant, and Scott's Restaurant. Many a war-era thespian from the nearby theatres must have ducked out of rehearsals and dashed here, most likely sitting down at the more economical Lyons. There were four Corner Houses in London and dozens of smaller Lyons teashops, precursors in ubiquity to today's Starbucks. The Corner Houses were mega-eateries, especially the Coventry Street premises, where 4,500 customers could be seated. And while the ordinary actors and stagehands were enjoying teatime at Lyons (or perhaps a more substantial meal of minced beef, carrots, and potatoes), director and stars may well have been enjoying oysters or lobster at the upmarket Scott's, opened at 18 Coventry Street in 1872 (and since the 1960s, located in Mayfair).

Coventry Street ends at Piccadilly Circus; turn right and head to Shaftesbury Avenue, the next street leading off Piccadilly Circus as you

Scott's Restaurant.

Bused Out

Some good wartime sightseeing can be done from atop a London double-decker bus, especially along these lengthy routes. As compared to a journey in the early 1940s on much the same streets, you will experience fewer bomb craters, less rubble, and, one hopes, no unexploded bombs.

Number 11—From St. Paul's Cathedral to Chelsea, via Ludgate Hill, the Strand, Trafalgar Square, Westminster, Victoria, and Sloane Square (a *great* sightseeing route)

Number 15—From Marble Arch to Aldgate, via Oxford Circus, Piccadilly Circus, Trafalgar Square, Aldwych, St. Paul's, and the Tower of London

Number 19—From Bloomsbury to Chelsea, via Piccadilly, Knightsbridge, and Sloane Square

Number 25—From Oxford Circus to Aldgate, via Holborn, and then either Bank (weekdays) or the Tower of London (weekends)

Number 53—From Oxford Circus to the Imperial War Museum, via Piccadilly Circus, Trafalgar Square, and Westminster

> *You see many more [ruins] on the drive through the City, on the 25 bus—these are really impressive, far more so than the East End....It makes slow going, as there are so many diversions because of craters.*
> —Author Rose Macaulay in a letter, October 3, 1940

circle northward. On the corner of Shaftesbury and Denman Street once stood London's largest Red Cross club for the Americans, **Rainbow Corner**, ready to help the enlisted man billeted in the big city or just arrived with a coveted three-day pass. Opened in 1942, the club had been cobbled together from two London landmarks—the Monaco restaurant and a Lyons, both previously blitzed and ready for reincarnation. Rainbow Corner quickly became Red Cross Central for all R&R activities in London and a safe haven for soldier boys adrift in the big city. Free London maps handed out to every visiting Yank featured a large photo of Rainbow Corner and the reminder, "If you get lost in London come here."

Lost or not, they came, more than 25,000 on a typical day. The Rainbow Club's staff (400-plus) catered to the crowds, providing entertainment, information, refreshments, and accommodations. Many soldiers headed downstairs to the "Dunker's Den," a faux corner drugstore right out of 1940 Middle America, to listen to gramophone records on the juke box, drink ice-cold Cokes, and devour fresh hot doughnuts or American-style hamburgers. Unlike most of London, the Den (and the entire Rainbow Corner complex) stayed open twenty-four hours a day. Two unexpected services: In one corner Adele Astaire, steady volunteer and sister to Fred, helped GIs write letters home, while nearby labored another woman whose only job was to sew on buttons.

The busy Information Desk, staffed by local young women, could answer the hardest of questions, from how to wire flowers to a sweetheart back home to what bus goes to the Tower of London. Rainbow Corner was also the place where GIs could get a good haircut, treatment for VD, or free tickets to West End shows. And attached to a lobby pillar were two wistful signs: "Berlin—600 miles" and "New York—3,271 miles."

For the men of the American 8th Air Force stationed outside of the metropolis, London beckoned irresistibly, and for every five missions flown, they got a three-day pass to the big city.

Upstairs was the hobbyist area, with space and equipment for anyone who wanted to model clay, play the piano, or draw. One room was devoted solely to the playing of classical records, another to hometown newspapers, a third to uniquely Stateside types of recreation—pool, pinball machines, playing craps (a room likely more popular than that for modeling clay). Two dining rooms offered filling meals to as many as 2,000 hungry Yanks at a time. Nighttimes the ballroom dance floor would be packed; one visiting Red Cross worker enjoyed "a great GI band...playing so enthusiastically the floor shook to the beat of the music." And, of course, there were plenty of bunks for soldiers who turned up overly intoxicated with the delights of the big city.

In its first year, Rainbow Corner served more than five million U.S. servicemen and their guests. The sad day the club closed in 1946 was enough of an occasion to draw Eleanor Roosevelt, Anthony Eden, and the American ambassador. In 1947 the building became a café, and then postwar redevelopment led to the construction of a bland, memory-less collection of shops and offices.

Nearby, up Great Windmill Street, is the site of the old **Windmill Theatre**, another wartime favorite. A London institution, the Windmill had two claims to fame. First, it never closed throughout the war except for the twelve days of government-mandated closure of theatres immediately after war was declared. And secondly, it presented the popular semi-vaudeville *Revudeville* featuring a continuous variety show (2:30pm to 11pm daily) of comics, dancers, and nude girls arranged in "artistic" poses. The revudebelles, as the showgirls were known, were constrained by local

regulations to flaunt their stuff under subdued lighting and without moving a muscle
once naked. Naturally the show was a sensation, especially with the appreciative men of
the Allied Forces. The theatre's motto, "We
Never Closed," was widely promoted during the war years and after, though many

**GREAT
WINDMILL
STREET**
CITY OF WESTMINSTER

thought "We Never Clothed" more appropriate. The Windmill did finally
close, however, in 1964 and then reopened as a strip club. Today it's still a
strip club of sorts: "London's most exciting table-side dancing club."

Continue along Shaftesbury where several of London's major **theatres**
march along the north side: the Lyric, Apollo, Gielgud (the Globe during
the war years), and Queens (well-bashed in September 1940 and closed
for the war's duration, in fact for almost twenty years). Wartime productions along this theatrical patch featured some of the greatest actors and
directors in the history of the English theatre, including Ralph
Richardson, Margaret Rutherford, Edith Evans, Peggy Ashcroft, Emlyn
Williams, Sybil Thorndike, Alec Guinness, Laurence Olivier, Michael
Redgrave, and John Gielgud. In fact Gielgud was the first on the scene
one Blitz night when the Globe Theatre caught a packet of incendiary
bombs. He and a friend dashed up the street "with the barrage going on
all around us, feeling very heroic and terrified, to find the fire out and the
stage deep in water—a lot of glass lying about and scenery soaked and
damaged but no one hurt."

To the right down Wardour Street is **Chinatown**, an area that developed primarily after World War II when London's Chinese community
slowly migrated here from the devastated Docklands area, ready to serve
the culinary tastes of soldiers returning from the Far East. For a quick
introduction to Chinatown, wander down Wardour Street, left along
Gerrard, then left again along Macclesfield Street back to Shaftesbury,
then backtrack to Wardour. If the sights, sounds, and mystery here intrigue
you—including those cute but tacky pagoda telephone kiosks and the

NOTICE

In the event of an Air Raid Warning an announcement
will be made by means of an illuminated box sign installed
immediately in front of the footlights. Patrons are advised
to remain in the Theatre, but those wishing to leave will be
directed to the nearest official air raid shelter, after which
the performance will be continued for so long as is practicable

somewhat more dramatic red and golden gates—feel free to go further afield. Gerrard and Lisle streets are the heart of Chinatown, but the Chinese supermarkets, restaurants, and shops of the district drift onto Newport Place and Leicester Place too. All will well repay your curiosity, and you can catch up with us back on the corner of Shaftesbury and Wardour Street.

German bombs wiped out two Soho theatres. The Shaftesbury on the southern side of Shaftesbury Avenue between Nassau and Newport streets was destroyed by a land mine in April 1941; for years its outer walls remained around a derelict car park. And on Dean Street across from Bateman Street once stood the Royalty Theatre, also a Blitz victim.

Soho, that "curious quarter" as one prewar guidebook put it, is roughly bounded by Oxford Street, Charing Cross Road, Leicester Square, and Regent Street—since it's not an official borough, there are no fixed borders. This district has always appealed to the adventurous who looked beyond the rundown shabbiness and could see, as did one wartime writer, that "when the sun shines on it, [Soho] looks more and more like a little part of Paris, say a turning off Montmartre or perhaps the market-place in the district École Militaire." Today, Soho's bohemian and exotic nature has been trending upwards a notch as the area rebounds after years of seediness that edged into sleaze.

One London observer has suggested that "the cooks and émigrés founded foreign Soho." The earliest enclaves of foreigners were probably the French Huguenots in the 1600s, and they brought their cuisine with them, as did later arrivals from Italy, Spain, Greece, Cyprus, Turkey, and Malta, with postwar arrivals from Japan, India, China, and Vietnam.

For seemingly forever, Soho has been filled with small restaurants serving a variety of cuisines, serviceable eateries where one could eat slightly exotic meals at a decent price. Unfortunately, many Italian émigrés also brought their Italian surnames and accents to Soho, and the days after Italy entered the war against Britain were both personally painful and sometimes dangerous for London citizens of Italian descent. Several Italian restaurants in Soho were trashed by rowdy groups; several others decided to become "Swiss" overnight. Many of Soho's longtime Italian and German residents were rounded up as enemy

No, Soho is not named after a trendy New York neighborhood. "So-ho" was the hunting cry used hereabouts by seventeenth-century hunters.

aliens and imprisoned to internment camps for the war's duration, a sad outcome of a difficult time.

From Shaftesbury Avenue turn north onto Wardour Street, passing **St. Anne's Churchyard**. The seventeenth-century quasi-Wren church (likely

built by one of the masons working for Wren)
was gutted in autumn 1940, first by a high
explosive bomb and then, the *coup de grace*, by
incendiaries. Only the ugly tower remained—
more compassionate viewers than I have called
it "a curious affair." Added to the church in the
early 1800s, it looks like a diving helmet atop a
postbox. It's now surrounded on the Wardour
side by a large grassy area several feet above street
level—this was once a burial ground, and thousands of people were buried here. We'll come
back to St. Anne's briefly in a moment, from the
Dean Street side.

St. Anne's tower.

From St. Anne's Churchyard continue to Old
Compton Street; a right turn and short block
bring you to Dean Street. German bombs diced the southwestern corner
of Dean and Old Compton streets in May 1941, devastating many of the
restaurants in the area, including the Patisserie Valerie, one of Soho's favorite
shops. Undaunted, the patisserie moved nearby to 44 Old Compton Street;
if you're ready for a rest stop, consider a chocolate truffle gateaux and a
cup of tea.

Old Compton Street is the High Street of Soho and worth a walk
from end to end—another day perhaps—to check out its boutiques, delis,
bars (gay and otherwise), quirky shops, and general high spirits. In the war
years, the area was filled with great little restaurants, plus dozens of gastro-
nomic support services: greengrocers, wine merchants, fruit stores, and
coffee merchants. This is the heart of Soho, where bookmakers and bootmakers, prostitutes and tailors, actresses and artisans, poets and pub-owners,
all lived or worked. Or drank...

...Which brings us inexorably to the **French Pub**. From the corner
of Old Compton and Dean streets, turn right a half-block to the French
Pub, officially the York Minster when it opened in 1914, now officially the
French House (renamed when it was sold in
1989), but known to all as the French Pub.
This was the wartime meeting place for
Free French expatriates and Belgian émigrés
(the owner was Belgian). Prewar and war-
time patrons also included French entertainer
Maurice Chevalier, poet Dylan Thomas, artist
Augustus John, playwright Brendan Behan

> **VISITOR DETAILS:** The French
> Pub is open Monday–Saturday
> noon to 11pm; Sunday 7pm
> to 10:30pm. The restaurant
> upstairs has slightly different
> hours. More information: 020
> 7437 2799.

Text continued on page 186.

December 16, 1899: Noël Pierce Coward is born at 131 Waldegrave Road, Teddington, Surrey (a plaque notes his birthplace).

1920s: Entertainer and playwright Coward lives at 111 Ebury Street, Belgravia, where his mother takes in lodgers (the building is now a bed and breakfast). His room is at the top back of the house, although as he becomes more successful he moves to rooms on lower floors: "As I rose in the world I went down in the house."

Early 1930s: Coward moves to 17 Gerald Road, Belgravia (a plaque notes his residence). He'll remain until 1956 when he sells the place (£11,000) and moves away from the high English taxes to Jamaica, Bermuda, and Switzerland.

1940: Coward spends time in Paris organizing a quasi-secret information link between the French and English. His frequent return visits to London almost always begin with a party at the home of author and artist Clemence Dane (pseudonym of Winifred Ashton) in her "rickety little house in Tavistock Street, Covent Garden."

> Be glad you missed that October day in 1941 when Noël Coward arrived at the Strand to find a mock tear-gas attack in progress. As he wryly noted, "At least the attack was mock, but the tear-gas was not."

April 16, 1941: Coward dines at the Hungaria (14 Regent Street), then takes a taxi home to Gerald Road in the midst of a bombing raid. There, after scrambling over rubble and broken glass in the street, he discovers his front door blasted off and the interior a shambles. Within minutes, a second blast brings down the skylight, shatters the windows, and sends two oak doors "skittering past us like ballet dancers." Coward moves temporarily into the Savoy Hotel on the Strand.

May 1941: In a single week Coward writes the script for *Blithe Spirit*, destined to become one of the longest-running comedies in the history of British theatre. It opens July 2, 1941, at the Piccadilly Theatre (still there, on Denman Street). Coward finds it ironic that the audience "had to walk across planks laid over the rubble caused by a recent air raid to see a light comedy about death."

July 1941: At dinner with Edwina and Louis Mountbatten, Coward listens raptly to Mountbatten's experiences during the sinking of the destroyer *Kelly* in the Battle of Crete. Coward soon discusses his idea for a naval propaganda film with officials at the Ministry of Information in Bloomsbury, then broaches the topic with Mountbatten, who is equally enthusiastic.

December 1941: Work begins on the *Kelly* film at Denham Studios in Buckinghamshire, northwest of London. Coward co-directs (with David Lean) and also plays the ship's captain, a role loosely based on the experiences of Mountbatten.

September 27, 1942: *In Which We Serve* opens at the Gaumont Haymarket. The London newspapers and the public cheer the dramatic story of a British destroyer, her captain, officers, and sailors. The film will be nominated for Academy Awards for best picture and best original screenplay.

May 8, 1945 (V-E Day): Coward begins the day by visiting his mother at Eaton Mansions in Chelsea, then wanders London's streets. His evening starts with a party at Clemence Dane's flat in Covent Gardens, where guests listen to speeches on the radio by King George, Ike, Montgomery, and others. Later Coward wanders down the Mall to stand outside Buckingham Palace ("we all roared ourselves hoarse"), and finally he's off to "Chips" Channon's party in Belgravia. "A wonderful day from every point of view."

February 4, 1970: Coward is knighted by the queen at Buckingham Palace.

March 26, 1973: Sir Noël Coward dies at his home in Jamaica, West Indies.

March 28, 1984: A floor stone honoring Coward is unveiled at Westminster Abbey: "Noël Coward / Playwright*Actor*Composer / 'A talent to amuse.'"

December 1998: The Queen Mother unveils a statue of Sir Noël Coward inside Drury Lane Theatre, Covent Garden, one of London's best-known venues for lavish theatricals.

(not to be confused with politician Brendan Bracken), and various other bohemians and bohemian wannabes. Sixty years later it's still a good place for an afternoon rest stop or evening meal, a real neighborhood bar (lots of photos) that's neither too seedy nor too trendy; perhaps a Pernod would be appropriate. Watch for the framed photo of de Gaulle over the bar and a copy of his June 1940 radio broadcast by the door.

> The ashes of mystery writer and church-warden Dorothy L. Sayers are buried beneath the floor in the tower of St. Anne's, Soho.

Across from the French House is the church side of St. Anne's, though it's hard to tell that from the street. For years after the war, the bombed area around St. Anne's was used as a car park, but by the early 1990s, redevelopment brought flats plus a community center and offices. The church is in the center of all this, down a covered passageway and much modernized; it's generally only open for services.

Continue north on Dean Street to Carlisle Street; a short block ahead is quiet **Soho Square**, an area laid out during the time of Charles II. That's a worn 1680s statue of the king near the pseudo-Tudor/Elizabethan structure in the square's center. The statue was originally erected in Soho Square but then removed, eventually turning up in the possession of W. S. Gilbert of Gilbert and Sullivan. Charles was returned here in 1938 after the death of Gilbert's wife—just in time for the Blitz. The king survived German bombs, though he stood for some years staring across the square at a burnt-out house.

As with many London squares, Soho Square started life as a residential enclave, then slowly slid into the office and agency realm. Because the Soho district was home not only to cinemas and theatres but to the companies connected with producing films and stage shows, many of the larger firms set up shop here. Gracie Fields, Tyrone Power, Leslie Howard, and other wartime film stars walked the pavements of Soho Square, heading to the London offices of Twentieth Century Fox Film Company. British Movietone News was here too, as well as offices of music publishing firms, cinema theatre proprietors, film printers, and many other movie-related businesses.

Time for a Pernod?

Air raid shelters were dug in the square's center, beneath the grass and flower beds, and the eighteenth-century cast iron railings were uprooted and taken off to be made into armaments. The garden wasn't restored to public use until 1954.

French Protestant Church.

Today Soho Square is surrounded by churches and offices, and unlike St. James's or Grosvenor squares, doesn't quite warrant a building-by-building circuit. But do walk by two important structures here: the French Protestant Church and St. Patrick's Catholic Church.

The **French Protestant Church**, or more officially the Eglise Protestante Française de Londres, is located near the square's northwestern corner at Number 9. It opened in 1893, dedicated "to the glory of God and in grateful memory of His Majesty King Edward VI who by his charter of 1550 granted asylum to the Huguenots from France." This red terra cotta and brick structure, in the Flemish-Gothic style, was much used by French servicemen during the war. Unfortunately it's usually closed.

Across the square is **St. Patrick's Catholic Church,** opened on St. Patrick's Day in 1893. In the 1930s, an illuminated cross stood on the tower, its wartime removal necessitated by the perfect target it provided Luftwaffe pilots. In November 1940, a German bomb crashed through the roof, banged off a column, and buried itself deep in the nave floor. It did not explode—the luck of the Irish. Step inside to view the gray and cream interior and dramatic barrel-vaulted ceiling.

VISITOR DETAILS: St. Patrick's is one of those wonderful churches that seem to be always open; for more information: 020 7437 2010, or www.stpatricks.uk.com.

Before heading to the nearby Tottenham Court Road Underground or the Oxford Street buses, pause a moment in Soho Square to remember all the working people of Soho and Covent Garden who lived through six years of war, enduring discomfort, hardship, and peril. King George had it right: "We are a nation on guard and in the line. Each task, each bit of duty done, however simple and domestic, is part of our war work. It takes rank with the sailor's, the soldier's, and the airman's duty."

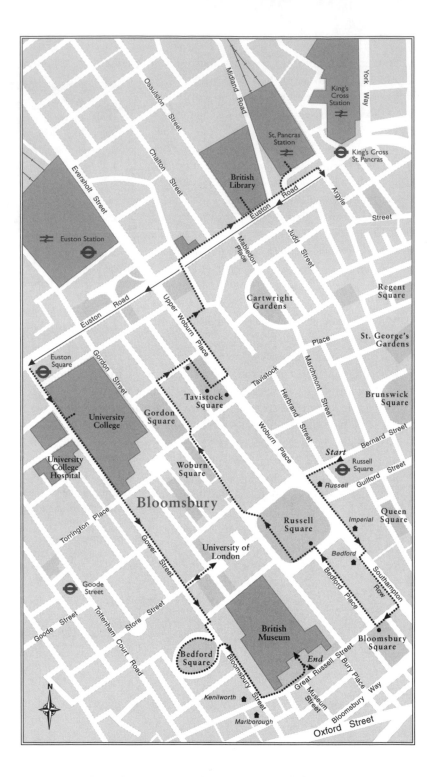

York Way

King's
Cross
Station

Ossulston Street

Midland Road

St. Pancras
Station

King's Cross
St. Pancras

Chalton Street

Eversholt Street

British
Library

Euston Road

Argyle

Street

Euston Station

Mabledon Place

Judd Street

Regent
Square

Upper Woburn Place

Euston Road

Cartwright
Gardens

Place

St. George's
Gardens

Euston Square

Gordon Street

Tavistock

Marchmont Street

Brunswick
Square

University
College

Gordon
Square

Tavistock
Square

Herbrand Street

Bernard Street

Woburn Place

Start

Russell
Square

Russell

Guilford Street

University
College
Hospital

Woburn
Square

Bloomsbury

Imperial

Queen
Square

Russell
Square

Bedford

Torrington Place

University of
London

Southampton Row

Gower Street

Goode
Street

Bloomsbury
Square

Bedford Place

Goode Street

Tottenham Court Road

Store Street

British
Museum

Bedford
Square

Bloomsbury Street

End

Great Russell Street

Museum Street

Bury Place

Bloomsbury Way

Kenilworth

Marlborough

Oxford Street

N

6
Bloomsbury's
Leafy Squares

You never escape the war in London....Very few buses.
Tubes closed. No children. Everyone humped with a gas
mask....A reversion to the middle ages with all the space
and silence of the country set in this forest of black houses.

—VIRGINIA WOOLF

London bobbies escort passersby to safety.

Highlights: Russell Square hotels, Blooms-bury Square, Bedford Place, Russell Square, Woburn Square, Gordon Square, Tavistock Square, Euston Station, St. Pancras Chambers and Station, British Library, Gower Street, Senate House, Bedford Square, British Museum, Great Russell Street

Underground Station: Russell Square

Photo Ops: Photo opportunities inside the British Museum abound, but don't overlook the outdoor sights of Bloomsbury: flowers in the squares, plaques honoring members of the Bloomsbury Group, or the ruddy façade of the British Library.

BEFORE LEAVING ON YOUR TRIP

■ **Travel Scheduling:** The springtime blooms and autumn color of Bloomsbury's spacious tree-lined squares are particularly appealing.

■ **Cultural Preparations:** Head to your public library for Virginia Woolf's *Letters*, especially the volume covering 1936 to 1941, or check out Graham Greene's *The Ministry of Fear*, filled with fifth-columnists, German spies, and a bomb or two. Music lovers: The second movement of Ralph Vaughan Williams' *A London Symphony* takes the listener on a slow and melancholy stroll through "Bloomsbury Square on a November Afternoon."

■ **Internet Best Bets:** Try the British Museum website: www.thebritishmuseum.ac.uk. Your favorite teenager may enjoy www.talkingto.co.uk, a chance to get some answers about Virginia Woolf and George Orwell.

War Words: Sireens, Wailing Winnies, and Moaning Minnies

Early in the war, when wailing air raid sirens first warned of danger over-head, Londoners sometimes referred to the alarms as **SIREENS** (rhymes with "Irenes"). Soon nicknames were coined for the ominous fluctuating or warbling signal: the nightly Monas, wailing Winnies, howling Horaces, moaning Minnies, screamies, all describing what author Evelyn Waugh called that "hideous, then unfamiliar shriek."

The "danger passed" siren, more commonly known as the All Clear, was a steadier tone but still quite similar to the warning siren (some shelterers couldn't tell one from the other). It garnered few nicknames except perhaps "Clara."

Today on a quiet London night, listen for the modern "sireens," distant police or fire sirens echoing the tone (if not the one- to two-minute duration) of those long-ago wartime warnings.

Bette Midler once said, "When it's 3 o'clock in New York, it's still 1938 in London," an apt description of Bloomsbury's streets and squares. Not the hectic lanes of New Oxford Street and Theobald's Road, Bloomsbury's southern boundary, nor bustling Euston Road to the north. And not Tottenham Court Street to the west nor Gray's Inn Road to the east, both busy London thoroughfares. That's the streetscape Angelica Garnett, niece of Bloomsbury's most famous wartime resident, described as the "sky-scapery rock-hard metropolis of today." Instead it's the less-traveled routes deep within this urban outline, and particularly those bordering some of the area's tree-shaded squares, that can produce a sensation of time warp.

This "inner" Bloomsbury, now as in 1938, is a place of few shops, fewer monuments, and many residents, an area characterized by offices, lodging places, and medical facilities. During the war, these streets filled with a wartime cast: government workers, soldiers, refugees, and medical people. London historian Richard Tames once compared Bloomsbury in the early 1940s to a transit camp. Indeed, streets here overflowed with the uniforms of a half-dozen armies, and an exotic mix of languages and accents was heard in every restaurant and shop. Meanwhile, Bloomsbury's permanent residents struggled with anti-aircraft guns bivouacked in the playground, the boarding-up of shattered windows, and the endless queuing for rationed food.

Today the soldiers are gone, and happily the "ack-ack" guns are too. Yet if one squints a little or focuses selectively, war and prewar reminders can still be found, ghosts of sixty years past. One might even imagine author Virginia Woolf striding down the quieter streets. Ah Virginia, so inextricably linked with this area, as are her husband, sister, brother-in-law, and a bevy of other Bloomsburyite relations, friends, acquaintances, neighbors, and employees (Hogarth Press, owned by Virginia and Leonard Woolf, operated here too). Although Woolf died in March 1941, she saw all too much of war's fury in this neighborhood, and her comments on the air raids and their effects on her beloved Bloomsbury give voice to London's homefront experience. So as Virginia Woolf herself so often did, let's go street sauntering and square haunting in Bloomsbury.

From the front of the Russell Square Underground, look back a moment to admire the maroon tile façade, much more appealing than the modern look of some Tube stations. The red postbox nearby bears the royal emblem of Edward VII, Britain's king from 1901 to 1910—watch for these older postboxes throughout the Bloomsbury/Holborn district. (For more on wartime postboxes, see Chapter 7.)

Straight ahead along Bernard Street is Russell Square, the largest of Bloomsbury's squares. Along the square's eastern side (and to your left as you head toward the square) is the red brick and terra cotta **Hotel Russell**, just over a hundred years old. This flamboyant hostelry provided wartime guests with a comfortable place to stay plus a winter-garden and restaurant. Bloomsbury-set aficionados might want to fortify themselves with a stop at the hotel's café, Coffee at VW's. Although the Hotel Russell has recently had a £10 million internal renovation, the worn red exterior

The prewar look of the Hotel Russell.

still remains an appropriate backdrop to imagine Virginia Woolf heading through the entrance for a meeting or an appointment. She probably paused to admire the building's intricate carvings and columns and the entranceway's unusual lamp standards. And what was the Hotel Russell's interior like during the war years? One young American Red Cross worker was sure it "must have been *some* stuff in Lillian Russell's time....It's furnished in such completely horrible taste it's magnificent. Nine shades of marble, bronze, and alabaster statues strewn among stained-glass windows, pillars and potted palms on red velvet carpets, converted gas lamps, and naturally the original plumbing fixtures."

> A Mrs. Gambier, proprietor of Belgrave House at 6 Montague Street, Russell Square, offered wartime lodging (bed, breakfast, and bath) for five shillings a night with no extras except, of course, for the air raid shelter.

Past this delightful extravagancy is Guilford Street; here the American Red Cross operated the Russell Square Service Club in the old Guilford Hotel, one of over a dozen U.S. service clubs in London. Nearby, the Red Shield, run by the Canadian Salvation Army, maintained a Canadian Allied Service Club.

Don't miss the marble sign advertising Turkish baths, visible in the pavement at the corner. It points you further along Russell Square's eastern side toward the bleakly modern **Imperial Hotel**. In the late 1930s, London visitors could stay in one of the hotel's 700 rooms, complete with central heating and Turkish baths, for 9/6 a night with full breakfast included. Today's rates range from about £75 to £100 (breakfast still included) for a night in the rebuilt 1960s hotel, a very plain replacement for the opulent early 1900s original here throughout the war. Alas, the Turkish baths are also long gone.

Beyond the Imperial and along Southampton Row are several other large hotels. In fact, the entire district is laced with hotels, bed and breakfasts, furnished rooms, flatlets, dormitory facilities, bedsits, boarding houses, and various other lodging places. It was much the same during the war, although several of the more popular Bloomsbury establishments were then known as temperance hotels. These were private hotels lacking a license "to supply intoxicating liquors," as a prewar Baedeker's guidebook puts it. Temperance hotels were also generally less pretentious and more affordable: "Many of them (e.g., in Bloomsbury) may safely be recommended to the traveler of moderate requirements." And wartime Bloomsbury was a place people *stayed at*, whether Belgian and Dutch refugees billeted in hotels along Great Russell Street, Canadian troops lodging in boarding houses on the northern side of the district, or American travelers spending a night or two in Southampton Row hotels.

Beyond Russell Square and across Southampton Row is the red-brick **Bedford Hotel**; cross at the light in front of the hotel. A plaque near the car park drive is a reminder that Londoners suffered in both world wars. Near here in 1917, twelve people were killed and many more injured by a 112-lb. bomb dropped from a German airplane in one of London's first nighttime air raids. The old Bedford Hotel was repaired soon after and has since been totally rebuilt—but perhaps you guessed that.

Continue down hectic Southampton Row to Great Russell Street; a right turn and a short block brings you to quiet **Bloomsbury Square**. Originally laid out in the 1660s, this is one of London's oldest squares. The trees, surviving both war and the underground car park, today frame the statue of Whig politician Charles James Fox at the square's northern end.

American Gertrude Stein and brother Leo lived at 20 Bloomsbury Square briefly in the early 1900s. Gertrude found the area a bit grim, though she did enjoy the British Museum. She soon left for France, where she and companion Alice B. Toklas spent World War II. Most of the really old Bloomsbury Square buildings are long gone, although Numbers 5 and 6 in the southwestern corner are of mid-eighteenth-century vintage.

Assuming the recently undertaken refurbishment and replanting of the square is completed, wander amidst the trees and lawns or warm a bench and people-watch, perhaps musing on what a wartime benchwarmer would have seen. Then the grass was scarred by trenches dug seven feet deep in the London clay, covered with concrete roofs and two feet of earth, then fitted with primitive airlocks to protect against poison gas, all providing a protective but not particularly comfortable air raid shelter.

North from the square is **Bedford Place**, connecting Bloomsbury and Russell Squares. The last time I walked here I had a major déjà-vu moment, noting the prosperous residential buildings on the left while the long block opposite was boarded up, with windows filled with "To Let" signs. I began imagining the residents had fled to the countryside as the air raids increased, or perhaps a high explosive bomb had eviscerated the building behind the still-standing façade, or maybe…. The watchman, ending my time travel meanderings, pointed out that the owner was in the process of selling the place for offices. But this block is typical of the dual nature of Bloomsbury—stretches of well-kept Georgian-era buildings facing blank-windowed run-down flats sporting "To Let" signs.

Good Homefront Reading

Dozens of homefront novels have been published—patriotic rants veiled as fiction, sentimental soap operas with two-dimensional characters, unbelievable espionage tales, and some reasonably sympathetic and spot-on portrayals of the city at war. Any suggested list is bound to be both personal and idiosyncratic. Nevertheless, these titles share readability, availability, and reasonably on-target fictional portrayals.

Don't miss *Atonement* (2001), Ian McEwan's complex novel of honesty, guilt, and consequences, set in prewar England, Dunkirk, and wartime London. This is one of those stories that'll reverberate through your consciousness weeks after you finish it.

Several interconnected families—working poor to upper-class—deal with the devastating effects of the German air raids on London in 1940 in Molly Lefebure's well-written *Blitz* (1988).

Need a good airplane read? Try *Blitz* (1979) by David Fraser—though the characters are a trifle on the cardboardy side, and the author almost too resolutely marches past every aspect of the homefront, it's nevertheless an engaging story.

In *Caught* (1950), author Henry Green focuses on an Auxiliary Fire Service firefighter in the Blitz.

Andrew Grieg's *The Clouds Above* (2001) is an intense novel of love and war, set on the homefront in the midst of the Battle of Britain. Keep a handkerchief handy.

The Fire Fighter (2002), a gripping adventure/romance/mystery, follows Jack Finley, recruited to prevent fires in several mysterious buildings in the City. Despite his efforts, there are blazes aplenty, and fire almost becomes the lead character. You'll stay up late to finish this one.

The Heat of the Day (1949) by Elizabeth Bowen is really about human relationships that just happened to take place with the war as background, though that background is vividly presented. Bowen's experience as a wartime ARP worker adds subtle details to her spy tale, a richness of

On the west side of Bedford Place, mid-block, Number 28 is where young T. S. Eliot stayed when he first arrived in London from the States in 1914. In quick order Eliot went to Oxford, married, became a teacher, worked as a clerk in Lloyd's Bank, met Ezra Pound and Virginia Woolf, started the literary magazine *The Criterion*, wrote *The Waste Land*, and in 1925 began work at the book publishers Faber & Faber, then located on the far side of Russell Square, straight ahead.

We'll see the Faber & Faber building in a moment, but first continue along Bedford Place to **Russell Square**. Beyond the fence stands the impressions and images that's also apparent in her much-anthologized short story "Mysterious Kôr."

In *Human Voices* (1980), Penelope Fitzgerald recreates the quirky world of an eccentric group of BBC broadcasters during London's early air raids.

Helen Humphrey's *The Lost Garden* (2003) reads like a carefully crafted luminous poem, but don't let that deter you. This is a short affecting book, the story of shy and solitary gardener Gwen Davis as she leaves London to serve in the Women's Land Army.

Graham Greene set two of his novels in wartime London—*The Ministry of Fear* (1943) and *The End of the Affair* (1951). His usual seedy undertow is apparent in both, though the taut mystery of the former is somewhat less grim than the Catholic guilt and angst of the latter.

Mrs. Miniver (1940) by Jan Struther is the book the very sentimental movie was based on, but these short vignettes bear little resemblance to the syrupy cinema version other than the title character. Mrs. Miniver's story is affecting in an early-days emotion-laden style.

Dorothy L. Sayers never finished *A Presumption of Death* (2003), but author Jill Paton Walsh took up the task and produced a corker of a mystery, featuring sleuths Harriet Vane and Peter Wimsey. Though the setting is primarily Wimsey's country village, homefront details are plentiful and accurate.

Evelyn Waugh set his satiric novel of society, *Put Out More Flags* (1942), in the first year of war, that long period when nothing much happened. Even so, the story of uppercrust Basil Seal, his family, friends, and mistresses, moves right along. His dealings with the Connollys, the war's most disgusting little evacuees, is one of the best—and funniest—aspects of the story.

Those nasty Nazis are at it again in *The Windsor Plot* (1981), planning to assassinate the king and Churchill and place that German sympathizer, the Duke of Windsor, on the throne. This fast-paced thriller by Pauline Glen Winslow is a good airplane-read for mystery fans, with enough Brit-details to satisfy anglophiles.

square's only statue, the fifth Duke of Bedford, overseer of development here in the early 1800s. He also served as a member of the first Agricultural Board, which explains the allegorical details—the sheaf of corn, the sheep, plow, and cherubs, the latter representing the seasons. In October 1941, someone saw fit to splash the word "Traitor" on the bronze statue, though it's difficult to see how the curly-haired duke or his passive sheep and cherubs could have committed wartime treason. Actually it was the twelfth Duke of Bedford who was being accused as he had refused to allow the railings around his home in Lowndes Square,

Imagine 1940...

Knightsbridge, to be dismantled for recycling into armaments.

One can enter Russell Square's garden at any of the corners, but from here the most direct route is to turn left at the duke and enter at the southwestern corner, just beyond the telephone kiosk. Head along the left inside walkway, enjoying another of Bloomsbury's recently renovated squares. And how might this area have looked in the 1940s? There were shelters here throughout the war—trench shelters at first, then later a large air raid shelter, and the trees were not nearly so tall. The multi-geyser fountain wasn't here (it's a twenty-first-century addition), and the corner café was then just a mobile canteen. During the later war years, a V-1 "robot" rocket fell nearby but failed to explode, leaving staunch pacifist Vera Brittain to mince no words in her description of it: "I had an...opportunity of seeing a fallen robot...in Russell Square; it bore a curious resemblance to a huge dead bat with a broken back."

VISITOR DETAILS: Russell Square is open dawn to dusk. Café, restrooms.

West of Russell Square stands Senate House, the towering administrative building for the University of London. You may catch glimpses of it while exploring this neighborhood, but save a closer look for later. For now, leave the square at the northwestern corner near the small green taxi hut. Ahead is 23–24 Russell Square, where T. S. Eliot served as a director with publishers Faber & Faber before and during the war—there's a wall plaque honoring him as "poet and publisher." From his second-floor office, Eliot looked out toward the trees in Woburn Square to the north while perusing the manuscripts of the likes of Djuna Barnes, Ezra Pound, Lawrence Durrell, W. H. Auden, and Marianne Moore.

In 1943, T. S. Eliot moved to Shamley Green, outside London, but continued to work in the city a part of each week, staying in a flat in the Faber building and serving nightly as firewatcher, checking for incendiary bombs on the roof. Since he suffered from mild vertigo, Eliot's rooftop duties were not particularly pleasant, though they did provide a memorable poetic image. While standing nighttime watch, he experienced the curious phenomenon of airborne ash. "During the Blitz," he later wrote, "the accumulated debris was suspended in the London air for hours after a bomb-

ing. Then it would slowly descend and cover one's sleeves and coat with a fine white ash." This became a telling image in "Little Gidding," the last of his *Four Quartets*, evoking the dawn after an air raid: "Dust in the air suspended / Marks the place where a story ended...." Eliot must have walked in Russell Square on many a wartime morning, perhaps brushing a night's ash off his coat sleeves.

Head past Eliot's old office and up narrow Thornhaugh Street toward Woburn Square. Note that the roadway ends but the sidewalk does not. Also note—how can you miss them?—the brutalist buildings to either side. **Woburn Square**, laid out in the 1820s, is another once all-residential square that has yielded to office buildings. But here Georgian homes weren't just transformed into offices. Many were demolished in what has been termed "one of London's great post-war acts of vandalism" to make way for yet more University buildings. Pause to enjoy what's left and imagine what's gone.

Straight ahead across from Woburn Square is the larger **Gordon Square**, a Bloomsbury Group locale par excellence, starting with 51 Gordon Square, where biographer and critic Lytton Strachey briefly resided. Strachey didn't live to see the war—he would have hated it. Next is 50 Gordon Square, where a plaque honors *en masse* the Bloomsbury Group of writers and artists. A young Virginia Woolf (then Virginia Stephen) lived in 46 Gordon Square, together with sister Vanessa and brothers Thoby and Adrian. John Maynard Keynes, one of the most influential economists of the twentieth century, lived at the same address from 1916 to 1946. A member of the Bloomsbury Group, he

> England's pacifists, including Vera Brittain, were frequent visitors at 6 Endsleigh Gardens, home of the Peace Pledge Union, an organization formed in 1935 by Dick Sheppard "to express the positive side of pacifism."

turned his economic skills to good use during both wars as an advisor to the Treasury. In fact, at various times (almost all shortly before the war), Bloomsburyites James and Alix Strachey, Ralph Partridge and Frances Marshall, Julia Strachey, and Clive and Vanessa Bell lived in Gordon Square.

Also here in the war years were actors Elsa Lancaster and Charles Laughton. Their Gordon Square flat was destroyed when a Luftwaffe dive bomber slammed into it after being hit by anti-aircraft shells. Luckily neither performer was home at the time.

And in the prewar years, in the midst of this unconventional crowd of artists, authors, and actors, right-wing Oswald Mosley established the offices of the periodical *Action* at 5 Gordon Square. Throughout the 1920s, Mosley was steadily moving more and more into the fascist sphere. In 1931, he founded the New Party, a third political party focused on nationalistic concerns. It lasted less than a year, and during that time published a few issues of *Action* from Mosley's offices

> Virginia Woolf must have walked here: "I could wander about the dusky streets in Holborn & Bloomsbury for hours. The things one sees—& guesses at—the tumult & riot & busyness of it all."

here. Harold Nicolson served as editor, a post he resigned when the charismatic Mosley moved even further into demagoguery to found the British Union of Fascists in 1932. Fascists, especially home-grown ones, were considered a threat and Mosley spent most of the war in jail.

After circumnavigating Gordon Square (or just walking along the eastern side), head a block east to **Tavistock Square**. You can enter the garden mid-block along the northern edge. First thing, a large boulder to your right honors the solidity and steadfastness of wartime conscientious objectors, a particularly difficult moral path in a war considered by many to be a "good war." A nearby tree honors the victims of Hiroshima. And in the square's center sits Gandhi, pacifist and leader of India's independence struggle. The statue's hollow base is often filled with floral tributes, candles, and burning incense.

From 1924 until 1939, Virginia Woolf lived at 52 Tavistock Square, a home she and husband Leonard shared with their Hogarth Press. This area fared particularly poorly in the war. In October 1940, the Woolfs' former home—they'd moved out of Tavistock Square just weeks before—was struck by German bombs. Virginia returned to view the ruin with melancholy mien: "Basement all rubble. Only relics an old basket chair...and Penmans board To Let. Otherwise bricks and wood splinters.... I cd just see a piece of my studio wall standing: otherwise rubble where I wrote so many books. Open air where we sat so many nights, gave so many parties." The remnants of the building are long gone, and the site is now part of the Tavistock Hotel, but for an idea of what the Woolfs' house was like, check out the buildings along the square's western side.

Across Upper Woburn Place, step inside the courtyard of the British Medical Association (be your usual charming self and the security guard will let you in). These iron gates of remembrance are a memorial to the members of the BMA who died in World War I. Beyond, a small pool and fountain in the courtyard's center are dedicated to the British medical men and women who died in World War II. The statues around the pool represent Sacrifice, Cure, Prevention, and Application, an earnest foursome. The British Medical Association building (then the Theosophical Society headquarters) was designed in the early 1900s by architect Sir Edwin Lutyens, designer of the Cenotaph; he was also responsible for the design of the gates of remembrance.

From the BMA, turn and continue along Upper Woburn Place. Woburn Walk to the right beckons with its quaint Georgian shop fronts and may be a good spot for a quick rest stop. Three rail stations and a library await, but perhaps you'd rather read ahead a bit, since a visit to at least the first of these is better done on the page than in person.

Rail stations may not be high on your list of London must-see sights, but the three clustered along Euston Road—Euston Station, St. Pancras, and King's Cross—do offer a compact reminder of London's wartime transportation scene. (For more on wartime train travel, see "Is Your Journey *Really* Necessary?" elsewhere in this chapter.)

All three stations are located across too-wide, too-busy Euston Road, built in the mid-1700s as a bypass for cattle being driven across town to Smithfield Market. Today it still has much the same feel— Max Beerbohm once called it the "awfullest of thoroughfares." Immediately after the war, in a misguided attempt to make Euston Road one of the finest thoroughfares in London, the roadway was widened. Alas, the traffic moves well but the street is gray and grim.

The immediate postwar years saw a slow but steady return to the well-kept landscaping that characterized Tavistock Square before the war. By the late 1940s, most of the wartime weeds had been cleared away, although in some areas, ropes were stretched from tree to tree to keep passersby on the paths and away from the tangled undergrowth.

Euston Station opened in the mid-1830s, the first main rail line into London. A monumental Doric arch originally on the Euston Road side of the station together with the dramatic Great Hall within suggested both the significance of the railroad itself and the grand beginning of a new transportation era for London. After a century of use, however, the Euston Station had become shabby, dated, and inconvenient. Major efforts were needed to renew it, and a total remodeling was planned for the end of the 1930s. Bad timing.

The old station survived German air raids although the roof of the Great Hall, a few offices, and part of the adjacent hotel were damaged. It took post-war improvements to *really* destroy Euston Station. Major reconstruction began in 1961 and the first to go was the once-triumphant arch, followed soon after by the Great Hall. The bland new terminal, opened in 1968, has been called both glib and depressing. Personally, rather than a

Text continued on page 204.

Walking the Streets of Bloomsbury East

Most Bloomsbury visitors stay close to the British Museum/University of London axis. Instead, this residential stroll meanders east of that well-traveled area to neighborhoods linked with Bloomsbury's wartime writers and artists.

Begin by walking down Guilford Street, away from Russell Square. Julian MacLaren-Ross, a peripheral member of Bloomsbury's wartime literati, toured the stretches of rubble here, noting a house where a bomb had ripped away one side. Presciently he mused, "Graham Greene himself had been seen staring with particular intentness at this particular ruin…he might be writing something about London in the air raids." Indeed, Greene's mystery *The Ministry of Fear* opens amidst the bleak wartime atmosphere of Guilford Street: "A bomb early in the blitz had fallen in the middle of…[Guilford] street and blasted both sides," he writes. "There were boards instead of glass in every room, and the doors no longer quite fitted."

> The Zepplein raids of World War I—with their 100-lb. bombs—were far less destructive than the mega-bombing raids of World War II.

For a brief square detour, take the narrow walkway to the right just past the car park drive. It leads to hidden Queen Square, laid out in the reign of Queen Anne although that's most likely Queen Charlotte standing in the garden. The square's northern side is primarily 1930s flats. A few older Georgian homes can be seen, mostly on the western side. World War I residents would have looked out onto a square with a huge crater in the center, the result of a Zeppelin raid. World War II residents fared slightly better.

Return to Guilford and turn right. On the corner of Lansdowne Terrace and Guilford Street stands Selwyn House, where Cyril Connolly, literary critic and editor of the journal *Horizon*, had his wartime offices. Connolly worked in a ground-floor flat shared for a time with poet and wartime fireman Stephen Spender. The place soon became a magnet for many of London's literary lights. Early in the Blitz, German bombs peppered this area, and for much of the following month, the neighborhood was cordoned off due to unexploded bombs. That left Connolly unable to get to his office and caused much distress to Bloomsbury neighbor Virginia Woolf. On a recent visit I found Selwyn House boarded up with an ominous Writ of Possession stuck on the door. On my next visit, the building was scaffolded and workers scurried about turning Selwyn House into "quality residential accommodation" for the University of London.

I also found the garden of Brunswick Square—further up Lansdowne Terrace—looking like World War II trench shelters were being constructed, but it was just major park refurbishment. Those brown scars across the lawns—like the war scars—should be well-mended by the time you visit. A young Virginia Woolf (then Virginia Stephen) lived at Number 38 Brunswick Square in the early 1900s, joined at various times by her brother Adrian, painter Duncan Grant, and economist John Maynard Keynes. Their home has since been demolished and a University of London building now occupies the site, a scenario enacted over and over in Bloomsbury.

Author E. M. Forster, another Bloomsburyite, lived at 27 Brunswick Square from 1929 until 1939 in a building also long

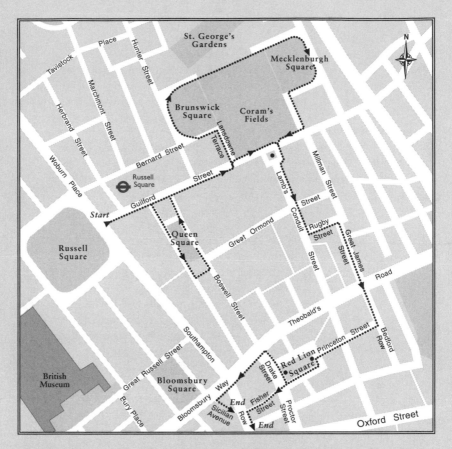

gone. During the war, both an anti-aircraft battery and a barrage balloon unit operated in Coram's Fields, the grassy area between Brunswick and Mecklenburgh squares. Getting to this second square, on the other side of Coram's Fields, necessitates back-tracking to Guilford Street, unless you're feeling adventuresome and want to take the narrow path behind the playing field that connects the two squares.

If you opt for the more conservative street route, return to Guilford Street and continue walking eastward past the street frontage of Coram's Fields, an enormous playground and sports grounds. The Foundling Hospital (1720s) stood here un-til the late 1920s, when it was demolished and the portion closest to the street made

a children's playground. The area still en-tertains Bloomsbury's youngsters: its outer fences carry notices that adults are not ad-mitted unless accompanied by a child. Watch too for the resident flock of sheep.

This is the same playground that the Selwyn House windows of Connolly and Spender looked out on from the west side. Author John Lehmann described that early Blitz attack as seen from this, the Mecklenburgh Square, side: "An enormous blaze was developing beyond the Balloon station in the Foundling grounds…sud-denly it struck me that it looked alarmingly close to Stephen's flat." Actually Brunswick Square survived the attack and the war in good shape; it was Mecklenburgh Square, where Lehmann was, that suffered.

From Guilford Street, turn onto Mecklenburgh Place and walk a block to Mecklenburgh Square, a U-shaped street connected at both ends to Coram's Fields. (If you've taken the connecting path, it ends on the back part of Mecklenburgh Square.) Poet John Masefield lived at Number 18 before the war; he would later write the poem "Remembering Dame Myra Hess," honoring Hess's wartime concerts in the National Gallery. (See Chapter 2 for more on Hess.) And Dorothy L. Sayers, creator of fictional detective Lord Peter Wimsey, briefly lived at 44 Mecklenburgh Square in 1920.

But perhaps the most famous Mecklenburgh Square residents were authors and publishers Virginia and Leonard Woolf, who in August 1939 moved into Number 37, a four-story row house. The house is gone, but check out the homes on the square's northern side closest to Coram's Fields for an idea of what the Woolf's home looked like.

> The Woolfs rented their Mecklenburgh Square home for £250 a year.

During early bombing alerts, the Woolfs could have stayed in the air raid shelter erected in the center of Mecklenburgh Square but decided against it. Leonard investigated the shelter arrangements, then declared, "We thought it better to die, if that were to be our fate, in our beds." The Woolfs didn't have to chose between shelter and bed during a September 1940 air raid. They were away at their country home in Sussex and returned to find Mecklenburgh Square roped off. Virginia's diary entry worried, "Wardens there, not allowed in. The house about 30 yards from ours struck at one this morning

by a bomb. Completely ruined. Another bomb in the square still unexploded."

The Woolfs returned several times, hoping to board-up broken windows and begin moving their Hogarth Press to a safer location. "The ruins are still smoking, a bomb timed to go off in an hour. But it didn't; and we went up again on Friday...but the bomb was still unburst in the flower bed." And when it did finally explode several days later, it blew out all their windows and ceilings, and smashed all of Virginia's china. After a land mine exploded at the back of the house a few days later, it was Leonard who surveyed the damage. "You could stand on the ground floor and look up with uninterrupted view to the roof while sparrows scrabbled about on the joists of what had been a ceiling."

Neighbor John Lehmann lived a few doors from the Woolfs in a flat with a view over the square's trees. After that September raid, he saw "broken glass everywhere, half the garden scorched with incendiary bombs....My flat has a chalk cross on the door to mark it unsafe—I thought of the Plague Year—but I got in...it was uninhabitable...and I suddenly felt very sad, standing by the windows and looking out on the ruin of the lovely old Square."

Early in the war, author Graham Greene also lived in Mecklenburgh Square in a pied-à-terre, away from his family in Clapham so he could more easily focus on his writing (and, as it turned out, his new girlfriend). Greene later moved to Gower Mews, a few blocks away and closer to the ARP headquarters where he served. He loved the Blitz, finding it "wonderful to wake up and know you were still alive and hear glass being swept up in the streets." There certainly was a lot of glass; by war's end, practically every house in Mecklenburgh Square was down or terribly blasted.

Return to Guilford Street, then backtrack a block toward Russell Square. At Guilford Place, by the slightly derelict Victorian statue/fountain (1870) of the good woman of Sumaria emptying her jug, turn left onto Lamb's Conduit Street. The statue and the surrounding houses here were much blasted and blitzed during the raids of 1940.

Watch for The Lamb at 94 Lamb's Conduit Street, a public house that served as the local for many Bloomsburyites. Visitors to the Hogarth Press would often step up to the wooden bar for a bolstering pint before dealing with the curmudgeonly Leonard Woolf and his quiet partner. The Lamb still serves lunch, and a visit may bolster you too.

From Lamb's Conduit Street, turn onto Rugby Street. A block on, at the juncture of Millman and Great James streets, a right turn brings you to a narrow residential block lined with eighteenth-century row houses. Dorothy L. Sayers lived at 24 Great James Street from 1920 to 1957, although a plaque here credits the writer of detective fiction only with the years 1921–1929. Sayers' air raid shelter was her basement: "We have a good cellar in Gt. James Street but just at present I understand we are surrounded by time bombs...we get a few bangs and bumps in the neighbourhood most nights." Indeed.

Great James's Street ends at busy Theobald's Road, where the war's bangs and bumps were simply catastrophic. Almost the entire northern side of Theobald's Road, particularly to the west, was shredded by German bombs and has since been rebuilt. Cross to Bedford Row, a wide avenue originally constructed in the 1700s, where a goodly amount of wartime destruction also occurred, with only a handful of original houses surviving. A right turn on Princeton Street and two short blocks

brings us to Red Lion Square, just beyond the traditional Bloomsbury boundaries but well worth an out-of-Bloomsbury experience. Along the way, you can practice your skills at determining what's prewar and what's postwar construction.

Take a breather in Red Lion Square to consider the effects here of Luftwaffe bombs. On the southwestern corner near Fisher Street was the Church of St. John the Evangelist, built in 1878 and blitzed in April 1941. The Victorian Gothic building was simply "blown to bits," as one wartime commentator put it, and not rebuilt. And along the eastern side of this seventeenth-century square, German bombing raids produced heavy damage.

Images of two pacifists bracket the small central garden: a bust of philosopher and mathematician Bertrand Russell sits at one end and a carefree statue of Fenner Brockway dances at the other. Brockway was a socialist politician, a member of Parliament, and a conscientious objector in World War I.

From Red Lion Square's western side, you have at least two options (check the map before setting off). If you feel daring (and the traffic is light) cross Drake Street mid-block. Follow narrow Fisher Street to Southampton Row, where a left turn and a short walk will bring you to the Holborn Underground. Alternatively, cross Drake Street at the corner of Theobald's Road, and walk two blocks west to Sicilian Avenue for a pleasant detour along a colonnaded pedestrian walkway filled with bookstores, quaint shops, and cafés.

Whichever route you select, note the train tunnel (not in use) in the middle of Southampton Row, part of the old Aldwych-Piccadilly Underground and the wartime lodging place for the Elgin Marbles and other British Museum antiquities.

The British Library.

visit to the rail station, I'd advise a quiet moment imagining the thousands of war-era journeys that began and ended there. Then cross Euston Road and head east—it's time for a bibliographic interlude.

The red brick of the **British Library** echoes the rusty color of St. Pancras Station beyond, just one of several architectural devices that make this new structure settle into its site. Before the war this was the Somers Town Goods Yard, part of the old Midland Railway. German bombs ended that, and the area, cleared of rubble in the postwar years, remained a car park until library construction began. The national library houses all the treasures once crowded into the British Library section of the British Museum—books, manuscripts, postage stamps, journals, patents, sound recordings, printed music, and maps.

The British Library was founded as part of the British Museum in 1753, became an independent body in 1973 though still housed in the British Museum building, and opened in new and independent quarters on Euston Road in 1997.

The British Library is not a *public* library—you can't stroll in and take a book to a table for a quick read, or check your e-mail. The book stacks and reading rooms here are meant for serious researchers. Nevertheless, a great deal is available for public viewing. Start with the free exhibition galleries near the entranceway where over 200 items are displayed, from the Magna Carta to handwritten Beatles' lyrics. Don't miss the illuminated manuscripts, the 1455 Gutenberg Bible, Shakespeare's First Folio, or the "Turning the Pages" digitized computer display. The exhibits, changed from time to time, recently included the typescript copy—with pencilled-in corrections—of the draft of the 1939 British ultimatum to Germany. Around the gallery walls, sound stations showcase brief recordings from the Library's audio collection. Listen to an excerpt from a BBC radio talk Virginia Woolf gave on "Craftsmanship." For a more sobering experience, Barbara Stimler describes her arrival at Auschwitz.

Beyond the lobby steps is the King's Library, housed in a glass six-story book stack. In 1823, King George IV presented his father's collection to the nation, and it now forms the center-piece of the Library's public area. And this is just a fraction of the library's holdings—over twelve million volumes are shelved here, most in the library's basements, deepest in London (they would have made great air raid shelters). Ask at the Information Desk about audio and guided tours.

Of the three Euston Road rail terminals, **St. Pancras Station** is the least modernized and the most architecturally intriguing to explore—in fact, the only one worth exploring. The station and the old hotel hug Euston Road in an extravaganza of terra cotta and brick, a turreted, towered, arched, and pinnacled fantasy, a red "high Victorian secular Gothic" structure that has to be seen to be believed. Turn-of-the-twentieth-century travelers arriving from the north of England could detrain in the station (opened in 1868), marvel over the magnificent glass-roofed train shed covering the platforms—690 feet long and over 100 feet high at the apex—then settle in to the station's Midland Grand Hotel.

Architect George Gilbert Scott designed the Midland to be the most opulent rail hotel in all London, offering guests over 250 rooms, a grand staircase, a dramatic curved dining room, the first revolving door in England, and even a (gasp) ladies' smoking room. Unfortunately the hotel had no central heat and a limited supply of bathrooms. By the 1920s, the Midland was struggling, finally closing in 1935 to be made over into British Rail offices. British Rail left in 1985, and **St. Pancras Chambers**, as it's known, stood vacant until recently. Herculean restoration lies ahead, plus eventual development as a twenty-first-century hotel. Visit it now so you can say you knew it when.

The war was a difficult time for St. Pancras Station. In October 1940, the terminal closed briefly when a large part of the roof was wrecked; three weeks later a rail platform and the Booking Office were badly damaged. The most devastating attack came the night of May 10, 1941,

St. Pancras Station.

VISITOR DETAILS: Guided tours of St. Pancras Chambers weekends 11am and 1:30pm. Limited to twenty (first-come, first-served); admission is charged. The ground floor (the entrance hall and former coffee lounge) is open weekdays 11:30am to 3:30pm. Note: The tour has lots of steps and no disabled facilities. More information: 020 7304 3921, or check the developer's website for a virtual tour: www.lcrproperties.com.

when a 1000-lb. high explosive bomb penetrated the station's roof, slammed down through the iron floor into the basement and buried itself twenty-five feet down in the solid clay…and exploded. Although damage to the station and tracks was major, heroic repair efforts meant rail service was restored within a week.

Take your own personal tour of St. Pancras Station by turning up the incline just past St. Pancras Chambers. At the top is the Booking Office—step inside and step back in time, when rail stations were wood-paneled, dim and held relatively little advertising. Another twenty feet and you're in the train shed itself, all red brick and stone, columns and glass. All it needs is a steaming locomotive to be complete.

Next in the triumvirate of rail stations is King's Cross Station, across Pancras Road; I personally have found it only worthwhile when I have a Harry Potter fan in tow, so I'd suggest skipping it and trying another form of transport—a #73 or #10 bus, caught on the far side of Euston Road and a transit shortcut that saves walking back along this "awfullest of thoroughfares."

Once the bus turns onto **Gower Street**, alight and start walking again. The quadrangle of University College is to the left. Stroll in for a closer look at the portico with its closely spaced columns and dome above. The latter, built in the late 1820s, was badly blasted and burned in wartime bombing but has been rebuilt. Back on Gower Street, don't get trampled by the throngs of aspiring thespians heading toward RADA, the

Royal Academy of Dramatic Arts, another building that suffered extensive damage in the raids of 1940.

A long block or so further south, turn onto Keppel Street. The first large building is the London School of Hygiene and Tropical Medicine, its cornerstone laid by then-Minister of Health Neville Chamberlain in 1926. During London's Blitz, author and air raid warden Graham Greene was assigned to Bloomsbury's ARP Post Number 1, located in the basement of the London School of Hygiene. He rather enjoyed his war work, despite frequently encountering the "untidy gaps" between Bloomsbury houses caused by German bombs. Early in the war Greene lived in a cottage on Gower Mews, a street now gone, with his very good friend Dorothy Glover, who shared air raid duties with him at ARP Post Number 1 (while Greene's wife and children were tucked away for safety in the countryside).

At the end of Keppel Street **Senate House** looms, Bloomsbury's most dramatic skyscraper (210 feet high) and the heart of the University of London. This hulking structure served as wartime headquarters for the Ministry of Information, a bureaucratic warren from which originated government press releases and pamphlets, entreating slogans, and endless wartime propaganda for both domestic and foreign consumption. This was also the headquarters for the censorship division, those pencil-and-scissors-wielding watchdogs who checked photos for publication and letters mailed across the seas, being sure no sensitive war secrets were inadvertently revealed.

Senate House.

Because writers were needed to produce all the verbiage pouring out of the ministry, practically every English author, broadcaster, and journalist, from Graham Greene to George Orwell to Evelyn Waugh to Agatha Christie to Dorothy L. Sayers, either worked here or wanted to work here. Greene, for example, labored in the propaganda section early in the war before he moved on to work for MI6, Britain's Secret Intelligence Service. Numerous American war correspondents also hung out at Senate House, ever hopeful that the ministry would release some fresh—and publishable—war details.

The building's designer was Charles Holden, also responsible for London Transport's skyscraper at 55 Broadway, Westminster. When Senate House opened in August 1936 it was the tallest building in England. Personally, the building's exterior reminds me of a 1940s-era radio, but others have seen more ominous overtones, comparing Senate House to the Ministry of Truth in George Orwell's novel, *1984:* "It was an enormous pyramidal structure of glittering white concrete, soaring up, terrace after terrace, three hundred meters into the air....A thousand rocket bombs could not batter it down." Well, at least four German bombs proved ineffective, damaging but not crippling the building, its ministry, nor its office minions. Incidentally, wartime posters may have given Orwell further inspiration for *1984*. Early in the 1940s, England's consumers were urged

During much of the war, rumor persisted that exactly 999 bureaucrats worked in the Ministry of Information.

to "Spend to Save, Save to Lend," perhaps a forerunner of the slogans on the side of Orwell's Ministry of Truth: "War is Peace, Freedom is Slavery, and Ignorance is Strength."

Today Senate House houses the University's administrative offices, the library, and various offices. For a hint of the drama of wartime work here, cross the plaza/parking area and step inside the cold Deco interior.

Return to Gower Street and turn left. Late Georgian row houses begin to dominate closer to the oval garden of elegant **Bedford Square**, ahead on the right. The well-tended trees and greenery are set in a key garden—only residents of the square have keys to the garden gates. Stroll

Is Your Journey *Really* Necessary?

If your London visit includes train travel northward, your trip may well start at one of the three rail stations along Euston Road. As you settle into your seat, imagine for a moment the difficulties experienced by the wartime traveler.

Even before boarding, the uncertainty and inconveniences of wartime journeys would have been apparent. Inside rail stations (and at Tube stations, and on hoardings everywhere), posters querulously asked, "Is your journey *really* necessary?" Military and war workers had priority on trains, as casual travelers were constantly reminded. Stations were crowded, and there were few porters and fewer luggage trolleys—wheeled luggage not yet having been invented. Departure times were constantly changed, trips were frequently interrupted (trains would be slowed or stopped along the tracks during air raids), and arrival times were vague at best.

Once on board, travelers had difficulty finding seats—imagine 2,000 passengers on a single train, many of them soldiers; standing for an entire trip was not unusual. Dining cars had been discontinued early in the war. Passengers were warned to "beware of pickpockets…. In crowded trains keep a weather eye on your money and belongings….There are tricksters in London as there are in every big city."

Because of invasion fears, station signs had been removed or town names obliterated; passengers were often unsure if they were at the correct stop. Window blinds were closed during air raids as a protection against flying glass and as part of the blackout, further adding to the difficulty of knowing one's location. Emergency—and very dim—blue lights were used, making navigating train aisles difficult and reading impossible. Despite all these negatives (including those wily tricksters), at least one ebullient train passenger of 1942 found "a certain exciting chanciness about the whole thing."

Wartime travel: soldiers to the front, children to the countryside.

the wide sidewalks around the garden, taking in the "unspoiled aspect of classic contentment" of the best preserved of Bloomsbury's squares. Watch for the many still-intact Georgian domestic features: fanlights over doorways, boot scrapers, and coal holes in the pavement.

Bedford Square retained its iron garden railings during the war, opposing the order to donate fences, gates, and other ironwork to be recycled for weapons. The decision prompted a spate of letters to the London *Times.* One from the Georgian Group of the Society for the Preservation of Ancient Buildings waved the flag for historic preservation. "These beautiful railings of elliptical formation designed by Thomas Leverton are not only in themselves a work of art, but contribute an important, if subtle, part to the beauty of the square....Bedford Square may be damaged by German vandalism...but let us at any rate not be answerable to posterity for any deliberate mutilation, however small, of the finest Georgian square in London." As George Orwell put it in late 1942, "Generally speaking, where there is money, there are railings."

A handful of plaques affixed to the buildings (most now offices) honor previous famous residents of Bedford Square, although two of these are as yet un-plaqued: architect Edwin Lutyens and critic Cyril Connolly. Lutyens, designer of Whitehall's war memorial Cenotaph and the fountains in Trafalgar Square, lived at 31 Bedford Square from 1914 to 1919. During this same period he also became architect to the Imperial War Graves Commission. Literary critic Cyril Connolly lived in a flat in the upper part of 49 Bedford Square from 1942 until just before the end of the war. Connolly, a brilliant but hedonistic curmudgeon, managed only

Text continued on page 212.

Tell Me a Story:
Homefront Books for Young People

Pre-trip reading will help make London's war experience come alive for youngsters. These books are aimed at first graders through high schoolers. An entire genre of books on the wartime evacuation of children isn't included here; your local librarian can help you locate them.

Album of World War Two Home Fronts. Don Lawson (1980; grades 4–8). Besides the London experience, this offers perspective on the equally bleak, blitzed, and battered homefronts of the Germans, French, Soviets, and Japanese.

Blitzcat. Robert Westall (1989; grades 6–8). Cat lovers of any age will enjoy this tale of a black cat that journeys across war-ravaged England in an effort to track down her beloved master. The author, like the Blitzcat, lived through the war.

A Child's War: Growing Up on the Home Front 1939–45. Mike Brown (2000; grades 5–8). A social history of England's war, *A Child's War* focuses on kids' interests: food, holidays, doing one's bit, school, evacuation, etc., with first-person accounts and many previously unpublished photos.

The Exeter Blitz. David Rees (1980; grades 6–8). It's May 3, 1942, and the Lockwood family is scattered all over Exeter—at work, at the cinema, at home—and young Colin is high atop the city's historic cathedral. Then the air raid begins.

Fireweed. Jill Paton Walsh (1969; grades 6–10). Two teenage runaways refuse to be evacuated and struggle to survive London's Blitz. This affecting novel is set in several recognizable London sites, including a just-bombed Mayfair house and a desolate St. Paul's Cathedral.

Good Night, Mr. Tom. Michelle Magorian (1981; grades 7–12). An old man, with a quiet life in the countryside and with painful memories of his own, adopts an abused London boy.

Horrible Histories: The Blitzed Brits. Terry Deary and Martin Brown (1994; grades 6–10). It's not your father's history book, that's for sure. This insouciant look at wartime England answers questions young people really want to ask (from blackout murders to disgusting rationing), and provides at least one adolescent use for a gas mask. This inexpensive paperback purchase—in print in the UK but hard to find in the States—will have to wait for your arrival in London. Be sure to read it yourself.

Kingdom by the Sea. Robert Westall (1991; grades 5–8). Young Harry ("an old hand at air raids now") survives a bombing raid, but the raid sets in motion a series of adventures as he wanders away, finds a stray dog, and embarks on an incredible journey. Lots of wartime details: "Henry began to count. If you were still counting at ten, the bombs had missed you. The last thing he remembered was saying 'seven.'").

Life in Wartime Britain. Richard Tames (1993; grades 7–10). Historian Tames considers Britain's homefront—from food to fashion—and adds seldom-seen photos and war-related trivia.

London. Michael Kronenwetter (1992; grades 5–9). A nonfiction look at the war's effects on Londoners, this details bombing raids and the evacuation of children.

On the Home Front: Growing Up in Wartime England. Ann Stalcup (1998; grades 4–6). The author spent the war in Lydney, and this story of her experiences, though a trifle stilted, offers many wartime details.

Paper Faces. Rachel Anderson (1993; grades 4–6). Wartime life in London was hard for Dot and her mother, and with the war's end, the young girl is frightened by the coming changes, especially the impending return of the father she's never known.

Randolph's Dream. Judith Mellecker (1991; grades 1–3). It's summer 1940 and young Randolph, whose family is separated by the war, dreams that he saves his father's life. This read-aloud tale has plenty of realistic wartime details.

Time of Fire. Robert Westall (1997; grades 6–8). A powerful novel set in Newcastle, *Time of Fire* follows Sonny, his mother dead from a German bomb and his father off in training, as he tries to understand the darkest truths of war.

War Boy: A Country Childhood. Michael Foreman (1990; grades 3–7). An account of the author's childhood in an English village, *War Boy* features charming illustrations by the author and much evocative detail. The sequel, *After the War Was Over*, has tales of beaches being cleared of barbed wire and mines, bomb sites being used for playgrounds, and food rationing going on...and on.

War Dog. Martin Booth (1996; grades 5–7). After her owner is arrested while poaching, Jet—a black Lab—is requisitioned by the British Army and her past "training" proves useful. She sees duty on Dunkirk's beaches, searching for survivors of bombing raids on English cities, and in Italy at war's end. This warm story gets better as it goes along.

When the Sirens Wailed. Noel Streatfeild (1976; grades 4–6). Rather than stay with a new family, three evacuees try to return to their London home after their country host dies. The author served in the Women's Voluntary Services during the war; though a bit dated, this book is considered a classic by many.

Winston Churchill. Fiona Reynoldson (2002; grades 4–10). An appealing compact biography of the war leader, this is filled with kid-oriented photos and asides (on Churchill's lisp, for example). Timelines, maps, cartoons, charts, a glossary, and short biographies of key people will help elucidate a distant time (for youngsters).

one night of wartime firewatching. He set off for his duties, according to a friend, armed with "a case of cigars, a hot-water bottle, and a heavy tartan rug." He did not stay long.

From Bedford Square, Gower Street subtly becomes Bloomsbury Street. During the war years, the next corner—Great Russell and Bloomsbury streets—boasted two temperance hotels offering accommodations to travelers of moderate requirements and means: the 200-room Kenilworth (still there) and the 300-room Ivanhoe (now the Radisson Edwardian Marlborough).

> Cyril Connolly entertained often at his Bedford Square home; a party held after D-Day included American author Ernest Hemingway among the guests.

Down Great Russell Street is the neoclassical **British Museum**; enter the large courtyard at the open iron gates. At least one wartime bomb cratered this area, shattering windows along the museum's frontage as well as those of nearby shops and flats, and breaking underground water and gas mains. Incidentally, the museum took a somewhat determined stance regarding the suggested wartime donation of its fencing and kept the 1850 gates and railings along this side. Railings on the north side along Montague Place did go off to war.

The collections of the British Museum (over seven million items arranged in two-and-a-half miles of galleries) can be daunting—and don't look for any World War II artifacts sandwiched between the Mesopotamian, Egyptian, Meso-American, Anglo-Saxon, and similar classical antiquities. This is a not-to-be-missed cultural resource and your first visit might best be spent wandering and weighing where to spend time on subsequent

The British Museum.

visits. Don't miss the standards: the Portland Vase, the Rosetta Stone, the Sutton Hoo and Mindenhall Treasures, the Egyptian mummies, Lindow Man, and the Elgin Marbles. (Pronunciation Alert: Save yourself the tiny bit of embarrassment I suffered— that's a hard *g* in "Elgin.")

One war-related connection is apparent as you walk up the museum's exterior steps onto the columned portico. The inscription to the right, carved by Eric Gill, is Laurence Binyon's poem "For the Fallen," with its sad line, "They shall grow not old, as we that are left grow old." The poem was written about the boys who didn't survive the trenches of World War I France, though it applies equally well to those who fell in World War II. Poet Binyon, an authority on Far Eastern art, worked in the museum's Department of Prints and Drawings for forty years.

> *And who had readers' tickets for the British Museum's Reading Room? Check just inside the doorway of the Great Court's Reading Room, where some familiar wartime names appear: Beaton, Benes, Brittain, Clark, Eliot, Greene, Huxley, Macaulay, McNeice, Orwell, Sitwell, Waugh, Wells, and Woolf.*

While strolling the museum's thirteen-plus acres, consider what a perfect target this massive structure, with its commanding central dome, offered to Luftwaffe pilots, and the dilemma wartime curators faced in protecting the museum's collections from explosive and incendiary bombs. There was no way to effectively hide the dome, but at least the museum's contents could be dispersed. Beginning in late August 1939, movable artifacts were packed and sent to various wartime retreats, from Wales to a stone quarry in Wiltshire, and finally to the much closer Aldwych-Piccadilly Underground tunnel. During just one of the moving days, museum staff evacuated over twelve tons of coins and medals, twelve tons of perishable antiquities, and fifteen tons of library materials.

The halls of the British Museum were left echoing and nearly empty for much of the war, with just a few exhibits left behind; these were moved to the

> *"For the Fallen" is a popular poem in war-related writings and ceremonies, though the words of the first line often appear transposed as "They shall not grow old."*

safest locations within the museum, often sandbagged and lodged behind hastily built temporary blast walls. In February 1940 some galleries reopened with special exhibitions, although, as the *Times* sniffed, "These will of necessity include no very important or irreplaceable objects, since such objects have all been evacuated or stored."

The collections dispersed, museum staff mobilized to protect themselves and the building. Air raid precaution measures were organized,

Text continued on page 216.

Leonard and Virginia Woolf

November 25, 1880: Leonard Woolf is born in Kensington.

January 25, 1882: Adeline Virginia Stephen is born at 22 Hyde Park Gate, Kensington. (Still a private home; a plaque honors Virginia's father, lexicographer Sir Leslie Stephen.)

1904: Virginia Stephen, brothers Thoby and Adrian, and sister Vanessa move to a Victorian row house at 46 Gordon Square, Bloomsbury: "The light and the air after the rich red gloom of Hyde Park were a revelation." This area will became part of the University of London's Birbeck College in the 1960s. (A plaque notes the site of her residence.)

April 1907: Virginia and Adrian move to 29 Fitzroy Square, Fitzrovia, just west of Bloomsbury and once the home of playwright George Bernard Shaw. They remain

until 1911. (Now offices, the building has a plaque honoring Virginia.) Her sister Vanessa Bell and artist Duncan Grant will later rent a large studio nearby at the back of 8 Fitzroy Street (1929–1940); incendiary bombs gut it in September 1940.

November 1911: Virginia Stephen moves to 38 Brunswick Square, Bloomsbury, a home shared at times with her brother Adrian, Duncan Grant, Maynard Keynes, and Leonard Woolf. Adrian Stephen and his wife later live at 50 Gordon Square. A psychiatrist, Adrian would make available fatal doses of morphine to the Woolfs early in the war, to be used in case of German invasion.

August 10, 1912: Leonard Woolf and Virginia Stephen marry in the St. Pancras registry office.

1912–1914: Leonard and Virginia Woolf live in tiny rooms at 13 Clifford's Inn, an Inn of Court flat (since replaced with a more modern structure).

1914–1915: Virginia's nervous breakdown (late 1913) leads Leonard to seek quieter surroundings; he rents 17 The Green in suburban Richmond, southwest of London (still a private home).

1915: Leonard and Virginia move to Hogarth House, Paradise Road, Richmond. The Woolfs' publishing company is founded here in March 1917. The printing press will sit in their dining room for nine years. (A plaque commemorates the Woolfs and their press.)

1919: For £700, Leonard and Virginia Woolf buy a country home in Rodmell, Sussex, located about fifty-five miles south of Bloomsbury. Until 1939, they will spend summer months, holidays, and alternate weekends here at Monk's House. (Open to the public for brief periods in the summer.)

1924–1939: The Woolfs lease 52 Tavistock Square, Bloomsbury. They occupy the basement and top two floors; a legal firm operates out of the ground and first floors. Hogarth Press is located in the basement, and Virginia's study is nearby. (The bomb-damaged building is eventually demolished; the site is now part of the Tavistock Hotel.)

August 1939: Leonard and Virginia Woolf (and Hogarth Press) move to 37 Mecklenburgh Square, Bloomsbury, just a few weeks before war begins. Later made uninhabitable by an unexploded bomb that finally did, the building is eventually torn down. The Woolfs move Hogarth Press to Letchworth in Hertfordshire, and themselves leave London for full-time residence at Monk's House in the somewhat safer Sussex countryside. At Rodmell, Virginia attends meetings on first aid and on escaping from bombed buildings; Leonard does fire-watching and ARP duties.

© London Borough of Camden

MECKLENBURGH SQUARE W.C.1.

March 28, 1941: Virginia Woolf, convinced she is once again sinking into madness, fills her coat pockets with rocks and walks into the Ouse River about a half-mile from Monk's House. Her body is found three weeks later. Leonard Woolf remains alone at Monk's House until his death in 1969.

including first-aid and firefighting teams, and construction begun on decontamination rooms in case the Germans resorted to poison gas.

The first bomb to hit the British Museum came on the early Blitz night of September 17, 1940. The 500-lb. missile passed through the Department of Prints and Drawings, then smashed into a girder and essentially broke apart without exploding, eventually falling harmlessly onto the museum's subground floor. Coincidentally, five nights later another high explosive fell through the same hole (only about three feet square!), this time landing unexploded on the mezzanine floor, where it stayed several days until the bomb squad could remove it.

> The British Museum's façade was cleaned in 1978, the first time in over a century. The wartime exterior would have been darkened by layers of Victorian-era grime and soot.

Such extraordinary luck did not continue. Another high explosive bomb fell into the King's Library area, a long book-lined corridor on the museum's eastern side. Much of the collection had been removed to safety, but the bomb shredded some 400 to 500 books and pulverized thirty feet of wooden bookcases and set others afire. More severe structural damage occurred a few weeks later when the Pediment Hall at the north end of the Parthenon Gallery (near where the Elgin Marbles are today) was struck, damaging the gallery walls and shattering the elaborate glass roof above. Luckily the Elgin Marbles had not yet been installed in the just-constructed gallery (completed in 1939); they were safely sandbagged in that nearby Tube tunnel.

Besides the explosive bombs, the British Museum was badly damaged by incendiary bombs on May 10, 1941, that horrendous night when so many London landmarks were hit. A shower of incendiaries penetrated the copper sheathing of the museum's roof, falling in a hollow space to

which there was no access and becoming, in the evocative words of the *Times*, a "raging furnace until...the roof crashed on to the floor below, a mass of flame and twisted metal." For the only time in the war, the London Fire Brigade was called in to help museum staff fight the resulting fire. Ten of the upper galleries were destroyed and the roof over the main staircase ruined.

That same night the southwestern corner of the bookstacks burned, with as many as 250,000 volumes destroyed. The library had

Air Raid Precautions badge.

been an integral part of the British Museum

building; its cavernous domed reading room, based on the designs of Sir Anthony Panizzi and completed in 1857, was the hushed sanctuary for many a scholar, philosopher, writer, and dreamer. Rare was the English author who didn't spend time here, paging through one of the 24,000 reference volumes or patiently awaiting books from the twenty-five miles of storage behind the circular walls (or impatiently— Thomas Carlyle started the London Library after he had to wait too long for an item). The Reading Room was closed to the public from September 1940 until June 1946, a frustrating bibliographic drought although the smaller North Library filled in for some of this time.

> **VISITOR DETAILS:** The British Museum is open Saturday– Wednesday 10am to 5:30pm; Thursday–Friday 10am to 8:30pm. Sound guides and guided tours available. Several shops, cafes, and restrooms; check the maps at the Information Desk for locations of these. More information: 020 7323 8838, www.thebritishmu seum.ac.uk.

The Reading Room's immense cast-iron dome—106 feet high and 140 feet in diameter—offered a dramatic bull's-eye to Luftwaffe bombers. One extremely sharp-eyed German pilot managed a direct hit, dropping an oil bomb that crashed down through the dome in a shower of bricks, demolishing a lamp on the table in the center of the room, but destroying only a single book. Luckily the bomb's load of flammable oil spilled on the outside of the dome, causing little damage. Although no explosives or incendiaries fell here after 1941, the building complex was rocked and its windows smashed by the Germans' late-war rockets, landing nearby.

When the British Library moved to new quarters on Euston Road, quite a bit of prime real estate was left empty in the museum's center. The intriguing solution is the soaring Queen Elizabeth II Great Court designed by architect Norman Foster, who coincidentally also put a glass roof over Berlin's Reichstag. A spectacular glass-covered courtyard with a circular public reading room in the center, the Great Court is fast becoming as much an attraction as the museum's artifacts. Enjoy and explore the antiquities, galleries, museum shops, and cafés here.

> *Bloomsbury has an even dozen squares— thirteen if you count the covered public square of the British Museum's Great Court.*

And as you walk across the Great Court, note the intricate glass-and-steel ceiling high overhead—and give a moment's thought to what an inviting target it would have offered sixty years ago.

As you leave through the British Museum gates, glance across **Great Russell Street** to the left. On the corner of Bury Place is Westaway &

Text continued on page 220.

George Orwell

June 25, 1903: Eric Arthur Blair, later known as George Orwell, is born in Bengal, India.

1921–1940: Orwell graduates from Eton, spends five years in Burma as a policeman, returns to London as a penniless writer, teaches school, works in a Hampstead bookstore, writes *Down and Out in London and Paris* and *Keep the Aspidistra Flying*, and heads to Spain to fight in the Spanish Civil War. He also becomes a socialist. When in London Orwell lives in various rooms and flats, including over the bookstore at Pond Street and South End Green in Hampstead, 50 Lawford Road, 22 Portobello Road, and 77 Parliament Hill, Hampstead. (All have plaques noting Orwell's residence.)

1930s–1940s: Author Orwell often visits his book publishers: Victor Gollancz has offices at 14 Henrietta Street, Covent Garden, and Secker & Warburg are located at 22 Essex Street near the Strand. He also frequents the pubs of Soho and Fitzrovia, particularly the Fitzroy Tavern on Charlotte Street and the Wheatsheaf and Marquis of Granby, both on Rathbone Place (favorites also of Dylan Thomas).

June 9, 1936: Orwell marries Eileen O'Shaughnessy in the parish church in Wallington, Hertfordshire.

May 1940: The Orwells rent a flat at 18 Dorset Chambers in Chagford Street, southwest of Regent's Park. "So many streets in...the quarter roped off because of unexploded bombs, that to get home from Baker Street, say 300 yards, is like trying to find your way to the heart of a maze."

Summer 1940: Despite his very poor health, Orwell joins "C" Company of the 5th County of London Home Guard Battalion in St. John's Wood, as a sergeant.

April 1941: The Orwells move to 111 Langford Court, St. John's Wood. In mid-May after a bomb damages the building, residents are evacuated: "I noticed afterwards that what I had taken was not my typewriter or any documents but my firearms and a haversack containing food, etc., which was always kept ready."

August 1941: Orwell begins work at the BBC in Portland Place as a Talks Producer in the Indian Section of its Eastern Service. His salary is £640 per year. His early radio training takes place at Bedford College in Regent's Park (now Regent's College). Eventually Orwell's office is moved to the Peter Robinson department store (200 Oxford Street), a site requisitioned in part by the BBC for wartime use. Orwell sometimes raises a pint at the nearby Argyll Arms at 18 Argyll Street (still there).

Summer 1942: The Orwells move to 10A Mortimer Crescent, renting the lower half of a semi-detached house in Maida Vale, west of Regent's Park; they raise chickens in the backyard to supplement their rationed diet.

November 1943: Orwell resigns from the BBC to become literary editor of the *Tribune*, an independent socialist paper with offices in the Outer Temple at 222 Strand (still standing).

June 1944: A V-1 rocket falls near the Orwells' Mortimer Crescent home; Orwell and his wife relocate, first to a friend's nearby flat and finally to a flat at 27B Canonbury Square, Islington; rent is £100 a year. (A plaque on the building notes his residence.)

Summer 1944: The Orwells adopt a baby boy, Richard Horatio Blair.

March 1945: Orwell leaves the *Tribune* and begins work as a war correspondent for the *Observer*. He is in Germany when his wife dies during an operation for cancer.

August 14, 1945: Orwell is in Fleet Street on Victory over Japan Day, and feeling testy. "There was quite a bit of jubilation in the streets, and people in upstairs offices instantly began tearing up old papers and throwing them out of the windows....For a couple of miles my bus travelled through a rain of paper fragments which glittered in the sunlight as they came down and littered the pavements ankle deep....In England you can't get paper to print books on, but apparently there is plenty of it for this kind of thing."

1945: Orwell's *Animal Farm* is published.

June 1949: Orwell's novel of totalitarianism—*1984*—is published. Suffering from advanced tuberculosis, Orwell has spent months in northern hospitals and sanatoriums, but now enters University College Hospital, Bloomsbury. He stays in the private patients' wing on Grafton Street.

October 13, 1949: Lying in his hospital bed, Orwell is married to Sonia Brownell.

January 21, 1950: George Orwell dies in University College Hospital. His funeral service is held at London's Christ Church, Albany Street, and he is buried in All Saints' Churchyard, Sutton Courtenay, Oxfordshire. The tombstone reads "Here lies Eric Arthur Blair."

Westaway, a clothing store that's always a pleasure to visit, especially on wintry days when new cashmere gloves sound inviting. The company has been selling warmth since 1937, though their wartime stock, then aimed primarily at the wholesale trade, was somewhat different from the well-priced cashmere items of today.

Wartime clothes rationing went into effect in June 1941 with the establishment of a points coupon program for new clothes. One paid money as well as coupons for clothing, and the allocation to adults of sixty-six coupons a year did not go far: a new overcoat cost sixteen coupons, a coat jacket thirteen, trousers eight.

British homemakers were encouraged to "make do and mend," and re-doing rather than purchasing was the trend. Curtains were re-made into dresses, and ratty old sweaters were unraveled and the wool knit into new versions. By war's end, most Londoners passing by the museum's gates would have looked a little drab and frayed around the edges, in patched overcoats and well-worn dresses or suits, with darned socks and scuffed shoes. If you do make a cashmere stop at Westaway & Westaway, be mindful of the austere shopping limitations a wartime Londoner would have experienced—and perhaps celebrate the fact that you never had to darn socks or gloves!

On the nearer end of this same block and almost directly across from the museum's gates sits the Museum Tavern. Reputedly Karl Marx was a frequent customer, stopping by after his studies in the British Library. One can imagine many visitors over the years—perhaps even wartime servicemen—explaining that they were late because of an educational stop at "the Museum." Enjoy your Guinness and fish and chips at the outdoor tables on a sunny day or in the Victorian interior anytime.

Great Russell Street, stretching from Tottenham Court Road to Southampton Row, offered wartime service personnel several havens, including the YWCA Central Club Hostel at 16 Great Russell Street and the YMCA London Central Club at 112 Great Russell Street (since rebuilt). The Graham Club YWCA at 107 Great Russell Street provided an overnight stop for Canadian women officers.

For wartime visitors who were essentially just passing through—the refugees, the soldiers, the newly employed office workers—Bloomsbury was a refreshing new neighborhood, its tree-shaded squares pastoral retreats

> *Static water tanks, holding upwards of 5,000 gallons and dotted along London streets, provided emergency water supplies for firefighters. They were also an attractive nuisance to London's youth who, despite barbed wire around the tank edges, tossed in bricks, bicycles, prams, and other debris. A static water tank stood on one side of elegant Bedford Square.*

in the midst of the area's urban byways. But for residents, the destruction that German bombs and rockets delivered to Bloomsbury was devastating.

Shortly before her death, Virginia Woolf briefly returned to her old haunts from her country home in Rodmell, where she and husband Leonard had moved after their second Bloomsbury house was blitzed. She wandered "in the desolate ruins of my old squares; gashed; dismantled; the old red bricks all white powder, something like a builder's yard. Grey dirt and broken windows. Sightseers; all that completeness ravished and demolished."

Sadly Virginia Woolf did not live to see the renovation and rebuilding of her beloved Bloomsbury haunts, those "desolate ruins" made complete and inviting once again. Today's Bloomsbury bustles with an intoxicating convergence of elegance, culture, and ever-so-slight down-at-the-heels style. It's 1938 all over again.

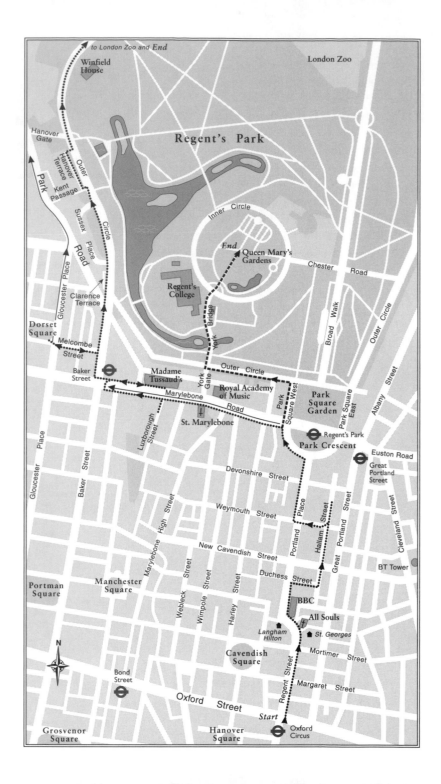

to London Zoo and *End*

Winfield
House

London Zoo

Regent's Park

Hanover
Gate

Hanover
Terrace

Kent
Passage

Outer

Park

Circle

Sussex
Place

Road

Gloucester Place

Inner Circle

Clarence
Terrace

End

Queen Mary's
Gardens

Chester   Road

Regent's
College

Bridge

Broad   Walk

Outer Circle

Dorset
Square

Melcombe
Street

York

Baker
Street

Madame
Tussaud's

Outer   Circle

Park Square West

Park
Square
Garden

Albany   Street

York Gate

Royal Academy
of Music

Park Square East

Marylebone

Luxborough
Street

Road

St. Marylebone

Gloucester   Place

Baker   Street

Regent's Park
Park Crescent

Euston Road

Devonshire   Street

Great
Portland
Street

Weymouth   Street

Portland   Place

Hallam   Street

Great   Portland   Street

Cleveland   Street

BT Tower

New   Cavendish   Street

Marylebone High Street

Welbeck   Street

Wimpole   Street

Harley   Street

Duchess   Street

Portman
Square

Manchester
Square

BBC

Langham
Hilton

All Souls

St. Georges

Cavendish
Square

Regent   Street

Mortimer   Street

Margaret   Street

N

Bond
Street

Oxford   Street

Start

Oxford
Circus

Grosvenor
Square

Hanover
Square

"This is London": The BBC, Marylebone, and Regent's Park

Some people have concluded that the Germans are devoting especial attention to this borough....When one sees the kind of damage they have inflicted, either they must be indulging in entirely indiscriminate bombing, or—they are very bad shots.

—ANTHONY WEYMOUTH, *JOURNAL OF THE WAR YEARS*

A bombed Broadcasting House.

Highlights: St. George's and Queen's Hall sites, Langham Hotel, All Souls Church, Broadcasting House, Portland Place, Murrow home, Sikorski statue, Regent's Park, Marylebone Road, St. Marylebone Parish Church, Madame Tussaud's, Dorset Square, Regent's Park terraces, Winfield House, London Zoo

Underground Station: Oxford Circus

Photo Ops: It's undeniably hokey, but you might want to have your picture taken with Charles de Gaulle or near King George VI in Madame Tussaud's.

BEFORE LEAVING ON YOUR TRIP

■ **Travel Scheduling:** If matters horticultural interest you, the roses of Queen Mary's

Garden in Regent's Park are at their best in May and June.

■ **Cultural Preparations:** The book *This Is London* contains transcripts of broadcasts made by Edward R. Murrow early in the war. As a counterpoint, Penelope Fitzgerald's novel *Human Voices* provides a droll look at the wartime BBC. Music lovers: Watch for Eric Coates' *London Again Suite*; the second movement, "Langham Place," is built on the notes B-B-C, and ends with the muffled midnight notes of Big Ben, just as they might have sounded in distant Langham Place.

■ **Internet Best Bets:** Madame Tussaud's at www.madame-tussauds.co.uk or London Zoo's wealth of information at www.zsl.org.

So, what *did* happen to the animals in the London Zoo during the war? Were the most dangerous animals really killed before the air raids began because of fears that a bomb would set them free to roam London? And what about the elephants? How did they survive wartime rationing? The answers to those questions and others—including "Has the BBC always been so stuffy?"—are found in this part of town and along our route.

> London radio listeners enjoyed the hilarious *"It's That Man Again"* (known to all as *ITMA*), the *"Brains Trust," "Hi Gang!"* with Americans Ben Lyon and Bebe Daniels, and especially the evening news.

We'll start from Oxford Circus north along upper Regent Street to Broadcasting House, home of the BBC, then head to Madame Tussaud's Wax Museum, a kitschy but entertaining stop even in the war years. The London wartime haunts of American radio broadcasters, including one of the greatest of newsmen, Edward R. Murrow, lie throughout this neighborhood, and we'll spot several of them. Finally, it's on to Regent's Park and the zoo. A guidebook published soon after World War II noted that in this part of London "the points of interest are somewhat far apart and the district does not repay minute exploration." There's still some truth in that, so keep your Travelcard or some loose change handy—bus possibilities will be noted.

Stroll north from the Oxford Circus Underground along Regent Street to the strange junction where Langham Place slides off to the left to become Portland Place, with the drum-like All Souls Church seemingly right in the middle of the street and the barrel-like Broadcasting House looming behind it. Off to the right on Riding House Street is St. Georges Hotel, built in 1963 on the site of **St. George's Hall**, originally opened as a concert hall in 1867. Sixty-six years later the growing BBC acquired it as a studio concert hall, and so it remained until late September 1940, when incendiary bombs smashed through the glass roof and fire leveled the hall.

Adjacent to St. George's Hall was **Queen's Hall** (1893), a popular concert venue with perfect acoustics. Sir Henry Wood began his Promenade

War Words: Doorhopping

A peculiarly urban phenomenon, **DOORHOPPING** involved a wartime style of travel, half-walk, half-run, in which the cautious pedestrian ducked into doorways briefly whenever bombs or shrapnel started falling nearby. It is replicated today when spring rains surprise Londoners.

The prewar look of the Langham Hotel.

Concerts here in 1895 (the "Proms" continue today at Kensington's Royal Albert Hall). Some months after the attack on St. George's Hall, incendiary bombs fell next door on Queen's Hall, all successfully extinguished until one landed unnoticed in an inaccessible location. The resulting blaze consumed the entire building, turning it into a roofless brick shell punctuated with twisted steel girders, looking much like an ancient Roman arena. The BBC's Henry Wood House, with St. Georges Hotel a part of it, now stands on the site of the two halls—watch for the plaque.

Along the southwestern side of this unusual intersection sits the **Langham Hotel**, opened in the mid-1860s. As one of the few luxury hotels in the area, it hosted some notable prewar guests, including conductor Arturo Toscanini and the exiled emperor Haile Salassie. With the outbreak of war, the BBC moved in, partitioning many of the stylish rooms into crowded offices. In September 1940, a bomb exploding at the hotel's eastern end sent blocks of masonry crashing to the street. This plus a second attack in December left the hotel badly shattered. To make matters worse, the 38,000-gallon tank on the Langham's roof, storing water from the hotel's artesian wells, proved an appealing target for at least one Luftwaffe pilot—the bombed tank flooded the hotel. Water, plus wartime and postwar occupation by the BBC, squelched the hotel's luxury reputation, and it wasn't until the 1990s and new ownership that the Langham returned to its sumptuous origins.

According to the wall plaque, **All Souls Church** was "severely damaged and made unusable by aerial bombardment" in December 1940. A land mine exploding here caused extensive damage, particularly to the roof and steeple, the latter known to generations of Londoners as the "candle-snuffer" spire. The steeple's point was so badly damaged that steeplejacks were called in to carefully remove the top section, giving the already unusual spire a stunted look throughout the war. The congregation moved temporarily (eleven years) to St. Peter's Vere Street, returning to All Souls in 1951 when postwar renovations were complete. Subsequent reconstruction resulted in Nash's unique exterior and a very modern gold and white interior. Step in and see if the combination works for you.

All Souls Church.

Just beyond All Souls Church is **Broadcasting House**, home to the British Broadcasting Company (now Corporation) since the early 1930s, though it was clear even then that the new building was too small, and the parceling out of BBC services and programs to other locations soon began. During the war this meant nearby St. George's Hall and the Langham Hotel, Bush House on the Strand, and Maida Vale west of Regent's Park, where studios were set up in a deserted ice skating rink. Today the BBC has scores of offices and studios throughout the UK (and the BBC monopoly on the airwaves has ended), but to the minds of many, Broadcasting House is Britain's Mother Studio.

Broadcasting House was the first building in the world custom-built for radio broadcasting, its soundproofed walls three feet thick and its studios located in a windowless "central tower" within the building's core. Look up—above the bronze entrance doors is Eric Gill's sculpture of Shakespeare's magician Prospero sending his brave spirit Ariel out into the world.

George Orwell once described the wartime BBC atmosphere as "somewhere halfway between a girls' school and a lunatic asylum."

It was John Reith, the BBC's first general manager (1922-1927) and then director-general (to 1938) who established England's radio broadcasting style for much of the twentieth century. From the start, the straitlaced Reith insisted that BBC announcers (all men, of course) wear black ties while at the microphone, symbolic of the BBC's lofty moral tone, high ideals, and staid, unswerving broadcasting responsibilities (no dance music to be broadcast on Sundays!). This slightly puritanical and haughty aura survived for years and was perfectly captured by Virginia Woolf in 1937; after spending time at Broadcasting House preparing a radio talk, she described the "sad discreet atmosphere" there as "oh so proper oh so kindly."

The BBC's Broadcasting House.

Things lightened up somewhat during the war years—at least the black tie policy was abandoned. And the suspense of the Munich crisis and the early war years meant regular news listening became an essential ritual for the English. News was broadcast at 7am, 8am, 1pm, 6pm, 9pm, and midnight, and especially for the 9pm news, half the adult population—sixteen million people—put aside their newspapers or knitting to listen.

The war was particularly unkind to Broadcasting House, both to its structure and its occupants. A wartime visitor would have immediately noticed newly installed defensive measures, none of them particularly attractive. The building's exterior was camouflaged a dark gray and surrounded with sandbags. Windows were covered, and security guards were everywhere. The front entrance was almost completely bricked-in except for a single narrow passage through which one squeezed, security pass in hand, into the gloomy foyer. Along the interior corridors, ominous gas-proof doors had been installed.

When the threat of bombing and invasion became more serious in late summer 1940, soldiers replaced the security guards; a pillbox fully equipped with machine guns and gunners guarded the front door; and six-foot-square concrete blocks ringed the building's perimeter, sturdy defenses against attacking tanks. Radio broadcasts continued during air raids, though often from emergency studios located in the

Although some sort of radio transmission was occurring as early as the 1900s (thank you, Guglielmo Marconi), formal radio broadcasting in the UK didn't begin until 1922, when the BBC was born. Ten years later King George V made the first live royal broadcast, and the world has not been the same since.

Text continued on page 230.

FOOTSTEPS OF THE FAMOUS
Edward R. Murrow

April 25, 1908: Egbert Roscoe Murrow is born in Greensboro, North Carolina; his family will move to Washington State in 1913, where, as an adolescent, Murrow begins using the name "Ed."

Summer 1930: College student leader Murrow spends eight weeks in Europe, finding England "a sort of museum piece...small...compliant, not important."

September 15, 1930: Murrow, still a student, makes his first radio broadcast for the two-year-old Columbia Broadcasting System.

October 27, 1934: Edward R. Murrow marries Janet Brewster.

Summer 1935: After working several years at the Institute of International Education, Murrow takes a job with CBS in New York as Director of Talks.

April 1937: As CBS's new European Director, Murrow moves to London. He and his wife settle into a flat on Queen Anne Street. Murrow begins work at the CBS office in Langham Place, across from Broadcasting House.

May 12, 1937: The Murrows, seated in the stands in front of Apsley House near Hyde Park, watch the coronation procession of King George VI and Queen Elizabeth. Twenty-six years later, Murrow will stand in the rain along the processional route and broadcast the coronation of Queen Elizabeth II for American television viewers.

Spring 1938: The Murrows move to 84 Hallam Street, several blocks from Broadcasting House. An air raid shelter is located in the mews behind the building, although the Murrows never use it, preferring to shelter under a large oak table in the study. (The Hallam Street building still stands.) Throughout the war, the Murrow flat serves as a combined office, club, and pub for Murrow's friends and co-workers, including the "Murrow Boys," the young, articulate journalists he hires as radio broadcasters: William Shirer, Eric Sevareid, Larry Le Sueur, Charles Collingwood, and Richard C. Hottelet.

September 3, 1939: Murrow is on the air from Broadcasting House soon after Chamberlain's war declaration, and his terse descriptive style—very new to radio listeners—is already in place: "Forty-five minutes ago the prime minister stated that a state of war existed between Britain and Germany. Air raid instructions were immediately broadcast, and almost directly following that broadcast the air raid sirens screamed through the quiet calm of this Sabbath morning."

August 24, 1940: At 11:30pm, Murrow broadcasts from in front of St. Martin-in-the-Fields, Trafalgar Square, picking up the sound of air raid sirens and people's scuffling footsteps as they hurry to bomb shelters, "like ghosts shod with steel shoes."

September 6–8, 1940: Murrow and two friends head down the Thames Estuary looking for a story on the coastal bombing. The night of September 7, from a hilltop in Gravesend, they watch London's East End pounded in the first attack of the Blitz. In his next broadcast from Studio B-4, deep in the bowels of Broadcasting House, Murrow will describe what he saw to his American listeners: "The guns were working all around us, the bursts looking like fireflies in a Southern summer night....Huge pear-shaped bursts of flame would rise up into the smoke and disappear. The world was upside down."

Most Americans are convinced Edward R. Murrow's wartime broadcasts began with a pregnant pause: "This...is London." Actually his opening was more of a declaratory statement with no marked pause: "This is London."

September 21, 1940: From atop Broadcasting House, Murrow begins the first radio broadcast ever made in the middle of an air raid. "Off to my left, far away in the distance, I can see just that faint red angry snap of anti-aircraft bursts against the steel-blue sky...."

1939–40: Murrow frequently dines at his favorite restaurant, L'Etoile at 30 Charlotte Street in Soho. He also finds time to purchase elegant—and expensive—suits along Mayfair's Savile Row.

Autumn 1940: Murrow's CBS office on Langham Place is wrecked by a near-miss explosion; he moves to a second office on Portland Place. When that too is bombed, he moves to 1 Duchess Street (still standing). A massive German raid on London will soon damage the Duchess Street office, necessitating yet another move, this time to 49 Hallam Street (still standing).

January 1942–April 1945: Murrow continues broadcasting and experiencing the war. He also finds time for a brief intense affair with Pamela Churchill, ex-wife of the prime minister's son.

May 8, 1945 (V-E Day): Murrow broadcasts from London: "As you walk down the streets you hear singing that comes from open windows; sometimes it's a chorus, and sometimes it's just a single voice raised in song. 'Roll Out the Barrel' seems to be a favorite."

March 10, 1946: Murrow makes his last radio broadcast from London, leaving England where, he said, "This reporter left all of his youth and much of his heart." He will return to the U.S., eventually move to television to host "Person to Person" and "See It Now," and serve as director of the U.S. Information Agency.

April 27, 1965: After a long battle with cancer, Edward R. Murrow dies in his home in upstate New York.

sub-basement, three floors below ground. The BBC moved into siege mode, ready for anything the Germans could throw its way.

These stout defenses plus the pressure of work meant many BBC employees remained in the building night and day, or used it as a shelter and went home only briefly after the All Clear to tidy up. A canteen provided meals, and early on, one end of the basement concert hall was carpeted with dozens of mattresses. Employees picked their way over sleeping colleagues and, with the help of dimmed flashlights, found the night's allotted spaces—a primitive arrangement but welcome after a fourteen-hour workday. Even American musician Glenn Miller slept here on occasion, although in general his experience with the BBC wasn't positive. Miller was fired after refusing to produce more even-toned music for the BBC's listeners, many of whom were unacquainted with the ebb and flow of the Glenn Miller sound. Later in the Blitz, numbered and reservable metal bunks were set up in the basement of Broadcasting House, discreetly arranged with men on one side of the room and women on the other, with a prim curtain in between.

Even faithful BBC listeners tuned in to German radio to catch the latest sneering pronouncements by Lord Haw Haw, British citizen William Joyce turned Nazi propagandist. Joyce had fled to Germany in 1939; his nickname came from the pseudo upper-class laugh he affected on the air. He was executed for treason early in 1946.

Broadcasting House experienced two major attacks, the first in mid-October 1940 (coincidentally just about the time the building was camouflaged). A 500-lb. delayed-action bomb crashed into the telephone switchboard room on the seventh floor, fell down through the newsroom, and eventually landed on the fourth floor outside the music library. The bomb took several long terrifying minutes to explode. When it finally did, one witness described "a deafening crash, or series of crashes, as if the entire top of the BBC was coming down on our heads." Bruce Belfrage had been reading the 9pm news on the air at the time the bomb fell—he knew there was an unexploded bomb ticking somewhere in the building, and he just kept on reading the day's news—when his radio listeners throughout England faintly heard the explosion. After the briefest of pauses from Belfrage and another voice whispering "It's all right!," the news broadcast continued.

VISITOR DETAILS: Broadcasting House is not open to the public; visit the BBC shop close by at 50 Margaret Street, open Monday–Saturday 9:30am to 6pm; Sunday 10am to 4pm. More information: 020 7631 4523, www.bbc.co.uk, www.bbcshop.com.

A jagged hole thirty feet long and twenty feet high had been blown in the exterior wall of the fourth and fifth floors on the Portland Place side of the building. The switchboard room was a jumble of tangled wires, and the music library was ravaged, with files, scores, and recordings shredded. The upper part of the building caught fire, though quick work by London's firefighters averted tragedy. At least six people were killed. The BBC was no longer just reporting the war; it was in the thick of it.

> *Sir Kenneth Clark, wartime director of the National Gallery, lived at 30 Portland Place in the 1930s.*

A few months later, a land mine exploded in Portland Place and pulverized every window in the building and smashed yet another hole in the exterior wall. All Souls Church and other nearby buildings were also damaged. This time there were fewer casualties, but fire inside Broadcasting House, combined with a broken water main and firefighters' hoses, caused extensive problems during the six hours it took to get the blaze under control. Witnesses described staircases like waterfalls, a pool of water in the lobby, and desks practically floating. The BBC continued broadcasting.

The very broad **Portland Place** (over 125 feet wide) was originally laid out by the Adams brothers in the 1770s, then enlarged by architect John Nash. Portland Place heads north to Regent's Park, but first, a short detour—at the first cross street after the BBC, take Duchess Street to the corner of Hallam Street.

It was at 1 Duchess Street that American radio broadcaster Edward R. Murrow settled in to new digs after being bombed out of two nearby offices—and he'd get bombed out of this one too. The building also served as a wartime club for American officers, run by the Red Cross. That elderly "Duchess Street" sign was undoubtedly spotted by many an American desperate for a good cup of coffee and a friendly face.

Up Hallam Street you'll soon pass Cavendish Mews South, the first of many mews in this neighborhood; explore any that appeal. And while you're thinking detour, Hallam Street is obviously a strictly residential enclave, but plenty of cafés and pubs line Great Portland Street, just a block east.

Number 49 Hallam Street was Murrow's fourth CBS office in London, convenient to **Murrow's home** up the block at Number 84. Murrow was CBS's point person in London during the early 1940s, hiring new broadcasters, grappling with British censorship regulations, making nightly broadcasts (and because of the time difference and because radio then was live, not taped, his broadcasts were very late), and interpreting the war for his American listeners. In the process, Murrow helped define American radio, essentially inventing the news commentary. His was a descriptive, straightforward style, seemingly emotionless; in reality Murrow's broadcasts exuded a subtle emotionality and were more powerful because of it. And every description, every fact, was backed with personal experience. Unlike the studio-based BBC news readers, Murrow was a news experiencer, living the events and happenings of the war. He stood atop Broadcasting House to record an air raid in progress, he flew in an RAF Lancaster bomber over Berlin, he went down inside the most fetid of East End air raid shelters, and he sought out and memorably described the look of London's blasted streets, the sound of Big Ben's resolute tolling, and—at war's end—the horrors of Buchenwald.

From the Murrows' flat at Number 84, retrace your steps half a block back to Weymouth Street, perhaps imagining what this narrow avenue was like on a late autumn night in 1940 as German explosives shook the buildings and the pavements heaved from the shock of nearby explosions. In the blackout, this would not have been a very happy stroll.

Turn right onto Weymouth Street and walk the short block to Portland Place. In the middle of the divided roadway ahead stands a **statue of General Wladyslaw Sikorski**, Polish prime minister and commander-in-chief of the Polish Armed Forces from late 1939 until July 1943. The bronze figure, looking toward the embassy across the street, was erected in memory of Sikorski, the Polish Armed Forces, and the Polish Resistance Movement. The embassy he's eyeing at Number 47 was the wartime focus for refugee Poles seeking work or assistance. The Polish Embassy's flag was lowered to half-mast after the announcement of General Sikorski's death in an airplane accident off Gibraltar, a somewhat suspicious and untimely accident given the international political jockeying of the mid-1940s. For more on Sikorski and the Polish participation in both the war and London's homefront, see Chapter 9, where the General Sikorski Museum is on the itinerary.

All along this stretch, these sizeable and very elegant buildings have long been turned to official rather than residential use. The Swedish Legation was at 27 Portland Place throughout the war, and during the early 1940s, Number 41 housed the Balfour Club, serving Jewish members of the Allied Forces. Number 49–51, the People's Republic of China Embassy, was simply the Chinese Embassy before postwar political machinations; note the ever-present

V for Victory

Winston Churchill, cigar in one hand and the other raising a defiant "V" sign, is a lasting image from the war's homefront, even though Churchill didn't start making the sign of the V until August 1941. Months before, the potent symbol was being chalked on Belgian walls, then seemingly scrawled almost everywhere in Occupied Europe, helped along by BBC broadcasters spreading the word.

The "dit dit dit dahh" rhythm of the opening of Beethoven's Fifth Symphony was used by the BBC as a time signal between broadcasts to Nazi-occupied Europe, a sound that perfectly matched the "dot dot dot dash" of Morse code for the letter V. Many a Frenchman huddling over his illegal homemade wireless used the distinctive notes composed by the German Beethoven to help tune in the BBC's broadcasts.

It was V for *vitezstvi* to the Czechs, V for *vitazstvo* to the Slovaks, V for *vrijheid* to the Belgians, and V for *victoire* to the French. To the Germans, it was damned annoying. Worse, V for victory was being incessantly hummed, sung, whistled, and honked everywhere—and even tapped on the sides of European coffee cups. Naturally the Germans tried to co-opt the V movement, insisting all those scrawled Vs in Vichy France stood for *viktoria* or Vive Hitler; the Nazis even erected a fifty-foot-high V on the side of the Eiffel Tower in Paris. The worst and perhaps most effective German move, though, was the V-1s and V-2s. V for *vergeltung*...vengeance.

> The V is the symbol of European solidarity and co-operation—an expression of the common will of the peoples of occupied territories to resist the Germans till the great day when they can rise up and throw them out.
> —Antonia White, BBC at War, 1942

Today, images of the twenty-second letter of the alphabet, in victory brooches, bracelets, earrings, and lockets—jewelry worn by a waiting sweetheart or mother—are a popular homefront collectible. Watch for V-related items in London's antique and street markets.

Metropolitan Police out front. The Turkish Embassy was located at Number 69, a building that still serves as the Turkish ambassador's residence. Even the American embassy was once here, extremely prewar (the 1860s), at Number 98.

At the northern end of Portland Place are the stuccoed terraces of Park Crescent, Regency-era buildings designed by John Nash in the 1820s. Several received direct hits from German bombs and were leveled—

"razed to the ground, leaving a cruel gap in the regular curved colonnade," mourned one resident. A great deal of rebuilding followed, with a move toward offices for learned societies and charitable institutions rather than residences, though a few flats remain. If you're house-hunting, flats start at about £210,000 ($325,000) for a small one-bedroom place.

Beyond Park Crescent to the north is Regent's Park Underground and beyond that, the formal tranquility of **Regent's Park** itself, all 480-plus acres. If the upcoming delights of Madame Tussaud's don't interest you, cross into the park—continue around Park Crescent to the left, cross Marylebone Road, go straight ahead on Park Square West, then *voilà*, turn left on the park's Outer Circle. The first major turn north on York Bridge will lead you toward the Inner Circle and Queen Mary's Gardens, including a walk past the red-brick buildings of Regent's College. This was once Bedford College, founded in 1849 to provide women a liberal education; the school moved here in the early 1900s. Soon after the outbreak of war, school staff and students were evacuated to Cambridge, and the buildings were turned over to the BBC as a training school for new hires—quickly dubbed "The Liars' School" by the irreverent radio trainees, untouched by the historic decorum and traditions of the BBC. George Orwell, among others, worked here.

> **VISITOR DETAILS:** Regent's Park is open daily 7am until dusk. Several cafés and tea houses, mostly clustered along Broad Walk, open daily 9:30am to 5:30pm. Check posted park maps for exact locations (ditto restrooms).

A wartime walker would have noticed a barrage balloon moored in the park's Inner Circle and couldn't have missed the high artificial hill hereabouts, made up of thousands of tons of sand dumped at the beginning of the war for sandbags. One's perambulations might, however, be restricted by immense roped-off areas where the bomb squad detonated delayed-action bombs. All in all, Regent's Park in wartime drab was far different from the manicured beauty so evident today. For more on London's parks, see "Parks in Wartime" in Chapter 2. And for more on the western and northern sides of Regent's Park, see the section below that follows Madame Tussaud's.

> *"Marylebone" is pronounced, roughly, MARL-uh-bun, so slurred that it's almost MARY-bun. It may help—or not—to know the word's origin: the church of St. Mary on the Bourne or stream.*

If the waxy amusements of Madame Tussaud's call more urgently to you than the bucolic lanes of the park, turn onto **Marylebone Road** from Park Crescent and head west for a half-dozen short blocks. This throughway, laid out in 1757 as London's first bypass, is today a thundering six lanes of traffic. If you wish to avoid the tumult, use that transit Travelcard or that handful of change and hop on a bus to Baker Street.

Your bus route (or walking route, if you chose) heads west along Marylebone Road; one of the first streets to the left (south) is Harley Street, together with nearby Wimpole Street long known as a center of upmarket medical offices. A hostel for Canadian service women moved in amongst the medicos late in the war at 68 Harley Street.

On the same side stands **St. Marylebone Parish Church**, erected in the early 1800s. By mid-war, Hitler's bombs had produced a particularly shabby look, with damage to the windows, walls, and a huge gash across the back of the altar. The nearby parish chapel was so badly damaged by explosives that it was demolished in 1949, its site now a small garden paralleling the pavement about a half-block down Marylebone High Street. Incidentally, if you're on foot and want a pleasant interlude in a charming neighborhood, Marylebone High Street fills the bill.

Luxborough Street is next, with flats along one side of the street and the University of Westminster on the other. Here was the wartime residence of author Rose Macaulay, at least until her home at Number 8 was badly bombed in May 1941. Macaulay was away at the time; she may well have been on duty as an emergency driver for the London Auxiliary Ambulance Services, her wartime job. After bombs left only a smoking, blackened ruin, she moved to Hinde Street near Manchester Square. The hardest loss for the author was her books. The night after her flat was gutted, she described her situation as "bombed and burnt out of existence, and nothing saved." She sadly added, "I am bookless, homeless, sans everything but my eyes to weep with." Perhaps you can guess on which side of the street she lived.

Cross Marylebone Road at Baker Street. On the corner is the Baker Street Underground, a rather elaborate multi-platformed labyrinth. Walk past Mr. Holmes standing outside and head eastwards to **Madame Tussaud's** and the London Planetarium. Madame Tussaud's delights over two million visitors annually and, especially during the summer season, this popular destination can be jammed. Even on a rainy

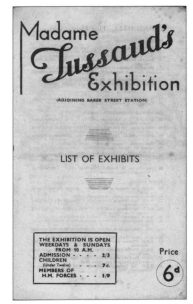

April weekday, I waited in line an hour. But remember, we visit not as tourists but as homefront enthusiasts, eager to see how an important London site experienced and survived the war, and how modern-day circumstances can illuminate the war years. So line up (or better, buy a timed ticket and know when you're getting in).

> Madame Tussaud probably preferred the French pronunciation "tyo-SEW," but grew used to "too-SAWD."

First a little prewar background—in fact, very prewar. Purchase a booklet at the ticket desk for more details on the museum's early history, but briefly the story began when Madame Tussaud (1761?–1850), a Swiss woman from France and well-skilled in the techniques of wax modeling, came to England in the early 1800s. She settled her waxworks exhibition in the Baker Street area in 1835 and moved to the present site in 1884. It proved a major visitor draw from the start, attracting over 750,000 annually by 1924. Just a year later, fire—the worst enemy of a waxworks—destroyed the building and all the figures inside. But the molds for the wax effigies were saved, and reconstruction began immediately. Within three years, Madame Tussaud's reopened. By the mid-1930s, Tussaud's had expanded, adding a cinema and Restaurant Tussaud, with dancing every evening.

> I know you've been wondering, so yes, all the figures in Madame Tussaud's do wear underwear—otherwise their clothing wouldn't hang quite properly.

In early September 1940, German bombs gutted the Tussaud Cinema, leaving nothing but the walls and part of the stage. The blast also shattered windows on both sides of Marylebone Road, blew apart the glass roof of the nearby Underground station, and smashed shop windows and wares all along Baker Street, but caused only minimal damage to the waxworks itself. Nevertheless, most of London—assuming the waxworks had been leveled—was dreadfully worried about Madame Tussaud's. Even Churchill wondered exactly who the casualties had been. Author H. G. Wells also assumed the museum had been destroyed and suggested that the waxen images of himself, the king and queen, Hitler and Stalin, and even Lady Astor had finally all been melted into one corporate state.

Our visit to this three-dimensional wax gallery begins with a lift ride to the main floor. Beyond, the cast of characters changes from time to time; currently the emphasis is on contemporary entertainment figures (Jerry Springer!?!).

I admit I was the tiniest bit disappointed with Ms. Tussaud's wares, perhaps because TV takes some of the thrill from "just like real life"—though judging by the delighted squeals of others here, my lack of enthusiasm wasn't shared. In the Grand Hall, where national and political leaders are gathered, overseas visitors line up to be photographed standing next to the ruler of their country—monarchs, princes, generals, and presidents. Stateside visitors must forego this pleasure—American presidents are gathered together in a tableau, separated from one-on-one photo possibilities. You'll have better luck with the British Royal Family; just recently a waxy Queen Elizabeth has made herself available for close-up photo ops. To me, the Royal Family here is a bit off, and I found myself checking captions to determine exactly who a figure was supposed to be. See if you agree.

> A figure of Churchill was first installed in Madame Tussaud's on his wedding day, September 12, 1908. In all, there have been seven different wax figures of Churchill.

It *is* fun, however, to discover each new image, marvel at the likeness (pro or con), check out the clothing, and see how tall people were. Watch for General de Gaulle (much more handsome and less imposing here than in real life), war-related U.S. presidents (including FDR and Ike, the latter's suit with some *serious* 1950s lapels), Winston Churchill in his polka-dot tie, and Harold Macmillan (smug-looking even in wax). And it *is* satisfying to put a face on some of the names so prominently a part of London's more distant past—the Duke of Wellington, for example, or Charles II.

A visitor to Madame Tussaud's in 1944 would have seen an entirely different cast of characters, although Churchill, Gandhi, and Lincoln are

A wartime tableau of American presidents at Madame Tussaud's.

Postboxes

It's a rare London outing that doesn't pass a half-dozen red postboxes, those cast-iron cylinders so unlike the hulking blue mailboxes found on Stateside corners. Postboxes bear the cipher of the reigning sovereign when they were installed, and replacements carry the current monarch's monogram. Thus the older models are slowly disappearing, making postbox spotting almost as much fun as shelter signspotting (see Chapter 3). Watch for Queen Victoria's cipher (V R for Victoria Regina) and that of her son, George (G R V). Closer to the war period, postboxes were marked E R VIII for King Edward VIII (good luck—only 161 boxes were cast during his short reign) and G R VI for King George VI. And since 1952, postboxes bear Queen Elizabeth's E R II. Here's some postbox and mail service miscellany to consider as you send those postcards home.

The pillar-box... an object full of civic dignity, the treasure-house of a thousand secrets, the fortunes of a thousand souls... there it stands at all our street corners, disguising one of the most beautiful ideas under one of the most preposterous of forms.
—G. K. Chesterton

• Author and post office official Anthony Trollope was the originator of the red pillar box. The first was installed in the Channel Islands in 1852 and is still in use in St. Peter Port, Guernsey. Postboxes came to London in 1855, the first at Fleet and Farringdon streets. The next five were erected on the south side of the Strand, and in Pall Mall, Piccadilly, Grosvenor Place, and Rutland Gate. All are long gone.

constants. Almost all the figures would have been arranged in themed tableaux. Contemporary sports figures and record makers were prominent, including Amelia Earhart and Charles Lindbergh. The grouping entitled "Their Glory Shall Live for Evermore" featured two early World War II heroes: Captain Warburton-Lee, awarded the first Victoria Cross in the war for gallantry at Narvik, Norway, and Lance Corporal Nicholls, a Victoria Cross recipient for gallantry at Dunkirk.

A waxy Mae West flaunted her best, attired in a clingy costume from her hit movie, *I'm No Angel*. Nearby stood Greta Garbo, Bette Davis, Marlene Dietrich, and Katherine Hepburn. Wartime tourists were greeted by American male film stars including Spencer Tracy, Charlie Chaplin, Mickey Rooney, and Leslie Howard. English entertainers included George Robey ("The Prime Minister of Mirth") and singer and actress Gracie Fields.

- The *Illustrated London News* reminded readers in 1941 that the collection and delivery of letters would continue as it had so far through the Blitz attacks, "even if the mail had sometimes to be rescued from pillar-boxes almost submerged beneath debris and delivered to addresses which had become overnight smoldering heaps of ruins." In fact, Londoners reminded their correspondents to add "House wrecked—will call at sorting office" on all letters addressed to residents who had been bombed out.
- Not only postboxes and homes were bombed— the Central Telegraph Office, then London's main postal office and located near St. Paul's Cathedral, was badly damaged in a Luftwaffe raid. Emergency mobile post offices, essentially counters under open-air awnings, were set up as needed in areas of heavy bombing to aid mail delivery to bombed-out Londoners and to fill in for damaged post office buildings.
- Early in the war, postboxes were painted with squares of yellow detector paint that changed color if there was poison gas in the air.
- "Postwomen" replaced many of London's male postal workers, releasing them for wartime military duty.
- Between 1939 and 1945 over sixty million civilian changes of address were filed.
- Letters sent to the States from England during the war could take anywhere from two weeks to two months to arrive...if a German U-boat didn't sink the ship carrying them.

The Grand Hall in 1944 was filled with English prime ministers and royalty (including two very young princesses), British admirals and air marshals, and the National Government Group, including John Anderson and Herbert Morrison, proponents of wartime air raid shelters. The United Nations group was particularly compelling as many of the figures represented leaders who had escaped from Nazism—General Sikorski of Poland, Czechoslovakia's Dr. Edward Benes, Queen Wilhelmina of the Netherlands, and King George of Greece.

Herr Hitler stood somewhat apart in 1944—in fact on a stair landing—with other shunned European leaders: Goering, Rommel, Goebbels, Mussolini, Rudolf Hess, and the French Vichy chief, Pierre Laval. Hitler remains separate today, standing alone outside the Chamber of Horrors, the next stop and a favorite of teenagers.

VISITOR DETAILS: Madame Tussaud's is open Monday–Friday 10am to 5:30pm; weekends 9:30am to 5:30pm. Admission is charged. Café Tussauds; restrooms. More information: 0870 400 3000, www.madame-tussauds.co.uk.

The concluding animatronic ride, "The Spirit of London," sits the visitor in a sort of time travel London taxi that lurches through a montage of London's past 400 years, including a very brief Blitz visit as Churchill stands nearby. Last stop is the chaotic shop.

From the waxworks, head west on Marylebone Road back toward the Baker Street Underground. At Baker Street turn right a block, then left on Melcombe Street. **Dorset Square** is ahead, and on the nearest corner is Number 1. Once the headquarters of Bertram Mills' circus and fun fair, this modest house served a different purpose during the war, housing members of the Free French Forces and their British comrades "who left from this house on special missions to enemy-occupied France." Many did not return.

Buses run northward along Gloucester Place; you can catch #274 for a pleasant ride around half of Regent's Park and on to the zoo. However, to check out several Regent's Park terraces, you could instead walk to the zoo, but be warned—it's quite a lengthy hike. If you opt for the bus, catch up with us in a few pages.

Okay walkers, from Dorset Square retrace your steps down Melcombe Street to Baker Street, turn left (north), crossing Park Road into the Outer Circle. We'll pass several magnificent **Regent's Park terraces** (there are altogether perhaps a dozen terraces circling the park), home to an impressive collection of war-era writers.

The summit of Primrose Hill, to the north of Regent's Park, had an anti-aircraft battery situated on it during the war.

Elizabeth Bowen lived at 2 Clarence Terrace, the first series of terraces on the left. Annoyed about being exiled for a week from her home while the bomb disposal squad wrestled with time bombs in Regent's Park, Bowen at first fretted about her uncovered typewriter, and then she slipped back inside the barricades several times to feed her cats. Then she just slipped back to live, ignoring the barricades.

"Around three sides of the Park, the Regency terraces look like scenery in an empty theatre," she wrote. "At night, at my end of my terrace, I feel as though I were sleeping in one corner of a deserted palace.... Blown-in shutters swing loose, ceilings lie on floors, and a premature decay-smell comes from the rooms. A pediment has fallen on to a lawn." Indeed, Bowen's terrace was badly blasted several times, and she finally moved out when the ceiling fell down and all the windows were broken.

Another literary light lived in nearby Sussex Place Terrace, now home to the London Business School. Critic Cyril Connolly, a good friend of Bowen's, moved into 25 Sussex Place Terrace in spring 1945. However, it's the elegant and restrained Hanover Terrace just beyond Kent Passage that's of particular interest.

Watch for 13 Hanover Terrace (there's a plaque), wartime residence of novelist H. G. Wells. The previous and more superstitious tenant had called it 12A, but Wells restored it to Number 13, and in fact had the number painted even larger once bombing raids began. Although most of his neighbors had moved away during the Blitz, Wells stayed on, feisty as ever, shaking his fist at the absent neighbor whose weeds blighted Wells's formal garden, fulminating against neighborhood dogs whose barking disturbed his work, and raging about a Salvation Army hostel set up at 1 Hanover Terrace—or more exactly, raging somewhat irrationally about the sign on the hostel, a battle waged in London's newspaper columns.

Impervious to bomb fears, Wells slept in an upstairs bedroom throughout the war. Asked after a particularly severe nighttime raid if he'd gotten any sleep, Wells sniffed, "Oh yes, I can sleep through all that row. I have the gift of sleep." Number 13 lost its windows, and the front door was blown in several times, but happily for the building and its sleeping occupant, no major damage was done. A year after war's end, almost to the day, Wells died here.

Continue around the western side of Regent's Park, passing on the left the minareted London Central Mosque, built in the 1970s. **Winfield House** is next, though little more is visible than the exit and entrance gates. It's currently the private residence of the U.S. ambassador and is surrounded by a very private garden rivaling Buckingham Palace's in size.

Winfield House was originally constructed for Woolworth heiress Barbara Hutton in 1937. Its wartime roles ranged from housing an RAF barrage balloon unit to serving as a reception center for prospective RAF recruits. It later saw duty as the Lord Tweedsmuir Club, a service club for

> In late 1941, after a visit to H. G. Wells in Hanover Terrace, author John Dos Passos "slipped out into the blackness, and felt my way down along the edge of the park toward Baker Street, smelling the autumnal leaves, hearing distant trains, the squawk of a bird from the zoo, feeling all about me the country quiet of the blacked-out city."

On the Homefront with London's Pets

War is particularly hellish on animals, and World War II was no exception. On London's homefront, the anticipation of catastrophic bombing prompted many pet owners, fearing they'd be unable to care for their cats and dogs, or worse, that the animals would be maimed, to take their beloved pets to the local veterinarian to be put to sleep. Over 400,000 cats and dogs in the London area met that sad fate in the first few days of war.

For those animals that remained, the subsequent air raids *were* unpleasant. The droning roar from the skies, the wailing sirens, the sudden flashes of light, the booming explosions all combined to terrify London's pets.

Gas masks were available for horses (though expensive at £2 each), but alas there was no such protection for cats and dogs. Several national organizations stepped in to offer assistance. NARPAC (National Air Raid Precautions for Animals Committee) distributed white registration discs for pets, and the RSPCA issued shelter cards to be posted on the front gate or door noting how many people, cats, and dogs slept inside. The National Canine Defense League offered a helpful pamphlet on first aid for dogs, and together with the RSPCA erected a London air raid shelter specially for dogs—pets were not allowed in public shelters. After the bombs fell, volunteers helped rescue animals, staffed Animal First Aid Posts, and reunited pets and owners.

Canadian officers. Several near-misses from German bombs meant boarded-up windows and cracked plaster, and then moisture seeped in to buckle the parquet floors. A flying bomb exploded nearby in 1944, killing an RAF cadet, injuring twenty others, and tossing debris about. By war's end, the still basically beautiful house was riddled with structural problems. Perhaps envisioning years of rehab, heiress Hutton, who'd spent much of the war in the States (where she married Cary Grant in 1942), gave the house to the U.S. government…for a dollar.

Winfield House also has interest for what once stood here: Hertford House, built in the mid-1820s and later renamed St. Dunstan's Villa. Beginning in 1917, the building served as a training center for blinded ex-servicemen, and within a year over 2,000 were being re-educated here. Many of the men from St. Dunstan's Institute for the Blind served as switchboard operators or shorthand-typists in government offices during World War II, refusing to be evacuated (besides children, the blind were given priority in evacuation plans). St. Dunstan's alumni found their visual situation of little consequence in London's blacked-out streets.

Continue walking (or riding) around Regent's Park to another of London's top attractions. Most visitors here are short and young, and all are delighted to be visiting London's Zoological Gardens—the **London Zoo**. This is a perfect place to mean-der, map in hand, visiting whatever aspects of zoodom interest you, in-cluding some unexpectedly intrigu-ing architecture. A comprehensive visit could take several days since more than 650 species (12,000-plus animals) are housed in the zoo's thirty-six acres. This, the oldest zoo  in the world, opened in the late 1820s for scientific use, then opened to the public in 1847, moving here from the Tower of London. Ever since, it has steadily grown and changed as practices have evolved regarding the treatment and display of animals in captivity. As you enjoy today's zoo, consider how the war's air raids and bombings, rationing and shortages affected both the zoo's structures and its residents.

First, the bad news. From the very moment war was declared, director Julian Huxley had to consider what would happen if zoo enclosures were hit by German bombs. "The first thing I did…was to see that the black widow spiders and the poison-ous snakes were killed, sad though it was." Thirty-eight specimens in all were dispatched, including an anaconda, two Blood Pythons, and a boa constric-tor. Then, Huxley continued, "I closed the aquarium and had its tanks emptied; and arranged that the ele-phants, who might well have run amok if frightened by the expected bombing (elephants are very nerv-ous creatures) be moved to Whipsnade," the zoo's country branch in Bedfordshire and open today as Whipsnade Wild Animal Park. Besides the elephants, Whipsnade became the wartime home to an ostrich, two yaks, two brown bears, five tawny owls, six black lambs, and myriad other zoo residents. The air raid squad of zookeepers, allowed by special dispensation to carry rifles, stood ready to shoot any dangerous animals that remained in London and might escape.

The London Zoo opened the first children's zoo in Britain in 1938, with young Bobby and Edward Kennedy, sons of the American ambassador, participating in the ceremony.

The good news is that other than a wandering zebra (chased by Huxley himself), a demoiselle crane (recaptured after a few days), and three hum-

George the camel helps clean up bomb rubble.

mingbirds (gone forever), no animals escaped their cages. And despite rationing of human food, the animals never went hungry since much blitzed food unfit for human consumption was sent along to the zoo. Huxley also organized an Animals Adoption scheme whereby organizations or individuals could pay for the upkeep of any zoo animal they fancied. Author Dorothy L. Sayers chose two porcupines, which she named Stickly and Prickly.

In all, the London Zoo—which remained open throughout the war—was a target for fourteen high explosive bombs, hundreds of incendiaries, one or two oil bombs, and a flying bomb; eighteen other flying bombs fell in the vicinity and caused damage to the zoo. George the camel was put to work pulling debris from damaged buildings, and the sea lion pool served as an emergency water tank for firefighters' hoses. Every pane of glass was broken once or twice, or more; the ravens' cage was bombed (and unfortunately raven Jill was likely a victim; her disconsolate mate Jack carried on); and the Zebra House was destroyed and the Clock Tower damaged (both rebuilt in the late 1940s). And the staff? Those that stayed to care for the animals used the pedestrian tunnels for air raid shelters, piling up sandbags at the ends and later building blast walls. Those that went to war and didn't come back are memorialized by the monument located near Three Island Pond.

> **VISITOR DETAILS:** The London Zoo is open daily 10am to 5:30pm; closes earlier in winter. Admission is charged. Several cafés (not inexpensive) and restrooms; use the free map. More information: 020 7722 3333, www.londonzoo.co.uk.

From the London Zoo, catch a bus back out of the park. Or if energy remains, walk through the park along Broad Walk or continue along the Outer Circle past yet more terraces on the park's eastern side. Whatever route or method you chose, spend a little time mulling over the questions—and answers—this district provides about London's homefront experience.

Checking London's skies for German aircraft.

8

Mr. Wren's Neighborhood: The City & Environs

Anne and I went into the City of London,
which from a distance seemed one vast bonfire.
It was the very image of hell. The sun could not
be seen at all…geysers composed of millions of sparks
shot up from time to time as another burnt-out building
fell in upon itself. One dared not get too near for fear
of collapsing walls and the infernal heat.
—ROBERT MENGIN, *NO LAURELS FOR DE GAULLE*

The story of St. Paul's survival—the cathedral threatened by fire and explosive bombs, rising majestically like a great ship floating above smoking, flaming debris—has reached almost mythic proportions. As well it should: it was a miraculous deliverance. In this chapter we revisit that much-told story, adding some lesser-known details, plus take several walks in the Cathedral's neighborhood, primarily (with a little westward drift) in the City.

This isn't the trendy, touristy West End—the City is London's financial and legal downtown, where the commercial business of the Empire transpires. Slightly over a square mile in size, it bustles weekdays with 285,500 workers, yet only about 6,700 Londoners actually sleep here every night.

In Chapter 1, we visited the several worlds at the foot of Big Ben. Here in the environs of St. Paul's, multiple spheres also co-exist. There's the legal community to the west, where lawyers muse through Inner and Middle Temple, the Royal Courts of Justice, and Lincoln's Inn. There's the religious district of St. Paul's Cathedral and the cluster of churches nearby, and then the more worldly neighborhood east and north of St. Paul's—the Bank of England, Guildhall, and the Museum of London.

Arbitrary divisions? Perhaps, but a useful way of approaching this complex history-strewn area. And tying together these three worlds is the work of that extraordinary architect, Christopher Wren. Born in 1632, the gifted Wren (he was also a scientist and mathematician) was named assistant surveyor general by King Charles II in 1661. Five years later the Great Fire swept through London, destroying 13,200 homes, 43 livery company halls, and 87 of 109 parish churches. In the following third of a century, Wren  re-designed and re-built more than fifty devastated churches in a spectacular burst of architectural energy. We'll visit many of these Wren-related structures, considering particularly their resilience in the second Great Fire of London, December 29, 1940. On that night, Red Sunday, the fire came from above—incendiary bombs rained down on the City, setting afire offices, warehouses, shops, and houses.

A number of factors combined to make a bad raid horrific. First of all, the City was more deserted than usual. Many residents had gone away for the New Year's weekend, and most businesses and churches were stoutly locked up. No regular schedule of firewatchers had yet been imposed, and worse, the Thames was at low tide. Fireboats couldn't get close to shore, and there was insufficient water for pumping from the river. And then the Luftwaffe came, the first planes dropping incendiaries, followed by a wave of bombers dropping high explosive bombs on the blazing target below. It was a very long night.

And it wasn't the last. On May 10, 1941, the rabbit-warren streets of the City were bright under a bombers' moon, and the German pilots again found their targets. By war's end, over 225 acres—a third of the City—had burned, leaving bleak vistas of rubble-filled desolation. Reconstruction followed, slowly in the cash-tight 1940s, then picking up speed in the 1950s and '60s. The process continues today as some of those hastily erected postwar buildings are replaced with newer construction. Even given the scaffolding, jackhammers, and cranes of the modern City, there are myriad war memories in the three worlds here, and we'll seek out many of them. But the destruction of the City was so pervasive that an entire book—*The City's War*, perhaps—could be written, guiding visitors to war sites, memorials, and memories here. Our steps, unlike Hitler's, shall be limited and selective, with the understanding that there's much more war-related history to be uncovered along every one of the City's narrow streets and crooked alleyways.

One final note: On weekdays this area can be exceedingly crowded, particularly during commute times and lunch hours; conversely, it's eerily empty on weekends—most shops are closed and the streets deserted. Choose your visiting time based on how you feel about crowds and solitude.

PART I
THE LEGAL WORLD AROUND
ST. PAUL'S CATHEDRAL

*A few months before the Blitz on London began
I wandered through the narrow alleys and passages which
lie to the north of Fleet Street, and I remember shuddering at
the thought of the devastation which a bomb would cause
amidst all these small houses and shops.*

—ANTHONY WEYMOUTH, *JOURNAL OF THE WAR YEARS*

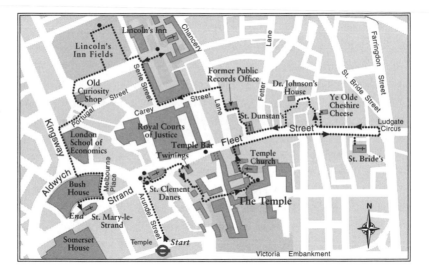

Highlights: St. Clement Danes, Royal Courts of Justice, Twining's, Inner and Middle Temple, Temple Church, Fleet Street, St. Bride's, Johnson's House, St. Dunstan's-in-the-West, Lincoln's Inn, Lincoln's Inn Fields, Old Curiosity Shop, Bush House, St. Mary-le-Strand

Underground Station: Temple

Photo Ops: I'm a sucker for bomb dings, cat statues, and little-known war memorials; this walk has them all.

BEFORE LEAVING ON YOUR TRIP

■ **Travel Scheduling:** The Lord Mayor's Procession and Show is held annually on the second Saturday in November. The new Lord Mayor, following dozens of floats and bands and marching groups, rides from Guildhall to the Royal Courts of Justice.

■ **Cultural Preparations:** Reading Charles Dickens (especially *Bleak House* or *The Pickwick Papers*) gives the flavor of the area, albeit extremely prewar; for something more contemporary, try Evelyn Waugh's 1930s novel of Fleet Street, *Scoop.*

■ **Internet Best Bets:** The Temple Church website (www.templechurch.com) has an excellent map of the Inns of Court. For more on the Guinea Pig Club, check out www.gpigs.fsnet.co.uk.

Searchlights

London's wartime skies held several levels of coordinated defense against nighttime bombers—barrage balloons kept Luftwaffe pilots flying higher than they would have liked as they tried to elude the city's searchlights, lights that showed anti-aircraft gunners exactly where the bombers were.

Much like barrage balloons (see Chapter 4), searchlight batteries were located in parks and other open areas. And like the cuddly balloons, they elicited warm affection from Londoners. When you next see a single searchlight in the London sky, heralding the grand opening of a store or a film premiere, imagine dozens of beams crisscrossing the heavens, "...lovely in shape, lovely in their moonlit colour, lovely in texture, so impalpable and fine that they give the notion that they must be pressing their pools of light against the darkness."

This walk combines the busy Strand with the peaceable kingdoms of the Inns of Court. We'll cross into the City near Temple Bar to check out some less frequently visited churches and several hidden courtyards and alleyways, an area where London's homefront became a battleground of conflagration and chaos.

From Temple Underground, walk up Arundel Street to the Strand, then cross to the churchyard of **St. Clement Danes**. To the north stands Sir Arthur Harris, wartime Marshal of the Air Force and chief of the RAF's Bomber Command. The plaque at the statue base honors not only Harris but the men of Bomber Command, more than 55,000 of whom died in the war. Harris has always been a lightning rod for controversy, as he advocated politically (and in retrospect, perhaps militarily) incorrect positions. It was "Bomber" Harris who pushed for the mass bombing of German cities, including the thousand-plane raids and the annihilation of Dresden in 1945. His statue has been the victim of several paint-splashed epithets: "War Criminal" and "Shame."

Many Londoners consider St. Clement Danes the church in the rhyme "'Oranges and lemons' say the bells of St. Clement's." It's more likely St. Clement, Eastcheap, but nevertheless the bells of St. Clement Danes play "Oranges and Lemons" daily at 9am, noon, 3pm, and 6pm.

Nearby is Air Chief Marshal Hugh Dowding, head of the RAF's Fighter Command. The wordy plaques around the statue's base provide an overview of Dowding's proud war achievements, especially his resistance to political pressure to commit his forces in France too early in the war and his commitment to the very new concept of radar. The bronze statue was unveiled by the Queen Mother, who, as we'll see, was kept busy throughout the City unveiling war-related memorials.

Imagine St. Clement Danes pre-Luftwaffe, when it was just the statue of Gladstone and the simple stone church here, with its long history stretching back to London's ninth-century Danish community. King Alfred expelled the Danes from England in the late 800s but allowed those with English wives to settle just outside London's walls. Thus St. Clement Danes rose on the high road between the cities of Westminster and old London

(today's City, with a capital "C"). William the Conqueror rebuilt the church in the eleventh century, and then Christopher Wren designed this third structure on the site (1681), with James Gibbs later adding the spire (1719).

German bombers found this historic building several times in the Blitz; the worst attack came in May 1941. When the last bomb had exploded and the last flame extinguished, only battered stone walls were left. The roof and all inside were simply...gone. For years after the war, St. Clement Danes stood derelict, a blackened ruin open to the sky. Then the move to rebuild gathered momentum (and money) with the suggestion to make this the official church of the Royal Air Force. St. Clement Danes was eventually reconsecrated in 1958 with a completely rebuilt interior and recast bells. Today the church stands proudly as a memorial to the men and women of the RAF who died in the defense of freedom.

> Visitors to St. Clement Danes wanting to check more than the day's opened page of a book of remembrance can use the nearby photocopied version.

Watch the floor here, starting with the rosette just inside, formed by the badges of the Commonwealth Air Forces surrounding the badge of the RAF. The wide aisle floors also invite a look—they're studded with almost a thousand slate RAF squadron and unit badges; the wall poster near the door offers a guide. Display cases showcase a range of church- and military-related silver plate, swords, and medals, and the ends of the pews toward the altar bear the coats of arms of RAF Chiefs of the Air Staff: Portal, Newall, Tedder, and others (Tedder's ashes are buried here). Ask the churchman on duty to show how the pews can be moved to double the church's seating capacity, a clever design introduced with the postwar reconstruction. The elegant pulpit—attributed to that master woodcarver, Grinling Gibbons—survived the war, safely tucked away in the crypt of St. Paul's Cathedral.

To one side of the altar, the names of RAF and WAAF recipients of the George Cross are inscribed; on the opposite side, recipients of the Victoria Cross. A memorial to the wife of Sir Douglas Bader, the wartime fighter ace,

sits nearby. Across the aisle is the McIndoe seat, given in memory of plastic surgeon Sir Archibald McIndoe by the Guinea Pig Club (note the flying pig crest). McIndoe saved the lives of untold numbers of savagely burned RAF pilots; they called themselves his guinea pigs and naturally McIndoe's hospital in East Grinstead became "the sty."

Note the embroidered kneelers as you walk along the north aisle toward the Polish Air Force memorial (look down). Along both aisles are remembrance books, including one for the U.S. Air Force just ahead. Finally, and especially if you lost a loved one in World War II, write a message in the guest book. On a

Bomb dings at St. Clement Danes.

recent visit, I found the most affecting message was one of the simplest: "To my dear brother, buried in France."

Before leaving St. Clement Danes, glance up at the windows. Over the centuries Wren's clear windows were replaced by stained and colored glass, but wartime explosions destroyed all that fancy glass. With the church's reconstruction came a return to Wren's original concept, and today sunlight streaming in lights up this jewel of a church. Finally, be sure to explore the crypt—more remembrance books, more RAF symbols, more plaques, all in a setting with decidedly medieval feel.

> **VISITOR DETAILS:** St. Clement Danes is open daily 8:30am to 4:30pm. Public restrooms outside, on the far end of the building and down the stairs. More information: 020 7242 8282.

Samuel Johnson—critic, essayist, philologist, wit, poet, talker—stands outside at the eastern end of the church. This was his parish church in the eighteenth century, though both his favorite pew and a memorial window were destroyed by twentieth-century bombs. The church wall behind Dr. Johnson was splashed and pitted by bomb fragments, a reminder of the utter ferocity of war's weapons. One wartime observer mused, "The Doctor did not even move on his plinth, or take his eyes from the pages of the book he is reading, as the landmines and the bombs came thundering down....The Doctor was a man of physical courage and would have made an unflinching air-raid warden." Soon after the worst of the war's bombing attacks, a large poster appeared on this blackened wall: "Hit back with war savings and stop this."

Across the Strand looms the **Royal Courts of Justice** or Law Courts, worth a visit if matters legal fascinate you. Yes, you can take a seat in the public galleries here; there are more than sixty courts hearing primarily civil, but some criminal, cases. The building, constructed in the 1880s in a down-to-earth Victorian-Gothic style, was the

> **VISITOR DETAILS:** The Royal Courts of Justice are open weekdays 9am to 4:30pm. The map near the door provides disabled access information. Tiny shop. More information: 020 7936 6751.

unwilling recipient of German explosives, destroying several courts. Given the wholesale destruction hereabouts, this sizeable complex—over 1,000

rooms, three-and-a-half miles of corridors, and thirty-five million bricks—got off easily.

Cross at the Belisha beacon to the Strand's south side for **Twining's Tea and Coffee Merchants** at Number 216. This narrow shop opened in 1706 as Tom's Coffee House, and today offers innumerable varieties and flavors of tea; purchasing single teabags allows for taste-testing later. A small tea museum is at the back, not as comprehensive as that near Tower Hill but free. And, of course, Twinings has war stories. The company supplied tea

Royal Courts of Justice.

and coffee to the British Red Cross for parcels sent to prisoners of war and provided coffee to the Army. Twining's also ensured the tea and coffee urns of the WVS canteens and YMCA service canteens remained full. Twining's tiny building was severely damaged in a January 1941 attack, but the shop moved temporarily to a nearby shop front and remained open, using furnishings salvaged from the ruins. Wisely, the company's ledgers and other historic materials had been evacuated.

> **VISITOR DETAILS:** Twining's is open weekdays 9:30am to 4:45pm. More information: 020 7353 3511, www.twinings.com.

Behind Twinings and to the south is the **Temple**, a secluded enclave of buildings and gardens, none of which look remotely like a temple. The name comes from the Knights Templar, a military religious order formed in the early 1100s to protect Christian pilgrims off to the Holy City of Jerusalem. They were introduced to England by King Henry I and in the second half of the twelfth century, settled on the north bank of the Thames, where they constructed some rather impressive monuments, including the

Temple Church. All was not well with the knights, however, and between their envious enemies and their own excessive pride (which did indeed goeth before their fall in 1312), their property was granted to another group—the Knights Hospitaller—which in turn lost

Most Temple buildings, gates, and lamp posts have an identifying symbol: either a lamb (the lamb of God) indicating the Middle Temple or a flying horse (Pegasus) indicating Inner Temple.

it all in the Reformation. Meanwhile, numerous lawyers had settled in as tenants and when the property finally passed to the Crown, the by-then-entrenched lawyers were allowed to stay.

Hence the Temple, where two of the four Inns of Court (Inner and Middle Temple) are located. These are England's legal societies, with the exclusive right to admit lawyers to practice at the English bar. The Temple has professional chambers for practicing barristers and residential chambers occupied historically by a variety of tenants, primarily lawyers, but also politicians and statesmen, novelists and playwrights, historians and dictionary writers. Yes, Samuel Johnson lived here (the peripatetic Johnson lived at a dozen City addresses), as did Oliver Goldsmith, William Makepeace Thackeray, and (at 4 King's Bench Walk in the 1930s and 1940s), wartime author and politician Harold Nicolson.

Today the Temple feels like an English university set in the midst of an urban park. To enter, backtrack about thirty feet west along the Strand toward St. Clement Danes. Just before The George, narrow Devereux Court beckons to the left.

Down the flagstoned walk past the side entrance of The George, turn left (note the war-related stone plaque on the back of Twining's), then turn right past the Devereux Pub, and then left again. It's simpler than it sounds. Once in New Court, step down to the sunken fountain, set in an area called, naturally, Fountain Court—there's been a fountain here since 1681. The fountain had a great deal of bricking added in 1940 so that it could serve as an emergency water tank for fire-fighting; a new fountain (this one) was built in the mid-1970s.

Walk around the fountain past the stately building situated south and east of the fountain. That's Middle Temple Hall, a magnificent six-teenth-century structure and the site of a 1602 performance of *Twelfth Night*—very possibly the first public performance of the play and likely with the playwright himself in the cast. The building has a fine double hammerbeam roof.

Temple Church knight.

Middle Temple Hall was hit five times in wartime bombings, the worst in mid-October 1940, when a hole was blown in the east gable and the clock tower was partly demolished. Most of the stained-glass windows had been removed and stored before the Luftwaffe came calling, but other windows were blown out. In fact, in a January 1941 raid, nearly every window hereabouts was shattered.

> *A pheasant appeared in the Temple environs in October 1940, no doubt frightened by wartime alerts, alarms, sirens, and bombs. Pursued by a Temple cat, it quickly moved on to a place of greater safety.*

Straight ahead across Middle Temple Lane and through the arched passageway is Elm Court, with the new Lamb Building behind you, Crown Office Row to the right, and Pump Court on the left (rebuilt following war damage). At the far end of Elm Court, the wall of Inner Temple Hall has a plaque indicating the site of Fig Tree Court, destroyed in London's Great Fire of 1666 and rebuilt in 1679, only to be destroyed by enemy action in 1940.

Left up the steps is Church Court. The arched cloisters here have an aged feel to them, though much of the original seventeenth-century

structure was rebuilt (1952) after being done in by high explosive bombs. The large courtyard has two Knights Templar atop that slender column, providing some idea of what the twelfth-century protectors looked like. Nearby (look down) a plaque marks the site of the old brick Lamb Building, built in 1667 and wrecked that ferocious May night in 1941. The four-story structure was reduced to one hollowed-out level, soon overgrown with weeds and vines, and eventually demolished.

To the north is **Temple Church**, one of a handful of round churches in England and the only one to be lacerated by wartime bomb and blast. The round nave of Temple Church—where the Knights Templar worshipped and were buried—was erected in 1185, its design based on Jerusalem's Church of the Holy Sepulchre. The rectangular Gothic-style choir was added in the mid-thirteenth century, then the busy Christopher Wren did some interior work here in the 1680s. Little of his efforts

> *Visitor Hint: If the Temple Church door doesn't open when you pull on that large ring, try turning the ring.*

survived the Victorian restoration of the mid-1800s, which included a conical roof added atop the Round Church.

Although open to the public, Temple Church serves as the private chapel of the lawyers of Inner and Middle Temple. It's off the usual tourist path—

I recently found myself the only visitor except for the cleaning man and his vacuum cleaner. Temple Church is particularly worth a wander if you let your mind wander too, back to the late hours of May 10, 1941, the last and worst night of the Blitz. It was then, in the evocative words of mystery writer P. D. James, that "the flames had roared with the tongues of an advancing army, the chapel had become a furnace, the marble pillars had cracked and the roof had exploded in a burst of fire to fall in blazing shards over the effigies. Then it seemed that seven hundred years of history were falling in flames." Outside, it was the steep roof above the Round Church that was afire, streaming molten lead and burning timbers onto the floor inside, badly damaging the medieval effigies of knights stretched out below. Blast shattered the east window, and the Victorian pews, altar, and choir stalls were swiftly reduced to a pile of smoking embers.

> **VISITOR DETAILS:** The Temple (Inner and Middle Temple) is open from 9am to 5pm; weekends try Tudor Gate, off Tudor Street, if the various Strand/Fleet Street entrances are closed. Middle Temple Hall is open weekdays 10am to noon and 3pm to 4pm. Temple Church is open Wednesday–Sunday, generally from 11am to 4pm. No services in August or September. Temple Gardens are open summer weekdays, noon to 3pm. No guest facilities. More information: 020 7353 3470.

It's a long time since May 1941: the stone effigies are repaired, the restored interior has new pillars, and replacement pews are aligned in collegiate order facing into the middle aisle (an appropriate arrangement as Inner Temple owns the southern half of the church and Middle Temple the northern half). Finally, the east window once again glows. A close look at the new stained glass shows St. Paul's in the Blitz and the Temple Church looking as it did before the war, complete with that odd roof. In the Round Church floor, a simple plaque amidst the recumbent knight effigies reads, "Remember in your prayers those who died in the Second World War 1939–1945."

From Temple Church, turn right, then right again; walking down the passageway toward the street's traffic and bustle, give a thought to this walk in the blackout, with sirens wailing, searchlights streaking the sky, and the nearby walls shuddering with every all-too-close bomb blast. Once through the covered passageway, you'll discover the Strand has become **Fleet Street** in our absence. Temple Bar,

Temple Church after the Luftwaffe's visit.

that griffin-bearing memorial to the
left in the middle of the roadway,
marks the change. Erected in 1880, it
stands on the site of the old Temple
Bar, a Wren-designed archway, but a
divider of sorts has marked the boundary between Westminster and the City
for 500 years. Traditionally when the
monarch visits on state occasions, the
custom is to stop here and request
formal permission from the Lord
Mayor before entering the City.

Temple Bar.

Turn right onto Fleet Street, the
"Street of Ink" in the prewar and war
years, home to England's national
newspapers as well as numerous foreign, Dominion, and provincial papers,
presses, and journalistic support services. Since the 1980s, the media has
steadily shifted offices and presses to
the less-pricey Docklands area. Reuters, the pioneer of news agencies, is
about all that remains, still at Number 85 where it moved in 1939.

Across the street, mosaics herald the offices of the long-gone *Dundee
Evening Telegraph*. Watch for more small signs, busts, and plaques along the
next three blocks, all suggesting the media's one-time omnipresence here.
A pair of buildings, also across the street, testify to that—Number 135 is
the old *Daily Telegraph* offices, its striking Egyptian
classical style of the 1920s still evident; nearby, that
modernist black glass edifice (1932) was once home
to the *Daily Express*.

Just past Reuters at Number 85, turn right to **St.
Bride's**, parish church of Fleet Street and known as
the Journalists' Church. Gazing at St. Bride's fanciful
spire, it's obvious why this "madrigal in stone" is considered the inspiration for the tiered wedding cake,
though some have likened it to a telescope on end.

A plaque inside reminds visitors that St. Bride's
was once a roofless ruin, devastated by enemy action
(i.e., bombs) on December 29, 1940. All that you
see—the oak reredos, the pews, the statues, the marble floor, the windows—is Wren-inspired but of

*When German bombs
first threatened, the
vicar of St. Bride's carefully stored the com-
munion plate in the
church safe. After the
battering of December
29, 1940, the scarred
and scorched safe lay in
the smoking ruins for
days. When opened
several weeks later, it
had protected its
contents completely.*

twentieth-century construction. Before looking more closely at these neo-Wren features,
step back 1,800 years by heading downstairs.
St. Bride's has always considered itself a historic church, but the same German bombs
that destroyed Wren's interior also uncovered
an additional thousand years of history. Well,
bombs plus postwar excavation. In the low-
ceilinged crypt, display cases showcase artifacts
from the Roman and Saxon eras, the eleventh
and twelfth centuries, and the Great Fire and
the Blitz. At the back of the altar lies a second-
century Roman pavement. Remarkably, there
have been at least seven previous churches on
this site; Saxon, Celtic, and Roman history is

St. Bride's today.

layered here, something to cogitate upon if you attend a morning service
at the crypt altar. In an odd juxtaposition, a
book of remembrance from the *Evening
Standard* newspaper is opened in the same
area, "in grateful and abiding memory of our
comrades who fell in the two world wars."

Retrace your steps to Fleet Street and
cross to the northern side at the next intersection, pausing near Ludgate Circus to look
eastward toward St. Paul's. Imagine this dis-

VISITOR DETAILS: St. Bride's
Fleet Street is open daily 8am
to 4:45pm. Crypt services
weekdays at 8:30am. Free
lunchtime musical recitals.
The crypt isn't wheelchair-
accessible. More information:
020 7427 0133.

trict in 1945. A railroad trestle crossed Ludgate Hill, just past Ludgate
Circus; beyond it, both sides of Ludgate Hill had suffered extensive bomb
damage. This wasn't the "a blown-up house here, a bit of rubble there"
damage. This no-man's land of desolation was leveled for 200 yards on
either side of the roadway. Conversely, turn west and look down Fleet
Street, where we just walked—war's effects were much less evident.
German bombs had fallen *behind* the street frontage, leaving the façades of
Fleet Street offices to camouflage the devastation just beyond.

Backtrack along the northern side of Fleet Street, and if it's lunchtime
consider Ye Olde Cheshire Cheese, a pub located up Wine Office Court;
downstairs is the less-touristy area. This relic, built in the mid-1660s, suffered little from wartime bombs, a good thing as those explosions would
have destroyed a historical watering hole, one frequented by wordsmiths
as varied as Samuel Johnson and, closer to the war-era, Dylan Thomas.

If you stopped at the pub, exit right to Dr. Johnson's house. If you're
still on Fleet Street, just twenty feet from Wine Office Court is Hind Court;

Looking west down bomb-rubbled Ludgate Hill toward Fleet Street.

turn right up the narrow passageway. Zigzag to **Dr. Johnson's House** at 17 Gough Square, a four-story brick building closely watched by Johnson's cat Hodge. Samuel Johnson lived and worked here from 1748 to 1759, toiling with a small cadre of helpers to compile his *Dictionary*, an innovative project characterized by much labor and little profit.

Throughout the war, the house remained open to visitors, although it primarily served as a rest center for neighborhood members of the Auxiliary Fire Service. Several of the firefighters were also members of the London Symphony Orchestra, and later in the war musical evenings were held in Dr. Johnson's parlor. When not firefighting, the AFS men occupied their time making toys; watch for the small model workshop on the top floor,

Johnson's cat.

made by firefighters and donated in appreciation for the care and attention they were given here in the war.

To prepare for the expected bombings, the pictures in Johnson's home were stored in waterproof tea chests, and his letters were tucked snugly inside two suitcases. Paintings were covered with felt and paper, then sewn into waterproof covers; books were packed into cartons and placed up on blocks in the basement. Given that this wasn't a government-funded museum with access to Underground tunnels or storage in distant castles, preparations were as good as they could be.

It wasn't until the night of December 29, 1940, that the City experienced the worst the Germans had to offer: that night the roof of Dr. Johnson's house was burned away, the garret's front wall set afire, and the basement flooded. Johnson's books survived, albeit a bit damp, as did his letters—the caretaker had grabbed the two suitcases and set off through the burning streets to find shelter in the basement of the *Daily Mirror* building in Fetter Lane.

In all, the war brought havoc to Dr. Johnson's neighborhood five times, including a June 1944 attack when several V-1 rockets fell nearby. Even before the V-1s, though, the area had suffered grievously. One visitor in 1942 failed to recognize Gough Square even when standing in the middle of it, "because as a Square it no longer exists. Dr. Johnson's House…is fortunately unharmed, but the whole of the east side and most of the north has disappeared, and one looks across an acre or two of devastation." Not exactly "unharmed," as Johnson's home required extensive postwar restoration. It finally re-opened, with Dr. Johnson's pictures, paintings, and books in place, in 1948.

> **VISITOR DETAILS:** Dr. Johnson's House is open Monday–Saturday 11am to 5:30pm; closes earlier in winter. Admission is charged. Unavoidable steps and narrow staircases; small shop. More information: 020 7353 3745, www.drjh.dircon.co.uk.

Continue down labyrinthine Johnson's Court, the passageway to the left as you and Hodge face Dr. Johnson's abode. This quiet wander eventually ends at the very unquiet Fleet Street. Turn right, cross Fetter Lane (a "lane" no more), and just past the *Dundee Evening Telegraph* Building we saw earlier is first the churchyard and then the church of **St. Dunstan's-in-the-West**.

There are several unrelated items in the churchyard, including the statue of Queen Elizabeth I over the parochial school entrance, the oldest (1586) public statue of a monarch. The good queen spent the war bricked in, ensuring her surviving in fine shape. Bricks also successfully protected the nearby bust of press baron Lord Northcliffe. The clock above—its two moveable giants ready to stiffly strike their bell—also came through German bombings intact. It had already kept track of London time for 270 years, including a century spent in Regent's Park on Hertford Lodge, where it gave its name to St. Dunstan's Institute for the Blind (see Chapter 7). The clock was returned here in the mid-1930s, just in time for the war.

> On the way to Lincoln's Inn, you'll pass a clutch of older telephone kiosks at the back of the Royal Courts of Justice.

St. Dunstan's dark octagonal building (1830s), built on the site of a previous St. Dunstan's, is now the home of the Romanian Orthodox Church. A German bomb pierced the roof but caused little interior harm;

the damaged tower has since been rebuilt. The nineteenth-century stained-glass window in honor of seventeenth-century writer and church vestry-man Izaak Walton survived, though the clerestory windows and the altar suffered. And as with so many London buildings, one can visit and have no sense of the war-time destruction, so seamlessly have repairs been made.

Lincoln's Inn gateway.

Turn right from St. Dun-stan's and almost immediately right again onto Cliffords Inn Passage. Wend your way to Chancery Lane and turn right. That's the old Public Records Office on your right, now the Library and Information Centre for King's College, London. Britain's most important historical documents were once stored here, priceless valuables evacuated during the war to a range of safe havens, from Belvoir Castle to Shepton Mallet Prison.

Head along Carey Street and within a block, turn onto Serle Street. At the southeast corner of Lincoln's Inn Fields, enter **Lincoln's Inn**, not a pub but rather the third of London's four Inns of Court. I can't tell you how many times I've gotten lost here, and I urge you to do the same. Watch for the monument to "our comrades" of the Inns of Court who died in the war, including the Duke of Kent. This stone structure is covered with plaques, inscriptions, and welcoming benches. And if your path wanders northward, watch for the tablet on the wall of the Inns of Court and City Yeomanry Signals Squadron Building, noting World War I bomb damage.

This is the third Inn of Court we've visited (Gray's Inn, the fourth, is to the north), and like the others, Lincoln's Inn provides its residents with living quarters and offices, plus a dining hall, library, and chapel. The other three Inns of Court lost much of the latter amenities to Luftwaffe

> **VISITOR DETAILS:** Lincoln's Inn is supposedly open to the public weekday mid-days only, but I doubt they'll throw you out if you're here earlier or later. Look purposeful.

bombs; Lincoln's Inn fared far better. Of its lawyers' chambers, many were damaged but none demolished, and its dining hall, library, and chapel escaped major damage. You can visit the chapel, an Inigo Jones design circa 1623, the only building here open to the public.

Leave Lincoln's Inn the same way you entered, then cross to **Lincoln's Inn Fields**. This twelve-acre square was once quite fashionable, but for decades the drift has been toward legal offices and away from residences. On the garden's northern side is a subdued memorial honoring Canadian wartime participation, including the 14,455 Canadian airmen killed. The marble block looks much like a podium, and if so, the speaker would face the street and houses along the northern side of the square. Number 20 was overseas headquarters for the Royal Canadian Air Force, providing support to the 85,000 Canadian personnel in RCAF and RAF squadrons (there's a plaque on the building). As you turn from the marble memorial and face south, the young tree opposite is a Canadian maple, dedicated to RCAF personnel stationed in Lincoln's Inn Fields in the war. Yes, this large area was decorated in wartime with trench shelters, barracks, and barrage balloons.

VISITOR DETAILS: Lincoln's Inn Fields is open daily from 7:30am to dusk. Outdoor café; restrooms just beyond the northeastern corner.

Enjoy the gardens of Lincoln's Inn Fields, the plane trees, the benches, and the Frisbee and tennis players as you head toward the southwestern corner. (Incidentally, in 1939, you could book a tennis court for just 1/6 an hour.) The Royal College of Surgeons was (and still is) along the square's

The Old Curiosity Shop.

southern side in a building badly damaged by Nazi bombs, though not as badly as the nearby College of Estate Management. That was so completely flattened that firefighters from the National Fire Service used the ruins to raise pigs.

Past the southwestern corner of Lincoln's Inn Fields and just down Portsmouth Street slumps the **Old Curiosity Shop**, "immortalized by Charles Dickens," except of course it wasn't. Dickens in his novel *The Old Curiosity Shop* was writing of a shop located elsewhere, one demolished long before his sad story of little Nell took place. Nevertheless this shop has had a similar inscription since the 1860s. One wartime effect was the destruction of the sign, since replaced.

Our route becomes a little zigzaggy here. Continue down Portsmouth to Portugal Street, then right toward Kingsway. At Kingsway turn left; the street ends at Aldwych, arching above the Strand. Ahead is **Bush House**, with the blue-and-white flag of the BBC overhead. The statuary in the building's pediment represents a friendly England and America bearing the torch of freedom. A Nazi flying bomb sheared off the arm of America, which allegedly fell to the pavement and killed several people below. The amputated limb wasn't replaced until the 1970s.

Bush House, conceived of in 1919 but not completed until 1935, was originally meant to be a trade center, a showplace for the display and sale of goods. For a variety of reasons, that never came to be and miscellaneous offices took over. Then the BBC needed wartime space for its ever-expanding overseas broadcasting, and Bush House has been home to the BBC World Service ever since. Walk around either side to the Strand, passing Australia House to the left or India House to the right. The excellent BBC World Service Information Centre and Shop awaits. Bush House itself isn't open to visitors.

> **VISITOR DETAILS:** BBC World Service Information Centre and Shop is open weekdays 10am to 6pm; Saturday 10am to 5:30pm; Sunday 12:30 to 5:30pm. More information: 020 7557 2576, www.bbcshop.com.

Ready for one last church? **St. Mary-le-Strand** (1714) is situated directly across from Bush House in an even smaller traffic island than that of St. Clement Danes. This parish church escaped major war wounds, so restoration isn't the byword here—it's remembrance. This is the official church of the Women's Royal Naval Service, the WRNS, commonly called Wrens—rather appropriate given the ubiquitous Mr. Wren hereabouts, though it was architect James Gibbs who designed St. Mary-le-Strand. A stunning gold alms dish honors the twenty-two Wrens lost aboard the *Aquila*, torpedoed in August 1941, and another memorial honors those aboard the *Khedive Ishmael*, torpedoed and sunk in February 1944. The book of remembrance honors all Wrens who died in

> **VISITOR DETAILS:** St. Mary-le-Strand is open weekdays 11am to 4pm. Lunchtime recitals. More information: 020 7836 3126.

service to their country. I've always felt this baroque church very attractive, with little of the harsh modernity of many bombed-then-renovated structures—though the blue glass is a little unsettling. See what you think.

Our route through the legal side of Mr. Wren's neighborhood ends near Temple Underground. Several buses surge along the Strand, providing a more relaxing transit option if you're done for the day. Or head east toward St. Paul's Cathedral to investigate the City's religious side.

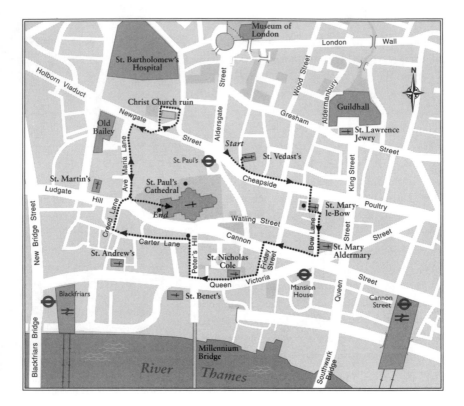

PART II
THEY NEVER GOT IT—
ST. PAUL'S AND NEARBY CHURCHES

Ave Maria Lane was gutted, smoke was still coming out of the buildings in Ludgate Hill itself. We walked around St. Paul's Churchyard. The place was desolation....Firemen were still hard at work; smoke and steam rose in various directions....Even in St. Paul's itself there was still that queer, dank, smoky smell.

—CHARLES GRAVES, *OFF THE RECORD*

St. Paul's stands unharmed in the midst of the burning City...

Highlights: St. Vedast, St. Mary-le-Bow, St. Nicholas Cole Abbey, Christ Church Greyfriars, St. Paul's Cathedral

Underground Station: St. Paul's

Photo Ops: The empty window frames of Christ Church Greyfriars provide a wrenching photo possibility, while the roses planted nearby offer a more optimistic one.

BEFORE LEAVING ON YOUR TRIP

■ **Travel Scheduling:** If visiting during the holidays, consider attending a carol service with a performance by St. Paul's Cathedral choir; check the newspaper for dates and times.

■ **Cultural Preparations:** Connie Willis's haunting short story about St. Paul's Cathedral, "Fire Watch," the title story in a collection of her work, is worth tracking down.

■ **Internet Best Bets:** Don't miss St. Paul's website: www.stpauls.co.uk. Another best bet for information on churches in the area: www.cityoflondonchurches.com.

St. Paul's Cathedral, the survivor, once stood alone (as did England), ringed by a flattened and battered landscape. Sixty years of redevelopment and construction have camouflaged but not removed the scars of London's homefront. There are lesser-known monuments and hidden memories here, many of them missed by tourists intent on "doing" St. Paul's and getting on to the next attraction. We won't rush. Our path circumnavigates the immediate environs of St. Paul's, makes a leisurely circuit inside the Cathedral itself, and ends with a relaxing glass of wine in the crypt of the "parish church of the empire." An alternative is to visit St. Paul's first thing in the morning, then head off to other sights and return for an evening organ recital or Evensong service. There's nothing quite like those first riveting organ chords to remind one of the majesty of St. Paul's Cathedral.

From St. Paul's Underground walk along the north side of Cheapside to **St. Vedast's** on Foster Lane. This seventeenth-century Wren church was ravaged by German bombs and com-

VISITOR DETAILS: St. Vedast's is open weekdays 8am to 6pm. More information: 020 7606 3998.

pletely rebuilt in the 1960s. Photos on display show the church's walls still standing amidst a chaos of destruction. As the caretaker confided about St. Vedast's wartime drama, "We didn't let it stop us, we just carried on." Such "London can take it" sentiments have become a cliché, but there's an entire generation for which they are a very personal and heartfelt emotional response.

Many of the church furnishings—the font, pulpit, organ case, even the Lord Mayor's sword holder—were rescued from or donated by other churches since many of the original furnishings were lost in the blaze that followed the bombing. The windows too are new, executed by stained-glass artist Brian Thomas—his work also appears in St. Paul's. Unlike other

Towering Infernos

So how come so many churches burned but their towers remained? Most church towers withstood bomb blasts simply because of the thickness and great weight of their walls. Then when fire swept through, towers served as chimney shafts, drawing flames quickly upward. Flooring and bell-frames would burn (and church bells would crash to the floor), and perhaps cupolas and lead-covered spires would be consumed, but the sturdy tower walls remained.

A desolate wartime Cheapside.

blitzed churches that have been rebuilt, St. Vedast's manages an appealing patina of use and warmth.

From St. Vedast's, turn left onto Cheapside—the bustling shopping street of medieval London. Sixty years ago Cheapside cut through one of the City's more devastated areas, and a walk along the next few blocks allows contemplation of the mid-war look of the City. Very little street traffic, of course, what with petrol rationing. And very few pedestrians—there was simply nowhere to go in this nightmare landscape. No Lyons Teashop or Boots Chemist. Particularly along the southern side of the street, German bombs had blasted most structures, followed by demolition experts who'd dynamited wobbly walls and unsafe structures. The rubbled acreage had been cleared, the demolition services carefully stacking bricks and smaller masonry to one side of each lot. Foundation outlines hinted at what and where structures had been. Wooden fences dissuaded the few pedestrians from taking shortcuts across poten-

> The Norwegian Chapel near St. Mary-le-Bow's altar was built in memory of those who served in the wartime Norwegian Resistance.

tially dangerous ruins, ruins made more treacherous when the basement foundations filled with rainwater. The tailors and rubber stamp makers, solicitors and moneylenders, typewriter ribbon manufacturers and starch merchants, all gone, their shops and offices boarded up, their premises declared unsafe. The look and feel and smell of mid-war Cheapside was lonely and barren. Except, of course, for the fireweed beginning to sprout in the rubble. (See "Wartime Plants" in Chapter 9.)

St. Mary-le-Bow sits on the southern side of Cheapside, about three blocks from St.Vedast's.The tiny green area toward the back of the court-yard held a wartime static water tank, built to provide emergency water to wartime firefighters; John Smith didn't arrive until the 1960s. This is the church of the Bow Bells (pronunciation hint: that's "bow" to rhyme with "know"), part of the folklore of London—to be born within the sound of the Bow Bells was the sign of a true Cockney. And remember the nursery rhyme? "'I do not know' says the Great Bell of Bow." The recorded sound of the Bow Bells was used by the BBC as a radio interval signal, and it's a good thing a recording had been made because the bells crashed to the ground, shattering, cracking, and splintering during the tumultuous night of May 10, 1941. Only the steeple, the crypt, and the scarred walls sur-vived. For the Luftwaffe, score another gutted church.

Church bell aficionados, this is the place for you. The twelve new bells, using metal salvaged from the shattered bells, were rung for the first time in December 1961. They range in size from about 625 pounds to just over 4,700 pounds, and each has been given a name. The largest, of course, is known as Bow.

VISITOR DETAILS: St. Mary-le-Bow is open Monday–Friday 6:30am to 6:30pm. Small fee for bell tower visit. Lunchtime concerts. Basement café ("The Place Below") is open week-days 7:30am to 2:30pm; enter through the tower. More infor-mation, and to make bell tower appointments: 020 7248 5139.

Use the entrance toward the back of the courtyard; it enters directly across from the altar. Watch for the stained-glass window with Mary cradling the church building, and the image of St. Paul surrounded by bombed city churches. Yes, this is modern stained glass, replacing the Blitz-shattered windows. St. Mary-le-Bow was rebuilt in the early 1960s "to meet the demands of a modern church," which means a much more contemporary feel than the seventeenth-century exterior suggests.You'll either love it or hate it. For a touch of antiquity, take a look at the crypt down the outside stairs by the iron fence.

Follow the narrow passage at the back of the church to Bow Lane and head south along this narrow pedestrian shopway. Cross Watling—look right for a sudden view of St. Paul's.You'll pass St. Mary Aldermary on the left, a Wren church that suffered minimal war damage. At the next big intersection, turn right onto Cannon Street, then left on Friday Street to Queen Victoria Street. Incidentally Friday Street was here as early as the 1300s, home to many of London's fishmongers. Much of this ancient street was "disappeared" by the German onslaught.

In 1945, **St. Nicholas Cole Abbey** was one of just two buildings remaining in the eight blocks surrounding it, and the church was but a

A war-ravaged St. Nicholas Cole Abbey, near St. Paul's.

gaunt and roofless stone outline, burnt out in that devastating May 1941 raid. Having been totally reconstructed in the 1960s, St. Nicholas became yet another church with an older exterior and a mismatched interior. It's been home most recently to the Free Church of Scotland, but now sits empty and unused.

Walk another block down Queen Victoria Street, then turn right up Peter's Hill, dodging skateboarders, toward St. Paul's. Three more churches are in the neighborhood, but unless you're determined to visit every single church in St. Paul's shadow, a brief description should suffice. Grab a bench along Peter's Hill and read on.

Back down Peter's Hill (that's the Millennium Bridge straight ahead) on Queen Victoria Street is St. Benet Welsh Church (formerly St. Benet, Paul's Wharf), a Wren church that suffered minor wartime damage. Also on Queen Victoria Street is St. Andrew-by-the-Wardrobe, another Wren church but this one gutted by bombing (Cecil Beaton called it "a hideous black mess") with only the tower left, hollow and spireless. Rebuilt in 1960, it has that modern feeling, although there are some fine older furnishings, some from other churches, some stored for safety during the war and thus missing Hitler's bombs. Up St. Andrew's Hill and across Ludgate Hill is St. Martin-within-Ludgate, a Wren church that survived the war essentially unscathed, a miracle considering the utter devastation around it.

Now caught up on nearby religious survivors, we're off to a ruin. Walk to the top of St. Peter's Hill—that bronze statue honors London's wartime firefighters, the thousand-plus men (and twenty-three women) killed in wartime firefighting efforts—and turn down quiet Carter Lane, a break from the bustle around St. Paul's. At Creed Lane, turn right, cross Ludgate Hill, and head to Newgate Street. There's construction going on here, so be flexible route-wise. Our next stop is that corner ruin, once **Christ Church Greyfriars**, and one of London's most evocative war memories, hinting at what could have been the fate of St. Paul's Cathedral.

> *Two blocks northwest of St. Paul's is the Old Bailey, the Central Criminal Courts, where the postwar trial of Nazi propagandist Lord Haw Haw (William Joyce) was held.*

Walk amongst the partial columns, looking west toward the arched window, their glass long gone but the metal window frames still standing. Christ Church Greyfriars was destroyed by firebombs, with only a shell of walls remaining beside the tower. The ruins of the church were eventually demolished, the steeple having been dismantled, repaired, and then re-erected in 1960. The wooden structures, with climbing roses twined about them, represent the original stone pillars; the box hedged rosebushes represent the alignment of the pews.

From one of the benches, look southward toward **St. Paul's Cathedral**, just visible past a great deal of new construction. First, a little background:

St. Paul's Cathedral.

St. Paul's, the fourth cathedral here, was completed in 1710 (after thirty-five years of work) and is the penultimate architectural achievement of Christopher Wren. Like Westminster Abbey, St. Paul's is packed with memorials and plaques, though many are in the crypt, leaving more grandeur and gloss for the main floor. The Cathedral serves as the principal church of the Anglican diocese of London and as the seat of the Bishop of London. It's also a busy tourist attraction; come early or late, but try to avoid a midday visit when tour guides are shepherding large groups about.

Construction Alert: Until recently one could walk south from Christ Church Greyfriars across windswept Paternoster Square to the Cathedral.

If ongoing construction warrants a detour, retrace your steps along to Ludgate Hill, then turn left toward the west door of St. Paul's Cathedral.

Before entering St. Paul's, check out a newer Blitz monument. On the Cathedral's northern side a massive limestone wheel sits flat on the pavement, a memorial to the 30,000 victims of the London Blitz. The inscription quotes Winston Churchill: "In war, resolution; in defeat, defiance; in victory, magnanimity; in peace, goodwill." And around the base, "Remember before God the People of London 1939–1945." It was unveiled in 1999 by the Queen Mother, then the most distinguished living survivor of the Blitz.

Queen Anne at St. Paul's.

Head back to St. Paul's western side and the front door. That's Queen Anne at the bottom of the steps—the Cathedral was finished during her reign. Glance to the right side as you face the steps, at a point about twenty feet out from the base of the southwestern tower, near where the last bollard is. One of those miraculous wartime stories began here on September 12, 1940, when an unexploded Luftwaffe bomb buried itself deep under the pavement—it landed fifteen feet down and then sank another twelve feet in the slippery London clay. The area was cordoned off and evacuated for blocks around, and the job of dealing

ST. PAUL'S CHURCHYARD EC4

with "Hermann" fell to Number 5 Bomb Disposal Company. The men first considered defusing the bomb, but it was a new type of UXB, fitted with an as-yet unsolved fuse mechanism; attempting to defuse the bomb in place would likely set it off. Not an option. An alternative was to just let the bomb sit until it exploded...also unacceptable. The only solution was unearthing it and carting it away.

The men worked very, very slowly for three days—one false move could wipe out London's finest architectural achievement, to say nothing of the demolition engineers themselves. To make matters worse, either Hermann or the preliminary excavation work had fractured a gas main and before the gas could be turned off, three workers passed out from the fumes. The risk increased when the escaping gas caught fire. Finally, the gas main off, the men returned to digging, seeking an eight-foot-long bomb weighing over a ton buried twenty-seven feet underground. Once the bomb was unearthed, they gently hauled it upwards with special tackle, then ever so slowly loaded it onto a truck. Lieutenant Robert Davies, head of the bomb disposal unit, drove through London's streets, heading for distant Hackney Marshes where Hermann was detonated. The explosion made a crater over a hundred feet across. This narrow escape was the first of many for St. Paul's Cathedral.

St. Paul's interior.

Up the steps and inside the Cathedral, you'll find a disconcerting swirl of humanity, but things will calm down once you're past the entry desks and in the body of the church. I recommend renting a recorded tour; an Acoustiguide provides helpful commentary, and you can intersperse your listening of the general story of the Cathedral with some of the following war-related highlights. The recorded tour takes you down the northern side of St. Paul's to the American Memorial Chapel, then back along the south side with a detour to the crypt. You can visit the Whispering Gallery on your own, if you'd like. (Vertigo Alert: Don't go.)

Be forewarned: The Cathedral has embarked on a major cleaning and restoration endeavor, and various sections of the interior are scaffolded and shrouded. The end result will be worth the interim chaos; if a memorial or statue you hoped to view is inaccessible, buck up—consider what the Cathedral must have been like at war's end.

I recently interviewed a wartime resident of London, a quite charming and articulate Englishwoman. As we sat down and before I could say a word, she leaned over and touched my arm. "They never got it, did they." It was a statement, not a question. "They never got it. St. Paul's."

Inside the west door, a floor plaque reminds visitors to "Remember men and women of Saint Paul's Watch who by the grace of God saved this cathedral from destruction in war 1939–1945." More of that story in a bit. As you set off on your sound guide tour, watch for the display case containing the Merchant Navy Roll of Honor and the memorial to Field Marshal Slim. There's also a wooden memorial to the Cathedral's choristers who died in both world wars.

Next up is Henry Moore's *Mother and Child*, installed in the north choir aisle near the high altar in 1984. Circle the Travertine stone sculpture to view this very contemporary work from all sides. Personally, I admire Moore's work but its modern presence here always jangles. Nearby is the elegant high altar with its massive oak columns, a memorial from the British people honoring the 335,451 service members of the Commonwealth and Empire Forces who died in the world wars. It replaces the Victorian-era altar, badly damaged by German bombs.

The solemn **American Memorial Chapel** in the Cathedral's apse (the recess behind the high altar) honors the 28,000-plus American soldiers and airmen based in Britain who lost their lives in the war. The chapel was a gift to America from the British, though the Americans donated the nearby roll of honor, a beautiful 500-page illuminated manuscript listing American dead. One page is turned a day. The paneled carvings at the back of the chapel feature American birds, plants, and flowers—even a rocket ship (check the far right panel). In fact, many symbolic elements decorate the chapel, including the dove on the altar cloth, symbolizing peace after war, and the carved and gilded eagle above the altar, indicating the sorrowing strength of survivors and victims alike. The stained-glass windows by Brian Thomas depict the service and sacrifice of the soldier; the borders contain the insignia of the fifty American states and the U.S. military. Finally, the panels on the ends of the stalls have medallions representing President Eisenhower and Queen Elizabeth II, the respective leaders of the U.S. and Britain when the chapel was installed.

> *Wondering about those brass grilles in the floor of St. Paul's? Installed in 1881, they were designed to allow air from a heating system below to rise and circulate throughout the Cathedral; in 1909 a more efficient system of hot-water heating was installed.*

Along the south aisle, there's usually a group gathered around the display case containing artifacts and articles about St. Paul's in wartime. Above hangs the famous photograph showing the Cathedral during the horrendous attack of December 29, 1940. This familiar shot crystallizes the entire Blitz—St. Paul's Cathedral, riding the waves of smoke and flames and providing, as one wartime observer put it, "the most inspiring and terrifying sight that Londoners had ever seen."

Walk back under the dome and take the stairs down to the crypt and its hundreds of memorials. Starting from the OBE Chapel on the eastern end, watch for the memorial to Cathedral staff who died in both world wars. Commemorative plaques and graves of several war-related individuals are here, including Sir Edwin Lutyens, architect of the Cenotaph; Alexander Fleming (discoverer of penicillin, the miracle drug that saved thousands in the war), and sculptor Henry Moore, whose Shelter Drawings captured the essence of the Tube-sheltering experience. Wall plaques near Wellington's tomb commemorate British Field Marshals and the men who served under them, including Monty, Slim, Ironside, Wavell, and Gort; nearby, a separate circular memorial plaque again pays tribute to Field Marshal Gort, and another acknowledges Naval Commander Philip Vian.

> Journalist Ernie Pyle saw the defiance: "The people of London...go to look at it [a bombed St. Paul's Cathedral] without sadness, and they say, 'We would rather have it that way in a free London than have it whole like Notre Dame in an imprisoned Paris.'"

Near Nelson's tomb, a half-dozen reminders of World War II can be found. One of the more touching is the memorial to RAF Pilot Officer William Meade Lindsley Fiske III, an American killed in the Battle of Britain. Interestingly, Fiske was no hotshot kid eager to get in his licks. According to Derek Boorman in *For Your Tomorrow* (a comprehensive study of Britain's World War II memorials), Fiske was a wealthy stockbroker living in England, married to the former Countess of Warwick. He joined the RAF the day war was declared and died almost a year later, pulled from the wreckage of his plane in Sussex. The plaque honors "An American Citizen Who Died that England Might Live"; below it a small display case contains Fiske's RAF wings.

Watch for memorials to the men and women in the Russian Arctic Campaign, to the Parachute Regiment and Airborne Forces, to Polish airmen, to the Middlesex Yeomanry, and to the men and women of the Air Transport Auxiliary, pilots who ferried aircraft from place to place, freeing combat pilots for what they did best.

> St. Paul's Cathedral took air raid precautions: The Wellington memorial and Nelson sarcophagus were bricked-in. Carved work by Grinling Gibbons and the Tijou screens were taken down and stored. And the effigy of John Donne, former Dean of St. Paul's, was moved to the crypt.

Enough memorials—head back upstairs and grab a chair for a brief rest stop. The Cathedral has been the site for dozens of important events, including war-related services in honor of President Roosevelt in April 1945, V-E Day services, and Victory Thanksgiving services at war's end. One of the most poignant was Winston Churchill's state funeral in January 1965. (See "Footsteps of the Famous" in Chapter 1.) A bronze plaque in the floor of the dome records the site of Churchill's catafalque during the service, but the enlarged everyday altar (as opposed to the high altar) has recently been constructed over it.

All these treasures, all these memorials, all this grandeur. It could have ended like Christ Church Greyfriars—a partial wall standing here, a few

Searchlights and St. Paul's.

half-pillars over there, a handful of memorials leaning against a cracked and broken wall. St. Paul's came so very close to destruction, despite the best firewatching plan in all the City. St. Paul's Watch, formed originally in World War I, had 200 volunteers available on a night and day schedule, posted at multiple points on the Cathedral roof and dome. After extensive training, they knew firefighting, and as St. Paul aficionados, they knew the vast building. They knew the dome (all 64,000 tons of it) was really two domes, with an outer lead-covered wood roof separated from the interior brick dome. They knew the Cathedral's immense roof, both the very meltable dome and the many flat expanses, provided innumerable crevices where an incendiary bomb could lodge and cause havoc. They knew where the water was: extra water tanks had been installed at all levels of the building in case the main water supply failed, and several static tanks had been erected at ground level to the north of the building. And they knew that additional doors and stairs had been built to speed firefighting access to previously inaccessible locations. The men and women of St. Paul's Watch, in their blue overalls and steel helmets, were trained and ready.

> *The Daily Mail headlined the famous photo of St. Paul's Cathedral "War's Greatest Picture: St. Paul's Stands Unharmed in the Midst of the Burning City."*

The saga of St. Paul's firewatchers began at 5:55am on October 10, 1940, when the Cathedral received its first direct hit—a bomb plummeted through the outer roof of the quire and exploded between the vault and the roof. A mass of masonry fell into the quire, destroying the high altar, smashing the chapel just behind it, and severely damaging the Victorian reredos. Several days later when Vera Brittain wandered St. Paul's, she found "the shattered fragments of the high altar still lie where they fell, strangely lit up by the sunlight which streams through the surrounding gloom straight on to the white remnants of stone." There were jagged holes in the Cathedral's stained glass at this end of the building, but miraculously no major fire had started.

A defiant St. Paul's still stands resolute.

Six months later, on the night of April 16, 1941, hundreds of incendiaries were dropped by Luftwaffe pilots, and the firewatchers raced about the roof, kicking the firebombs off or dousing them with sand. Then, far worse, a heavy explosive bomb crashed down on the north transept, pierced the saucer dome, and detonated inside the church. The explosion and attendant debris broke through the floor into the crypt, leaving a gaping twenty-five-foot-wide hole in the floor. One exhausted firefighter wrote the following day, "8 solid hours fighting to save St. Paul's. We put out every sort of fire and saved it from *that* but couldn't cope with the terrific H.E. crashes....It rocked so much once we were sure it was over."

Between these two epic nights was the nightmare of December 29, when businesses and churches were locked up tight and incendiary bombs fell like rain as over 300 German bombers concentrated their efforts on the City. Only St. Paul's had an organized firewatching brigade, but with water mains broken and the river at low tide, the firewatchers had to resort to stirrup pumps and buckets, even sandbags, to attempt to smother the incendiaries or fight the fires

VISITOR DETAILS: St. Paul's Cathedral is open Monday–Saturday 8:30am to 4pm (last admission). Admission is charged; guided and recorded tours available. Cathedral Shop is open Monday–Saturday 9am to 5pm; Sunday 10:30am to 5pm. Crypt Café (same hours as the shop) and the tonier Refractory Restaurant (11am to 5pm) are in the crypt, as are restrooms. Disabled access is on the south side of the building; ring for assistance. Note: Shopping, eating, and restrooms are accessible without paying admission; use the north side entrance. More information: 020 7246 8348, www.stpauls.co.uk.

For the Fallen—The City's Blitzed Churches:

It would be a very long walk indeed to visit every churchly war survivor in the City. And personally, after a while they all blend into each other. Rather than trekking to the much restored (and sometimes far too modernized) churches that outlasted the Blitz, watch for memories and reminders of these long-gone churches.

St. Augustine (Watling Street). St. Augustine's, designed by Christopher Wren in the 1680s, was burnt out in 1941. The tower still stands, part of St. Paul's Choir School.

St. Dunstan-in-the-East (Great Tower Street). Another Wren church (1702), St. Dunstan's was wiped out by German bombs in 1941. Open-air services were held beside the surviving tower in 1943 and 1944, the congregation called to worship with a handbell. The shell remains as a public garden with the tower at one end.

St. Mildred (Bread Street). Badly bombed in April and May 1941, this war casualty became a weed-filled bomb site. Thirty years later, the little that remained was demolished and a bank built on the lot.

St. Stephen (Coleman Street). Essentially only four walls were left after wartime bombing, and these ruins have since been demolished. This too was a Wren church.

St. Swithun, London Stone (Cannon Street). This late 1600s building was sufficiently damaged in bombing raids that it was eventually demolished.

they started. That night over two dozen incendiaries landed on the Cathedral, but only a handful caused appreciable damage. The worst was the firebomb that pierced the Cathedral's lead roof and fell into the wooden timbers of the inner dome below. Firelight glowed out through the hole—it looked like the entire building was afire. Edward R. Murrow, sighting the blaze from afar, tersely broadcast to his American radio listeners, "The church that means most to Londoners is gone. St. Paul's Cathedral…is burning to the ground as I talk to you now." Burning, yes, but not to the ground. The incendiary burned through the dome timbers and fell to the floor; the fire above did not spread beyond the singed roof timbers. That was the night of the famous photo, when so many buildings in St. Paul's shadow *did* burn to the ground.

Now, having investigated the immediate neighborhood of St. Paul's and having seen the splendors of the Cathedral—and how close this symbol of Britain's wartime defiance came to destruction—return your Acoustiguide and head to the crypt café or restaurant for a long grateful pause. Raise a glass (or sandwich or bag of crisps) in remembrance of St. Paul's Watch, the small band of volunteers who saved a national monument.

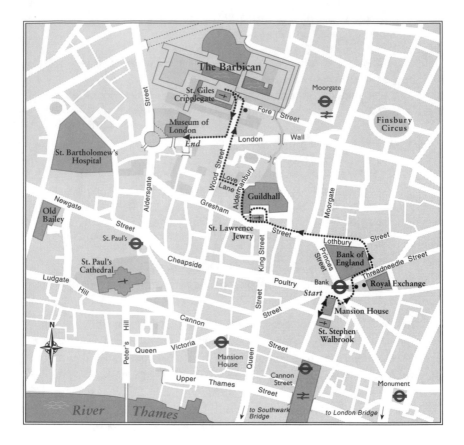

The Barbican

Moorgate

Finsbury
Circus

St. Giles
Cripplegate

Fore   Street

Museum of
London

End

London   Wall

St. Bartholomew's
Hospital

Street

Aldersgate

Wood Street

Love Lane

Aldermanbury

Gresham

Guildhall

Moorgate

Newgate

Old
Bailey

Street

St. Paul's

St. Lawrence
Jewry

Street

Lothbury

Street

Bank of
England

Threadneedle Street

St. Paul's
Cathedral

Cheapside

King Street

Princes
Street

Royal Exchange

Ludgate

Hill

Poultry

Bank

Start

Mansion House

Cannon

Street

St. Stephen
Walbrook

N

Peter's   Hill

Queen

Victoria

Street

Mansion
House

Queen

Street

Cannon
Street

Monument

Upper   Thames

Street

River   Thames

to Southwark
Bridge

to London Bridge

PART III
THE CITY'S WORLDLY SIDE

The maze of little streets threading through the wilderness, the broken walls, the great pits with their dense forests of bracken and bramble, the vaults and cellars and deep caves, the wrecked guild halls...empty shells of churches with their towers still strangely spiring above the wilderness....

—ROSE MACAULAY, *THE WORLD MY WILDERNESS*

The hectic City stills after bombs fall near the Royal Exchange.

Highlights: St. Stephen Walbrook, Mansion House, Royal Exchange, Bank of England, St. Lawrence Jewry, Guildhall, St. Mary Aldermanbury, St. Alban's, Barbican, St. Giles Cripplegate, Fore Street sign, Museum of London

Underground Station: Bank

Photo Ops: Whip out that camera for some unusual shots of Oscar Nemon's Churchill statue at Guildhall, the Fore Street sign announcing the first bomb dropped on the City, or the lovely lonely garden of St. Mary Aldermanbury.

BEFORE LEAVING ON YOUR TRIP

■ **Travel Scheduling:** London's churches often close for repairs and vacations in August; if viewing church interiors is important to you, consider a non-August visit.

■ **Cultural Preparations:** Rose Macaulay's novel *The World My Wilderness*, quoted above, provides telling descriptions of the havoc wreaked on London's homefront.

■ **Internet Best Bets:** Check out the Museum of London's upcoming exhibits at www.museumoflondon.org.uk.

Our route in the worldly district of the City moves diagonally northwest from Mansion House, the Royal Exchange, and the Bank of England to Guildhall and the Museum of London, stopping along the way for several churches and some dramatic ruins.

From the Bank Underground, walk south to **St. Stephen Walbrook**, a Wren masterpiece hidden behind Mansion House.

ARP warden sends a message.

This church is considered one of Wren's finest, with "the most perfectly proportional interior in the world." In 1941, a bomb ripped a hole in the dome, destroying about two-thirds of it and setting aflame the pews below, damage sufficiently reparable that services were able to resume in 1944. More focused restoration was done first in the early 1950s and then again in the 1980s. The result is a nontraditional interior with blond

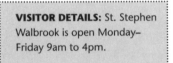

VISITOR DETAILS: St. Stephen Walbrook is open Monday–Friday 9am to 4pm.

wood benches circling a massive marble altar table by Henry Moore, all sitting quite modernly below the stunning dome. This is one of London's less-visited churches (one more time, I was the only one here); climb the worn steps and see if the modernity inside grows on you.

Retrace your steps back to the frantic Bank intersection, where seven streets (it seems like more) come together. **Mansion House** (the building with six fluted columns across the front), erected in the mid-1700s, is the residence of the City's Lord Mayor. A nearby wartime explosion caused minor damage. Cross to the **Royal Exchange** (opened by Queen Victoria in 1844), with Wellington astride in front. The war memorial here honors the officers and men of London who served King and Empire in the Great War, with the usual addendum adding World War II warriors to the list. The columned portico (eight plain columns) of the Royal Exchange was usually festooned with wartime banners urging "Buy War Bonds" and the like. When a German bomb crashed onto this intersection in January 1941, jumbling

How times change: According to Katherine Sturtevant in Our Sisters' London, *until World War II a female clerk at the Bank of England couldn't go from one part of the building to another without a chaperone.*

ragged hunks of pavement and leaving dozens dead in the Underground station below, it was a bitter irony that a "Dig for Victory" slogan hung across the front of the building. Both Mansion House and the Royal Exchange are closed to the public.

To the north stands the **Bank of England**, the nation's central bank. This massive building, constructed between 1788 and 1833, houses an absorbing museum (entrance on Bartholomew Lane), especially if you like money. You can heft a gold bar, examine the intricacies of bank note design, and spot (or miss) some forgeries. Watch for details of wartime Operations Andreas and Bernhard, German attempts to forge millions of Bank of England notes to destabilize the British economy. This was a major reason that wartime production of paper money (above £5) was halted.

Before the Blitz, several bank departments were moved out of London for safety. The remaining staff donned air warden hats and Fire Guard armbands and kept a vigilant watch for the Luftwaffe from the roof. A direct hit early in September 1940 meant most departments moved to more secure underground rooms and offices in the depths of the building. War's end brought back staff from the countryside and up from the underground offices but the Bank of England faced even more of a cataclysm ahead—nationalization by the Labour government in 1946.

> **VISITOR DETAILS:** The Bank of England Museum is open Monday–Friday 10am to 5pm. Sound guides available. Small shop. No eating facilities; restrooms are located along the self-guided tour route. More information: 020 7601 5545, www.bankofengland.co.uk.

Turn left from the Bank of England Museum door and then left again on Lothbury Street, a roadway that soon executes a typical London morphing, into Gresham Street. Ahead about three blocks is **St. Lawrence Jewry**, yet another Wren church (1680) and yet another victim of the Luftwaffe. It was almost completely destroyed by fire in 1940, "a result of action by the King's enemies," an archly euphemistic way to put it. St. Lawrence Jewry had been securely locked up the night of December 29, and firefighters were unable to get inside. Only the walls and piers survived the fire, plus the masonry tower. St. Lawrence Jewry was rebuilt in the mid-1950s, a light-filled and elegant structure, all gold and white with wooden pews.

> **VISITOR DETAILS:** St. Lawrence Jewry is generally open weekdays 7:30am to 2pm. More information: 020 7600 9478.

Just beyond St. Lawrence Jewry is **Guildhall**, another building done in by the king's enemies. The center of municipal government for the City of

London, it's a City Hall, mayor's office, and council chambers all rolled into one. It also serves as the major ceremonial center for the City—here's where Churchill and Eisenhower were given the Freedom of the City, and where London celebrated the fiftieth anniversary of V-E Day.

The City's Guildhall.

This building, constructed in the early 1400s, survived the London blazes of both 1666 and 1940–1941, though the latter caused severe damage. Particularly hard hit was the Great Hall—on the night of December 29, 1940, sparks and pieces of burning wood from the roaring fire of nearby St. Lawrence Jewry set the hammerbeam roof ablaze. It crashed to the floor, and the fire soon spread to the Council Chambers. The Great Hall's gallery was completely burnt out, reducing the imposing wooden figures of Gog and Magog, here for several hundred years, to ashes. Most of the stained glass in the Hall was destroyed (and since replaced); the one small plain glass window, circa 1435, survived (to the right as you enter the echoing hall). In the rebuilt gallery above, you'll see two new figures of Gog and Magog erected in 1953. Note the phoenix on Magog's shield, a symbol of renewal.

Statues and monuments deck the Great Hall. Tucked back against the walls, most survived the flames from the roof, the crashing masonry, and the falling timbers. Lord Nelson did lose his wreath and one of the figures below was broken, and the Duke of Wellington had pieces of stonework about his base smashed. The seated bronze figure of Winston Churchill by Oscar Nemon, installed in the late 1950s, missed the trauma of the Great Hall's destruction. Visit the crypt (if it's open) and watch for the dramatic stained-glass window showing the Guildhall rising from the flames.

VISITOR DETAILS: Guildhall is open (barring some ceremonial function) daily 10am to 5pm; closed winter Sundays. Expect a security check. Library Bookshop is open Monday–Friday 9:30am to 4:45pm. Art Gallery is open Monday–Saturday 10am to 5pm; Sunday noon to 4pm. Admission is charged. Public restroom outside the library. More information: Guildhall 020 7606 3030 ext. 1460; Bookshop 020 7260 1858; Art Gallery 020 7332 3700.

Red Telephone Kiosks

London's wartime streets sported hundreds of telephone kiosks—not everyone had home service and only Dick Tracy's two-way wrist radio approximated the ubiquitous cell phones of today. Two slightly different models saw wartime use, and today's observant visitor can spot them both.

The older kiosk—the K2—was designed by Sir Giles Gilbert Scott, later designer of the rebuilt House of Commons. In 1926 the first production K2s were installed in Kensington and Holborn (now long gone); wooden prototypes can be found today in the entrance archway of Burlington House on Piccadilly.

> If you needed to call Mr. Churchill mid-war, the number at 10 Downing Street was WHitehall 1234. If, however, you were more interested in ringing up Harrods, you'd dial SLoane 1234.

The more recent design, also by Scott, was the K6 (models K3–K5 being less than serviceable and never widely produced), introduced in 1936. By 1940, there were 35,000 red K6 kiosks in England. In the postwar years, and with the privatization of phone service in the late 1980s, the cast-iron kiosks were routinely removed and replaced with soulless open-air plastic booths. Eventually—and wisely—preservation of the older red kiosks was mandated in London's tourist and historic areas. Here's how to tell the *really* old models from the merely old ones:

K2 (circa 1926 to 1936): red, cast iron; nine feet three inches tall; crown in pediment pierced; three panes of glass wide, six panes high, all panes of equal size

K6 (circa 1936 to 1968): red, cast iron; eight feet three inches tall; crown in pediment embossed; three panes of glass wide, eight panes high, panes of unequal size.

Stop by the Guildhall Bookshop for London-related books, maps, prints, playing cards, and postcards, much of it unavailable elsewhere in the metropolis. One of my favorites is a map by Cecil Brown, titled in part "A Prospect of the City of London from the south-east in the year 1945 showing its architecture [and] the destruction caused by the King's enemies during the previous five years...." In short, a map of bomb damage

Aldermanbury, circa 1941.

in the City, and so detailed you can see pigeons at St. Paul's and pedestrians on Cheapside.

Across the plaza is Guildhall Art Gallery, established in 1885 to house and display the paintings and sculpture of the Corporation of London. The present building opened in 1999, replacing the building destroyed in the Blitz.

Head to the corner of Aldermanbury and Love Lane, to what appears to be a small park. Walk past Shakespeare to the site of **St. Mary Aldermanbury**, a Wren church decimated by Nazi air raids. Two decades later the building stones were taken to Westminster College in Fulton, Missouri, where the church was rebuilt as a memorial to Winston Churchill. The foundation and column fragments remain, surrounding a public garden; a marble tablet toward the back chronicles the church's history and the move.

From one somber sight to another—walk westward along Love Lane to Wood Street. Directly ahead is **St. Alban's**, or, more exactly, St. Alban's tower, all that's left of the Wren church after the Luftwaffe wrecked it in December 1940. The tower sits isolated on a traffic island in the middle of Wood Street.

The area around St. Giles' Cripplegate was so well-bombed that it was humorously suggested that the church should be renamed St. Giles in the Clearing.

Turn up Wood Street, passing the police station on your right, then head up the steps and over London Wall to Fore Street, entering one side of the Barbican complex (and complexity). Incidentally, a barbican is a fortification in a medieval city; *the* **Barbican** is a massive postwar development of residential tower blocks, shops, open space, schools, and theatres. I usually take the stairs labeled Alban Walk leading to Alban High Walk, which in turn leads to The Postern. Are you unwinding a ball of string? Fear not, this route is less byzantine than most of the Barbican and more pleasant than staying on street level. When a sign announces St. Giles' Church, do what it says and head down those steps to both a church and a memorable sign.

The church first, **St. Giles' Cripplegate**, a Blitz survivor (though wounded) while all around was leveled. Portions of the small stone building date to the 1390s although it was much extended after fires in 1545 and 1897. Here Oliver Cromwell was married and John Milton buried; a statue of Milton, erected in 1904 in the churchyard to the north, was perhaps the first statue in London to be bombed in World War II. He took a tumble on August 24, 1940, thrown on his back in the first air attack on a City church. Milton was replaced on his pedestal, was hit again by later bombs, and then wisely was removed to safety.

> **VISITOR DETAILS:** St. Giles' Cripplegate is open weekdays 11am to 4pm. More information: 020 7638 1997, www.stgilescripplegate.com.

After a visit by German bombers that nasty night of December 29, 1940, fire destroyed the roof of St. Giles' Cripplegate, and when the rafters fell, most of the pews and other interior furnishings burned, and the church bells were shattered or cracked. The church's interior was heavily restored after the war, but its exterior stands as a medieval reminder in the midst of Barbican modernity. Watch for that statue of Milton, now inside, and the tablet on the floor in front of the pulpit, marking his grave site.

A wounded Fore Street, looking much different than today.

Wartime Sandbags

Millions of jute bags plumply filled with sand—the most elemental of protections against bomb blast—were stacked everywhere in wartime London. They shored-up walls, surrounded doorways, protected monuments, and covered windows. Sand was excavated from London sites (including Hampstead Heath below Jack Straw's Castle, and Hyde Park near South Carriage Drive), then trucked to various parts of the metropolis and dumped. Volunteers and soldiers stepped forward to fill bags by hand, which were then distributed to and piled around "vital points": at first government buildings, hospitals, machine gun pillboxes, and stat-

ues, and later offices, shops, and even homes. Stacked in rows fifteen to twenty bags high, this ordinary defensive measure shielded Hyde Park's anti-aircraft batteries, Mayfair's restaurants, and the treasures of Westminster Abbey.

It is, however, in the nature of sand to be uncontainable. Sandbags were sometimes stabbed open and handfuls grabbed to put out incendiary fires. And then as time passed and the waterlogged bags rotted and burst open, gritty sand would fly about London on windy days, some of it quite evil-smelling, given the attraction the bags had for London's dogs and cats. Finally, by the later war years, many of London's remaining antique sandbags could be seen with grass growing out of them.

Retrace your steps across the clearing, but go past the pub and the steps, then across the intersection to Fore Street and the wall **sign** near the corner noting when the war began for the City. The text gives no indication of the devastation that occurred in the nine months after that August beginning. Every building in sight, including this one with the plaque, was constructed after all-too-effective German bombings.

On to the Museum of London. Climb back up the steps and start retracing your path—shortly a sign will indicate a right turn for the museum. Have faith, turn right, and soldier on—though stop for sustenance at any of the cafés along the way if the labyrinth of passages has unnerved you.

The walkway parallels the modern street below called London Wall and also portions of the actual second-century London Wall below on the other side. Ahead, the **Museum of London** is the perfect conclusion to a walk focused on the worldly side of the City. The museum's collection traces the urban history of the metropolis from Roman times to the present. Popular galleries and attractions are the Roman interiors, the Great Fire Experience, London shopfronts, eighteenth-century Newgate Prison, the Lord Mayor's coach, and the Early Twentieth Century. Watch for the newest gallery: World City—London 1789–1914.

This building, constructed as part of the Barbican development, opened in 1976. The Museum of London grew out of two collections: the London Museum, originally housed in Lancaster House then later in Kensington Palace, and the Guildhall Museum. This structure allows the display of these combined and much-augmented collections in an inviting fashion, and offers much more of an emphasis on unearthing the city's past. It's an entertaining way to steep yourself in London's history.

> **VISITOR DETAILS:** The Museum of London is open Monday–Saturday 10am to 5:50pm; Sunday noon to 5:50pm. Shop; Museum Café; restrooms. Note: Café and shop are accessible without paying admission. More information: 020 7600 0807, www.museumoflondon.org.uk.

From the museum door, check out the directional signs and select your path—you can wander more in the Barbican (a euphemism for getting lost) or follow the signs to St. Paul's Underground.

Legal, religious, worldly. We've walked the three worlds of the City, a compact square mile with dozens of war memories. The perspective gained on this and other walks in *London's War* should enable you to uncover memories of World War II on your own. Whenever and wherever you walk the capital's streets, that process of discovery will continue to illuminate and enrich your experience of one of the most exciting—and dreadful—times in London's history.

9
Around London

*It would take ten years, at the present rate, for half the
houses of London to be demolished. After that, of course,
progress would be much slower.*

—WINSTON CHURCHILL, HOUSE OF COMMONS, 1940

London is too big. It was too big for Hitler to destroy, and it's too big to walk everywhere to experience the wartime homefront. Our focus has been on the much-frequented, compact haunts of central London: Westminster and Whitehall, Trafalgar Square, St. James's, Mayfair, Soho and Covent Garden, Bloomsbury, Marylebone, and the City. But across the southern swath of the metropolis, sweeping from Kensington to the East End, dozens of important wartime sites and present-day attractions add nuance and texture to a homefront visit...they're just so darned far apart. A broad range of locations are included here, not as part of a walking route, but rather as a selection of priority stops to arrange in your itinerary as you see fit. Several are noted as absolute must-sees, but all will add to your understanding of London's homefront.

Left: Cleaning up yet another London church after enemy action.

Londoners at work filling wartime sandbags in Kensington.

PART I
KENSINGTON, SOUTH KENSINGTON, & KNIGHTSBRIDGE

I've seen a good many blitzed buildings in the past few years, but somehow one I saw in Queen's Gate gave me an unusually unpleasant shock. It must have sustained a direct hit, for what had been a typically ornate Victorian house of the red tiles and bricked rococo kind...was merely a gigantic heap of brick and rubble.

—ANTHONY WEYMOUTH, *JOURNAL OF THE WAR YEARS*

Checking-in to a Knightsbridge service club.

Highlights: Kensington Palace, Albert Memorial, Royal Albert Hall, Sikorski Museum, Victoria and Albert Museum, Harrods

Underground Stations: High Street Kensington or Queensway for Kensington Palace area; South Kensington for the V&A; Knightsbridge for Harrods

Photo Ops: Bomb scars along the west side of the V&A make for an unusual shot. The displays in Harrods' food halls may tempt you, but alas, photography isn't allowed.

BEFORE LEAVING ON YOUR TRIP

■ **Travel Scheduling:** Tours of the Albert Memorial take place on Sundays, March through December. The Promenade Concerts ("The Proms") at Royal Albert Hall are mid-July to mid-September. Harrods' big sales are in January and July.

■ **Cultural Preparations:** The diaries of photographer and designer Cecil Beaton provide an insight into this complex man living in a complex time: check your public library for *The Years Between: Diaries 1939–44*. And for a view of Beaton's photographic skills, watch for *Cecil Beaton: The Royal Portraits*.

■ **Internet Best Bets:** Shop Harrods at www.harrods.com. Or check what's coming up at Kensington Palace at www.hrp.org.uk.

Kensington Palace has been a royal residence since the 1680s when Christopher Wren enlarged the building for William and Mary. Since then, the palace apartments have housed members of the extended Royal Family—Princess Victoria was born here in 1819 and remained until she became queen in 1837; Princess May, later to become Queen Mary, was born here in 1867; and more recently, Princess Margaret, the Duke and Duchess of Kent, and Princess Diana have all lived in Kensington Palace. The lavish State Rooms and Royal Ceremonial Dress Collection annually draw thousands of visitors.

The London Museum, formerly housed in Lancaster House, also found a home here. Its collections were moved into Kensington Palace postwar and remained until 1975, when the museum went on to its current City site. More recently, Kensington Palace was the focus for public grief after Princess Diana's death.

The war experience of Kensington Palace was characterized by military occupation (the Army took over part of Clock Court) and bombs. The State Rooms were initially closed to visitors but reopened in mid-1940, only to be closed on and off throughout the duration. Firebombs falling on the royal apartments of Princess Beatrice and Princess Alice left the roof a ruin of blackened timbers and gaping holes. Late-war flying bombs compounded the damage.

> **VISITOR DETAILS:** Kensington Palace in Kensington Gardens is open daily 10am to 6pm; closes earlier in winter. Admission is charged. Sound guides available; shop. The Orangery is open daily, 10am to 6pm; closes earlier in winter. Restrooms near the Orangery and along the Broad Walk toward Kensington Road. More information: 0870 751 5170, www.hrp.org.uk.

The cumulative effects of blast, fire, and water were particularly dismaying, but repairs were eventually completed, and Kensington Palace returned to a semblance of normal—normal for a palace, that is.

It's hard to miss the **Albert Memorial**, and Queen Victoria would be pleased that you're not going to. Prince Albert was the Queen's Consort, and his death from typhoid in 1861 sent Victoria into four decades of deep mourning. One result was the construction of this neo-Gothic memorial by Sir George Gilbert Scott, architect of the fanciful St. Pancras rail station. It took twelve years to build the cast-iron, lead, bronze, glass, mosaic, and stone memorial, a monument that Londoners have never been particularly fond of. However, after the restoration program stretching through most of the 1990s, even locals are finding the gaudy memorial attractive. It helps that Albert has been restored to his original gold; he had been painted black in 1915 allegedly because of fears the gleaming statue might attract bomb-dropping Zeppelins (though the German-born prince wasn't very popular at the time anyway). More likely it was cash shortages that prohibited Albert's needed regilding.

> War correspondent Ernie Pyle caught the general feeling: "Londoners pray daily that a German bomb will do something about the Albert Memorial....As the British say, they could bear its removal with equanimity. But the contrary Germans have only taken a few little chips out of it."

Walk all the way around for a sense of the allegorical themes, starting with the groupings at each corner representing the continents. The marble frieze encircling the base features figures from the arts, agriculture, manufacturing, and the industrial arts—but alas, count how many women made the cut. The mosaics shine and glint in the sunlight, giving the structure the appearance of a very large jewel box. And serenely above all sits Queen Victoria's own jewel of a man, the three-times-larger-than-life Albert holding a catalog from his penultimate project, the Great Exhibition of 1851.

Albert Memorial.

As for the war and Albert: Neither the memorial nor the statue were sandbagged or protected. An October 1940 incident (possibly a bomb but more likely shrapnel or an unexploded shell from Kensington Park's artillery guns) knocked the cross off the top and dethroned one of the angels. Falling debris (cross, angel, etc.) did in ninety feet of paving and a stretch of railings at the northeast corner.

High explosive bombs later that same month and again in the Little Blitz of 1944 caused further minor damage. Somewhere in all this, the right breast of the figure representing Asia was rather cleanly sliced off. The cross, angel, and breast were all replaced soon after the war. And through it all, London's victory gardeners tended their allotments in the memorial's shadow.

If Albert were to glance up, he'd see **Royal Albert Hall** (1871) across Kensing-

> **VISITOR DETAILS:** The Albert Memorial is viewable at all hours. Guided tours behind the railings are available Sunday, March–December; admission is charged. Albert suggests you head to Kensington High Street for a choice of restaurants, and due west or northeast for park restrooms. More information: 020 7495 0916.

Royal Albert Hall.

ton Gore. This venue, home to the Promenade Concerts after they were blitzed out of Queen's Hall, suffered the usual wartime wear and tear: broken windows, blackened walls from nearby fires, and extensive blast damage, but amazingly no direct hits. Today the Proms are held here; besides the performance, attendance offers a chance to see the interior of Royal Albert Hall, compared by one wartime observer to "like being inside of a Christmas silver ball."

VISITOR DETAILS: For performance details at the Royal Albert Hall, check London's newspapers. More information: 020 7589 8212, www.royalalberthall.com.

The round structure was intended as yet another monument to dear Albert and his progressive and innovative ideas, as noted in the 800-foot-long frieze circling the building. Incidentally, the domed hall inside is elliptical, not round, and now seats about 5,000. During the war, concerts started earlier (usually about 6:30pm) so concertgoers could get home before the blackout—or the bombing—got too serious. You can expect a later curtain.

The **General Sikorski Museum** on Prince's Gate sits in a neighborhood of embassies, consulates, and official residences. Nearby Number 14 was the American ambassador's residence in the late 1930s; it now houses the Royal College of General Practitioners. A plaque here honors John Kennedy; he visited while his father was U.S. ambassador, although the plaque makes it sound as if JFK lived here when president.

VISITOR DETAILS: The Sikorski Museum at 20 Prince's Gate is open Monday–Friday 2pm to 4pm, and the first Saturday of the month 10am to 4pm. Admission and guided tours are free. More information: 020 7589 9249.

The Sikorski Museum (officially the Polish Institute and General Sikorski Museum) houses a varied mix of militaria and memorabilia, from a gleaming airplane engine to regimental badges to swords to fine china. All are related to the role of the Polish armed forces in the defense of their country's freedom, with an emphasis on the life of General Wladyslaw Sikorski. Students of the Cold War will remember that after World War II, Poland was occupied by the Russians, and a Polish government-in-exile remained in London until 1990. Expect the tour to open your eyes to both the World War II Polish experience and the realities of postwar European politics.

The **Victoria and Albert Museum**, the national museum of art and design and the world's largest collection of the decorative arts, is a must-see. Start outside with the western wall along Exhibition Road, where

Look Out in the Blackout!

In retrospect it makes little sense but at the time everyone was convinced—vehicle headlamps or a light shining out a window or an illuminated sign or even a lit match could be seen by German pilots flying miles above London. A blackout was decreed—no lights to be visible from the street, a rule strictly enforced by ARP wardens who aggressively tracked down any glimmer of illumination. London became primeval, darker than in Julius Caesar's time.

Impermeable window covers had to be devised from curtains, old blankets, cardboard, sheets of thick paper, or wood, then put up and taken down daily. Because of the fearful conditions on the capital's nighttime streets, both for drivers and pedestrians, many Londoners just stopped going out after dusk. Even so, pedestrian deaths rose dramatically in the first few months despite urgings to cross streets with care, good advice even today: "Bear this constantly, *consciously* in mind: there is death in the streets. Don't think that *you* can get away with taking any chances."

The blackout gave rise to ingenious methods to increase nighttime visibility, including the painting or whitewashing of curbs, light poles, tree trunks, gateposts, pillars, kiosks, barriers, steps, building corners, and even sandbags. A white line was painted down the center of streets, an obvious safety measure but never done before and so new that many drivers drove along the line instead of to one side. Bicycles were required to have six inches of the mudguard painted white, and auto mudguards, bumpers, and running boards were also painted. Headlight regulations varied, early on allowing no lights at all, later allowing headlights covered with layers of paper or with specially designed hooded lamps.

Individuals were urged to "Wear White for Visibility": white armbands, white shirts untucked, white hatbands, or white coats. Or carry something white—a newspaper, a white handbag, a painted walking stick, a luminous disk, a buttonhole of flowers, or even a small white dog.

In a triangular island across from the V&A, a memorial honors those who died as a result of the tragic Yalta agreement in 1945, repatriating Russians and other East Europeans back to Russia, in most cases to be murdered by Stalin's orders.

some serious wartime bomb damage has been left as a memorial "to the enduring values of this great museum in a time of conflict."

Once inside, pick up a free map—you'll be lost without one, wandering the seven miles of corridors, off track in the Ivory Carvings or adrift in Arms and Armour when you really wanted to be in the Dress Gallery or the Cast Courts. At least those are two of my favorite galleries (of the more than 140 here). The Dress Gallery, with clothing and accessories from 1600 to the present, answers those burning questions: What *is* a Trilby hat? What were English women wearing right before the war? What exactly was Utility clothing and was it as plain as it sounds? And what about wartime socks? And shoes?

After finding the answers, head to the Cast Courts. No, not casts as in broken bones, but as in reproductions of sculptures and architecture cast in plaster, from Michelangelo's *David* to Trajan's Column. Most have little wartime relevance, though there are casts of five Templar Knights from the Temple Church, taken in 1938 before a German bomb bounced the

Bomb memories at the V&A.

War Words: Allotments

ALLOTMENTS were small plots of ground, allotted (loaned or rented) during the war to local residents for the growing of essential foodstuffs. Onions, kale, carrots, beetroots (beets), marrows, and other vegetables were grown to supplement rationed food. This wasn't one's own yard or garden, which no doubt was also being cultivated, but a portion of land in a common area, somewhat similar to the community gardens of today. These small victory gardens were found along roadways, in factory grounds, beside tank traps and bomb craters, on golf courses, and in community areas—the Warders at the Tower of London tended their allotments in the Tower's filled-in moat. Posters urging "Dig for Victory" were everywhere, and by 1943 over 1,750,000 allotments and 3,000,000 private gardens were annually producing vegetables valued at £15,000,000.

originals around. These galleries just have an otherworldly, ethereal quality that makes me hyperventilate every time I enter; see if they affect you as dramatically.

Bombing fears prompted the closure of the V&A in August 1939, and staff packed up most exhibits and evacuated them to the usual places of safety including the Aldwych-Piccadilly Underground. The Raphael cartoons (drawings of planned tapestries for the Sistine Chapel, done by the Renaissance artist) were too big to move; they were bricked into a specially constructed bomb shelter outside the Gamble Room. The museum's director or another staff member slept here nights, ready if an attack came to help determine what needed to be saved first.

Empty galleries were put to new uses—the huge South Court became a canteen for the RAF and then for Bomb Damage Repair Squads; the smaller Morris, Gamble, and Poynter rooms were used as storage; and part of the museum became classrooms for schoolchildren evacuated from Gibraltar to South Kensington—truly an "out of the frying pan, into the fire" move. The V&A reopened in November 1939 with a relatively small collection on display, then closed briefly seventeen months later after German bombs damaged the building. In July 1944, a V-1 flying bomb fell on Exhibition Road

Early in the war, poet T. S. Eliot lived at 33 Courtfield Road in South Kensington, where he served as an air raid warden. To prepare for incendiary bomb fires, he practiced on bonfires set in nearby Emperor's Gate. Eliot also lived (and died, in 1965) at 3 Kensington Court Gardens off Kensington Road.

VISITOR DETAILS: The V&A on Cromwell Road is open daily 10am to 5:45pm; Wednesday 10am to 10pm. Guided tours are free. Extensive shop; restaurants and restrooms. More information: 020 7942 2000, www.vam.ac.uk.

and caused sufficient damage to again close the museum for some months.

Today, enjoy the portrait miniatures, the European Ornament Gallery, the Rodin sculptures and the tapestries, the Gallery of Japanese Art, and the Gallery of Indian Art. And don't miss the Dress Gallery and the Cast Courts.

Harrods as a war-related site? Yes, indeed, though you may want to shop first and then enjoy teatime in one of Harrods' cafés while considering department-store-as-homefront-battleground.

But first, a little background. There *was* a Mr. Harrod: Charles Henry Harrod, a wholesale grocer and tea merchant who founded Harrods in 1834. The store's motto is "Omnia Omnibus Ubique," clear to even the Latin-challenged: All things, for all people, everywhere. Today the immense building (four-plus acres) in Knightsbridge offers the best in British style and quality, to say nothing of London's most spectacular food halls.

Shopper Alert: Harrods sells "Winston Churchill" bow ties, polka-dotted (or as the English would say, white-spotted) and dark blue.

But what about the war? First of all, there was the blackout. Covering the store windows involved over a ton of cardboard and more than three miles of wooden battens to make removable cardboard screens; then, of course, there were the three miles of blackout curtain fabric. Most of the various blackout contraptions had to be put in place nightly and removed every morning. Harrods' staff also filled 18,000 sandbags and lugged them into place around the building's exterior. Such duties kept them from their appointed rounds—store deliveries were cut back drastically, and West End customers went from the possibility of four deliveries a day to hopes of once a week. Business fell off—petrol rationing plus the general exodus to the countryside meant many customers simply couldn't make it to the store. Open hours were reduced, and even at upmarket Harrods, there was no packaging for purchases.

A nighttime visit to Harrods provides an opportunity to count the light bulbs outlining the exterior; if the thought is overwhelming (as is the sight), there are 11,500 bulbs. The tradition began in 1959, so wartime blackout restrictions weren't a factor.

Staff and shoppers "kept at it" during air raids; shopping continued on the ground and first three floors while spotters watched for hostile aircraft from a concrete pillbox on the store's roof. A warning was sounded when the Luftwaffe got too close, and shoppers were shepherded to the shelter in—guess where—the food halls.

Harrods.

Harrods' workers on ARP duty (forty-eight hours a month) slept in the basement. Store staff sewed uniforms in the Clothing Workrooms, and Harrods' factories turned to aircraft parts and parachutes. Employees knitted "comforts" in their spare time, mittens and scarves destined for chilly soldiers at the front. There were many fewer workers here; over the course of the war, 1,900 saw active service. Of these, more than fifty were killed in action and over thirty spent time as prisoners of war.

Harrods was very lucky, bomb-wise. Early on, a small bomb slammed through the store's roof and started a fire in the Ladies Hairdressing Department, rapidly extinguished by staff ARP workers and the building's sprinklers. In fact, water from the sprinklers was more of a problem than the fire, but all was quickly made right and Harrods opened on time. May 1941 bombs—including one high explosive and three dozen incendiaries—meant multiple fires and the loss of most of the store windows. Then came a doodlebug, a direct hit on the Estate Office opposite the main store along Brompton Road. The blast shattered what windows Harrods had left and scattered glass and dust throughout the store. The Estate Office was not so lucky; the blast left an ugly gap in the shopfronts along the street, with the building essentially vaporized into a small pile of chunky rubble.

VISITOR DETAILS: Harrods on Brompton Road is open Monday–Saturday 10am to 7pm. Entrance guards ensure a certain level of propriety, so behave yourself and forget the shorts. Cafés and restaurants; alternatively, gather a picnic feast in the food halls and head for Kensington Gardens. Restrooms (ladies, be ready with a pound entrance fee). More information: 020 7730 1234, www.harrods.com.

Firefighters contend with dying embers on London's wartime streets.

PART II
BELGRAVIA, CHELSEA, & PIMLICO

...Number 38 [Eaton Square] is empty; others have been turned into soldiers' hostels. The garden...is now disfigured by asphalt pavement, under which are public air raid shelters....The garden to the east is filled with huge emergency tanks for the fire brigade....Came home footsore and weary.
—GENERAL RAYMOND E. LEE, *LONDON JOURNAL*, APRIL 27, 1941

A Londoner considers her shelter options.

Highlights: Belgrave and Eaton squares, National Army Museum, Chelsea Royal Hospital, Chelsea Physic Garden, Chelsea Old Church, Westminster Cathedral, Tate Britain

Underground Stations: Hyde Park Corner for Belgrave Square; Sloane Square for Eaton Square and Chelsea; Victoria for Westminster Cathedral; Pimlico for Tate Britain

Photo Ops: Plaques honoring London's notables abound in posh Belgravia. For a more global perspective, photo the metropolis from the bell tower of Westminster Cathedral.

BEFORE LEAVING ON YOUR TRIP

■ **Travel Scheduling:** Art lovers, if you have some travel flexibility, check the Tate's website for upcoming exhibitions and plan accordingly.

■ **Cultural Preparations:** It may be time to rediscover Glenn Miller. Two great CD collections are *The Best of Lost Recordings and Secret Broadcasts* and *In the Mood: The Very Best of Glenn Miller*. And check your PBS-TV listings to see if *Goodnight Sweetheart*, the bittersweet story of a man who can slip between the 1940s and 1990s at will, is being broadcast locally. Great homefront details and humorous too.

■ **Internet Best Bets:** Chelsea Old Church's website includes photographs and detailed information on the wartime bombing: www.chelseaoldchurch.org.uk.

Consider walking two elegant Belgravia squares: Belgrave Square near Hyde Park Corner, and Eaton Square, between Sloane Street and Grosvenor Place, both with homefront connections.

Belgrave Square was the wartime home of Henry "Chips" Channon; we've met this political bon vivant, diarist, and gossip earlier in these pages, and finally we see where he lived. In 1935 Channon and his then-wife Lady Honor Guinness (the money in the family—think beer) moved into Belgrave Square. Their exquisite home at Number 5 was the unfortunate recipient of wartime bomb blast, badly damaging the portico and splashing masonry and broken columns everywhere. Windows on the south side of Channon's home were blown in, and a guest's car parked nearby was left battered and charred. Even the resilient "Chips" found the experience distressing, although he managed to laugh and joke about the destruction. He made sure his guests and the local ARP warden had drinks (though not, of course, the Krug '20 from the wine cellar—there *are* limits), then he toured his blasted home, and so to bed.

> At least one visitor found staid Belgravia a bit formidable. "Walking through Belgrave Square, I suspect the flash of a lorgnette at the window, and, as I hurry away, am pursued by a dowager's unstrung voice asking, 'Who was that person?'"

Other wartime occupants in Belgrave Square included the British Red Cross Society at Numbers 7 and 8, the Portuguese Embassy at Number 11, the Austrian Legation at Number 18, the Spanish Embassy at Number 24, the French Red Cross at Number 25, the Polish Hearth at Number 45—well, you get the idea. To the north stands Robert Grosvenor, a telling quote from John Ruskin on the statue's plinth: "When we build let us think we build forever." Walking Belgrave Square, note the classy touches—fanlights, wood doors, marble steps, wooden interior shutters, and everywhere, elegant cream-colored stucco, built to last forever though all well-jolted by the bombs of London's war.

Eaton Square, a much larger area, is actually a six-part rectangle in mid-Belgravia. The trench shelter constructed in the garden area in front of Numbers 40 through 48, surrounded by garden allotments, took two direct hits from high explosive bombs in May 1941, killing six people and injuring another eleven. Tree bark was stripped off, the iron railings (not yet gone for armaments) were blasted to the ground, and the garden plots were plowed under, a devastation that's hard to believe looking

at this pleasant area today. It's almost as hard to imagine the dignified atmosphere of Eaton Square broken with the clucking and crowing of poultry, but ARP wardens kept a large flock of chickens here in 1941 and 1942.

> *If you walk to the National Army Museum along Chelsea's Flood Street, watch for the garden of remembrance at the corner of Redesdale Street.*

Numerous plaques on Eaton Square walls highlight the homes of former residents. Prime Minister Neville Chamberlain lived at 37 Eaton Square in the mid-1920s and 1930s. Stanley Baldwin lived at Number 93 from 1913 to 1923; he was prime minister just before Chamberlain, during the 1936 abdication crisis. Number 86 was home to Lord Halifax, Foreign Secretary from 1938 to 1940 and British ambassador to the U.S. in the early 1940s. A player in other dramas, actress Vivien Leigh, lived at 54 Eaton Square; her greatest movie, *Gone with the Wind*, was a popular wartime hit in London. Number 103, the wartime (and current) Belgian Embassy, has a large wall plaque honoring Belgian volunteers.

> **VISITOR DETAILS:** The National Army Museum on Royal Hospital Road is open daily 10am to 5:30pm. Shop and small café; restrooms in the lower level. More information: 020 7730 0717, www.national-army-museum.ac.uk.

Chelsea's **National Army Museum** on Royal Hospital Road follows the British soldier from the Middle Ages to the Victorian age and on through two world wars. There are enough dioramas, photos, sound effects, and models here to satisfy the most attention-challenged. The World War II section, "From World War to Cold War—The British Army 1914–1968," features several campaigns, including Dunkirk, Operation Overlord, and the Far East. The major homefront touch is a diorama depicting weapons training in a countryside village hall. Several homefront uniforms are on display, including the gear of the LDV (Local Defense Volunteers, later the Home Guard) and the ATS. There's even a "demob" suit, the demobilization clothing issued to soldiers after war's end. If the uniforms, fancy medals, small arms, and large tanks begin to make your eyes glaze over, pause at the grave marker in the middle of the Japanese POW camp display. Its inscription will bring you back to the reality of military conflict: "When you go home, Tell them of us and say, For your tomorrow, We gave our today."

> *The museum at the Chelsea Royal Hospital includes a 250-kg. bomb dropped on the hospital.*

The **Chelsea Royal Hospital**, next door to the National Army Museum, opened in the 1680s as a refuge for old soldiers "broken by war." It still houses elderly unmarried war veterans having no other source of income, and you'll see them about London in their long red coats (in summertime) or blue winter coats.

Blue Plaques, Brown Plaques, and Other Plaques

Plaques marking war-related residences or sites can be found throughout London. The following addresses, either beyond areas we've walked or not appearing in "Footsteps of the Famous," are worth seeking out if you're in the neighborhood. Postal codes are added to aid in locating addresses.

North of Central London

54 Delancey Street, NW1: Poet Dylan Thomas (who had worked on wartime documentary film screenplays and BBC broadcasts) lived here briefly after the war.

20 Frognal Way, NW3: Wartime singer and comic Gracie Fields "built this house for herself" in 1934.

31 Pond Street, NW3: Biologist Julian Huxley lived here from 1943 to 1975; as secretary to the Zoological Society of London, he effectively served as Zoo director in the early war years. Another plaque, shared with Huxley's brother Aldous and father Leonard, is at 16 Bracknell Gardens, NW3.

3 The Grove, Highgate, N6: Wartime playwright and author J. B. Priestley lived here.

West of Central London

11 Wymering Mansions, Wymering Road, W9: Vera Brittain lived here; the author and pacifist also resided at 58 Doughty Street, WC1, where she shares a plaque with friend Winifred Holtby, a novelist and feminist.

2 Maida Avenue, W2: Comic actor Arthur Lowe, Captain Mainwaring in *Dad's Army*, lived here. If you're a fan of the TV series, a plaque at Barons

This place seemed particularly singled out for attention by the Luftwaffe. Frances Faviell in *A Chelsea Concerto* noted that after multiple bombings, the pensioners insisted that "Hitler knew that the place was under the administration of the War Office, and that it was bombed with intention." More likely it was its location along the Thames between two bridges. Whatever the reason, the 500 or so residents grumbled the requisite soldierly amount and remained calm, "as befits war veterans." Out by Royal Hospital Road, wartime trenches were dug, and various hospital sites were designated as shelters—including the beer cellar.

During one attack, German bombs showered down upon the complex of buildings, and several time bombs necessitated temporary removal of

Keep, Hammersmith, W14, marks the home of comic John Le Mesurier, who played Sergeant Wilson.

Porchester Square, W2: Szmul "Artur" Zygielbojm lived here; a Polish-Jewish wartime leader and representative to the Polish Parliament-in-exile, he "took his life in protest at the world's indifference to Nazi extermination of the Jews."

33 Melbury Court, Kensington High Street, W8: Wartime political cartoonist David Low lived here.

2 Warrington Crescent, W9: Alan Turing, codebreaker, scientist, and chief scientific figure at Bletchley Park, was born here.

South and East of Central London

26 Gwendolen Avenue, Putney, SW15: Dr. Edward Benes, president of Czechoslovakia, lived here from 1938 to 1940, the beginning of his seven-year exile from his homeland.

44 Craigton Road, Eltham, SE9: American comic Bob Hope was born here in 1903; Hope spent the war years entertaining troops overseas.

55 Archery Road, Eltham, SE9: Herbert Morrison, Home Secretary in the war cabinet and proponent of the Morrison shelter, lived here from 1929 to 1960.

277–281 New Cross Road, SE14: This is the site of Britain's worst V-2 attack; 168 people were killed.

Bethnal Green Underground Station, E1: This is the site of the war's worst civilian disaster; 173 men, women, and children died descending the steps to the Bethnal Green Underground air raid shelter.

Railway Bridge, Grove Road, Bow, E3: This is the site of the first V-1 flying bomb to fall on London, June 13, 1944.

24 Rossendale Street, E5: This is the site of the Air Raid Precaution Centre for North Hackney, built in 1938 and used throughout the war.

the residents. When one of the bombs finally exploded, a section of the largest barracks building was crushed, with splintered oaken beams and rubble strewn about. A somewhat overwrought *New York Times* journalist sent this report home: "Here were three floors lined with cubicles that have sheltered veterans who have fought for the empire under Marlborough on the Continent, Clive in India, Wolfe at Quebec, Wellington in Spain and Flanders. The cubicles, laden with medals and mementos, cascaded to the ground, while the torn building itself trembled like a wounded veteran." In a mid-April 1941 attack, a parachute mine badly damaged the infirmary, causing sufficient damage that the building eventually had to be demolished. There were thirteen casualties among the

VISITOR DETAILS: Chelsea Royal Hospital on Royal Hospital Road is open Monday–Saturday 10am to noon and 2pm to 4pm; Sunday 2pm to 4pm. Museum and shop open the same hours, but only April–September. Chapel services are open to the public. More information: 020 7730 5282.

hospital's old soldiers, and five died in a January 1945 rocket attack on the North East Wing in Light Horse Court. Maybe the Germans *were* aiming for the place.

Bomb rubble, usually piled up and hauled off from London's demolished houses and buildings, was here carefully cleared away, every brick and tile put in safe-keeping for use in the eventual repairs, and restoration has been seamlessly completed on this elegant Wren–designed landmark. Call to arrange a tour (a week's notice is usually required) or take an unguided wander through the Great Hall, Chapel, and excellent small museum.

Plant lovers, don't miss **Chelsea Physic Garden**. There's no fireweed here (the weed that grew in London's bomb sites), but you'll find plenty of medicinal plants, a restored 1773 rock garden, carnivorous plants, and even a grass garden, all in a sheltered idyllic setting.

The garden's statue of Hans Sloane (a copy of the one in the British Museum) was bricked-in for the duration, though sandbag pressure broke one arm. Staff did duty as firewatchers, retreating to bomb shelters erected in the medicinal plant area of the garden when the going got rough. Wisely, some of the rarer plants were evacuated to Kew Gardens, as German bombs shattered greenhouse glass and essentially rototilled plant beds. And with the Embankment rail-ings taken away for armaments and local children sneaking into this magical place, staff feared they'd either poison themselves on the medicinal plants or fall into one of the ponds. A protective fence of chestnut stakes was erected around the riverside.

VISITOR DETAILS: Chelsea Physic Garden on Royal Hospital Road is open April–October on Wednesday noon to 5pm, and Sunday 2pm to 6pm. Admission is charged. Tea room; restrooms. More information: 020 7352 5646, www.chelsea physicgarden.co.uk.

On The Wednesday, that mid–April night near the end of the Blitz, **Chelsea Old Church** on Old Church Street and Cheyne Walk was shredded by German bombs in an attack that would continue for eight hours, killing over a thousand Londoners and injuring twice that many. Much of Chelsea was affected but the area around the church was the worst, with mountains of rubble, dozens of people buried, dust rising

A typical London street postwar...or prewar?

like fog, droning German planes overhead, bombs still falling, and the phrase heard over and over, "The church is gone. The church is gone."

What had been bombed into oblivion was a lovely building, its chancel dating from the thirteenth century, its More chapel the private chapel of Thomas More. And reputedly Henry VIII married Jane Seymour here. Luckily many of the memorials and monuments inside had been removed to safety or were reparable. And amazingly some parts of the building did survive, including much of the east end and the More Chapel. Around the survivors a new Chelsea Old Church was built. In an effort to recapture some sense of history, the churchwomen instituted embroidered kneelers in the 1950s. Hundreds have been made over the years, each commemorating a former parishioner or someone connected with the church—saints, kings, landowners, and ordinary folks. Walk the aisles and check them out. Toward the

> **VISITOR DETAILS:** Chelsea Old Church on Old Church Street is open daily 2pm to 5:30pm, when volunteer guides or the verger can show you around. More information: 020 7795 1019, www.chelsea oldchurch.org.uk.

back is a kneeler honoring Yvonne Green, a Canadian fire warden who died here on that devastating April night in 1941; nearby is a kneeler honoring the five firewatchers killed.

North of Victoria Station, you can't miss **Westminster Cathedral** towering over its Pimlico neighborhood. It's the principal Catholic Church in England and the Mother Church of the Diocese of Westminster. The

striking design is unmistakable—
the early Christian Byzantine style
features red brick with Portland
stone bands. Westminster Cathedral
opened for worship in 1903, and the
interior remains unfinished. Consider the vaulted ceiling and how
spectacular it will be when the marble work and mosaics are completed.

Religious services continue most
of the day, but generally in one of the
smaller side chapels, so it's easy and
acceptable to walk around the nave,
the widest in England. Sculptor Eric
Gill's fourteen Stations of the Cross
adorn the columns. On the left is
the Chapel of St. George and the
Martyrs of England, with several
memorials honoring war partici-
pants, including Catholic officers of

Westminster Cathedral.

the Royal Army Service Corps. Long tablets here are inscribed with the
names of church members who died in World War II, and a third memorial commemorates the Polish Armed Forces. The
funeral mass for Polish General Sikorski took place
here, attended by members of the Polish government-in-exile and Prime Minister Churchill.

> It's only three blocks
> from Westminster
> Cathedral north to
> Politicos Bookstore (8
> Artillery Row), London's
> most intriguing political
> bookshop and coffee
> house.

The Cathedral has a renowned choir, and musical CDs and cassettes are available in the shop,
which tends more toward the Roman Catholic
than the English Heritage retail effect. Downstairs
Cathedral Kitchen, an old-fashioned eatery, is per-
fect if you've been longing for beans on toast. This area most likely served
as a wartime shelter—though no shelter signs remain, the thick walls are a
sure indication of a place of safety and undoubtedly provided a comforting solidity to parishioners while ARP firewatchers battled incendiaries
on the Cathedral's roof. You can get a hint of the wartime firefighting
experience by looking out over London from the tower, 280-plus feet
above the pavement.

Tate Britain (formerly the Tate Gallery) is a bit out of the tourist
mainstream, but it's a must-see not only for art lovers but also for anyone

seeking wartime nuance in unexpected places. This gallery of British art (primarily 1600 on) was established when Sir Henry Tate donated his art collection and £80,000 for a new building to house it. Erected on the site of the Millbank Prison on land donated by the government, the Tate opened in 1897 and quickly became one of London's most popular galleries. If you'd like to pay homage to Sir Henry, think kindly of him the next time you put a sugar cube in your tea; he invented that sweet package.

Just a week before war was declared, the Tate Gallery closed to the public. As the last visitor filed out, gallery director John Rothenstein mused on what a momentous step

> **VISITOR DETAILS:** Westminster Cathedral on Victoria Street is open daily 7am to 7pm. Charge for the tower lift (open daily, April–November 9am to 5pm; winters, Thursday–Sunday, 9am to 5pm). Sound tours are available. Small shop and café; head to Victoria Station for restrooms. More information: 020 7798 9055, www.westminstercathedral.org.uk.

was being taken: "I wondered how many years would pass before these doors were opened.…Books were obtainable almost everywhere; music could be broadcast, but these doors (and those of the National Gallery, which were closed at about the same time) were shutting out the people from visual arts."

After the doors closed, the work began: packing and crating 4,000 art works for transport to various distant and much safer locations. Rodin's *The Kiss* stayed behind, but so well-sandbagged as to be unrecognizable. Early in September 1940, Rothenstein decided to spend nights as well as days at the Tate, and he and his wife moved in. Staff had carefully outfit-

The prewar look of the Tate Gallery.

ted one of the empty galleries with a carpet, bedside table, and a vase of flowers. The well-meaning decorators, however, had forgotten to look up: Rothenstein did, noting "there was nothing between us and the huge glass roof and, before the night was over, at many points there was nothing between us and the sky." The next night Rothenstein and his wife moved to the Tate's basement, a wise move as within a week really serious bombing began.

In mid-September 1940 an explosion of unbelievable violence shook the entire building, followed by rumbling crashes and the ever-ominous sound of breaking glass. Glass

shards and masonry fell with every thunderous shaking shot from the nearby anti-aircraft guns. "Acres of glass roofing had disappeared, and daggers of glass, some as high as a man and others minute, were lodged upright in the surrounding lawn." The blast had been strong enough to toss street paving-stones on to the top of gallery walls and roof beams, and to essentially vaporize the upper part of the Tate's east wall.

One way to put out a fire...

That was the worst night of devastation, but not the last. Later in September another bombing raid shook the building, blowing out what glass remained; a few weeks later, rain began to fall and the galleries flooded. Even when the roof was finally covered by tarpaulins, the damp, dark galleries never really dried out—and then there was the burnt flooring, the result of a clutch of incendiary bombs in January 1941. By Blitz's end, the Tate had no roof and few doors or windows. Repairs, it was estimated, would take years.

Some of the grassy areas around the Tate Gallery were turned over to wartime garden allotments.

Although the Tate suffered more severe damage than any other London art gallery or museum, the collection survived intact except for the loss of one painting being restored; unfortunately, the restorer's studio was bombed. And when the war was finally over, the Tate had to stand in line with other museums, galleries, organizations, businesses, and just plain folks trying to get repairs made. It took a year and some governmental arm-twisting, but six small galleries were finally restored, their gleaming new paint in sharp contrast to the desolation around them. In April 1946, with dozens of paintings retrieved from storage in the English countryside, the Tate Gallery re-opened,

> *Those chips and pits along the Tate's exterior walls, especially on the west side, are from wartime shrapnel and bomb dinging.*

featuring works by Braque, Cézanne, Rouault, and modern British painters. A huge crowd welcomed the "phoenix risen from the ashes," a crowd that may well have included every artist in London.

Bomb damage at the Tower of London, 1941.

PART III
ACROSS AND ALONG THE THAMES

Driving about one sees remarkable contrasts. You come across a huge crater or a row of wrecked houses, but, also, near the Tower of London I found magnificent dray-horses still quietly pulling their loads…and the old grey Tower itself sat there in the afternoon light as squat as it did centuries ago. There's something of the same enduring quality in Londoners themselves. They are sticking it out.

—JAMES LANSDALE HODSON, *THROUGH THE DARK NIGHT*, 1941

The Battle of London begins, September 3, 1939.

Highlights: Imperial War Museum, Britain at War Experience, HMS *Belfast*, Tower of London, Tower Bridge, Docklands and the East End

Underground Stations: Lambeth North for Imperial War Museum; London Bridge for Britain at War Experience and HMS *Belfast*; Tower Hill for Tower of London and Tower Bridge; the Jubilee line or Docklands Light Railway for Docklands and the East End

Photo Ops: The guns by the Imperial War Museum, with raised barrels sometimes lost in low-lying fog, make for a good shot.

BEFORE LEAVING ON YOUR TRIP

■ **Travel Scheduling:** You can't beat a gun salute for drama—and a reminder of war's ferocity. These take place at the Tower of London at 1pm on the day of Royal events (or the next day if the date falls on Sunday): February 6, Accession Day; April 21, the Queen's birthday; June 2, Coronation Day; and June 10, the Duke of Edinburgh's birthday.

■ **Cultural Preparations:** Read David Fraser's novel *Blitz* for graphic scenes of fire-fighting along the Thames.

■ **Internet Best Bets:** The Imperial War Museum (www.iwm.org.uk) has a fine online shop plus links to other IWM sites, including the HMS *Belfast*. Don't miss www.britainat war.co.uk for the Britain at War Experience; be prepared for online warning sirens and the sound of bombs exploding.

The **Imperial War Museum** is set in a dreary part of London, with streets wider and lonelier than the posher bits on the other side of the river. Buildings tend toward the ugly modern or slightly unkempt two-story brown brick, and it's likely a weed-filled lot or a gap in a row of houses is evidence of a successful German air raid. But once through the museum gates, the drab surroundings are forgotten—the Imperial War Museum is a surprise from the moment one enters. It focuses on the wars of the twentieth century, neither glorifying nor avoiding the horror. This isn't a dry and dusty museum of the distant past, but six floors of history, art, and artifacts focused on "the heroes, the villains, and the millions who are neither" at home and on the battlefield.

> The Holocaust exhibit at the Imperial War Museum is a haunting experience. But I must confess—I haven't yet been able to visit the entire exhibit. Every time I've tried, some desperately poignant item stops me cold, and I decide I'll finish another day.

Start with the light and airy Large Exhibits Gallery in the lobby, where a U.S. Army jeep, a 90cm searchlight, and a V-2 rocket share floor space with tanks, a howitzer, an armored car, a U-boat, and a one-man submarine. Overhead swarms a V-1 flying bomb, a P-51 Mustang, a Spitfire, and more.

The downstairs galleries focus on World War I, World War II, and conflicts since 1945. In the World War II gallery, line up for the Blitz Experience, a reconstruction of an air raid shelter and a blitzed neighborhood. You and your fellow shelterers can join in singing "Roll Out the Barrel" in the darkened bomb shelter and then wander a blasted London street, with the sights, sounds, and smells of war all around. Okay, it's a bit hokey, but the Blitz Experience offers some idea of what war-torn London was like. Just multiply today's tingle of apprehension when the lights go out or that surge of adrenaline when the "bomb" hits by about a thousand and you'll have a hint of the emotions experienced by millions of Londoners as the Luftwaffe's planes droned overhead.

Follow your Blitz Experience with a walk through displays featuring the Phoney War, the German Blitzkrieg of Western Europe, and military campaigns in the Mediterranean, Far East, and Russia. Closer to

Imperial War Museum.

Wartime Plants

With the focused intensity of the English, much note was taken of the plants taking root in the nooks and crannies of London's bomb sites, and many a letter to the *Times* pointed out the latest blooms discovered in the rubble. Green and golden fennel sprouted, as did vetch and nettles, purple milkwort and spiked purple loosestrife, coltsfoot and the ever-determined bramble. Two of the most remarked-upon plants were Oxford ragwort, a plant that usually flourished in the volcanic ash on Sicily around Mount Etna, and rosebay willowherb, commonly known as fireweed. This tall perennial with its rose-tinted blooms and long pointed leaves popped up in areas devastated by fire, a verdant camouflage for London's scars.

The vicar of St. James's, Piccadilly, counted twenty-three different varieties of wild plants behind his bombed altar.
—Cecil Beaton, *Memoirs of the 40s*

home, the Battle of Britain and homefront galleries are filled with artifacts, posters, photos, uniforms, signs, and more. You'll see what the bombs falling on London really looked like (the nine-foot-tall parachute mine is especially nasty), listen to a woman who was at the Café de Paris the night it was bombed, and watch an amateur film showing London wartime scenes. And check out the cozy Anderson shelter.

Don't overlook the art galleries on the upper floors, with memorable artwork by Paul Nash, Henry Moore, Graham Sutherland, John Piper, and other World War II artists. Check at the Information Desk for current exhibit details.

The Imperial War Museum is London's most sobering, most absorbing collection of wartime history. It's a must-stop for the homefront enthusiast and for anyone interested in the mechanics and memories of recent wars. However, you may want to balance your visit with a walk in the nearby Tibetan Peace Garden, dedicated by the Dalai Lama in 1999.

The **Britain at War Experience** near Tower Bridge is a theme museum focused on homefront details—sheltering in the Underground or an Anderson shelter, food and clothing rationing, American soldiers at the Rainbow Club, a ticking time bomb, BBC radio broadcasts, a Drury Lane dressing room, and much more. Posters, photos, sound effects,

VISITOR DETAILS: The Imperial War Museum on Lambeth Road is open daily 10am to 6pm. Excellent shop and café; restrooms downstairs. More information: 020 7416 5320, www.iwm.org.uk.

and a recreation of a blitzed street are all here—but a trifle worn and dusty. On the other hand, more obscure items are on view, like a Morrison shelter and a wedding dress made from parachute silk. Best may well be conversations with other visitors—this place sparks lots of memories for older visitors. My co-shelterer in the Anderson shelter leaned over and confided, "When I hear the sirens, even now, I get an awful feeling in the pit of my stomach."

VISITOR DETAILS: The Britain at War Experience on Tooley Street is open daily April–September, 10am to 5:30pm; closes earlier in winter. Admission is charged. Small shop. More information: 020 7403 3171, www.britainatwar.co.uk.

HMS *Belfast* is Europe's only surviving big gun warship, a cruiser launched on St. Patrick's Day in 1938. The ship saw duty in both World War II and the Korean War, though her service in the former was interrupted by a two-year respite for repairs from a German magnetic mine. The *Belfast* was in service with the Royal Navy until 1965, and has been moored on the Thames since 1971. Maritime aficionados will want to know that the ship's overall length is 613 feet and 6 inches, her maximum speed 32 knots, and nearly 800 crewmembers called the *Belfast* home.

Today all nine decks of this floating museum are open. Explore the flag deck, the quarterdeck and fo'c'sle, all the way down to the boiler room and engine room. My favorites are the messdecks, the sickbay and dental surgery, the bakery and laundry—the shipboard homefronts where the crew lived. Incidentally, use that map on your ticket—every time I visit, the signage gets a little better, but every time I still get lost.

VISITOR DETAILS: HMS *Belfast* is open daily 10am to 6pm. Admission is charged. Disabled access to the main deck is good, but many of the other decks are inaccessible. Shop; Walrus Café; restrooms near the ship entrance and a level up. More information: 020 7940 6300, www.iwm.org.uk.

Across the Thames is the **Tower of London**, popular for its ancient history and its modern anachronisms; you might also want to consider its World War II connections.

Since the late 1000s, the Tower of London has served as palace, prison, fortress, arsenal, and treasury; its walls are thick, its towers high, and its moat wide. A variety of accused (guilty and not) have been imprisoned here: Lady Jane Grey, Sir Walter Raleigh, Thomas More, Elizabeth I, and Thomas Cromwell. Here too are the Crown Jewels—the Royal treasures and regalia—and more armor and medieval weapons than you can shake a sword at. The Yeomen Warders, known as Beefeaters, conduct guided tours laced with anecdotes and atmosphere, and costumed guides stroll the grounds and buildings, ready to answer questions.

The Tower of London closed to the public with the outbreak of war and remained closed for the war's duration. Tours for visiting members of the Allied Forces were eventually established, however, led as today by Beefeaters; it's estimated that 75 to 80 percent of American troops who came to England toured the Tower of London. Unfortunately, they all missed the Crown Jewels, which had been evacuated to a far safer location.

The Tower's Yeomen and their families remained in residence throughout the war, and several military units were also garrisoned here, including an RAF detachment that operated a barrage balloon from the west moat. Members of the Women's RAF later took over balloon duties and lived in huts constructed in the moat. Not to worry— the moat had been drained almost a hundred years before. Besides serving as a balloon tethering spot, the moat was also used for victory garden allotments and was bombed at least twice. No air raid trench shelters were dug in the Tower of London, but several basement rooms—including one in the White Tower—were used as refuges for families and Warders not on duty.

> **VISITOR DETAILS:** The Tower of London near Tower Hill is open Monday–Saturday 9am to 5pm; Sunday 10am to 5pm; closes earlier in winter. Admission is charged. Many steps and cobblestoned walkways. Café, snack kiosks, and restaurant; restrooms. More information: 0870 756 6060, www.hrp.org.uk, www.tower-of-london.org.uk.

In the course of the war, over a dozen high explosive bombs fell within the Tower's environs and several flying bombs exploded nearby. Uncounted incendiaries were dropped, and it was only the vigilant firewatchers that kept the medieval precincts from going up in flames. None of the really older buildings were destroyed, but German bombs demolished several newer structures, including the North Bastion, Queen Victoria's Canteen, the Master of the Assay Office on the Tower's western side, and the Main Guard building. The last was a victim of German incendiaries combined with low water pressure and high winds. It burned to the ground and has since been rebuilt.

The Old Hospital Block on the eastern side served early on to house German prisoners. By May 1940 they had all been removed for detention elsewhere; just four months later German bombs partly demolished the building. Actually, every building

The Tower soon after the war.

Text continued on page 320.

Photo Ops with Cecil Beaton

January 14, 1904: Cecil Walter Hardy Beaton is born at 21 Langland Gardens, Hampstead in north London, where he lives until 1911. (A plaque there notes his residence.)

Early 1920s–late 1970s: Beaton's childhood interest in photography grows more serious as the amateur photographer eventually becomes an internationally known professional society, fashion, and portrait photographer. His other talents enable him to become a diarist, caricaturist, author, social historian, wit, and set and costume designer for stage and film.

July 1930: Beaton rents Ashcombe, an eighteenth-century home in the Wiltshire hills near Salisbury, about eighty miles southwest of London. He will remain here until 1945.

September 3, 1939: Beaton and his mother, sitting together in the Ashcombe parlor, hear Chamberlain's wireless announcement of the declaration of war.

September 1939: Eager to help in the war effort and aware that his society connections provide a weak resume, Beaton offers his services to various governmental agencies: he's willing to use his artistic experience in the Camouflage Department, or he'll even drive refugees to safety in the countryside. Neither offer is accepted. Eventually Beaton staffs an ARP Control Center telephone switchboard in Wiltshire.

Winter 1939: Beaton moves into 8 Pelham Place, South Kensington (still standing, it remains a private home). Built in the 1820s, the small row house was later described by "Chips" Channon as "a tiny but super-attractive snuff-box of a house." Beaton will use this as his London home and workshop for many years.

1940–1945: Beaton's skills are finally put to use: he photographs military leaders (General Ironside, Chief of the Imperial General Staff) and cabinet ministers (Anthony Eden and Ernest Bevin). Other wartime commissions include Edwina Mountbatten, Clementine Churchill, and King Zog of Albania. Beaton also works for the Ministry of Information taking documentary photographs on special assignment. One of the most famous—a young girl with bandaged head sitting in a hospital bed, clutching a stuffed toy—appears on the cover of *Life* magazine (September 23, 1940).

Autumn 1940: Beaton and James Pope-Hennessy begin collaborating on the book *History Under Fire* (1941) to show that "while certain things are frankly gone for ever, London on the whole is not so badly damaged."

September 1940: Beaton visits 10 Downing Street to photograph Clementine Churchill. "She insisted on showing me the whole house, and I was an avid sightseer."

November 10, 1940: Arriving at 10 Downing Street to photograph the prime minister, Beaton must deal with a very grouchy subject. The result is one of the best photos ever taken of Churchill.

1941: Beaton continues photographic work for the Ministry of Information, later writing about his experiences in *Winged Squadrons* (1942).

March 1942: Beaton journeys to the Middle East for more war photos, traveling for several months in Egypt, Palestine, Iraq, and Trans-Jordan. Later in the war he spends nine months capturing the war on film in India and China.

October 23, 1942: Beaton arrives at Buckingham Palace to photograph the Royal Family with their American visitor, Eleanor Roosevelt.

October 1944–May 1945: Beaton is in Paris organizing a photo exhibit "to show the people of France what happened to England during the last four years."

June 1947: Beaton buys Reddish House (£10,000) in Broadchalke in Wiltshire. He will live here the rest of his life.

April 30, 1958: *My Fair Lady* opens at Drury Lane's Theatre Royal (still there) near Covent Garden after two years in New York; the play showcases fabulous costumes by Beaton. Later he will design the costumes for the movie *My Fair Lady* and garner an Oscar for costume design, an award that will go well with his Oscar for costumes in the movie *Gigi*.

February 3, 1972: Beaton is knighted at Buckingham Palace.

January 17, 1980: Cecil Beaton dies at Reddish House. The funeral is held at All Saints' Church in Broadchalke; Beaton is buried in the nearby churchyard.

Tower Bridge roadways were raised during wartime air raids, and there was probably as much sand and dust in the air then as there is now when the road goes up. For Tower Bridge opening times, call the Bridge Lift Line at 020 7940 3984.

in the Tower of London suffered war damage: broken windows and window frames, roof damage, falling ceilings, cracked plaster, dinged exterior walls. Over 1,200 alerts were sounded in the Tower's vicinity; the highest total—fourteen in one day—on July 21, 1944, when flying bombs were literally whizzing over London.

Naturally the war meant prisoners for England's most historic of prisons—besides the German POWs mentioned above, Herr Gerlach, German Consul in Iceland, was briefly imprisoned here in 1940. Most famous of all, though, was Rudolf Hess, Hitler's deputy, who inexplicably left Germany, flew to Scotland, parachuted to earth, was captured, and spent the rest of his life in prison, including four days here in the King's House, near the Tower's southwestern corner and now known as the Queen's House. A German spy was executed in 1941 near the miniature rifle range on the Tower's northeastern corner.

Tower Bridge—the one with the two towers joined by a roadway with a walkway 140 feet overhead—has spanned the Thames River since 1894. A walk across this Victorian edifice at street level is free and the views are spectacular. For an even more exciting adventure, including details on bridge history and machinery, take in the Tower Bridge Experience. The war experience of Tower Bridge was relatively benign. The control cabins, where the machinery is located that raises and lowers the central bascules, were covered with steel sheathing and piled high with sandbags, precautionary measures that proved prudent once the Blitz began. Explosions broke windows and roof slates and dinged and chipped the structure. The closest call came when a bomb exploded near the south shore span, injuring a handful of people with flying glass and debris. But yet another defiant symbol of London—along with Big Ben and St. Paul's Cathedral—survived Hitler's bombs intact.

VISITOR DETAILS: Tower Bridge is open all the time (except when a ship passes underneath); Tower Bridge Experience is open daily, 9:30am–5:30pm. Admission charged. Small shop. More information: 020 7940 3985, www.towerbridge.org.uk.

The London Blitz began at 4:56pm on September 7, 1940, when air raid sirens wailed a warning over the capital's streets. In a night-long attack, German planes unleashed a conflagration on **London's docks and**

Tower Bridge.

the East End, killing over 400 and injuring more than 1,600. The onslaught continued for a week, and then, inexplicably, Hitler's Luftwaffe ranged further westward, away from the valuable docks and crowded slums of the East End toward central London and the West End. The worst of the Blitz was to last for fifty-seven nights in a row.

Today this huge area is enjoying an enthusiastic rebirth, helped along by much improved transit access and the construction of the maligned Millennium Dome—many consider it one of the most exciting, fast-moving areas of the capital. And, even more so than the City, this area is characterized by an "if it's empty or new, it's probably because of the war" feel.

Investigate and enjoy the new pubs, markets, and shops of East London and the Docklands, wander Canary Wharf, stroll Greenwich Park. And imagine what this area was like during those devastating Blitz nights in September 1940, with German bombs dropping on Woolwich Arsenal, on the gasworks at Beckton, on the Surrey and Limehouse docks, and on the West Ham power station.... "All that night the sinister glow deepened under the enemy's ruthless bombing, and only paled before the slowly approaching dawn."

As German bombers droned over London in 1941, journalist Virginia Cowles wondered "if future historians will be able to visualize the majesty of this mighty capital; to picture the strange beauty of the darkened buildings in the moonlight; the rustle of the wind and the sigh of bombs; the long white fingers of the searchlights and the moan of shells travelling towards the stars. Will they understand how violently people died: how calmly people lived?"

A London lorry crowded with V-E Day revelers.

London: May 8, 1945

[I am] speaking from our Empire's oldest capital city, war-battered but never for one moment daunted or dismayed...the years of our darkness and danger in which the children of our country have grown up are over and, please God, for ever.

—KING GEORGE VI, MAY 8, 1945

At last, London's war is over. After five years, eight months, and four days of war, it's over. London's homefront is quiet. The only fires today will be bonfires to dance around, the only explosions those from firecrackers.

The day the war in Europe ended—V-E Day—begins with torrential rain, coincidentally the capital's biggest thunderstorm since a similar downpour early on September 3, 1939. London's morning slowly brightens, though, as flags are raised and bunting is draped and crowds gather, mostly in the West End, in the heart of the metropolis.

As usual, Prime Minister Winston Churchill starts his day working in bed at 10 Downing Street. On the morning of May 8, 1945, his work is a victory speech.

In Knightsbridge, a huge sign on Harrods proclaims "God Save the King" and above it rises a five-story-high "V." Queues line up early, then wind down Hans Crescent and around the corner. On this national day of celebration most stores are closed, but the government has approved the opening of the food halls and bank at Harrods. Customers are eager to buy something, anything, to celebrate and to remember victory. Harrods closes at 1pm, though it takes some effort to urge all the customers out.

At noon the prime minister and the king have their usual lunchtime meeting at Buckingham Palace. Unlike several meetings earlier in the war, they will not eat in the palace's air raid shelter.

At 3pm, from the Cabinet Room at 10 Downing Street, Churchill rumbles into a BBC radio microphone in that familiar voice: "Yesterday morning at 2:41am at [Eisenhower's] headquarters, General Jodl, the representative of the German High Command...signed the act of unconditional surrender....Hostilities will end officially at one minute after midnight tonight, but in the interests of saving lives, the cease-fire began yesterday....The German war is therefore at an end....Advance, Britannia! Long live the cause of freedom. God save the King!"

Thousands of Londoners have jammed into Parliament Square and on up Whitehall—the streets are closed to traffic and loudspeakers have been set up to relay Churchill's broadcast to the crowd. Pacifist Vera Brittain, feeling a little grumpy, is among those standing in Whitehall listening to Churchill's announcement. "Typically he ended with the words 'Advance Britannia' & introduced no phrase of constructive hope for a better society which renounces war." Luckily for Brittain, Churchill's message had

What if Britain Lost?

A recurring theme in postwar fiction is the "what if we lost?" scenario; here's a selected list to start you thinking.

The brief "diary" of *I, James Blunt* by H. H. Morton (1942) begins, "It is now five months since Germany won the War." What if German military bands played in Green Park, Trafalgar Square became Hitler Square, and worse, what if free speech were a memory and local dictators ruled the land? What if that ominous knock on the door meant...?

Norman Longmate's *If Britain Had Fallen* (1974) is part history, part fiction, and breathlessly wonders what if the Nazis invaded London, took Trafalgar Square, advanced across St. James's Park, and headed down Downing Street where a defiant Churchill stood with revolver in hand, and then...?

Operation Sealion by Richard Cox (1977), another historical/fictional mix, considers what if an elite force of German paratroopers landed on the beaches near Folkestone...?

In Len Deighton's *SS-GB: Nazi Occupied Britain, 1941* (1982), the master of wartime fiction asks what if the German Army occupied London and took King George prisoner...?

Finally, for a mesmerizing and unnerving cinematic experience of the "what if" variety, watch *It Happened Here*, a classic available on video. This black-and-white film re-imagines history: what if the Germans defeated the English in 1940, occupied England, and, worse, many British citizens become pro-German collaborators...?

> But it oughtn't to need a war to make a nation paint its kerbstones white, carry rearlamps on its bicycles, and give all its slum children a holiday in the country. And it oughtn't to need a war to make us talk to each other in buses, and invent our own amusements in the evenings, and live simply, and eat sparingly, and recover the use of our legs....However, it has needed one: which is about the severest criticism our civilization could have.
> —Jan Struther, *Mrs. Miniver*

been balanced by a talk she'd
attended earlier at the London
Mission at Kingsway Hall where
she heard an inspiring address
on thanksgiving, penitence, and
dedication.

Harold Nicolson is also in
the Whitehall crowd, one he
later describes as cheerful but not
exuberant. He stands in Parliament's Palace Yard where he
hears Churchill's radio announcement from loudspeakers there.
Then Nicolson enters the Palace
of Westminster, heading to his House of Commons seat to await the
prime minister's arrival.

With the conclusion of Churchill's announcement, the noise begins—
ships and boats along the Thames blow whistles and toot horns, sounding
the "dit dit dit dahh" of the V for Victory along the waters of the Thames.
Church bells peal, planes fly low over London, and most of all, people
gather to talk and sing, to dance and chant and shout.

Churchill leaves Downing Street via the garden gates onto Horse
Guards Parade, riding in an open car that slowly moves through the
crowd toward the House of Commons. It takes thirty minutes to travel a
quarter of a mile. Once inside Commons, he concludes his brief remarks
by suggesting, as occurred at the end of World War I, that the members
adjourn to St. Margaret's Church for a service of thanksgiving. Churchill
and his fellow MPs (including Harold Nicolson, Lady Astor, John
Anderson, and Herbert Morrison) walk through St. Stephen's Hall, across
the road, and into the small church. There they give thanks for this day
and remember the twenty-one Parliament members who fought and died
in the war. As the historic service ends, the bells of St. Margaret's ring out
in victory celebration.

At much the same time, more than 200 members of the House of
Lords attend similar services in Westminster Abbey, where the dean of the
Abbey reads a short prayer adapted from Abraham Lincoln's second inaugural address: "Grant, O merciful God, that with malice toward none, with
charity to all, with firmness in the right as thou givest us to see the right,
we may strive to finish the task." A few blocks away, outside the ruins of
the Guards Chapel, blasted apart by a V-1 rocket in June 1944, an
impromptu thanksgiving service is held.

War Words: Baedeker Raids

The **BAEDEKER RAIDS** or Baedeker blitz, a series of unexpected and devastating air bombings by the German Luftwaffe, took place from mid-April through May 1942. The nonmilitary English cities of York, Exeter, Bath, Canterbury, and Norwich were hit at various times during this period, and over 1,600 civilians were killed. Ostensibly, the term came from the German assertion that, in reprisal for British raids on the historic cities (i.e., nonmilitary targets) of Lübeck and Rostock, every building in Britain marked with three-stars in the well-known Baedeker's travel guide would be bombed. The horrific raid on Coventry in November 1940 was *not* a Baedeker Raid. In that instance, the Germans were more concerned with the factories of Coventry than with revenge.

Meanwhile "Chips" Channon is, as usual, hobnobbing about London, including lunch at the Ritz Hotel on Piccadilly where "everyone kissed me." Outside, the crowds are growing along the West End streets. American GIs and soldiers of the many other Allied Forces billeted in London have started climbing atop the boarded-up Eros Fountain in Piccadilly Circus, then sitting there and watching the crowds mill about below. The signs beneath their dangling legs urge "Support Your Savings Group. Save for the Future." Buses are immobilized by the crowd, and every lamppost has two or three agile young men clinging to it.

The hoardings around Nelson's Column in Trafalgar Square read "Victory over Germany 1945" as thousands sit on (and in) the fountains, climb astride the lions, dance in long conga lines, and generally gather. London's policemen, like Nelson high above, turn a blind eye on the revelry.

In Leicester Square, a huge "V" sign on a building greets the singing, dancing, shouting Londoners in the streets below. In Regent's Park, 2,669 people take time from their victory celebrations to visit the London Zoo. In the City, the Mansion House balcony is bedecked with crimson bunting, while Dominion flags fly above. The bells of St. Paul's Cathedral begin pealing at 11:30am, drawing crowds all along the nearby bomb-scarred streets. Informal thanksgiving services go on all day at St. Paul's, about one every hour, with hymns sung with "rare fervor."

Moving vehicles, those that still can navigate the jammed streets of the West End, attract first passengers, then riders, then hangers-on. Down the Strand comes a small truck, horn honking, with at least thirty celebrants clinging to it. Today, the petrol ration be damned.

Fires are lit. A huge bonfire blazes under the trees in Green Park, and an even larger fire lights up Hampstead Heath in north London, another in St. James's Park, and one near Oxford Circus. In fact, most London streets sport a bonfire somewhere along their length. For some Londoners, though, the reaction to the fires is mixed. A friend of pacifist Frances Partridge later writes, "Some bonfires were wonderful, bringing back the old ecstasies of staring into a fire, but also having that appalling smell of burning debris, too terrifyingly nostalgic of blitzes."

> *A communal grave for victims of the Blitz is located at the Westminster Council Cemetery, Hanwell, West London.*

Things are more positive inside the Savoy Hotel Restaurant on the Strand where Victory Night is just beginning, a "cheering, jostling carnival" with dozens of extra tables squeezed in to hold all those who'd been making reservations for this special evening ever since early 1941. Noël Coward is at Clemence Dane's flat in Covent Garden, listening to radio speeches by Churchill, Ike, Montgomery, and others. Then he heads toward Buckingham Palace, joining the thousands of other Londoners walking in the same direction. The new arrivals mix with those who've stood outside the palace gates for most of the day, enjoying the red tulips, munching lunch, listening to the prime minister on the loudspeakers, clambering about the Queen Victoria Memorial.

The London *Times* later describes this as a red, white, and blue crowd, with seemingly every other woman adorned with a rosette or ribbon in her hair. But perhaps, the *Times* allows, they owe something of their brightness "to the sombre background of the palace itself, with its myriad glassless windows and only a few of its clustered gateway lamps undimmed." Only the balcony was bright, bedecked with gold-fringed crimson cloth. Now the chants begin: "We want the king. We want the king." Finally out comes the Royal Family onto the balcony, first the queen in a hat, of course, and a dress of powder-blue, then King George bareheaded in naval uniform, and finally the two princesses, Elizabeth in her ATS uniform and Margaret in a blue dress. They wave, the crowd cheers, they step back inside.

Photographer Cecil Beaton is in the crowd in front of Buckingham Palace, shouting with them, louder this time, "We want the king! We want the king!" There they are again on the balcony, and then Beaton notes, "Something remarkable happens. The diminutive personages bring forth another figure. It is none other than Winston Churchill. That he, a commoner, is here on the balcony with the reigning family is a break with tradition, but no one denies him this honor since he is the man who, perhaps more than anyone else, has brought us to victory."

> Over 50,000 memorials commemorate and honor participants in, and events of, Britain's wars.

The cheering rises to an unbelievable crescendo, continuing for five minutes as the great man smiles at the crowd, waves his cigar, flashes his V for Victory sign, and steps back inside Buckingham Palace.

John Rothenstein, director of the Tate Gallery, is here too, mingling with the crowds outside the palace gates; but he has work to do at the "derelict Tate" and stays only briefly. He misses the repeat appearances of the Royal Family as they are called to the palace balcony again and again by the enthusiastic cheering, eight times in all. The two young princesses, eager to join the excitement, are allowed to slip out a side door with a group from the palace, heading down the Mall. "We cheered the King and Queen on the balcony and then walked miles through the streets. I remember lines of unknown people linking arms and walking down Whitehall, all of us just swept along on a tide of happiness and relief." It was a night a princess—a queen—would remember decades later.

Meanwhile Edward R. Murrow is on the air from Broadcasting House, reporting London's victory reactions to his radio listeners in America. They range from voices overheard singing "Roll Out the Barrel" to those who appear unmoved by the joy. "Their minds must be filled with memories of friends who died in the streets where they now walk." Outside Broadcasting House, the Russian, American, and British flags flutter above the entrance, and down the side of the building another twenty-two Allied flags are unfurled. And then the floodlights are turned on.

> *Wars come to an end, but London goes on.*
> —H. V. Morton, *The Ghosts of London*

Slowly, throughout a city that has lived in medieval darkness for over five years, the lights come on. Big Ben stands bathed in light. The Palace of Westminster glows. Westminster Abbey, the lake in St. James's Park, Admiralty Arch, the National Gallery, St. Martin-in-the-Fields, St. Paul's Cathedral, the Tower of London, even the Chelsea Town Hall, all are floodlit tonight.

There will be another appearance by Churchill, just before 6pm. From the bunting-decorated central balcony at King Charles and Parliament streets, Churchill stands waving to the assembled multitudes stretching from the Cenotaph to Parliament Square. Microphones are set up to broadcast on the radio and to the loudspeakers below. On a nearby balcony proudly cluster several of the war's military leaders: Marshal of the RAF Sir Charles Portal, Field Marshal Sir Alan Brooke, and Admiral of the Fleet Sir Andrew Cunningham. The crowd: We want Winnie! We want Winnie! The prime minister steps to the microphone and begins by shouting to the ecstatic throng below, "This is your victory!" Then, "It is the victory of the cause of freedom in every land. In all our long history we have never seen a greater day than this. Everyone, man or woman, has done his best. Everyone has tried. Neither the long years, nor the dangers, nor the fierce attacks of the enemy, have in any way weakened the deep

War Words: Land Girls

LAND GIRLS were young urban women sent to the countryside to work as farm workers in place of the many rural men who had gone to war. A fictional retelling of the experience is *The Land Girls* by Angela Huth (1996), a sweet story that details the arduous wartime farm work involved and how remarkably well most young women adapted. The book has been made into a 1998 movie by the same title, available on video. When traveling through England's countryside, consider that many of the farms you pass were kept going through the war years by hairdressers from London, stenographers from York, and library clerks from Birmingham.

War Words: Buzzbombs and Doodlebugs

The V-1 flying rockets falling on England in 1944 and 1945 elicited several nicknames from their human targets, including **BUZZBOMBS** (from the splutter of the rocket) and **DOODLEBUGS** (probably referring to their randomness). A few carefree characters even referred to the rockets as "Bob Hopes" ("bob down and hope for the best"). At first the authorities—worried about the public's response to the unpredictability of the attacks—refused to explain the flying bomb concept, announcing instead the mighty explosions of local gas mains. So the pilotless planes were jokingly referred to by some as "exploding gas mains." The noise of the "beastly flame-tailed" things was actually preferable to the utter silence of the V-2 rockets. There were no nicknames for the V-2.

resolve of the British nation. God bless you all." At the conclusion of Churchill's brief remarks, the crowd sings "For He's a Jolly Good Fellow."

From the balcony of the Rainbow Club on Shaftesbury Avenue, an Air Force band plays for the crowd below, including that old standard, "Pack up your troubles in your old kit bag and smile, smile, smile." The street is tightly packed with flag-waving celebrants who know all the words and sing along.

At 9pm loudspeakers stationed around the capital's gathering places carry yet another speech to the celebrating crowds, the words of King George broadcasting a victory message to his people. Some 60,000 stand listening in Trafalgar Square, and at the speech's end, they enthusiastically sing "God Save the King."

And then oh my, the searchlights. A few had swept the skies earlier, but starting at 11:45pm the official dance begins as the capital's searchlights, hundreds of them, careen for a half hour across the skies, for once not seeking tiny silver crosses of German airplanes.

Beneath the searchlight beams, Londoners gather in silence at the foot of Big Ben, thousands standing along Westminster Bridge, filling Whitehall's streets, waiting in Parliament Square. At midnight, Big Ben tolls the hour, slowly, twelve long times. Tolling for the dead, tolling for the survivors, tolling for this magnificent city.

And then at one minute past midnight, the war in Europe—London's war—is really over.

A Homefront Chronology

PREWAR

January 30, 1933: Adolf Hitler becomes Chancellor of Germany.

May 28, 1937: King George VI names Neville Chamberlain as prime minister.

November 16, 1937: The House of Commons votes in favor of the building of air raid shelters in Britain's towns and cities.

March 12, 1938: German troops invade Austria.

September 1938: Shelter slit trenches are first dug in London's parks; gas masks are to be issued to Londoners.

September 29–30, 1938: Chamberlain meets with Hitler in Munich, then returns home to announce "peace in our time." The agreement approves German acquisition of Czechoslovakia's Sudetenland.

October 9, 1938: The first barrage balloons rise over London.

1939

March 1939: German troops invade the rest of Czechoslovakia. Chamberlain announces that Britain and France have agreed to guarantee unqualified support to Poland "in the event of any action which clearly threatened Polish independence."

August 1939: As war clouds gather, London museums and galleries begin to evacuate their treasures from the metropolis.

August 10, 1939: London's lights, except at the railway terminals, are turned off for a practice blackout.

August 23, 1939: Germany and Russia unexpectedly sign a non-aggression pact.

September 1, 1939: German troops invade Poland. Blackout regulations go into effect. The evacuation of children, expectant mothers, and the blind from London begins. Gas masks are to be carried at all times. England's nascent television service is shut down.

September 3, 1939: At 11:15am, Prime Minister Chamberlain announces, "This country is at war with Germany." Within minutes a lone airplane flying over England's east coast sets off air raid warnings; a false alarm, it appropriately marks the beginning of the eight-month Phoney War. Later in the day King George broadcasts to his people: "There may be dark days ahead, and war can no longer be confined to the battlefield."

September 12, 1939: ENSA (Entertainments National Service Association) is formed.

September 21, 1939: Petrol rationing begins.

September 29, 1939: National Registration begins; identity cards are issued.

October 1, 1939: Winston Churchill, First Lord of the Admiralty, makes his first wartime radio broadcast.

October 10, 1939: The first concert in London's National Gallery is held.

November 30, 1939: Russia attacks Finland.

September–December 1939: Almost twice as many London pedestrians are killed in this four-month period as in the same four months a year ago; blackout regulations are blamed.

1940

January 8, 1940: Food rationing begins. England tightens its belt: 4 oz. of butter, 4 oz. of ham, 4 oz. of bacon, and 12 oz. of sugar a week, per adult. The Royal Family receives their rationing cards.

April 9, 1940: German troops invade Norway and Denmark.

May 10, 1940: German troops invade France and the Low Countries (Belgium, Luxembourg, and the Netherlands). Neville Chamberlain resigns; King George VI names Winston Churchill as prime minister.

May 14, 1940: The Local Defense Volunteers, later renamed the Home Guard by Churchill, are formed. Within twenty-four hours, 250,000 Britons volunteer.

May 14, 1940: Holland surrenders to Germany.

May 26, 1940: The British Expeditionary Forces begin to retreat from Dunkirk's beaches in northern France. By June 4, hundreds of British ships, fishing boats, and sailing dinghies bring more than 300,000 stranded troops across the English Channel to safety.

May 28, 1940: Belgium surrenders to Germany.

Spring 1940: Over two million Anderson shelters are issued in Britain.

June 10, 1940: Italy declares war against France and Britain.

June 14, 1940: German troops goosestep down the streets of Paris.

June 17, 1940: France falls to Germany.

June 18, 1940: Two radio events: Churchill broadcasts his "Finest Hour" speech, and French General Charles de Gaulle exhorts his countrymen.

June 22, 1940: German terms for a formal French surrender are read to the French delegates in the Forest of Compiègne, the same place where the French read terms of surrender to the Germans at the end of World War I.

June 30, 1940: After two days of bombing, German forces begin invading Britain's Channel Islands. German troops will remain on British soil until war's end.

August 8, 1940: The Battle of Britain begins, though some would later suggest July 10 or even early June as the real beginning.

August 13, 1940: *Aldertag* (Eagle Day) begins, Germany's more focused attempt to break British morale and gain air superiority in southern England before the planned German invasion.

August 17, 1940: Germany announces a shipping blockade of Britain.

August 20, 1940: Winston Churchill lauds the Royal Air Force: "Never in the field of human conflict was so much owed by so many to so few."

August 24, 1940: The first daytime bombs fall on central London as German bombers, unable to find their targets, drop their bomb loads aimlessly.

August 25, 1940: In response to the bombs dropped on London the previous day, the RAF bombs Berlin—something German leaders had assured German citizens would never happen.

September 7, 1940: The Blitz begins; hundreds of Luftwaffe planes attack London's East End. Air attacks on the metropolis will continue, first steadily and then intermittently, until May 1941.

September 10, 1940: The Dig for Victory campaign begins extolling the benefits of allotments, gardening, and fresh vegetables.

September 11, 1940: Churchill orders every anti-aircraft gun in the south of England to London, and a deafening night-long barrage begins. Churchill will later call it a "roaring cannonade." The guns are totally ineffective in downing German aircraft and wildly effective in lifting Londoners' morale.

September 15, 1940: Battle of Britain Day: The RAF scores a major victory in England's skies (60 of 900 German planes are downed).

September 17, 1940: Hitler postpones Operation Sea Lion, the invasion of Britain. Major daylight raids on London are halted; nighttime targets shift from the East End and the docks westward to central London.

September 18, 1940: A major Luftwaffe raid (300-plus planes) drops 350 tons of high explosives on London.

September 1940: According to the London *Times*, 6,954 civilians are killed and 10,615 seriously injured in September as a result of German air raids on Britain.

October 13, 1940: Princess Elizabeth makes her first radio broadcast.

October 14–15, 1940: Another immense German raid: this time 400 bombers leave 430 Londoners dead.

October 1940: Signs go up in London's Underground: "The trains must run to get people to their work and to their homes. The space at the tube stations is limited.

Women, children, and the infirm need it most. Be a man and leave it to them." Authorities allow Underground stations to be used as air raid shelters, making official a situation that has existed for weeks.

October 1940: According to the London *Times*, 6,334 civilians are killed and 8,695 seriously injured in October as a result of German air raids on Britain.

November 3, 1940: The first night since September 7 that there is no Luftwaffe raid on London, though with tomorrow's raid another ten consecutive nights will follow. Over the previous fifty-seven nights, an average of 165 German planes attacked London, dropping 200 tons of high explosives a night.

November 14–15, 1940: More than 500 tons of bombs are dropped in a ten-hour German attack on Coventry, destroying a third of the city's homes and gutting the cathedral.

December 8–9, 1940: A 400-bomber raid kills more than 250 Londoners and injures over 600; 1,700 fires are started.

December 29–30, 1940: On a windy Sunday night, the Luftwaffe concentrates on the City. Incendiary bombs, falling on deserted warehouses, businesses, and churches, start over 1,400 fires. As a direct result of this raid, compulsory firewatching is instituted.

1941

January 1941: The Peter Pan statue in Kensington Gardens just misses being hit, but the bomb crater 200 yards away provides something new for children to climb around in. The crater, and others in the park, will soon be filled in with debris from bombed buildings.

March 19–20, 1941: Over 500 German bombers make a huge raid on London's docks and the East End.

April 16–17, 1941: "The Wednesday." The heaviest air raid on London yet, with 685 bombers dropping 890 tons of explosives and 4,000 incendiaries. The focus is central and south London.

April 19–20, 1941: "The Saturday." More tons of high explosives and incendiaries are dropped than in any other London raid. This time the docks and East End take the brunt.

May 10, 1941: German official Rudolf Hess parachutes into Scotland and is taken into police custody.

May 10–11, 1941: Bombers' Moon: Heavy German raids cause extensive damage to Parliament, Westminster Abbey, St. Margaret's Westminster, St. James's Palace, Queen's Hall, St. Clement Danes, the Tower of London, and other London landmarks. Over 1,450 Londoners are killed.

June 1941: Clothing rationing is introduced in Britain.

June 22, 1941: German troops invade Russia.

July 14, 1941: Thousands of London's civil defense workers line up in review in Hyde Park and hear Prime Minister Churchill remind them that Germany's indiscriminate air attacks "could not prevail against British tenacity and resolution."

December 7, 1941: Japanese planes attack the United States naval fleet at Pearl Harbor, Hawaii. The following day the United States and Great Britain declare war on Japan.

1942

January 1942: American soldiers begin to arrive in England.

February 1942: Soap is rationed to 3 oz. a month.

Mid-April–May 1942: Hitler orders the Baedeker raids on several English cities as a reprisal for Allied bombing of Lübeck. Exeter, Bath, Norwich, Canterbury, and York are all bombed.

May 30, 1942: The first 1,000-bomber raid on Cologne takes place.

November 15, 1942: Civil Defence Day is observed throughout Britain commemorating civilian valor and fortitude in the heavy air raids of 1940 and 1941. A huge parade of air wardens, rescue first-aid workers, nurses, WVSs, and others march in review past the king and queen at St. Paul's Cathedral.

November 26, 1942: The Stars and Stripes flies from Westminster Abbey during Thanksgiving services for American service personnel.

1943

March 6–12, 1943: Wings for Victory Week, yet another nationwide campaign to raise funds to fight the war. A Lancaster bomber sits in front of London's National Gallery; on March 8, a military parade of Allied Forces marches through Trafalgar Square.

May 16, 1943: Church bells ring out over England celebrating victory in North Africa.

July 25, 1943: Italy's Mussolini is overthrown.

September 10, 1943: German troops invade Rome; in a month (October 13, 1943) the relationship of the former Axis allies is formally sundered when Italy declares war on Germany.

December 1943: 542 Londoners die in air raids in 1943.

1944

January–April, 1944: The Little Blitz brings renewed Luftwaffe bombing raids over England.

February 1, 1944: Clothing restrictions are lifted; it's now possible to buy clothes with pleats and cuffs, though some form of clothes rationing will continue to 1949.

June 6, 1944: D-Day. Allied troops land on the beaches of Normandy; Operation Overlord begins.

June 13, 1944: The first flying bomb (V-1) lands in London.

August 24–25, 1944: Paris is liberated by Allied troops.

September 8, 1944: The first flying rocket (V-2), traveling at over 3,000 mph, explodes above Chiswick, London.

September 17, 1944: Blackout restrictions begin to be lifted in England, with the move from a full black-out to a dim-out, officially known as "half-lighting." But, warned the *Daily Mirror*, "Don't throw your black-out material away. If the siren should sound, you must be ready to black-out completely again."

September 19, 1944: Restrictions on radio broadcasting of weather details begin to be lifted.

December 3, 1944: The "stand down" of the Home Guard.

1945

March 20, 1945: The last bombs to be dropped on Britain in World War II land in Norfolk. Three days before, bombs landed on Hull; although damage wasn't serious, twelve people died, the last civilian casualties of the war caused by bombs from a piloted aircraft.

March 27, 1945: The last V-2 flying rocket falls on England, causing the final casualty of the homefront. Over 2,500 Londoners were killed by V-2 rockets and nearly 6,000 injured.

March 29, 1945: The last V-1 flying bomb falls on Hertfordshire.

April 12, 1945: President Franklin D. Roosevelt dies; Harry Truman becomes America's new president.

April 23, 1945: The blackout officially ends.

April 28, 1945: Mussolini is executed by Italian partisans.

April 30, 1945: Adolf Hitler commits suicide in a Berlin bunker.

May 2, 1945: The national air raid warning system and the industrial alarm scheme are discontinued; air raid sirens will no longer warn of raiders. Bomb alerts had sounded 1,224 times in the war years—on an average about once every thirty-six hours.

May 8, 1945: Victory in Europe Day (V-E Day).

May 14, 1945: King George, Queen Elizabeth, their daughters, Queen Mary, Winston Churchill, members of the diplomatic corps, cabinet, and all ranks of the fighting services, plus hundreds of representatives of Britain's working men and women attend Thanksgiving services in St. Paul's Cathedral.

Mid-1945: Many of London's galleries and museums begin to move their collections back to the metropolis.

July 5, 1945: General Election Day. Just weeks after V-E Day and with the war in the Far East continuing, Churchill is voted out of office (election results are announced July 26). King George VI names Clement Attlee as prime minister.

August 14, 1945: Japan agrees to surrender unconditionally. World War II ends.

POSTWAR

April 5, 1946: Workers begin removing the Elgin Marbles and other art treasures from the safety of the Aldwych-Piccadilly Underground.

April 10, 1946: The last National Gallery concert is held.

June 8, 1946: A massive Victory Day parade winds along a grand processional route in central London.

June 1947: Eros is returned to his spot atop the fountain in Piccadilly Circus.

April 3, 1949: Piccadilly Circus's nighttime lights, extinguished for almost a decade, are switched on as thousands cheer.

1950: Petrol rationing finally ends.

January 24, 1965: Winston Churchill dies in his London home, aged ninety.

Marquis Childs wrote at war's end, "Yet London is still the London we knew before. Battered, shabby, with many a gaping hole, there the city stands. Paris was saved by surrender and humiliation. Rome was preserved by the protecting wing of the Vatican. London was saved by her people—their fortitude, their stamina, their patient loyalty."

Where Are They Now?

Here are the current locations, so to speak, of some of the Londoners we met in the pages of *London's War*.

Nancy Astor (1879–1964). First woman to take a seat in the House of Commons, representing well-bombed Plymouth throughout the war. Her ashes were buried in the Octagon Temple on the grounds of Cliveden in Berkshire.

Cecil Beaton (1904–1980). Photographer, costume designer, and author. Buried in All Saints' Churchyard, Broadchalke, Wiltshire.

William Maxwell "Max" Aitken, Lord Beaverbrook (1879–1964). Served in Churchill's wartime cabinet as Minister of Aircraft Production and Minister of Supply. His ashes were placed in the plinth of a bust by Oscar Nemon in Newcastle, New Brunswick, Canada.

Ernest Bevin (1881–1951). Minister of Labor in Churchill's wartime cabinet. Buried in Westminster Abbey in the north aisle of the nave.

Laurence Binyon (1869–1943). Poet; author of "For the Fallen." Buried in the churchyard in Aldworth, Berkshire.

Elizabeth Bowen (1899–1973). Novelist. Buried in the graveyard in Farahy, County Cork, Ireland.

Vera Brittain (1893–1970). Pacifist and author. Her ashes were scattered over the grave of her beloved brother Edward in Granezza, Asiago Plateau, Italy.

Neville Chamberlain (1869–1940). Prime minister 1937–1940. His ashes were buried in Westminster Abbey beneath a memorial stone in the nave.

Henry "Chips" Channon (1897–1958). Conservative member of Parliament, consummate diarist, and man about town. Buried at Kelvedon, his Essex home.

Winston Churchill (1874–1965). Prime minister 1940–1945 and 1951–1955. Buried in St. Martin's Churchyard, Bladon, Oxfordshire, about eight miles from Oxford and less than a mile from Blenheim Castle. A memorial marble floor stone is by the west door of Westminster Abbey.

Kenneth Clark (1903–1983). Art historian and author. Buried in the graveyard of the parish church, Saltwood, Kent.

Cyril Connolly (1903–1974). Author, journalist, and literary critic. Buried at Berwick Church near Lewes, Sussex.

Noël Coward (1899–1973). Playwright, composer, author, actor, and director. Buried in Montego Bay, Ocho Rios, Jamaica.

Charles de Gaulle (1890–1970). French general and leader of the Free French forces. Buried in Colombey-les-Deux-Eglises in eastern France in the church graveyard.

Hugh Dowding (1882–1970). Chief of the RAF's Fighter Command during the Battle of Britain. Buried in Westminster Abbey's RAF Chapel.

Anthony Eden (1897–1977). Politician and statesman. Served as Foreign Secretary during the war and later as prime minister. Buried in the graveyard of St. Mary's Church, Alvediston, Wiltshire.

Edward VIII (1894–1972). King 1936. Buried in Frogmore Mausoleum at Frogmore, Windsor Home Park, Windsor, Berkshire.

Dwight Eisenhower (1890–1969). Allied wartime general; U.S. president 1953–1961. Buried at the Eisenhower Center, Abilene, Kansas.

T. S. Eliot (1888–1965). Poet and playwright. Buried in St. Michael's Church, East Coker, Somerset. A memorial floor stone is in Poets' Corner, Westminster Abbey.

Elizabeth, the Queen Mother (1900–2002). Wife of King George VI, and mother of Queen Elizabeth II. Buried next to her husband in St. George's Chapel, Windsor Castle, Windsor, Berkshire.

Gracie Fields (1898-1979). Entertainer and singer. Buried in the Catholic Cemetery, Capri, Italy.

George VI (1895–1952). King 1936–1952. Buried in St. George's Chapel, Windsor Castle, Windsor, Berkshire.

Pamela Digby Churchill Hayward Harriman (1920–1997). Diplomat and socialite; wartime daughter-in-law of Winston Churchill. Buried in Arden, New York.

Lord Haw-Haw (William Joyce) (1906–1946). Broadcaster of anti-British propaganda from Germany. Convicted as a traitor and hanged at Wandsworth Gaol; buried in Bohermore Cemetery, Galway, Ireland.

Myra Hess (1890–1965). Concert pianist; organized and performed concerts in the National Gallery throughout the war. Cremated at Golders Green in north London.

Rudolf Hess (1894–1987). High-ranking German politician who fled Germany by plane in 1941; briefly imprisoned in the Tower of London. Died in Spandau Prison in West Berlin; buried in Wunsiedel, West Germany.

Adolf Hitler (1889–1945). German Chancellor. Committed suicide in a Berlin bunker as the war ground down. His body and that of wife Eva Braun were subsequently burned.

Joseph Kennedy (1888–1969). U.S. Ambassador to Great Britain 1938–1940. Buried at Holyhood Cemetery, Brookline, Massachusetts.

Bea Lillie (1894–1989). Comedienne. Buried in the churchyard cemetery in Henley-on-Thames, Oxfordshire.

Charles Lindbergh (1902–1974). American aviator and advocate of wartime neutrality. Buried at Kipahulu Congregational Churchyard, Kipahulu, Maui, Hawaii.

Edwin Lutyens (1869–1944). Architect of the Cenotaph and other war-related memorials. Cremated at Golders Green in north London.

Vera Lynn (1917–). Wartime entertainer and vocalist. Currently living in Ditchling, East Sussex.

Glenn Miller (1904–1944). American trombonist and bandleader. His plane crashed into the English Channel and his body was never found. Memorial at Arlington National Cemetery, Arlington, Virginia.

Nancy Mitford (1904–1973). Novelist and biographer. Buried in St. Mary's Churchyard, Swinbrook, Oxfordshire. Her sister Unity (1914–1948), a friend of Hitler, is buried nearby.

Bernard Law Montgomery (Monty) (1887–1976). Field marshal and military leader, best known for victory at El Alamein. Buried in Holy Cross Churchyard in Binsted, Hampshire.

Henry Moore (1898–1986). Sculptor and artist. Buried in the village churchyard in Perry Green, Ware, Hertfordshire.

Louis Mountbatten (1900–1979). Commander of the *Kelly*, Chief of Combined Operations, and First Sea Lord. Buried in Romsey Abbey Church in Romsey, Hampshire.

Edward R. Murrow (1908–1965). American radio broadcaster stationed in London during the war. His ashes were scattered outside his home on Glen Arden Farm near Pawling, New York. A plaque set in a boulder marks the area.

Harold Nicolson (1886–1968). Politician, diplomat, journalist, and novelist. His ashes were buried in Sissinghurst Churchyard, Kent, near his home, Sissinghurst Castle.

George Orwell (1903–1950). Author and journalist. Buried in All Saints' Churchyard, Sutton Courtenay, Oxfordshire.

J. B. Priestley (1894–1984). Novelist, playwright, and radio broadcaster. His ashes were buried in the parish churchyard of St. Michael and All Angels Church at Hubberholme near Buckden, North Yorkshire.

Ernie Pyle (1900–1945). American journalist. Killed by a sniper's bullet on an island just off Okinawa. Buried in Punchbowl Memorial Cemetery, Honolulu, Hawaii.

Andy Rooney (1914–). American author and broadcaster; worked as a journalist in London during the war.

Eleanor Roosevelt (1884–1962). Wife of U.S. President Franklin Roosevelt. Buried next to her husband in Hyde Park, New York.

Franklin Roosevelt (1882–1945). U.S. president 1932–1945; good friend to Britain throughout the war. Buried in the formal garden at his home in Hyde Park in upstate New York.

Dorothy L. Sayers (1893–1957). Author. Her ashes were buried below the tower of St. Anne's Church, Soho, London, where for many years she was a churchwarden.

George Bernard Shaw (1856–1950). Playwright. His ashes were scattered in his garden, Shaw's Corner, Ayot St. Lawrence, Hertfordshire, near St. Alban's.

Wladyslaw Sikorski (1881–1943). Polish general and leader of the Free Polish resistance in London. Buried in Newark Cemetery, Newark-on-Trent, Nottinghamshire.

Wallis Warfield Simpson (1896–1986). Wife of Edward VIII (after he abdicated and was named Duke of Windsor). Buried beside her husband in Frogmore Mausoleum at Frogmore, Windsor Home Park, Windsor, Berkshire.

Edith Sitwell (1887–1965). Poet and author. Buried at St. Mary's Churchyard extension, Weedon Lois, Northamptonshire.

Dylan Thomas (1914–1953). Poet and author. Buried in St. Martin's Churchyard, Laugharne, Dyfed in southern Wales. A memorial floor stone is in Poets' Corner, Westminster Abbey.

H. G. Wells (1866–1946). Author and historian. Died in London; his ashes were scattered at sea near the white cliffs between Swanage and Studland in Dorset.

John Gilbert Winant (1889–1947). U.S. Ambassador to Great Britain 1941–1946. Committed suicide in Concord, Massachusetts; buried at St. Paul's School, Concord.

Virginia Woolf (1882–1941). Author and critic. Committed suicide; her ashes were buried at Monk's House, Rodmell, Sussex. The ashes of her husband Leonard (1880–1969; author, literary critic, and publisher) are buried nearby.

When this is all over, in the days to come, men will speak of this war, and they will say: I was a soldier, or I was a sailor, or I was a pilot; and others will say with equal pride: I was a citizen of London.
        —Quoted by Eric Sevareid, *Not So Wild a Dream*

PICTURE CREDITS

All illustrations are by the author or are from items in the author's collection, except as noted below. Please note that every effort has been made to acknowledge correctly and to contact the source and/or copyright holder of each picture. Apologies for any unintentional errors or omissions, which will be corrected in future editions of the book.

Photos and illustrations in *London's War* are courtesy of:

All Hallows by the Tower: Page 288

American Memory/Library of Congress: Page 42: LC-USW33-19093C; page 157: LC-USZ62-25600 DLC; page 291: LC-USW33-042473

B. P. Co. Ltd.: Page 39

Churchman cigarette cards: Pages 21, 56, 63, 216, 248, 280, 286, 310

Dorchester Hotel: Page 148

Franklin D. Roosevelt Library: Pages 2, 31, 128, 159

G. Pond & Company: Page 22

Harrods Ltd.: Pages 47, 144, 153, 262

Imperial War Museum: Page xxii: NYT 7633D; page 10: HU 36145; page 15: HU 91218; page 53: D14940; page 93: HU 36183; page 119: HU 57684; page 223: HU 91219; page 244: HU 91220; page 279: HU 91221; page 290: 55686; page 301: HU91224; page 312: HU 91222; page 322: HU 91223

Janet Fraser Jennings: Pages 40, 317

J. J. Corbyn: Page 309

Le Meridien Russell Hotel: Page 191

National Archives, Washington, DC: Page ii and page 265: 306-NT-3173V; page xiv: 306-NT-901(71); page 189: 306-NT-901C(20); page 209: 306-NT-3170V; page 246: 306-NT-901B-3; page 300: 306-NT-901C (11); page 313: 306-NT-2743V; page 325: 111-SC-205398; page 327: 111-SC-178801

Photochrom Co. Ltd.: Pages 100, 113, 116, 256, 259 top, 267, 269, 284, 285

Photos.com: Pages 86, 91

Raphael Tuck & Sons Ltd.: Pages 227, 257

Scott's Restaurant: Page 178

Valentine's: Pages 8, 54

W. Straker Ltd.: Page 261

Index

Major sites, streets, and personalities are indexed; photographs are not indexed.

About the Author

Travel editor Sayre Van Young has spent nine years uncovering the effects of World War II on the people and landscape of the world's most interesting city. When not exploring central London's wartime memories, she works as a research librarian and community historian at the Berkeley Public Library. Her business, InfoWeaver, provides publishing services to San Francisco Bay Area publishers and authors. She lives in Berkeley, California, and walks everywhere.